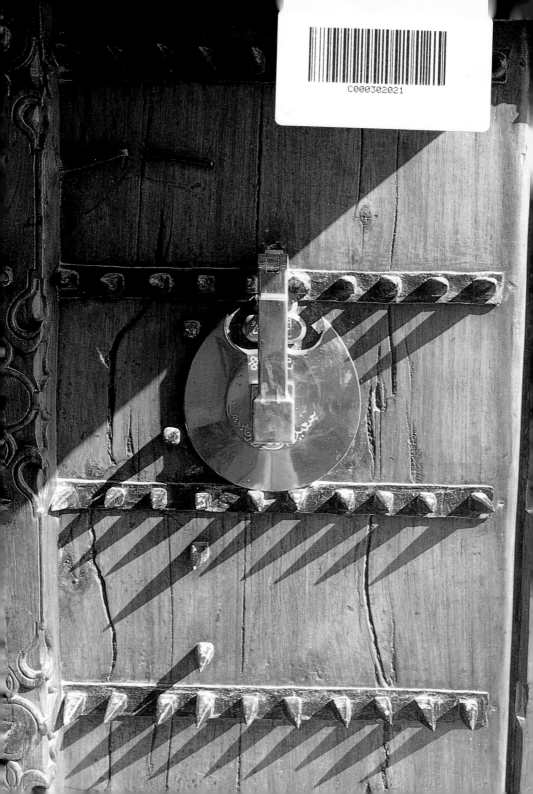

Spectrum Guide to
UNITED ARAB
EMIRATES

Camerapix Publishers International
NAIROBI

Spectrum Guide to United Arab Emirates

First published 1998 by
Camerapix Publishers International,
PO Box 45048,
Nairobi, Kenya

© 1998 Camerapix

ISBN 1 874041 29 6

This book was designed and produced by
Camerapix Publishers International,
PO Box 45048,
Nairobi, Kenya

Fax: (254-2) 448926/7
Tel: (254-2) 448923/4/5
E-Mail: info@camerapix.com
Website: http://www.camerapix.com

Colour Separations: Universal Graphics
Pte Ltd, Singapore
Printed and bound: UIC Printing & Packag-
ing Pte Ltd, Singapore.

The **Spectrum Guides** series provides a
comprehensive and detailed description of
each country they cover together with all
the essential data that tourists, business
visitors, or potential investors are likely to
require.

Spectrum Guides in print:
African Wildlife Safaris
Eritrea
Ethiopia
India
Jordan
Kenya
Madagascar
Maldives
Mauritius
Namibia
Nepal
Oman
Pakistan
Seychelles
South Africa
Sri Lanka
Tanzania
Uganda
Zambia
Zimbabwe

Publisher and Chief Executive:
Mohamed Amin
Editorial Director: Brian Tetley
Picture Editor: Duncan Willetts
Text: Jennifer Sturgis and Peter Stewart
Associate Editor: Ibrahim Al-Abed
Consultant Editor: Salim Amin
Projects Director: Rukhsana Haq
Production Editors: Roger Barnard and
Gail Porter
Cartographer: Terry Brown
Art Editor: Calvin McKenzie
Designer: Lilly Macharia
Typesetter: Rachel Musyimi
Editorial Assistant: Maryann Muiruri
Photographic Research: Abdul Rahman

Editorial Board

The latest in a rapidly growing list of full-colour, high-quality and in-depth guide books to the world's nations, *Spectrum Guide to the United Arab Emirates* adds new perspectives and insight to a nation young in years yet as old as its desert sands.

The *Spectrum Guide* series — originated by the three-man travel book team of world-renowned photographer **Mohamed Amin,** his equally renowned friend and colleague **Duncan Willetts** and Kenyan writer **Brian Tetley** — add depth, vision and understanding to each nation.

The text of *Spectrum Guide to the United Arab Emirates* was written and researched by **Jennifer Sturgis** and **Peter Stewart** who travelled the length and breadth of the seven emirates that make up the UAE.

Formerly with the UN in Hong Kong, Jennifer Sturgis, author of a country guide to Pakistan, has travelled widely throughout South and Southeast Asia.

Cambridge University Arabic graduate Peter Stewart has worked in London, Japan, Hong Kong and the UAE. He is the author of a guide to Korea and his interests include the study of hot mineral springs.

Spectrum Guide Publisher and Chief Executive Amin and Picture Editor Willetts recorded the breathtaking images of the UAE while Amin also handled the complex liaison and logistics involved.

The text of the guidebook has drawn on an ever-growing body of tourist and business publications from UAE federal and local authorities. These include the *UAE Almanac* and a variety of supporting publications by the Ministry of Information in Abu Dhabi and a number of brochures and the UAE chambers of commerce. Dubai Chamber of Commerce and Tourism were particularly helpful in providing information on the emirate of Dubai and the Jebel Ali Free Zone.

The Sharjah Natural History Museum, opened in 1995, proved to be a mine of information for the section on wildlife in the UAE. The museum, backed up by a large number of natural history publications, such as the *Tribulus*, provided detailed knowledge about flora and fauna while the Emirates Natural History Group and the Dubai Natural History Group were also a valuable resource.

The museums of the United Arab Emirates, especially the Dubai Museum and the Al-Ain Museum, provided much first-hand information about the heritage and culture of the UAE. The authors also consulted a number of histories of the UAE of which Dr Muhammed Abdul Nayeem's Prehistory and Protohistory of the Arabian Peninsula, with its detail of archaeological sites, was especially helpful.

Finally the *Gulf News*, *Gulf Today*, *Khaleej Times* and *Emirate News* provided much useful detail on every aspect of this fast-moving federation. In particular, the *Gulf News* gave advice on the off-road outings.

And the book could never have been completed without the tireless help of **Ibrahim Al-Abed**, adviser to the UAE Ministry of Information and Culture's department of external information.

Editorial Director Brian Tetley led the Spectrum in-house team of Art Editor **Calvin McKenzie,** and Graphic Designer **Lilly Macharia** who handled the design, and **Rachel Musyimi** who was responsible for typesetting. Maintaining *Spectrum Guide's* in-house style, and compiling a treasury of information for the end sections was the outcome of much diligent work by Projects Director **Rukhsana Haq**, Production Editors **Roger Barnard** and **Gail Porter**, helped by long-term Editorial Assistant **Maryann Muiruri**.

Consultant Editor **Salim Amin** kept track of the copy and production deadlines while **Rukhsana** also compiled the index. And finally Photo-librarian **Abdul Rahman** undertook picture research.

TABLE OF CONTENTS

LISTINGS

MAPS

Half title: A typical old Islamic wooden door; Title page: Tower at Khatt, Ras al-Khaimah.
Following pages: Timeless scene as sun sets over dhow at Abu Dhabi; Modern high-rise
buildings reach skywards in Dubai; Illuminated graceful mosque near Hatta Road, Dubai

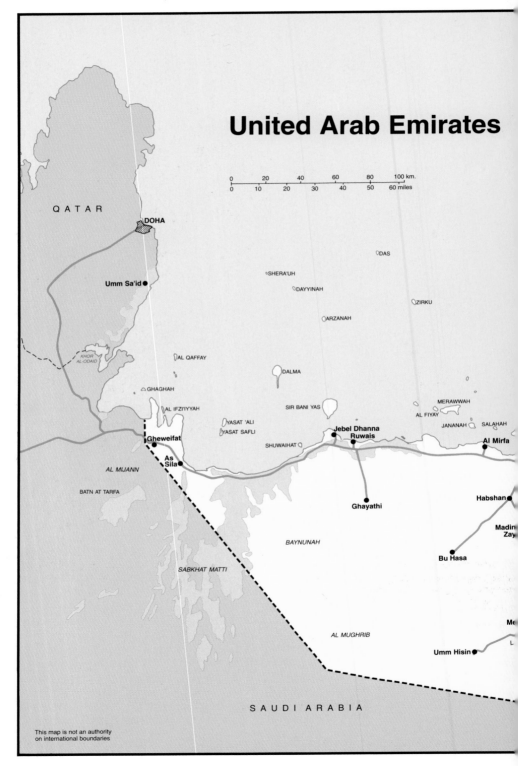

United Arab Emirates

QATAR

DOHA

Umm Sa'id

DAS

SHERA'UH

DAYYINAH

ZIRKU

ARZANAH

AL QAFFAY

KHOR AL-ODAID

DALMA

GHAGHAH

MERAWWAH

AL IFZI'IYYAH

AL FIYAY

JANANAH   SALAHAH

YASAT 'ALI

SIR BANI YAS

YASAT SAFLI

Jebel Dhanna
Ruwais

Al Mirfa

Gheweifat

SHUWAIHAT

As
Sila

AL MIJANN

Ghayathi

Habshan

BATN AT TARFA

Madin
Zay

BAYNUNAH

Bu Hasa

SABKHAT MATTI

Me

AL MUGHRIB

L

Umm Hisin

SAUDI ARABIA

This map is not an authority
on international boundaries

14

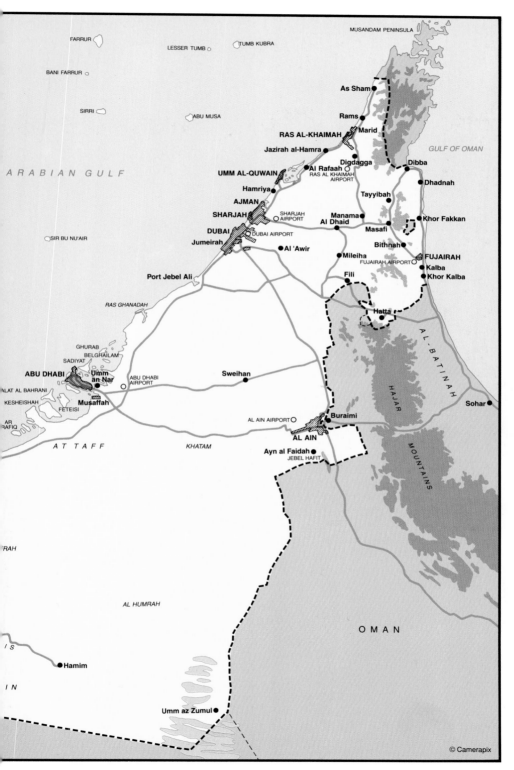

15

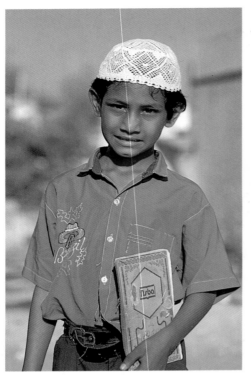

The United Arab Emirates' Experience

The United Arab Emirates is a melting pot of different cultures and people, tied together in a federation that sees itself increasingly as a nation. As one of the world's youngest nations, founded in 1971, it celebrated its 25th anniversary in 1996. The country has developed rapidly on the back of its massive oil wealth; the main cities of Abu Dhabi, Dubai and Sharjah are first and foremost commercial centres, with gleaming skyscrapers, excellent roads and many luxury hotels, little different from modern cities in Asia or Europe. For the holidaymaker, the UAE offers well-developed sporting facilities, including scuba-diving, shopping galore and wonderful sandy beaches. A closer look, however, reveals the United Arab Emirates consists of more than good living and good shopping.

Despite the increasing sense of nationhood, each of the seven emirates that make up the UAE retains its special identity and a degree of autonomy from the federal government.

Whereas Dubai is free-wheeling and cosmopolitan, Abu Dhabi, the centre of government, has a more conservative feel.

In Sharjah, the mercantile history is felt most strongly in the hundreds of Arab and Persian dhows that line the seafront. In the Northern Emirates — Umm al-Quwain, Ras al-Khaimah and Ajman — there is a sense of tradition where you sense something of the austerity of desert life. In the east Fujairah reflects the country's varied terrain as the mountains fall away steeply towards the Indian Ocean coast. This area is an ideal get-away from the bustle of the cities.

The Emirates are inhabited by a diversity of ethnic groups. In addition to the UAE nationals, there are various Arab groups, with different coloured headdresses denoting their country of origin, as well as Iranians, Indians, Baluchis, Filipinos, along with large numbers of Europeans and Americans.

The country has grown rich quickly. The title of a recent book, *From Rags to Riches*, reflects the pace of development. Black and white photos of Abu Dhabi, taken as early as the 1960s, show a city with only a few houses and shops. Now, its modern skyline is replete with skyscrapers and the latest architectural designs. But a half-hour's drive to the north brings you into the desert, where you can travel for miles without seeing any sign of habitation.

The skyline of all the key cities reflects the dynamism of the economy. But while buildings such as the Etisalat Towers in Abu Dhabi and Dubai are impressive in their modernity, business in the souqs is done pretty much as it was a hundred years ago. The merchants, some of them Arabs, but mostly Indians or Iranians, might only be haggling over the price of a melamine bowl, but equally you can find old carpets, spices and antiques.

Images of sheets of blue and silver glass, sharply reflecting modern buildings in their mirror, are just as much a part of the UAE as the reds, oranges and browns of Indian silks in the souqs; and the whiff of exhaust fumes from the cross-border trucks that ply all the way from Syria and Jordan is as much a scent of the UAE as the sweet smell of coffee brewing in one of the local coffee-shops.

For the UAE is a society in transition. But people make a country as much as monuments and sights. The people of the UAE are friendly and helpful, and the traditional virtues of generosity and hospitality are alive and well.

Whether it is reflected in the offer of guidance in response to a lost look on the part of a tourist, or the traditional offer of coffee or tea when bargaining begins in one of the souqs, the same concern for the visitor is shown by many locals.

The UAE is one of the easiest Middle East countries to visit, and the country has opened its doors wide to tourists. So, in the tradition of the UAE's fabled Arab hospitality and the greeting heard throughout the UAE when entering the offices and houses of its citizens, *Ahlan wa Sahlan* — Welcome.

Left: Faces of the Emirates – the country boasts a wide diversity of ethnic groups.

Travel Brief and Social Advisory

Some dos and don'ts to make your visit more enjoyable.

Getting There

Travel to and from the UAE is easiest through the country's several major international airports. Dubai International Airport, served by around 65 airlines, is the busiest. There are also international airports at Abu Dhabi, Al Ain, Sharjah, Ras al-Khaimah and Fujairah, though the last two are used very infrequently by international travellers, while Sharjah Airport is most frequently used by the increasing numbers of Tourists arriving from eastern Europe.

The UAE's own airline, Emirates, flies to most major destinations worldwide. Flights to the UAE are therefore readily available from many destinations either in Europe or in Asia and in fact many airlines stop in Dubai or Abu Dhabi en route from Asia to Europe or vice-versa (see Facts at Your Fingertips, Part Five).

Overland routes are uncommon but it would be possible to cross the Omani border at Ras al-Khaimah or near Hatta, or at Buraimi if you were coming overland from Muscat. It is also theoretically possible to cross the border from Saudi Arabia at Gheweifat or to take a boat from Iran if you're actually able to get a visa to any of the UAE's neighbouring territories.

Visa Requirements
The UAE's visa rules are quite relaxed compared to many other Gulf Nations, especially for British citizens. But the rules change periodically and visitors should check with the nearest UAE Embassy before making their journey.

GCC nationals, that is citizens of Oman, Saudi Arabia, Kuwait, Qatar and Bahrain, do not require a visa to enter the UAE. In 1996 UK nationals were given a 30-day visa on arrival but this may change. Other nationalities need a sponsor to arrange a 14-day transit visa. The sponsor can be a friend or relative living in the UAE, a UAE hotel or sponsoring company. These transit visas cannot be renewed so if you plan to stay longer, it is necessary to pre-arrange a 30-day visa which can be renewed.

Larger hotels act as sponsors for tourists or business travellers. Whoever acts as your sponsor is responsible for you while you are in the UAE and it is incumbent upon them to ensure that you leave the country. The usual system for visas is that the hotel or sponsor arranging your visa will leave it at the airport awaiting your arrival. Visas can be arranged on an emergency basis within three or four days but it is best to apply well in advance. The sponsor needs a copy of the first two pages of your passport and your flight details. It is in theory necessary to spend the duration of your stay at the hotel which has arranged your visa, but check with the hotel concerned. Alternatively, visas can be arranged through your local UAE Embassy.

If you have any evidence of travel to Israel in your passport, you will not be allowed to enter the UAE.

Vaccination requirements largely depend on any second destination. Although residents are required to undergo a test for various diseases including HIV and AIDS, there are no such requirements for tourists or other short-term visitors.

Getting Around

By Road
The UAE has an extremely modern and efficient road system and this, combined with a lack of other transport options, makes a car pretty much essential if you're going to do any travelling in the Emirates. Depending on the length of your stay and

Left: Jet touches down at Dubai airport.

Above: Most road signs are in two languages, Arabic and English, with a few also in Urdu.
Opposite: Many of the desert traditions now exist principally for the tourists.

---

your budget it is possible to hire a car fairly cheaply: around AED 100-150 a day or around AED 1800 a month for a small four-door saloon. 4WDs are substantially more expensive.

There is little difference in price between a manual and an automatic vehicle. One firm, Rent-A-Wreck, rents out cars that are usually just a year old. Normally no deposit is required and visitors may use their own licence or an international licence.

The rates mentioned apply to the more reputable car hire firms. Cars do come cheaper, but the smaller agencies may not have an efficient insurance policy.

Insurance is one area that should be carefully checked. Under UAE law, anyone involved in a fatal accident is obliged to maintain the family of the deceased, so make sure that the insurance covers *diyah* payments in the event of a bad accident. In the case of any accident, however small, always report it to the police. Also, do not move the car. The police expect to find it

exactly where the accident occurred so they can make a report.

There are many taxis available in the main towns; most have meters but some do not. If there is no meter, check with your hotel what you should pay and agree the price before you get in. Taxis cost a fraction of those in Europe — and it is rare for drivers to cheat, for instance, by taking a longer route than needed.

Roughly, taxis charge a minimum of AED 5 for the shortest journey, while AED 10-15 will be charged for a journey of as many minutes. Reasonable long-distance rates are also available by negotiation.

As an approximate guide, in 1996 you could expect to pay about AED 250 for the two-hour journey from Abu Dhabi to Dubai. For a bargain taxi ride, you could team up with other travellers at one of the taxi ranks and share the cab, an option which may be worth considering for longer journeys. After midnight expect to haggle, even in those cabs with meters which tend not to be switched on.

Reasonable maps of the UAE, produced by GEOprojects, are available in most bookshops or hotels. Routes are also reasonably well signposted though certain areas may be a bit confusing. In particular, Sharjah could be much better signposted.

One confusing aspect everywhere is that the names on maps do not always correspond to the names of the roads. Spellings and pronunciations also differ greatly. Except for the main roads through cities, locals tend to locate places by saying 'it's near the Ramada Hotel' or 'just past the Spinneys supermarket on the beach road'.

This is because many roads or streets have no names. The best way of dealing with this is to ask for help. If you're actually on the road, ask at a filling station. The staff are often friendly and knowledgeable.

One thing to bear in mind in a two-wheel-drive vehicle is that it is not advisable to go 'off-road'. Though some tracks may look passable, it is actually very dangerous to attempt them without taking the proper precautions (see the 'off-road' section, Part Four).

Also, though the UAE may seem modern and civilized, it is also a desert region and if

Above: Camels graze by the roadside in Ras al Khaimah. The sense of tradition is best preserved in the Northern Emirates.

you're stuck anywhere for any length of time, it can be extremely hot and unpleasant. Always make sure you carry water.

Finally, it is worth noting that the local style of driving may be a little surprising, especially if you're used to Western ways.

Cars pull out in front without indicating and weave in and out of lanes to gain a few metres. Speeding is common and there is little consideration for other drivers. The speed limit is usually 60-80 kilometres an hour in the cities and towns and 100-120 kilometres an hour on motorways.

By Air

There is a shuttle service between Dubai and Abu Dhabi called the Citylink Seaplane. The journey takes half an hour and costs AED385 return (see Listings) Otherwise air links between the Emirates do not really exist; nor are they necessary, given the small distances between the major areas.

By Train or Bus

There are no railways in the UAE but cheap rate buses run between Dubai, Abu Dhabi and other key towns, if infrequently.

There are also local buses within the cities which are used mainly by Indian and Pakistani migrant workers but there is no good information on where buses run to and from. On the whole, public transport is almost non-existent.

However, the fact that taxis are reasonably priced and easily obtainable, and car-hire rates are substantially lower than in Europe, especially if you hire a car for longer periods, compensate. Water taxis, *abras,* to get from one side of the creek to the other, are available in Dubai for 50 fils.

On Foot

Walking is not the best way to get about in the UAE, especially outside the main cities.This is partly because roads are often very dusty and without sidewalks, and partly because anything as energetic as walking in the heat of the summer is unpleasant.

Most shopping centres are in air-conditioned malls, thus nullifying the need to take a stroll in the heat. It is considered

Above: Traditional dress; modern technology: a businessman keeps in touch.

strange, for Westerners particularly, to be seen walking and taxi drivers will assume that you're waiting to hail one. In fact, a short walk of maybe five minutes often results in about four or five taxis beeping to let you know they're there, or even· stopping. If you actually want to walk somewhere, this can be most annoying.

Despite the endless opportunities in the Emirates for sport and leisure, walking is thus almost out of the question, apart from in the many parks which are dotted about the UAE.

For example, the Corniche in Abu Dhabi is popular with walkers and joggers of all nationalities, especially during the cooler months.

The People

It is possible to spend a week or two in the UAE without ever encountering a local but in general, the people that you will encounter are friendly and helpful. The UAE is a wealthy nation and, as such, you will be unlikely to come across poverty or beggars and are much more likely to be struck by the modernity of the place and the high

level of service in the stores, restaurants and hotels in the emirates.

If you. are unlucky enough to run into any trouble on the road, such as a car breakdown or losing your keys, you will find the Arab people very unwilling to leave you until the problem is solved. Maybe this is a custom which has been necessary for a desert people and which has remained with them.

Iranians are often seen in the dhows, smoking the *sheesha* and taking a simple meal on the wooden decks; but equally they manage a trading empire from modern skyscrapers – such as Arbift Tower that overlooks Dubai Creek – that has helped make the re-export business one of the largest foreign exchange earners in the emirates.

Russians swooped on the UAE as the Iron Curtain went down and their own economy opened up; many of the signs in the local shops have been translated into the Cyrillic script and it is not uncommon to hear an Indian merchant selling the latest in electronic equipment calling visitors from the East Bloc into his shop in a pidgin version of the language of the Moscow streets.

On rest days, the Filipino and Sri Lankan men and women, as they do in the green spaces and shopping malls of Hong Kong or Singapore, congregate in the main parks and avenues, exchanging gossip and chit-chat.

Cosmopolitanism is the country's hallmark; and this has been so for centuries, especially in the trading centre of Dubai. Visitors compare the UAE to Hong Kong or Singapore in its mix of races, and the country resembles these also in its prevalence of skyscrapers in the large cities.

But equally, the UAE is proud of its Arab roots and its Islamic identity. It is not uncommon to see a UAE national step out of his air-conditioned Mercedes or Buick on the highway and kneel beside it on the sand facing Mecca in prayer at the appointed hour.

The national dress comprises a loose-fitting white robe and a white headdress that is held on by a double-twisted black thong of rope. This has been worn by the local sheikhs for hundreds of years, and variants on this dress can be found across the Middle East, although the design of the headdress often gives clues as to the individual's country of origin and, in some cases, his tribal allegiance. Thus Syrians tend to wear red-and-white checked head-coverings, Saudis wear a similar design but with a wider check, while Palestinians wear the black-and-white checked head-covering made famous by Yasser Arafat, the legendary leader of the PLO.

Arab women in the UAE still wear the black over-garment and head-covering that has become a potent symbol of Islam in the West; a UAE variation of this is that many also wear an angular mask over their nose and mouth, known as a *burqa*.

Many women in the UAE, however, are from South Asia, including Pakistan, Bangladesh, Sri Lanka and India. Particularly in the Northern Emirates, women wear multi-coloured over-garments that have an altogether brighter look than the traditional black coverings

worn by Muslim women who choose to be 'covered'.

Local customs

Although the UAE, in particular Dubai, is a relaxed and tolerant nation, especially compared with the other Gulf sheikhdoms, it is a Muslim country and visitors should bear this in mind, no matter how progressive the society seems in some ways. Gender is much more of an issue than it is in the West.

Theoretically, men and women must be married to cohabit, and that applies also to tourist couples. In practice, there is wide tolerance of foreign custom; unmarried men and women can share a hotel room without any problem, but will invariably be treated as a married couple.

There seems to be little concept of the maiden/married name issue, so while you may be both expected to give in your passport, different surnames are not a problem.

Two women or two men sharing a hotel room is considered normal, rather than a sign of being gay, which is strictly taboo in Muslim society. Public displays of affection are generally frowned on. However, men walking hand in hand — surprising to many visitors — is perfectly normal.

Dress

Women in particular should dress modestly when out in public. A display of *déshabillé* that would not turn a head in the south of France is almost certain to meet with raised eyebrows, if not open resentment.

The rules apply particularly to female visitors, but even men should be careful to dress conservatively, particularly in the more traditional Northern Emirates.

This does not mean that you need to follow the local customs. Arab women, when they go out in public, almost invariably wear a full-length black wrap-around, often covering their eyes; for the men, a white *dishdash* and headdress is usual, if not de rigueur.

European women are not, as they would be in Iran or Saudi Arabia, expected to wear a headscarf and full-body clothing; but anything much shorter than a knee-length dress will, at least in public, risk being considered an affront.

Mini-skirts and hot pants are definitely frowned upon. Generally, the Northern Emirates are more traditional than Dubai and Abu Dhabi, where it is not uncommon to see Western tourists in fairly skimpy clothing, but it is best to follow the above dress guidelines throughout the UAE.

The beach is the exception. Although Arab and South Asian women either do not bathe at all, or go in the water dressed in a loose-fitting cotton sari, it seems to be accepted that Western women wear bikinis, although these will certainly attract some attention on the public beaches. Thongs and topless bathing, however, are stretching the point too far.

Muslim traditions

Muslim traditions extend beyond mere dress sense, however. One of the most common expressions the visitor will hear in the UAE is *Insh'allah,* which translates: 'by the will of God'. This occurs in almost every sphere of social intercourse. If you say you will see a Muslim friend tomorrow, he is quite likely to reply *Insh'allah;* the same response will often be made if you try to make any particular arrangement that could conceivably not go according to schedule.

Many Westerners find this irritating but they should not. It is usually not a subtle way of hedging one's bets, or a form of deliberate evasion, but a simple habit or tradition.

Consequently, if you make a request or appointment and get the response *'Insh'allah',* do not be concerned. In most cases Muslims would feel impious if they did not say this, as it would overstate the volition of the individual, and deny the will of God in determining events.

The Muslim religion is observed most strictly in the Muslim holy month of Ramadan. At this time Muslims maintain a dawn-to-dusk fast, which for most means not even drinking water; orthodox Muslims will not even swallow their own saliva.

Daytime smoking or eating in public during Ramadan are forbidden, and in some of the Emirates results in legal action, although in the hotels both are condoned. No one will have any problem if you eat, drink or smoke in your own dwelling: for instance, the hotel room in which you are staying. However, as a general rule, visitors to the UAE should never eat, smoke or drink in public during the period of Ramadan between sunrise and sunset.

The timing of Ramadan is based on the lunar calendar and the holy month is declared from the first sighting of the full moon; as such, the exact day that it begins varies from year to year. Visitors are advised to check in advance to see if their visit coincides with the holy month.

Alcohol

The Muslim holy book, the Qur'ân, also proscribes the drinking of alcohol by Muslims at any time. Specifically, what is proscribed is the drinking of *'khamr,* fermented grape juice, but by extension all forms of alcoholic beverage are off-limits to Muslims. In theory Muslims are not allowed to drink alcohol. The availability of alcohol for foreigners varies from emirate to emirate. In Dubai and Abu Dhabi, generally it is available at all good hotels, as well as at restaurants associated with them.

In Ajman, Ras al-Khaimah, Fujairah, Al Ain and Umm al-Quwain, hotels often sell alcohol, but not always. Restaurants may also sell alcohol discreetly, but not publicly. Sharjah is completely dry and even the bigger hotels do not sell alcohol.

Visitors should offer alcohol to UAE nationals, and indeed all Muslims, with caution. Although many do drink, much depends on the circumstances; someone who was quite happy to down a few pints in one of the UAE bars a few nights back may have a very different outlook at a formal meeting when other Muslims are present.

You cannot buy alcohol outside the hotels unless you have a special permit which is only issued to non-Muslim residents.

Etiquette

Etiquette is another potential minefield. Certain gestures, quite innocent in the West, often give offence to the Arab. Having

Top: Hubble bubble pipes have been a popular feature in many traditional coffee shops, although Abu Dhabi has tried to limit their use because of health concerns. Above: Few citizens retain a nomadic lifestyle today but the traditional Bedouin tent still provides a welcome escape from air-conditioned office blocks and the pace of modern life.

said that, Arab hospitality is legendary and foreigners are given a much wider latitude than locals in what they can and cannot do.

As UAE society is also a society in transition, and many of the indigenous population have travelled abroad, there is a high degree of tolerance of foreign custom. Anything but an obviously deliberate affront is likely to be met with good humour rather than hostility. Much depends also on the age, sex and background of the people you are talking to.

The following list contains some dos and don'ts for the visitor. But it should not be seen as exhaustive or definitive. A sense of humour can also make up for breaches of protocol.

• Don't show the soles of your feet while talking to an Arab host. This does not mean you have to keep your feet firmly planted on the ground throughout; but the expansive American gesture of crossing one leg across the opposite leg's thigh may be seen as rude.

• Don't point with your feet to indicate direction or, for instance, to indicate the item you want to buy at a market stall.

• Do take off your shoes when entering the home of a UAE national. Many will tell you not to bother, but the gesture is appreciated. Also, always remove your shoes when entering a mosque; in Muslim society, cleanliness is an important virtue, and the Qur'ân places high emphasis on it. Bringing dust into the mosque will invite a stiff rebuke, if not outrage.

• Do be sensitive to gender distinctions when visiting an Arab's home. Again, customs vary with age, class and level of education. Many Arab men will invite male guests into the living room, and usher the female guest into a separate room to chat with their wife. In other households it is considered acceptable for all the guests to be in the same room, but too much familiarity between the male guest and the host's wife might be frowned on. At any rate, don't expect an Arab man's wife to be present if you are invited into his home.

• Do rise and shake hands on greeting someone, or when leaving.

• Do exchange courtesies. These are more involved than in the West; traditionally on meeting someone again, one asks after the Arab man's family, in particular the children, but without going into the detail that people in the West often do. A hearty greeting will be remembered with affection; if it is a Muslim holiday, the name of the holiday (for instance, the Eid, at the end of Ramadan) followed by the word *mubarak* (blessed or holy), is the approved formula.

If it is a personal achievement that is being noted, a simple *mabruk* (congratulations) will do the trick. For those who prefer it, however, congratulations can be in English; the main thing is to recognize an event in simple, sincere and friendly terms.

• Do always accept light refreshments such as coffee or tea when offered. Taking coffee is part of Arab tradition; accepting or making the offer of coffee is a traditional sign of friendship in Bedouin society, and refusal was thinkable only when bad relations existed between two groups. Even if you only take a few sips, this symbolic acceptance means that offence is avoided.

• Do express appreciation at meals, but don't belch loudly, as recommended by the western folklore about Arabs. Most UAE nationals are a cosmopolitan bunch and etiquette norms while eating are similar to those in the West.

• Don't express admiration for ornaments and personal possessions. The comments will not be resented, but Arab tradition means that the host is obliged to cater to his guest's every whim. An Arab saying, *baiti baitak*, means 'My house is your house' and an Arab host will feel obliged to give his guest any object that is specifically admired, and if the offer is made, the host is unlikely to brook a refusal. The guest would then be obliged to give a present at a later date of an equal value.

The above list may sound daunting, and therefore it is important to emphasize a final don't:

Don't let the etiquette rules make you so careful to avoid offence that you end up sitting sullenly and appearing not to enjoy yourself.

An Arab friend of mine once expressed a great deal of affection for one foreigner among the many he had met — who did most things 'wrong' on their first meeting, at least according to the rules of etiquette.

A Westerner who makes mistakes can garner as much sympathy through openness, warmth and a sense of humour as the visitor who has read up all the right background, but seems ill at ease and inhibited.

Where to Stay

The UAE offers a wide range of hotels in the main cities, from budget options to the most luxurious five-star varieties. Rates are reasonable; for top name hotels you could expect to pay AED 500-700 a night. Medium-range hotels cost around AED 200-300 a night. There are also a few youth hostels and very cheap hotels at around AED 100 a night.

It is worth noting also that, as with other business negotiations in this area, you can bargain about hotel rates. The listed price of some hotels is as much as AED 100 above what they actually charge.

Outside the main cities, the choice of hotels is more limited. Government sponsored rest houses tend to be simple, clean and moderately priced. Hotels outside the cities are often booked well in advance, especially the beach hotels along the east and west coasts on the weekend. If you're planning a trip to the Northern Emirates or Fujairah it is best to book in advance.

When to Go

The UAE boasts sunshine all year round, with occasional showers at the start of summer and winter. Typically the temperature ranges from around 15-20°C in December to around 40-50°C and 100 per cent humidity in August. There is little rainfall at any time but when it does rain it often comes down 'in buckets'.

The hot season runs from June to September, with July and August the peak months in terms of humidity. The summer heat is at its worst on the coast and many Bedu and others traditionally retire inland during the summer monsoon, either to the mountainous areas in Fujairah, or the oases in Abu Dhabi on the border with Oman, to escape the heat.

Now, the move is often to holiday destinations in Europe; many Western expatriates also choose this time of year to get away.

In October, temperatures begin to fall, as does the humidity. The weather is balmy from November to April, though it can be cool and dull for weeks between December and February. May remains comfortable, but you can sense the summer torpor just around the corner.

Spring or autumn is probably the best time to visit the UAE. The water is warm but still refreshing, the sunshine nonstop — apart from occasional dust-storms — and the skies perfect, blue and cloudless.

Alternatively, a break over Christmas might be a welcome getaway from the long north European winter, although the water, while still swimmable, is perhaps a touch on the chilly side. The skies are sometimes cloudy, and this is the most likely time of year for rain.

Above: National flag of United Arab Emirates.
Right: Hotels of the highest international quality are to be found throughout the Emirates. Guests relax at Le Meridien, Abu Dhabi.
Following pages: Plains stretch out as far as the eye can see on both sides of the dual-carrigeway to Fujairah and the east coast.

Above: A visitor cools off in the heat of Abu Dhabi.

What to Take

Clothing

Obviously, a visitor's choice of clothing depends partly on the time of year although as a general rule of thumb it never gets really cold so a summer wardrobe should suffice. It is rarely, if ever, necessary to wear a coat in the UAE. In the 'winter' season from October through April, in addition to the light clothing worn in summer, you might need a cotton sweater, cardigan or jacket. This is particularly the case in the evenings, especially in the mountains and the desert.

Rainfall in the UAE averages about five days per year, usually in December or January. Even if you're visiting in these months, it's not really necessary to take an umbrella although gum boots can come in handy when the rains do come as there is little drainage and it doesn't take much for roads to turn into muddy rivers.

During the hot season, most of all July and August, no matter how little you wear it is difficult to remain comfortable without air-conditioning.

Water in swimming pools is like a luke-warm bath, affording little refreshment, and car steering wheels become too hot to handle if you park in the direct sunlight. While the obvious solution to the dress problem in such oppressive heat might seem simply to abandon as much of your clothing as you can, there are two objections: sunburn and local custom.

The strength of the sun should not be underestimated. Even in spring, a couple of hours on the beach may leave those with sensitive skin painfully roasted. In the summer, especially when swimming, severe sunburn and even sunstroke are a definite risk after a few hours out of the shade.

Even those endowed with a swarthy skin and heaps of melanin may suffer unexpectedly. It's best to use a good quality sun lotion or sun-block and avoid sitting in direct sunlight for any length of time. Also

Above: In the UAE when it rains, it pours. Winter 1996 in Sharjah.

avoid the midday sun. Sun lotions are readily available in the UAE.

Strangely enough, during the summer months it's sometimes necessary to wear a light sweater, jacket or cardigan due to the chill of the air-conditioning in restaurants and shopping malls.

Health

The UAE is fully equipped as far as medical facilities are concerned: well-stocked pharmacies, opticians, dentists and hospitals are available in the case of sickness. That said, health care in the UAE does not come cheaply, so it is worth taking out travel insurance. As is the case before travelling anywhere, it is advisable to have vaccinations against hepatitis A and B, typhoid and polio. Though there are mosquitoes, malaria is rare but does exist, so the use of malarial prophylactics may be advisable.

Photography

There is no problem in obtaining colour or black and white film, or having it proc-

essed. Taking photographs also poses few problems, unless around military bases – or sometimes oil fields and industrial areas. Whilst normal tourist photography is acceptable, it may be considered offensive to photograph Muslim women. It is courteous to ask permission before photographing men.

Overleaf: A water taxi provides a unique way to travel around town.

33

PART ONE: HISTORY, GEOGRAPHY AND PEOPLE

Above: A string of 5-star hotels, modern skyscrapers, lovely seafront drive and sandy beaches make Abu Dhabi's Corniche a magnet for visitors.
Left: Qasr-Al-Hosn, Abu Dhabi.

Land of Black Gold, Bazaars and Beaches

Formed in 1971, the United Arab Emirates — *Al Umarat al Arabiyah al Muthahidah* as it is known in Arabic — is one of the world's youngest nations. Yet in the quarter century since it was founded, it has achieved a distinctive 'personality' typified by tolerance, cosmopolitanism and its unique outward-looking development philosophy that has made it one of the Middle East's favoured business and leisure destinations.

The UAE celebrated its 25th anniversary in 1996. In its brief history it has transformed itself from a regional backwater into a central player in the area's development and the path to maturity has been gradual and steady.

The speed of its development has given it one of the highest living standards in the world, and one of the world's newest infrastructures. Yet change has not happened so fast that traditional values have been eroded.

The UAE, a key member of the Gulf Co-operation Council, has a reputation as a shrewd moderate in the complex regional politics that have pitted the oil giants of Saudi Arabia and Iran, Iraq and Kuwait against each other.

Oil has been the engine of this thrust to modernity. Crude oil, formed millions of years ago under the desert sands, was discovered in Saudi Arabia in the 1930s; about 20 years later, the emirates — then not federated but surviving individually as the Trucial States, and at times in conflict with their neighbours in what became the UAE — signed concessions with Western oil companies to exploit the 'black gold' under the sands.

It was a turning point in the history of the Emirates. The country's oil reserves were beyond the wildest dreams of the sheikhs who ruled a population that, at the time, eked a living from trade and date-cultivation, tending meagre stocks of live-stock, backed up by fishing. The UAE's reserves put it among the top five in the world in terms of years of sustainable production. Much of the credit for subsequent development lies with the ruling families of the oil-rich emirates. In Abu Dhabi, in particular, oil wealth was seen as the means to an end, and many socially beneficial investments in infrastructure, especially water resources, were made.

Oil wealth has also increased the influence of Abu Dhabi as the most important of the emirates, and the natural leaders in the delicate power-sharing that makes up UAE politics.

Oil reserves are unevenly distributed among the members of the federation. Abu Dhabi holds more than 90 per cent, enough for more than 100 years, while Dubai — although its free-wheeling trade made its own crude oil one of the most widely traded internationally and therefore a key price-determinant for the rest of the Gulf producers — has relatively meagre reserves, expected to last no more than about 30 years.

Sharjah and Ras al-Khaimah also have small pockets of condensate, a very light grade of crude oil, but not enough to develop an indigenous sustainable industry such as has been established in Abu Dhabi. However, Sharjah does have gas reserves.

The oil industry saw the transformation of UAE from a string of tiny impoverished principalities to a regional, and increasingly international, economic power in barely a quarter of a century. The UAE has a production capacity of 2.5-million barrels a day: in the same league as Russia or the North Sea.

It has been a member of the Organization of Petroleum Exporting Countries since it was formed. Abu Dhabi was a founding member of OPEC even before the federation was formed. Although, under

Right: Impressive fountain at Sharjah seems to imitate a gushing oilwell – symbol of the Emirates' prosperity.

Above: Not all industry is oil-based. Dubai Aluminium Co. at Jebel Ali in Dubai Emirate is a major employer. Right: Abu Dhabi's Baynunah Tower. Following pages: Abu Dhabi, the most conservative of all the Emirates, still allows plenty of scope for leisure activity.

the 1971 constitution, each of the emirates could individually elect to join OPEC, none of them did and Abu Dhabi gave up its own membership in favour of membership as a federation.

Traditionally, the UAE survived on trade, much of it related to the pearling industry until the 1930s, when Japanese cultured pearls swept the market and the worldwide economic depression combined virtually to wipe out an industry that had lasted for thousands of years along the littorals of the Arabian Gulf.

Trade remains the country's mainstay, but now it is petroleum rather than pearls that underpins the economy. The key export grades of crude oil — Murban from Abu Dhabi and Fateh Blend from Dubai — are among the most widely traded internationally, finding markets as far afield as Japan and the USA.

But the UAE economy is also rapidly diversifying; the re-export business to Iran has grown quickly in recent years and the emirates, particularly Dubai, are

striving to develop a variety of service industries.

The fruits of the oil boom have been re-invested in industrial and service sector projects: the UAE now has a thriving aluminium industry, while its ports at Mina Zayed, Sharjah, Fujairah, Jebel Ali and Dubai are important transhipment centres for goods from the Indian subcontinent and elsewhere.

It has also become a regional tourism hub with its own airline, Emirates, and some of the best hotel facilities in the Gulf. Desalination plants provide the fresh water that was so precious to the desert communities of the past, and the greening of the desert is being attempted by planting a number of hardy strains of vegetation which, it is hoped, will gradually bind the arid sands.

The speed of change is commented on by almost everyone. A recent book, *From Rags to Riches*, provides a moving portrait of this nation on the move. Recalling a childhood memory of hanging upside-

Contrasting styles in Dubai: Angular lines of old tower (left) contrasts with graceful modern housing development (above).

down from a camel after he inadvertently slipped off its back on a journey across the desert to Al Ain, Mohammed al-Fahim remarks:

'Nearly fifteen years after I had hung helplessly from the side of that camel, building had begun in Abu Dhabi. At the time, the island sand was used to make the concrete that went into everything that was being constructed. Our teacher told us that a day would come when there would not be enough sand in Abu Dhabi to build all the roads, houses and buildings we would need for our city. We scoffed at this impossibility. We had enough sand in Abu Dhabi to last until forever and beyond. Less than five years later, the impossibility became a reality when we had to bring sand from the desert to meet our construction needs.'

The pace of development is reflected in the bewildering mix of the old and new that typifies the main towns. Modern palaces, albeit using traditional architectural motifs, line the corniches and beaches of Abu Dhabi.

Skyscrapers stud the creek of Dubai, towering above the wooden *abras* that still ply its waters. In Sharjah, hundreds of dhows line the seafront, reflecting the continuity with the region's maritime traditions, while just to the west along the Corniche, engineering companies service the offshore rigs that have opened up a second frontier for oil exploration in the shallow waters of the Arabian Gulf.

The mixture of the old and new, the exotic and the kitsch means that travellers who want 'authenticity' may find the main cities of the UAE something of a disappointment.

Those who want a deluxe beachside holiday with a choice of international cuisines and night clubs that open until the early hours will be spoilt for choice, but will miss the interesting nooks and crannies that make the UAE a distinctively Middle Eastern nation.

Those who want the taste of 'the Orient' will probably be disappointed by the

45

انتح هنا
OPEN HERE

صندوق الرسائل

NEXT COLLECTION AT مواعيد التفريغ التالية للساعة

LETTER BOX

apparent dearth of ancient monuments, and the fact that — while everything from camel-riding to off-road desert trips are available — it is all largely laid on for the benefit of tourists.

Service industries are a growth area for the UAE and if it means being driven into the desert in a Japanese jeep by a Pakistani staff member of a European five-star hotel chain surrounded by Germans and Russians, that is the price of progress.

However, there is another side of the UAE, a far cry from the spanking newness of the cities. The countryside around the emirates provides beautiful natural scenery, from craggy mountains to stretching plains, from the dark red sand-dunes of the desert to the undulating white sands of the beaches along the Gulf and east coasts.

To avoid disappointment, however, these should be seen in their proper context; the UAE is a newcomer among tourist destinations and, despite what the government literature says, the UAE is not a place of stunning monuments and many of the sights would be easy to miss, even if they were well signposted, which is all too often not the case. There are numerous old forts, wind- and watchtowers, affording glimpses into the past, but these are often undocumented.

This situation is changing. The country's rulers have put much effort into reviving the people's awareness of their traditional heritage, and in exploring sites of historical and archaeological interest. This rich heritage ranges from local cuisine to sports such as falconry, as well as some modern cultural pursuits. The UAE also harbours a surprising variety of animal, bird and plant-life; the features on wildlife, birdlife, plants and sea-life attempt to reflect this. (See Part Four, Special Features.)

Undoubtedly in this *mélange* of the old and new, the new predominates. The UAE offers excellent modern hotels, with every variety of convenience, often fronted by beaches that are clean and sandy.

Although the top-range hotels are not cheap, comfortable accommodation can be had in all the emirates for around US$100 a night, and often cheaper.

The shopping malls, particularly in Dubai, offer a huge range of modern electronic items, particularly popular in recent years with Eastern European tourists. But bazaars and souqs offer traditional handicraft items: old coffee-pots, Oriental carpets, and a wide variety of antiquities, usually from India.

Yet one hour into the desert interior the tourist experiences a real feel of how the UAE must have been in the old days, when camels outnumbered cars, and you could travel for miles without seeing a single town. This remains the case; but the telltale signs of progress are all around, in the form of billboards all along the excellent paved roads, advertising everything from air-conditioners to poultry.

Though there are few monuments, for the tourist there is a variety of things to do. The UAE has the only 'green' golf courses in the Middle East, long stretches of fine sandy beaches, an almost perfect climate — at least for sun-lovers — and beautiful clear coastal waters that are ideal for snorkelling, scuba-diving or such water sports as wind-sailing and water-skiing.

Many tourists are content to soak up the sun in the five-star hotels, but forget to soak up the atmosphere in the souqs and bazaars. This is a pity, but a fact; many visitors stay only a few days, their interest limited to catching a few rays at the end of a business trip.

But the country has hidden depths. Increasingly, the UAE is focusing on its ecological variety as a tourist attraction. The waters around it abound in marine fauna rarely seen elsewhere, including a variety of dolphins and porpoises, and a kaleidoscope of tropical fish.

In the desert, the sparse arid environment is host to a number of endangered species of animals, including the oryx and the Arabian leopard. Meanwhile, in a number of locations such as parks, gardens and nature reserves, these arboreal habitats make the emirates ideal for bird-watching.

Left: The emirates' colonial ties with Britain are reflected in this 'pillar-box red' postbox.

Glittering attractions in shopping mall, Dubai, (above) and Sharjah (right).

As far as local culture is concerned, traditional handicrafts are still practised, as are entertainments such as dances and camel-racing, and there is a nascent interest in archaeology, with a number of Stone and Iron Age sites excavated.

The problem for the modern tourist is how to find these traces of the UAE's past. A number of tour companies offer attractive glimpses of these traditional pursuits but it is also still possible to come on them unexpectedly.

This is probably the real thrill for the tourist anywhere; and although in the UAE, modern-day living has transformed the towns and cities, coming across a traditional coffee-shop in a back alley by the souq, or an old antique shop selling coffee-pots from Oman or Saudi Arabia, offers a taste of the unexpected that is manna for the modern adventurer.

The UAE's commercial success means that such intriguing insights into the old days are few and far between, however. As a result, many visitors prefer to use the UAE as a jumping-off point for other destinations. The UAE is ideally placed as a gateway to visit the Far East, the Indian subcontinent or Central Asia. Excellent communication links, and a competitive travel trade, mean that travelling on from the UAE to another holiday destination is convenient, comfortable and cheap.

Nearby Oman offers insights into a society that has only emerged from its reclusive past in the last 20 years; a two-hour flight to India or Pakistan takes the visitor to the cradle of ancient civilizations; the emerging central Asian republics are only three to four hours away by plane; and, in half-a-dozen hours, one can relax on the beaches of Maldives, Thailand or Malaysia, or try the exotic Comoros or the countries along the eastern seaboard of Africa.

Birth of a Nation

The United Arab Emirates became a nation on 2 December 1971 when six of the seven emirates that currently form the UAE federation formed the Union Government, which took over the running of the country's internal and external affairs.

The original union was formed by Abu Dhabi, Dubai, Ajman, Sharjah, Umm al-Quwain and Fujairah, after the British decided to withdraw from their Indian Ocean territories in 1968. Ras al-Khaimah was a latecomer, joining on 10 February 1972. Originally, it had been mooted that Qatar and Bahrain might also become part of the federal system, but these declined.

Britain's withdrawal from the Gulf may seem surprising given the discovery of oil in Abu Dhabi only shortly before. But with India's independence in 1947, Britain lost much of the impetus for its role in the Arabian Gulf, which was never intended to be outrightly colonial but aimed primarily to protect its Indian territories. The British focused control on the sea-routes and foreign affairs, but left domestic policy largely to the locals.

The head of state is Sheikh Zayed bin Sultan al-Nahyan, ruler of Abu Dhabi and the founder of the federation. Zayed has been re-elected to successive five-year terms as president since 1971 by the Supreme Council of Rulers, which groups representatives from all seven of the Emirates.

The prime minister is the ruler of Dubai, Sheikh Maktoum bin Rashid al-Maktoum, who succeeded his father, Sheikh Rashid bin Saeed al-Maktoum, in 1990.

Government is by consensus among the rulers and their executive organs. The Supreme Council of Rulers is the top policy-making body of the state, and the rulers of each of the seven emirates has a seat on the council.

When the council was founded, each of the emirates had its own government mechanisms under the local ruler; the seven rulers thus agreed to set up a constitution, setting out which powers were to be allocated to the federal institutions, and which would remain the prerogative of individual emirates.

The federal government is generally responsible for foreign affairs, security and defence, nationality and immigration issues, education, public health, currency, postal, telecommunications, air-traffic control and aircraft licensing, labour relations, banking, delimitation of territorial waters, and the extradition of criminals.

But the relationship between federal and local government is complex and changing. Under the constitution, individual emirates can assign responsibility for certain aspects of the exercise of government to the federal authorities. In the mid-1970s, the army was unified and is now run at a federal level.

The main executive body is the Council of Ministers, the country's *de facto* cabinet, while the country's parliament, the Federal National Council, is made up of 40 members drawn from each of the seven emirates. The cabinet includes the usual ministerial portfolios, and is headed by the prime minister, who is chosen by the president and the other members of the Supreme Council.

The ministers may be drawn from any of the emirates, although in practice representatives are from the more populous emirates; part of the delicacy of government stems from the balancing act that is constantly necessary to ensure the best ministerial staff, while at the same time avoiding a skewed, unrepresentative cabinet.

The make-up of the Federal National Council is determined by fixed ratios of representatives from the various emirates, based on their population: the 40-member council currently has eight members each from Abu Dhabi and Dubai, six each from Sharjah and Ras al-Khaimah, and four each from Fujairah, Umm al-Quwain and Ajman. The council bears the responsibility of examining and, if necessary, amending legislation passed at a federal level. The

Opposite and following page: Exhibits at Al-Ain Museum.

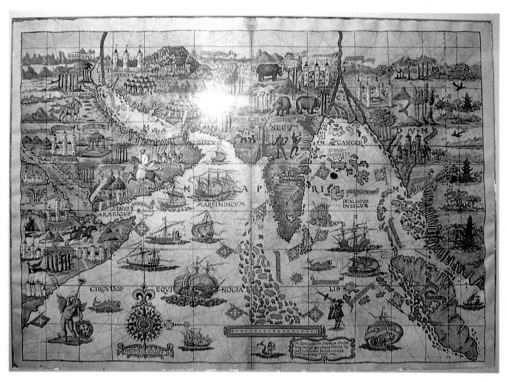

UAE has an independent judiciary at a federal level, guaranteed under the national constitution.

Each of the emirates has its own government, although these vary in size and also in complexity. In Abu Dhabi, the National Consultative Council is composed of members from some of the oldest tribes and families in the emirate.

The work of the Executive Council is split into two regions, each headed by an official with the title of the Ruler's Representative. The main cities are administered by municipalities, each of which has a Municipal Council.

Early history of the UAE

Although the recorded history of the UAE is relatively short, people have been living in settled communities on the peninsula for at least 7,000 years. However, evidence in the Arabian Peninsula has been found of human habitation since early Pleistocene and Lower Palaeolithic periods; Stone Age tools found in the UAE date back as far as 5,000 BC.

Stone Age (Neolithic) sites in the UAE indicate that the people who lived there had already established rudimentary agriculture systems, domesticated animals and probably both ate and cured fish.

Stone Age arrows and other hunting implements have been found in the Hajar Mountains. The settled communities which emerged in the fifth millennum BC have left their mark in many parts of the UAE, but unfortunately no written records or inscriptions have been found.

However, there are plentiful Neolithic pottery sites, including the well-known Ubaid pottery which has been discovered in Sharjah, Umm al-Quwain, Ras al-Khaimah and the Dalma Islands.

An increasing number of archaeological discoveries date back as far as 2,000-3,000 BC, at the beginning of the Bronze Age. Major archaeological sites have been discovered at Umm al-Nar and Hili, near Al Ain in Abu Dhabi, as well as in Sharjah, Ras al-Khaimah and Fujairah. Remains dating from 3,000 BC to the early-mid Islamic period have also been found at Hatta, Al-Qusais and Jumeirah in the emirate of

Above: Model communal grave, Dubai.

Dubai. Archaeological evidence suggests that in the prehistoric Bronze Age the area was closely associated with the mysterious civilisation of Magan, which is referred to as a major source of copper in the cuneiform texts of the Sumerian civilization, which was centred across the Gulf in the region of Mesopotamia.

The Magan region probably also included parts of Oman, whose rich copper deposits at Sohar were reputed to be the original site of King Solomon's Mines, and which are still being worked.

The ancient region of Dilmun, referring to the Bahrain peninsula and an area along the coast as far as Failaka, competed with Magan as a source of materials for the Sumerian and Akkadian civilizations. A third civilization, Meluhha, also traded with Mesopotamia during this period: it has been variously identified as India, some areas in what is now southern Iran or Pakistan, or the Nile countries.

Little is known about the kingdom of Magan. The first reference to Magan comes during the reign of Sargon of Akkad between 2,370-2,316 BC, and it is also mentioned in later Assyrian texts and in the epic of Gilgamesh.

It seems likely that the region — as well as its lifeblood, copper, which was largely exported as ingots rather than finished bronze items — also exported pearls, wood, diorite and limestone marble to the more heavily populated Mesopotamian region. Cuneiform texts also suggest that Magan supplied reed and vegetables, including onions, to Mesopotamia, as well as precious stones.

Copper was transported from areas including the Jebel Hafiz and Hili to trading centres on the coast, including Umm al-Nar, and exported either directly to Mesopotamia or via the adjacent empire of Dilmun. A host of copper objects have been found in the digs at Umm al-Nar, including copper slag, suggesting that some copper may have been smelted locally.

Records of the Magan civilization simply stopped after the second millennium BC. The Magan area may well have been more fertile than is the area that makes up the 20th-century UAE, and the gradual desertification of the area may have accounted for the decline. The growing importance of iron in making weapons and tools may also have diminished the importance of Magan as a source of copper. Iron Age sites, those dating from 1,000 BC to about 300 BC, are fewer in the UAE than Bronze Age sites; however, some remains have been found at Rumeilah, Hili and to the east and north of the modern town of Mleihah in the Northern Emirates.

Colonial Times

Before union, from the mid-1850s onwards, the emirates were known as the Trucial States, under a system in which each of the individual emirates had separate treaty agreements with the British colonial administration.

Each of the states was ruled by a sheikh, traditionally the leader of the most powerful tribe; individual tribes and their subsections each had their own ruler, who through influence or petition, and usually a mixture of both, would seek to influence the ruler in directions they saw fit.

The *majlis* remains a link between modern government and the traditional exercise of power. In the past, rulers and other senior leaders would hold regular *majlis* at which any citizen could turn up and make their pleas: anything from a request for a piece of land to complaints about ministerial behaviour, or weightier policy issues.

All the rulers of the emirates still preserve the institution of *majlis,* despite the modern apparatus of government that was created by the founding of the federation.

Already, in colonial times, substantial trade and cooperation existed between individual emirates but the history of the individual emirates have left their mark on the society of today.

Some states were little more than fishing villages, although Ras al-Khaimah had significant sea-power and, on occasion, attacked British forces.

In 1853, following a British decision to suppress the slave trade in the early 1800s, the sheikhs of the Gulf signed agreements to suppress the traffic and transport of slaves from their territory. It was a period of great and complex change, both demographic and political. The 19th and 20th centuries saw the formation of nations in the Middle East from what had been scattered provinces ruled largely by tribes or foreign governors.

Borders were often loosely defined, and allegiances makeshift. When borders were defined, they were likely to be done so by the colonial powers at the stroke of a pen. The system of protectorates was introduced at the beginning of the 20th century in order to carve up the Middle East into areas of influence among the colonial powers, notably Britain, France and Germany.

Under the protectorate system, the colonial power agreed to 'protect' a nation against any aggression, while the nation itself agreed not to cede its territory to a foreign power, nor to develop relations without the protector nation's agreement.

Such a treaty was imposed on the sheikhs of the UAE, partly reflecting British determination ahead of World War I to keep France and Germany out of what it saw as its area of influence.

Such treaties were signed with Sharjah and Fujairah as late as 1952 and it was at this time that the UAE principalities defined their current boundaries.

Above: Selection of coffee pots and other items at heritage exhibition, Abu Dhabi.

British rule has been the subject of much controversy, given the anti-colonial backlash that typified Arab nationalism. The UAE regards the period of British influence in a broadly negative light; 'benign neglect' is how it is described in the latest edition of the *UAE Yearbook*, which notes that the British paid little attention to the economic, let alone social, development of the region.

On the positive side, Britain held a role in the administration of the sheikhdoms, and British civil servants still play a part in the bureaucracy to this day; also in the 1950s Britain took a lead in solving a number of border disputes between Oman, Saudi Arabia and Abu Dhabi, including the rights to the Buraimi Oasis.

However, the UAE's formation as a nation state has left a number of border issues unresolved, both at land and at sea. Moreover, the existing sovereignty both within the UAE itself, and neighbouring Oman, is highly complex; little enclaves of one emirate are found within territory owned by another, and small tracts of Omani territory exist within the bounds of what is now the UAE. Throughout this period the Arabs of the Gulf retained their own identities. Nationhood was a product only of the 19th and early 20th centuries; until then, allegiance was chiefly to tribe, and then to clan and extended family.

These traditional allegiances still remain, despite the UAE's increasing self-identity as a modern nation. Each of the seven emirates' ruling families is descended from a tribe or group of tribes, and the rulers are proud of that association.

It was during British colonial rule that the current definitions of the territory of the various emirates emerged.

Tribal Territories

Even before the coming of the British, the four main tribal groups in the emirate of Abu Dhabi, were the Bani Yas, the Manasir, the Dhawahir and the Awamir. The Bani Yas was a federation of more than a dozen tribes which dominated the towns of Abu Dhabi and Al Ain, as well as areas of the Liwa Oasis.

The Bani Yas comprised a number of important tribes, including the Al Bu Falah,

who traditionally provided the rulers of Abu Dhabi. To this day, the Al Bu Falah, or the Al Nahyan as they came to be called in the 20th century, are at the helm of government in Abu Dhabi. The town of Abu Dhabi was founded, according to tradition, in 1762, well before the coming of the British.

Other significant tribes among the Bani Yas included the Rumaithat and the Qubaisat – both heavily involved in the pearling industry until the 1930s – as well as the Mazari, the Hawamil and the Sudan.

The Manasir have traditionally inhabited the vast stretches of land along the borders with Saudi Arabia; the Dhawahir lived in the eastern parts of the emirate, while the Awamir lived west of the Buraimi Oasis.

The Bani Yas emerged as the single most important tribal group in the UAE during the 18th and 19th centuries, gradually coming to dominate the Al Ain area, and also fighting off incursions from Saudi Arabia's hard-line Muslim Wahhabist movement in the early 1800s. The rule of the Bani Yas was further consolidated during the period of rule of Sheikh Zayed bin Khalifah Al Bu Falah, who reigned in Abu Dhabi between 1855 and 1909.

The historical ties between the Al Bu Falah and the areas of Al Ain and Liwa remain a factor in Abu Dhabi's planning. The current ruler, Sheikh Zayed, has poured huge amounts of energy and money into developing these areas, which had been largely neglected before the discovery of oil.

The emirate of Dubai was also established under a branch of the Bani Yas, but in this case the relationship has often been strained by rivalry with branches of the tribe settled in the Abu Dhabi area.

But the history of the town predates this: an Italian explorer in 1580 described Dubai as a prosperous town, dependent largely on pearl-fishing, and it is also located on Abraham Ortelius' map of 1570.

In 1833, 800 men from the Al Bu Falasah tribe settled in the area that is now Dubai, on the excellent creek that has become the lifeline of the city. The group settled at Bur Dubai under Maktoum bin Butti.

The town became independent and, eight years later in 1841, the group extended their domain to Deira, just over the creek, later also moving to Shindagha. In 1894, tax exemptions were made by Maktoum bin Hasher al-Maktoum.

By the beginning of the 20th century, Dubai was a small town three kilometres by one kilometre in area. In 1908 there were 350 shops in Deira and 50 in Bur Dubai. The souqs included: Al Kabilm, Al Manazer, Al Tomoor, Al Arsa and Al Sabkha.

Dubai's creek is located on one of the most favourable coastal strips in the whole UAE and its convenient anchorages soon attracted Persians, Indians and Baluchis — from the area that is now Pakistan — who were rapidly assimilated into the community.

The creek used to be much more extensive, stretching all the way to Al Ain, but silt reduced the water-level during the 20th century. In 1902 it was the main anchorage for boats coming from India and East Africa but, by the 1950s, silting caused by the north wind had reduced the volume of dhow traffic. During the 1950s, Sheikh Saeed bin Maktoum ordered dredging, a decision which, though costly, was a turning point.

Illegal or quasi-legal trade in gold also thrived: lack of customs duties meant that Dubai became an important transhipment centre for gold mined elsewhere, largely supplying the massive market in India.

The beginning of modern Dubai also stems from this period. In 1943 the first clinic was built and, in 1946, the first bank was established. Deals were struck with the UK for oil development.

Al Maktoum Bridge was built in 1962, the Shindagha Tunnel in 1975 and the Garhoud Bridge in 1976. In 1977 the population was 207,000. New dhow wharfage was added in 1993, under the new ruler who came to power in 1990.

Left: Woman collects water from an ancient well, Dubai.

The Northern Emirates have for a long time been dominated by the Qawasim, who originated in the 18th century as a clan of the powerful Huwalah tribe. The Qawasim formed their own empire, based at Ras al-Khaimah but stretching over areas that included large parts of modern day Sharjah.

References to the Qawasim have been found in a Portuguese document of 1648. The Qawasim depended largely on their prowess at sea, but also held sway in the central mountainous regions of the Northern Emirates. As a sea-power, it is no surprise that the Qawasim clashed frequently with the British who regarded the Gulf as a strategic link with India.

In part, the Qawasim were responsible for the colonial designation of the Gulf as the Pirate Coast. The sobriquet has subsequently been proved unjustified: the naval raids by the indigenous tribes were a natural response to the warmongering activities of what they saw as an intrusive foreign power.

The emirates of Ajman and Umm al-Quwain emerged from separate tribal groupings from the 19th century. Ajman is ruled by members of the Al Naim tribe, which originated in the Buraimi area.

The current day rulers of Umm al-Quwain are descended from the Al Ali tribe, who appear originally to have inhabited a large islet at Sharak, on the southern coast of Persia, and the nearby island of Qays. According to some authors, the tribe was related to the Al Ali of Oman. The Al Ali tribe was living in the Ras al-Khaimah area as far back as the 17th century.

The current separation of Sharjah and Ras al-Khaimah, both of whose current rulers bear the name Al Qassimi, resulted from a split in the tribal grouping in 1910. The current ruler of Sharjah, Sheikh Saqr bin Mohammed al-Qassimi, was the grandson of the first ruler, Salim bin Sultan.

Sharjah was located on maps as far back as 1580, and is mentioned in Dutch documents of the 18th century as one of the few inhabited places between Qatif, on the Nejdi coast of Saudi Arabia, and Ras al-Khaimah.

These accounts say the town was under the authority of a sheikh belonging to the Qawasim, which it lists as a branch of the Huwala tribal group. Although there is some confusion among the various names applied to the settlement, which is listed as Sir, Zur and Sara by a number of sources, it seems probable that all these accounts referred to Sharjah.

The current ruler of Ras al-Khaimah is also a descendant of the Qawasim tribal group. The key town in this area used to be Julfar, a few miles north of modern Ras al-Khaimah.

Another powerful tribal group, the Sharqiyyin, were spread across much of the area that is now Fujairah, inhabiting large tracts of the Musandam Peninsula south of the areas now held by Oman.

The tribe was one of the largest in the area, ruling the region east of the Hajar Mountains, but the area was only officially recognised as an independent emirate in 1952. In Arabic *sharq* means 'east', and it was their position on the eastern side of the peninsula that gave them the name Sharqiyyin.

The tribe established itself around the town of Fujairah, eking a living by planting date palms, and by building maritime trade, including fishing. The tribe remains homogenous, despite the pressures to internal migration in the oil-rich UAE.

Traditional Roots
Despite their separate tribal origins and identity, an important factor binding the separate emirates into a single system has been their shared heritage.

Until the early 20th century, the lifestyle of the Arabs brought disparate tribal and family groups together in a common interest. All Islam has been a touchstone of identity, defining the indigenous population against

Previous pages: Majestic aerial view of the creek, Dubai. Right: Dhow at harbour, Dubai.

Above: Traders inspect pearls at Dubai's diving village during Shopping Festival 1996.

the European colonial powers, just as family roots tended to define individual tribes against each other.

Traditionally the people survived on trade, notably pearl-fishing, but also by doing business in spices and other jewels and precious metals. For all but a few until the oil-boom, poverty was a part of everyday life. Families would get by on fishing, rearing camels or goats, and small-scale cultivation of crops, including dates, in the inland areas.

Families formed a web linking the coast to the inland oases; often, the men would go to the coast during the spring to dive for pearls, and would then migrate inland during the hot summer months. The Bedouin tribes would remain in the desert, roaming according to the season but in contact with the settled families in the oases on the coast.

The system has been followed for hundreds of years, back to the early days of Islam. As a result, borders in the past meant little. Traditional grazing grounds or water-rights at oases meant more than

sovereignty determined by lines drawn in the sand or on maps.

Friends or members of a tribal group would be welcome at one oasis, and driven away at another if hostility had broken out with a competing tribe. The drinking of coffee was a traditional sign of friendship; a refusal to offer the guest coffee, or a refusal by the guest of the proffered cup, would indicate that differences had arisen; only when these were sorted out was hospitality offered or accepted.

Such a society did not result in the building of great monuments. Culture was transmitted orally, in the forms of songs and stories, as well as the handing down of one's lineage. Those with reading and writing ability learned their skills largely from the Qur'ânic schools, where study of the Muslim holy book was conducted by simply learning the whole book by rote. Literacy thus derived set apart the scholar from the illiterate population, and he would then join the ranks of either the merchants, or the religious leaders.

Above: The Diving Village. Diving for pearls was an established industry long before the oil boom.

Maritime UAE

The UAE has borders on two of the world's great maritime trading routes: the Arabian Gulf and the Indian Ocean. In particular, because of its shallow waters and hot climate, the Gulf area was ideal for encouraging the growth of pearls; pearl-fishing was one of the region's major industries until the invention of the cultured pearl in the 1930s by the Japanese.

But traders in dhows have plied the waters of the Gulf and the Indian Ocean for hundreds of years, bringing spices from India, cooking oil from East Africa and taking back goods from Iran and neighbouring countries.

Through the centuries the maritime pursuits of the local people have been recorded. Marco Polo mentions the trade between the area and India in his book *The Travels*, although he is generally unimpressed by the quality of the vessels:

'Their ships are very bad, and many of them founder, because they are not fastened with iron nails, but stitched together with thread made of coconut husks. They

soak the husk till it assumes the texture of horse hair; then they make it into threads and stitch their ships. It is not spoilt by the salt water, but lasts remarkably well. The ships have one mast, one sail, and one rudder, and are not decked; when they have loaded them, they cover the cargo with skins, and on top of these they put the horses which they ship to India for sale. They have no iron for nails; so they employ wooden pegs and stitch with thread. This makes it a risky undertaking to sail in these ships. And you can take my word that many of them sink, because the Indian Ocean is very stormy.'

At the beginning of the 20th century, about 50 dhows visited Dubai annually and it was an important dhow-building centre. The dhow builders, *al-galaliif*, worked with traditional tools to make a variety of different boats, from simple vessels hewn from a single tree-trunk, for use in the local creek, to large ocean-going dhows. The *dawar shami*, a kind of pulley, was used to pull boats from the sea.

Left: Smiling traders at Dubai's fish market. Above: The Creek, Dubai, is a hive of activity.

The variety of boats on the creeks and the high seas reflects the sophistication of the UAE's maritime culture. These included: *sambuk,* a wooden boat with a wooden pole as a mast, used for fishing; *baggara,* used for pearling, and often decorated red, but with no mast; *banoush,* a slightly larger vessel about six metres long used for transporting people about the creek, and made of a single tree-trunk; *houri,* a small boat, between three and six metres long, made from a single tree trunk; *abra,* about seven metres long, used to transport people on the creek. *Abras* in particular are used in the creek for transportation to this day.

Various dhows were also used, depending on the size of journey and the types of water and wind conditions expected. *Al baghlah, al boom* and *al bateel* were used for long-distance travel, going as far afield as India or East Africa. *Al shouee, al baggarah,* and *al jalbout* were used for pearling and fishing in the Arabian Gulf or in the shallow waters near the Indian Ocean coasts.

Much smaller boats were used for transportation around the sheltered waters of the creeks along the coast of the Arabian Gulf, including Al Houri and Al Shahouf. Most boats were made of wood, but a smaller vessel, *al shasha,* was made from palm leaves and ropes fabricated from the fibres of the coconut palm.

Fishing was a source of both sustenance and revenue for those wealthy enough to own a simple boat. The Gulf waters of the UAE teem with more than 300 different types of fish drawn from 111 species. Generally, it was the men who went to sea to bring in the catch, while women traditionally sold the fish.

Fish were also dried for export, when they were known as *al ouma.* A wide variety of fishing techniques, both from land and at sea, has been developed along the coasts over the years. Among the most popular is the use of nets, *al aliakh,* to trap the fish; also used are *al garagir,* special cages made from palm leaves.

While fishing offered sustenance and some money, pearls opened up the possibility of becoming suddenly and incredibly wealthy. In the early 20th century there were 300 pearl divers' dhows and 7,000 people were engaged in the hard business of diving for pearls.

The pearl merchants were known as *al tawashin*, and the captains of the pearling dhows as *al nokhaza*. The pearl beds, *al hiraat*, were located along the shores of the Gulf and were especially rich around Bahrain.

The equipment used by the merchants included: brass sieves for separating out various sizes of pearl, copper pearl scales to weigh the pearls and brass pearl scoops for sorting the different qualities.

The divers themselves would use turtleshell nose clips as they dived for as much as three minutes down to depths of 30 metres or more; leather finger-protectors which were soaked in coconut milk to keep them supple were worn as protection against the sharp corals. Pearls were valued by their colour, size and shape, using special grading tools such as *al toos* and *al ghrabeel*.

Before the British

History before the coming of the British was defined by the competing claims of a succession of colonial powers whose influence rose and fell with the fortunes of their own empires.

For hundreds of years two powers held sway in the Arabian Gulf region — first, the Ottoman Empire, centred on what is now Turkey, and then successive Persian empires, centred on what is now Iran. Later, from the 1500s onwards, a number of Western powers began to vie for influence: first the Portuguese, followed by the Dutch, in the 1600s and 1700s, and then the French and British in the 1800s. The rise of Oman as a naval power began in the 1600s and the Western powers cooperated, alternately with the Persians, Ottomans and Omanis, in the execution of their colonial ambitions. Trade ties with India, the Central Asian lands and China in the east, and in the west with Europe, have been a continuum from ancient times; but this has largely been mediated by the colonial powers of the day. Similarly, the Europeans did not attempt to colonise the area, merely to control the maritime areas to influence trade and consolidate their colonial possessions elsewhere.

The Portuguese held the strategic town of Hormuz from the 1500s and it is largely from Portuguese accounts, supplemented by those of Venetian traders, that the first reports of the Gulf are known. Among them is that of Marco Polo, who vividly describes the climate and shipping:

'The people here are black and worship Mahomet. In summer, they do not stay in the cities, or they would all die of heat; but they go out to their gardens, where there are rivers and sheets of water. Here they build arbours of hurdles, resting at one end on the bank and at the other on piles driven in below the water, and covered with foliage to fend off the sun.'

The heat in the area clearly impressed Marco Polo, who also describes the intense wind that blows off the desert:

'It is a fact that several times in the summer there comes a wind from the direction of the sandy wastes that lie around this plain, a wind so overpoweringly hot that it would be deadly if it did not happen that, as soon as men are aware of its approach, they plunge neck-deep into the water and so escape its heat.'

A unique list of names of ports and towns is found in the account of a Venetian traveller, Gasparo Balbi, and from this it is clear that such towns as Dubai, Ajman, Sharjah and Umm al-Quwain were settled at least as far back as 1580.

Balbi lists many places not mentioned elsewhere until the end of the 18th century, including Sir Bani Yas, a reference which establishes that the Bani Yas tribe was active as far back as the 15th century.

The territorial extent of the state of Hormuz is uncertain, but it is likely it consisted of a loose empire of towns and cities on both the southern and northern shores of the Gulf. Hormuz was ruled by a Portuguese captain, who exercised his authority over the Shah of Hormuz in the name of the king of Portugal.

The Dutch exercised their influence through the Dutch East India Company, between which and the rival English East India Company tensions slowly developed.

The Persians tried to get help from England and the Netherlands to break the hold of the Portuguese in the Gulf, who at the start of the 17th century held sway over the Strait of Hormuz through the vassal kingdom of Hormuz.

Persian ambitions to expand from being essentially an inland power by moving outwards to the coasts, however, were hampered by their lack of naval power, and by the fact that the English and Dutch East India companies were proscribed by their directors from taking decisive military action.

Despite what regional representatives saw as opportunities for conquest, and no matter how closely local staff became embroiled in the machinations of local politics, the directors first and foremost looked at the bottom line. They were averse to risking large military expeditions that might do little to bolster trade. Thus Persian ambitions collapsed in the 18th century.

The Ottoman Empire, meanwhile, had its own problems in maintaining its position in the Gulf and, during the 18th century, it ceased to play an active role.

The Coming of Islam

Before Islam, the UAE was influenced by successive incursions from Persia, in about 200 BC, and in the second century AD by the Yazdites, a group of Yemeni extraction.

These two groups shared power in the peninsula, with the Azdites becoming a dominant force along the western slopes of the Hajar Mountains by the sixth century AD, and the Persians or Sassanids occupying areas around the Jebel al-Akhdar. At this time the population appear to have practised a form of animism, as in other parts of Arabia, mainly worshipping fire and the sun.

The UAE's Islamic identity has been established since the early days of the first caliphs who held sway after the death of the Prophet Muhammad, who received the revelation of the Qur'ân in the seventh century AD in the holy cities of Madinah and Makkah, in what is now south-west Saudi Arabia.

The death of Muhammad was followed by a rapid expansion of Islamic territory by the Ummayyad and Abbasid dynasties that embraced the Gulf area before the end of the first millennium.

The caliphs who succeeded Muhammad in spiritual authority codified his teachings into a body of Islamic law called the *Shari'a*, based on the Qur'ân itself, and the *Hadith* — a vast collection of sayings of the Prophet, or sayings attributed to him from a number of sources. The *Shari'a* forms a body of law which is still valid in many parts of the Islamic world today.

Sites in the UAE associated with this era include Bithnah, which houses the oldest mosque in the UAE, and the nearby town of Dibba, where a battle was fought between local tribes and the Muslim army from Makkah in AD 632 that finally ushered in the Islamic era. The battle resulted in thousands of deaths. The fallen are buried in a large cemetery in the plain behind the town.

Traditionally the UAE has belonged to the Sunni Muslim branch of Islam, which also was practised in Saudi Arabia. A second branch of Islam, the Shi'ite sect, formed around the fourth caliph Ali, who was murdered at Qarbala in Iraq. Shi'ites believe that the descendants of Ali, a cousin of the Prophet, are the source of ultimate spiritual authority in the community. Shi'ism became widely practised in Iran; the Ayatollahs of modern-day Iran are said to have blood ties with the family of the Prophet. Although Sunni Islam is the main religion, many Iranians living in the UAE are Shi'ites.

Overleaf: Ancient mosque at Badiyah, near Khor Fakkan, is the oldest in the UAE.
Following pages: A happy meeting at Sharjah's fish market.

The Land: Mountains, Dunes and Mangroves

The UAE is located between latitude 22° 50' and 26° 50' north and longitude 50° and 56° 25' east, in the north-eastern corner of the Arabian peninsula. It shares something of the harsh desert climate that has become legendary among desert travel writers.

Most of the UAE's territory is made up of lightly shrubbed and sandy desert, with only a narrow coastal strip that is semi-fertile, sometimes as a result of irrigation. Only in the extreme south of the country however, do you enter the barren wastes of the Empty Quarter so vividly described in the works of Wilfred Thesiger and Charles Doughty.

The Arabian Gulf desert forms part of the Saharo-Arabian desert, the world's most extensive dry zone.

In the UAE the simple term desert masks a wide variety of different micro-climates and micro-ecologies: mountains and hills, deep valleys, flood plains and alluviums, and dunes – which can be non-calcareous as at Kalba, ferrusiliceous, the deep red-coloured dunes that are typical before the oasis town of Dhaid, and white calcareous dunes that typify the west coast, for instance at Hamriyyah. Salt marsh is also found on the littorals of the UAE, both in the east and west, as well as clumps of mangrove forest.

The Emirates have a territory of about 85,000 square kilometres, of which about 65 per cent is desert, extending from the westernmost tip of Abu Dhabi, where it borders Saudi Arabia, eastwards to the land border with Oman and the Indian Ocean.

In the north, the coast runs along the Arabian Gulf as far as Oman, which lies at the tip of the peninsula opposite the Strait of Hormuz. Six of the emirates have a coastline on the Arabian Gulf, which stretches between the Musandam Peninsula and the Qatar peninsula; one emirate, Fujairah, lies on the Gulf of Oman.

About 750 kilometres of coastline runs along the Arabian Gulf, while a 75-kilometre strip lies on the eastern side along the Arabian Sea. To the north of the UAE, on the strategic Strait of Hormuz, the Musandam Peninsula spans the Arabian Gulf and Indian Ocean and is under Oman's sovereignity.

Abu Dhabi, the largest emirate, extending over approximately 65,000 square kilometres, covers almost all the western and central areas of the UAE. The border with Dubai is near Jebel Ali; in the south, Abu Dhabi has borders with Oman at the Buraimi Oasis and beyond the Liwa Oasis with Saudi Arabia; in the west, it extends as far as Khor al-Odaid. Some of the land and sea borders remain disputed.

A number of Gulf islands belong to Abu Dhabi, including Umm-al-Nar, an important archaeological site, and Sir Bani Yas, which the ruler has made into a nature reserve, and which harbours endangered animal species.

Dubai is the second largest emirate, with an area of around 3,900 square kilometres. It extends from the industrial zone of Jebel Ali in the west to the neighbouring emirate of Sharjah to the north-east. To the east the enclave of Hatta, lying on the border with Oman, is part of Dubai territory.

Sharjah lies directly to the east of Dubai along the Gulf coast, with small enclaves of its territory on the eastern coast at khor fakkan, to the north of that at Dibba, with a further small strip to south of the southern half of Fujairah. The total land area is around 2,600 square kilometres.

The emirates of Ajman, Umm al-Quwain and Ras al-Khaimah are often referred to as the Northern Emirates, a designation which often includes Sharjah. Although a convenient designation, the emirates are autonomous units from each other. In geographical terms these emirates are relative minnows.

Right: Jebel Hafiz, near Al Ain, Abu Dhabi, is one of several mountain ranges in the Emirates.

Above: Solitary watch tower stands guard near Hatta.

Ajman, the UAE's smallest emirate, a tiny enclave of only 260 square kilometres, is bordered to the west by the Arabian Gulf and along the rest of its territory by Sharjah. A small enclave of Ajman exists just to the west of Fujairah, with a slightly larger enclave situated along the border of Dubai territory at Hatta. Umm al-Quwain, an area of 780 square kilometres, consists of a narrow lagoon of territory just to the north of Sharjah. Ras al-Khaimah, the most fertile of the seven emirates, lies to the north of Umm al-Quwain, covering 1,690 square kilometres.

The most remote emirate, Fujairah, to the east of the Northern Emirates is connected only by a couple of roads to the other emirates. It covers 1,170 square kilometres.

Agriculture is the region's mainstay, although some nascent industry is under way in some coastal areas, and the emirate is rapidly developing its tourist industry.

The UAE's topography is varied: a line of low mountains stretches all along the eastern coast, before giving way to the sandy coastline of Fujairah. In the west and north the desert changes unpredictably from sandy, with spectacular, often reddish or pink-coloured sand-dunes, to arid scrubby sand or gravelly rock, before giving way to sandy beaches and salt flats all along the Gulf coast.

Only about five per cent of the overall land area is said to be cultivatable, and only about five per cent of that fraction is actually used for cultivation.

More than two-thirds of the UAE's total area is covered by sandy desert, studded by the occasional oasis. The two great stretches of desert are the desert foreland, which extends westwards to the coast from Ras al-Khaimah and Al Ain, and the westerly desert towards the borders of Abu Dhabi.

The latter location is the northern edge of the Empty Quarter of Saudi Arabia;

there are oases in this area at Al Ain, Buraimi and Al Liwa.

In such terrain, water was crucial and oases were a key source of drinking water during the journeys that might last as much as two weeks from the coast to the centre. Wells would be dug, the distance from the water depending on the season, i.e. winter or summer.

Ghaf trees were associated with oases, the roots of these majestic trees stretching as much as 60 metres. Date palms were also a key crop; their leaves were used for a range of household products, as well as for making sailing vessels. *Falaj* irrigation, using stone water courses, was employed to water the crops, and to provide water for the people and animals. The mountains are dominated by the Hajar (rock) Range in the east of the country. The Arabs picturesquely divide the UAE and neighbouring Oman into the *dahira* (back) and *batina* (belly) separated by the backbone of the Hajar Mountains, which lie in between the Gulf Coast and the deeper waters of the Indian Ocean.

The Hajar Range rises to around 1,200 metres (4,000 feet) in the UAE, and up to 3,000 metres (10,000 feet) in its northern extension into the Oman peninsula. A number of other mountain ranges exist, including Jebel Hafiz near Al Ain in Abu Dhabi emirate, as well as Jebel Buhais, Jebel Huwayyah, Jebel al-Saidirn, Jebel Fai'ya and Jebel Rumailah.

The mountains are impressively rugged, with some cliff faces almost vertical. They were largely formed by striations of a number of ancient sediments, overlayered by ancient oceanic lava flows. The uplifting of the mountains means that the various sedimentary layers can be seen above the surface, particularly in the Al Ain area.

In the dim and distant past, mountains were important centres of civilization and a number of important archaeological sites have been found there.

The coastal area comprises the salt flats, or *sabkha*, immediately after the desert sands. The flats stretch in a 32-kilometre-wide littoral about 320 kilometres (200 miles) all along the coast from Ras

Ghanada in eastern Abu Dhabi to the border with Qatar in the west.

The *sabkha* comprises Pleistocene and Holocene sediments, bordered on the land side by tertiary rocks. It was formed over the last 7,000 years by wind erosion of dunes and the movement of the tides sloshing about the sediments thus deposited. The coastal plain is wider in the Abu Dhabi area, but narrows gradually as you head north to Ras al-Khaimah.

Bordered with reefs, shoals, lagoons and low-lying islands, the UAE claims more than 200 islands, of which Abu Dhabi is the largest and most important. Sovereignty over three of the islands is disputed with Iran, which occupied Abu Mussa and the Greater and Lesser Tunbs in 1971. The inter-tidal zone sometimes contains mangrove swamps or mats of algae and seaweed, while lime muds lie in the waters immediately off this area. Coral reefs are found but the very salty water is not conducive to a wide range of species. More often, the reefs are rocky, abounding in small fish such as parrot fish.

Sometimes offshore the *sabkha* re-emerges in the form of a rocky or sandy island. These areas are ideal for snorkelling or scuba-diving. The waters of the Gulf coast are mostly shallow, most no deeper than 90 metres (300 feet), which although making navigation difficult, also made them ideal for the growth of pearl oysters.

Between the mountains and the *sabkha* area, a number of fertile, upland plains exist, mainly in the region of Ras al-Khaimah and Sharjah. In some of these, a layer of salt, *diapir* is overlaid with layers of sediment from the sea, in which oil and gas fields have been trapped. Occasionally the salt may be visible on the surface, but usually the cover is of sand or hard sedimentary rock.

Such widely different ecological habitats have spawned a wealth of different animal and plant-life, delicately adjusted to the harsh conditions. A cross-section across the middle part of the UAE reveals on the east coast, mangrove lagoon and beaches. This gives way as you head west to the coastal plain of the Arabian Sea.

Further west, as the land rises, you find wadis along the sides of the Shumayliyah Mountain, followed by upland plains and gravel canyons. Once over the brow of the mountains, the terrain gives way to low foothills, and further west, alluvial inland plains.

Small mountains, such as the fossil-bearing Jebel Fai'ya and Jebel Milaihat give way to red ferrusiliceous sand-dunes in this central region, but the dunes gradually turn white as you reach the Gulf coast.

Each of these micro-habitats has its own animal life, including birds, snakes, lizards, as well as a number of rare mammals and a surprising variety of different types of plant-life: **Mangrove:** Khor Kalba is well-endowed with birdlife, including the black-winged stilt. **Eastern plains:** at Ghail Plain shrubs include: 'safar' (Acacia tortilis); 'amuu aruu' (Abutilon panrosum); 'nuffakh' (Pseudogaillonia hymenostephana); 'aziij' (Euphorbia larica).

Mountain wadis: shrubs include 'habn' (Nerium muscatense); 'ayn al-qatt' (Anagalius aruensis); 'sadr' (Ziziphus spina-christi); 'baliilah' (Lippia nodiflora); 'muraar' (Centaurium pulchellum); and typical wadi grass.

Upland wadis: These have been cultivated for centuries with date groves, which in turn support crops including wheat, sorghum, alfalfa, mangoes, bananas, limes and grapes. The wadis are irrigated by open channels. Examples of this type of wadi are Wadi Ham (at Bithnah); Wadi Hiluw; Wadi Munayi; and Shees.

Upland plain and peaks: There are various zones, including those of Musandam, Shimailliyah and Hajar. These plains were formed by the uplifting of the Arabian plate about 65 million years ago.

This was followed by erosion, which created the upland plains, for example those at Masafi and Tayyibah; and by rainy periods, which in turn created small canyons, for example the gravel plains at Masafi.

Wildlife in these upland plains includes sand partidge, red-tailed wheatear, blue-tailed lizard and plain tiger butterfly. The plants include: 'shaliyyakah' (Echinops spinosissimus); 'zhafrah' (Tephosia apollinea); 'shu' (Moringa peregrina); 'shiibaan' (Geranium muscatense).

Western foothills: These are characterized by wadis which drain off the mountain range, sluicing off sediment. The upper foothills are stony, but often cultivated, as for instance at Wadi Shawqah which is covered in rain pools in the spring months. This habitat is endowed with the following wildlife: little owl, rock thrush, carpet viper, spinyfoot lizard. Plants include: 'shuweikah' (Atractylis carduus) and 'ruuq' (Erucaria hispanica).

Inland plain: These were formed by alluvium from the eroding mountains. The plains are protected by the north-south barrier created by the Jebel Fai'ya and Jebel Milaihah. Areas such as Dhaid, Milaihah and Fili are rich farming areas. They are covered by Acacia and grassland, giving them the appearance of savannah.

The wildlife in these areas includes great grey shrike, monitor lizard and blue-headed agarid. Plants found in this region include 'khaniiz' (Diplotaxis harra); 'qaSr' (Lycium shawii) and 'kuuthir' (Asphodelis fistulosis).

Red siliceous sands: These are blown by the shamal winds from the north-west. Inhabiting the sands are numerous ghaf trees, especially near Dhaid, as well as reptiles and mammals.

The Jebel Milaihah and Jebel Fai'ya (fossil rock) are of marine origin, hence the large numbers of fossils that are found there. Good red sands are found at Jebel Murra.

The wildlife that inhabits this area includes desert warbler, cream-coloured courser, black-crowned finch lark, houbara bustard, sand skink and the dhub (spiny-tailed lizard); also, the sand viper, the sand boa, the domino beetle, dung beetle and desert-white butterfly. The plants include:

Right: Daunting road to Jebel Hafiz from Al Ain. Following pages: Aerial view of spectacular Jebel Hafiz mountains, Abu Dhabi.

'ghaf' *(Prosopis cineraria)*; 'ghariira' *(Eremobium aegyptiacum)*; 'sharii' or 'hanazhil' *(Citrullus colocythis)*.

White calcareous plains: These merge with the red sands, like them also harbouring *ghaf* trees, but also the distinctive Sodom's apple trees.

Found in this habitat are yellow-throated sparrows; Arabian babblers; hoopoe lark; purple sunbird; Arabian rearfang – a type of snake – and sand snake. Plants include 'zamluuq' *(Caratropis pro-cera)*; 'qarmil' *(Zygophyllum simplex)* and 'khad-ram' *(Cyperus conglomeratus)*. Various tracks can be found in these plains for instance, of the hedgehog, gerbil, hare, lizard, fox, sidewinder and the camel.

Gulf coast: This includes tidal lagoon and mangrove between Ajman and Hamriyyah. At Hamriyyah saltbushes or *sabkha* are also found. Birds there include: Saunder's little tern; greater flamingo; slender-billed gull; western reef heron; crested lark and socotra cormorant. Plants include: 'khuriiz' *(Halopeplis perfoliata)*; 'thaliith' *(Halocenmum strobila-cerum)* and 'abu thariib' *(Frankenia pulvurulenta)*.

Prehistory

The UAE has been shaped by the great forces of plate tectonics over hundreds of millions of years. The plates, the outermost 100 kilometres (60 miles) of the earth's crust, move about because of heat at the centre of the earth.

The UAE is situated on the Arabian plate, which is moving gradually northeast. It is sandwiched between the Persian subplate of the main Eurasian plate to the north, the Somalian subplate of the main African plate to the south and west, and the Indian plate to the east.

Such forces of nature endowed the UAE with rich reserves of oil formed in underground pockets millions of years ago. The origin of oil is still disputed, but most experts suggest it was formed by the anaerobic decay of plants and simple animals under specific conditions. Subse-

quently pockets of gas often formed on top of the oil reservoirs.

The UAE has huge reserves of oil, about half of it formed under what is now land, known as onshore oil, while the rest lies under the waters of the Gulf.

The UAE also has plentiful mineral resources, including copper, gold, silver, chrome, asbestos, marble and manganese.

Although now largely desert, the terrain has changed over hundreds of millions of years, and long ago both the climate and the geography of Arabia were very different.

It is difficult to imagine that the mountains that now run along the spine of the Musandam Peninsula were once underwater, even more so that the area was influenced by the Ice Age in Europe.

The oldest rocks in Arabia date back 1,000-700 million years when Arabia was believed to be located on the edge of a large continent known which scientists have named Pangaea.

This super-continent consisted of what is now North and South America, Africa, Madagascar, India, Arabia, Malaya and the East Indies, New Guinea, Australia, and Antarctica. Gradually the super-continent was pulled apart by the forces of continental drift. Evidence of these ancient land movements have been found all over the UAE. The oldest rocks date back hundreds of millions of years. Volcanic ash deposited at least 600 million years ago has been found at Sir Bani Yas in Abu Dhabi and also at Sir Abu Nuair in Sharjah. The oldest multi-celled fossils are from between 600 and 570 million years ago, in the pre-Cambrian period.

More recently, over a 300-million-year period when plate tectonics pushed up the land, the Arabian Shield was formed. Flowering plants emerged during the last 65 million years.

The rocks of the Hajar Mountains used to be under the ocean. About 70 million years ago, the movement of the earth's plates caused a slab of oceanic crust to slide up and over the north-east edge of

Left: The rocky Hatta Road, Dubai. Previous pages: Majestic desert sand dunes flank the Hatta Road.

Above: Mangroves line the water's edge at Khor Kalba, Sharjah.

the Arabian continent. The rocks of this slab are now visible in the Hajar Mountains.

As the island of oceanic rocks drowned, patches of reefs made up of corals and large bivalves called rudists formed around its coasts. Rudistids lived in the Cretaceous period.

Arabia split from the African continent at the end of the Miocene period, 23 million years ago. Faulting caused the formation of the Jebel Faiyah and Hafiz, while uplifting caused that of the Hajar Mountains, continuing until the Miocene-Pliocene period.

Between ten to two million years ago, Sharjah rose above sea level and there was a large river system in western Abu Dhabi, well-populated with animals including *Samotherium, Palaeotragus, Cercopithecium, Hipparion.*

In the late Quartenary (Pleistocene) period, during the Ice Age in Europe, rivers formed and beaches were raised along the coasts. Wadis formed in the Pleistocene, a much wetter period two million to 10,000 years ago, when rivers cut into the hills, drying out only later. Since then, the sea level has fallen.

Chronology

Scientists studying plate tectonics, the movement of the earth's lithosphere (outer crust) which produce faults, joints, folds and cleavage, or cause magma to rise to the surface, have produced a fairly authoritative account of how the continents have drifted, divided and collided over the past 200 million years. The picture before that is incomplete, and beyond 400 million years the image is somewhat hypothetical.

The pre-Cambrian period in the UAE, 600 million years ago, saw the evolution of the first primitive life forms, such as simple bacteria and algae. At this stage, the UAE was in the southern hemisphere, about 40° south of the Equator in latitude and 60° east in longitude.

The land comprised largely igneous rocks forming north to south blocks such as the Qatar Arch.

During the Cambrian period, 500 million years ago, the UAE moved further north, to latitude 35° south and longitude

Above: Green colours of the mountain terrain are a refreshing contrast to the deserts below.

55° east. Then the UAE was underwater, and a salt basin formed stretching all the way from the Zagros Mountains, now in Iran, across the Arabian Gulf. At this stage, the earliest invertebrates evolved, including jellyfish and sponges, and the sea was populated with trilobites, ancestors of modern-day insects and spiders.

By the Silurian age, 400 million years ago, the UAE had moved a further 5° north, but was still in the southern hemisphere. The melting of the glaciers of the South Pole caused water levels to rise sharply, drowning the whole area of what is now the Arabian peninsula. The sea was alive with strange-jawed fish and sea-scorpions, with the simple algae of the pre-Cambrian and Cambrian age evolving into developed sub-sea plants.

Two hundred and fifty million years ago, the UAE occupied roughly the position of Madagascar today, but remained underwater for much of the Permo Triassic period, as this era is called.

But as the waters gradually receded, insect life evolved in the swamps and forests that grew in the shallow waters of the sea.

Parts of this habitat resembled the lagoons and *sabkha* of the modern day UAE; but the areas east of Dubai and Al Ain remained sub-sea, a fertile breeding ground for ammonites, reptiles and turtles. This was a period of major volcanic activity in and around Oman.

The early Jurassic period saw the emergence of dinosaurs across the Arabian peninsula. By now, 200 million years ago, the UAE was located just 8° south of the Equator and 45° east of the Greenwich meridian. The North American Continent had broken away from Pangaea leaving the UAE on the edge of the supercontinent which is known as Gondwanaland. Uplift raised the ground above the waters and the land, originally covered with forest, gradually became more arid.

The Middle and Upper Jurassic periods, dating back 150 million years, saw a fresh inundation of the UAE area by the sea, and it was at this stage that a wide range of reptiles, including birds and marine dinosaurs, began to proliferate. About 10 million years later the Cretaceous period saw the evolution of the first small mammals.

Above: Traditional healer with a patient.   Right: Beautiful desert sunset, Dubai.
Following pages: Setting sun over Al Ain and the Jebel Hafiz mountains reveals a scene untouched by time.

At this stage, the UAE was located in the same latitude and longitude as modern day Kenya, across the Equator.

Gradually the climate became drier, and about 70 million years ago, tectonic activity pushed up the folds of the earth's core, forming the mountain ranges of Oman. By now, the UAE was located 8° north of the Equator and 50° east in longitude.

During the Oligocene period, about 25 million years ago, the collision of the Arabian landmass with Asia pushed up the land, forming the Zagros Mountains in Iran, lifting the UAE out of what gradually became the Gulf. Although the north was still under water, areas to the west of Abu Dhabi and the mountains east of Al Ain were above sea-level, while mammals and flowering plants continued to evolve and develop.

By the Miocene period, about seven million years ago, the present day topography of the UAE was clearly visible, al-though the Gulf did not extend as far west. As a result, the land west of Abu Dhabi was threaded by tributaries of the Euphrates and Tigris rivers in modern-day Iraq, which formed wide deltas near the sea.

Dubai and the Northern Emirates were still largely covered with water. Elephants roamed the land and other mammals evolved gradually, as the Quaternary period approached, into the ancestors of modern day camels, goats and horses.

From about 10,000 years to 3,000 years ago, the last glacial period, the area that is now the Gulf gradually filled up with water, covering most of the rivers and separating the southern from the northern Gulf.

The People: Traditional qualities and virtues

The UAE's population has grown rapidly since federation, when it stood at just 180,000 people. Today it is a country of almost 2.5 million people, who enjoy among the world's highest living standards, largely as a result of the nation's oil wealth. The 1995 census put the total population at 2.377 million; males outnumber females by a wide margin, totalling some 1.579 million people or 66 per cent of the total population, mainly as a result of the large numbers of immigrant workers, who come to the UAE without their families.

Abu Dhabi is the most populous emirate, with more than 900,000 people, some 39 per cent of the total. Dubai, the next most populous, has 675,000 people, about 28 per cent of all the population, followed by Sharjah with a little over 400,000 people, representing 17 per cent.

The other emirates are relative minnows in terms of their population: Ajman's population is going on 120,000; Ras al-Khaimah's citizens number just over 144,000; Fujairah has about 75,000 people; and Umm al-Quwain only 35,000.

These figures include foreigners. Indeed, UAE nationals constitute less than a quarter of the total, the majority of whom are expatriates. Nationals have their own distinctive dress and almost invariably, whether man or woman, have their head covered.

National dress for women is the *abba*, also called *shaili* or *abaya*, a black full-length covering. Under the *bba*, women wear loose *sirwal*, or trousers, and a *kandura*, a dress often embroidered in gold or silver and the *thaub*. The *burqa* is the black mask covering the nose and mouth.

For men, the white full-length shirt is called the *dishdash*. The head-cloth, usually red-chequered or plain white, is the *gutra*. The black rope wrapped around the head to keep the *gutra* in place is called the *agal* and, under this headdress, men wear a small skull cap, or *taqia*. A cloak may be worn outside the *dishdash:* it is called an *abba* or *bisht*, usually coloured black.

Most visitors' first glimpse of the UAE national dress will be in a glitzy shopping mall, or in a gleaming Buick or Cadillac. Women are allowed to drive in the UAE, unlike in such fiercely traditional Gulf nations as Saudi Arabia.

Anyone who gets to know the nationals soon realizes the traditional qualities and virtues associated with the lifetyle of yesteryear are still alive today. These qualities are not easy to characterize.

Legendary Hospitality
Arab hospitality is so legendary, it has become something of a cliché. In the desert camps of the Bedouin, any stranger in need would first be welcomed with cups of coffee, and then royally fêted, as far as the harsh desert existence allowed.

Left: Dignified patriarch near the Oman border close by Dibba.
Right: Waterfront meeting, Dubai.

But the visitor should not expect the open-armed *bonhomie* to strangers he might experience in Mediterranean countries; indeed, UAE nationals tend to be somewhat reserved, in such a way that sometimes you might wrongly mistake it for surliness. Even so, anyone looking a little lost in the street is likely to be embarrassed by the persistence with which they will be helped to their destination.

Spontaneous generosity is another quality that is frequently associated with these proud desert nomads; and the tradition remains to this day. But the Arabs of the Gulf are also astute, if at times ruthless — but honest — traders; and business is business when it comes to arguing the bottom-line of a deal, whether you are a guest in the country or not.

The same kind of approach is likely to be found in most business transactions that the tourist enters into, whether it is buying a rug or negotiating a taxi fare. You are unlikely to be cheated, but equally a fair mark-up will be charged, however many cups of coffee you drink with the vendor.

The forefathers of the UAE's indigenous population across the Arabian Peninsula migrated in successive waves between 2,000 and 3,000 years ago. The various communities gradually mingled and, with the coming of Islam, were united not only by heritage but also by religion.

Muslim Identity

Islam is the state religion, and its Muslim identity is perhaps the most important unifying aspect of the UAE culture. The call to prayer echoes throughout the streets five times a day. But, unlike several neighbouring Gulf states, other faiths are tolerated, and indeed officially sanctioned.

Christian churches may be found in many of the main population centres. Moreover, the concept of tolerance is emphasized in the UAE; the hard-line militancy that has given Muslims such a bad press outside the Islamic world is frowned on in the UAE, however pious individually the citizens may be.

Citizens also avoid the wilder excesses associated with wealth that afflict some of the other Gulf nations, or at least that are associated with Arab wealth in the West. Whereas sudden access to riches has led to conspicuous ostentation being regarded as a virtue in some of the Gulf nations, nationals in the UAE tend to shy away from this.

The government discourages the flaunting of wealth in the interests of social harmony. Of course, this is not to say that people don't enjoy their wealth — in the shopping malls, any number of hugely over-priced novelties are sold, and presumably find a market.

Family Ties

The family structure remains the cement that holds together this richly varied society. In the past, part of the UAE population comprised nomadic herdsmen, or Bedouin, who moved with their camels and goats from one pasture to another, and from one watering-hole to another.

The Bedouin would seek out the oases, for instance at Liwa, where a few palm trees and vegetables were cultivated.

Although the romance of desert life, in its harsh struggle with the forces of nature, has captured the imagination of Westerners, the Bedouin — or Bedu — only ever formed a minority of the overall population. The word 'Bedouin' comes from the Arabic triliteral root b-d-w, meaning 'to live in the desert'. Most people lived in settled communities, at least for most of the year, working in agriculture or the maritime sector, often along the coast.

The traditional heritage remains a factor influencing the life of the indigenous population. It is reflected in conservative attitudes to women that typify many Islamic nations. The women of the family stayed at home, looking after the date-palm gardens and the children.

The communities belonged to tribes and then to clans. Among the key tribes that make up the indigenous UAE population, the Awamir were largely nomadic tribes

men, the inland oases were settled by the Manasir and the Bani Yas, while various sections of the Bani Yas such as the Qubeisat, the Rumaithat and the Sudan were frequently engaged in pearl-fishing and fisheries.

Along the edges of the Hajar Mountains, blessed with subterranean water supplies, tribes like the Dhawahir spent the whole year tending their date palms and farms, watered by *falaj* irrigation channels, but it would be wrong to identify too closely a tribe or clan with one particular activity only.

Many spent part of the year at the oases and some time on the coast, or at sea. Nevertheless, tribal allegiances led to traditional friendships which to this day partly determine a national's social status, and also influence what career they may follow.

Despite the sudden changes in their society, in some ways the UAE Arabs still function as they have done for centuries; the ruling families still have close ties with the tribes who roamed the desert in the days before oil.

Their religion, culture and traditions remain although there is clearly an influence brought about by the opening up of the UAE and the contact with the West and things Western.

Traditional Roots

The focus on heritage is a vital part of the UAE's identity. Living conditions were immeasurably harder in the days before the coming of oil. People went barefoot, without water and electricity and had no access to education or medicine. As a result many women died in childbirth. Traditional houses were made mainly of date-palm fronds, although stone houses were built by wealthier citizens, often located along the creeks that stud the Gulf coast of the UAE. Such stone houses consisted of a central *majlis* surrounded by verandas along the square of the inner building, and with a zigzag entrance.

The house would often have a square wind-tower or *baadgeer*, open on four sides to catch the gusts of wind and funnel them inside as a form of air conditioning, with the highest of these located above the bedroom.

These wind-towers might be built of stone, but equally were made from date-palm leaves, in the traditional *barasti* buildings. Because of the strict sense of family privacy, the houses had no windows.

In a typical *barasti* house, the front room was the public area, while the bedroom was found at the back. The wind-tower straddled the main living room and the bedroom, and there were no windows, preserving the shady atmosphere. Inside the main living room, furnishings were sparse, perhaps just a few wooden chests, mats and baskets. A simple *manama* bed, consisting of a rush mattress elevated above the ground with a ladder going up to it, was used for sleeping outside in the summer.

Formal education was introduced relatively late. Before that, most men were educated at *al katateeb,* the elementary schools in which study consisted entirely of learning to recite the Qur'ân. Both morning and afternoon sessions were held. In 1912 a new type of school, focused on developing skills for trading, as well as scientific knowledge, was founded at Al Ahmadiyah. Girls' schools were introduced in 1959.

In the desert, water was a key concern. The well was a focal point of the community and water was drawn in a basket made of animal hide, known as a *dallu*, often hoisted from the depths by a simple system of wooden rollers acting as a winch. The *fintas* was used to store water. It consists of a wooden water-tank, shaped rather like a modern-day panzer tank, about 2.5 metres (8 feet) long by 2 metres (6 feet) wide, with a funnel and lid at the top. Because of this predominant concern, oases were important population centres.

Nowadays, almost all the water is supplied by desalination plants. In 1993, for instance, water consumption in Dubai was 74,920 million gallons (340,600 million litres) a day of which 93 per cent was supplied by desalination plants. The rest of the water came from 56 water wells, mainly in the Hatta, where the traditional *falaj* irrigation is still used. In the days before the oil boom, however, the *falaj* water system was much more extensive.

Above: Arab women enjoying a visit to the market.

Lack of water also made the camel the single most important livestock. Camels were widely used for transport, both of people and goods, hence their nickname 'the ship of the desert'. The camel's incredible ability to conserve water is its chief quality; it can go without water for two weeks in the summer and for three months in the winter. As a result, camels were used in the UAE as a traditional measure of *dyah*.

Date palms, centred on the oasis were the most frequently cultivated crop. Known as 'the bride of the desert', it was used in most aspects of daily life, to make housing, tents, agricultural implements, fishing nets *(al garagir)* and simple boats *(al shasha)*. There are various types of date palm; *al loulou, al kheneizi, al hilali* and *al khasaab* are just four of more than 60 different varieties in the UAE.

The leaves of the date palm were cut to make the following: *al sarood* circular mats for food, *al makab* conical mats to cover food, *al mashab* fans, also used for lighting fires, *al mahafah* to fan the face, *al makhrafah*, a basket to collect dates in, *al mezmah* to carry dates home, *al jefeer*, a basket which women used to carry wares from the market and *al geffa* used by women to carry their personal items. Straw was also used to make the traditional *Qahfiyah* caps, and *shebdan* for holding perfume and kohl in.

The souqs were the centre of village and town life, divided into separate quarters associated with the different activities that were conducted in them. In the old days, the scene was very different from that in the modern day souqs: as late as the 1950s, people would ply the narrow streets on donkeys, and the alleys were filled with children, often playing with wooden toys, hopscotch or a spinning wheel.

The souqs sold food of all sorts, including dates and beans from Iran and Basra, cooking oils from East Africa, and spices. Spices were sometimes sold in the specialist spice souqs: for instance, the one at Al Ras in Dubai.

The spices, carried in jute bags, were shipped from India, Iran, Yemen and East Africa. They included: canella *(al qirfah)*, black pepper, sweet pepper, cloves, cumin and cardamom.

Above: Arab man from Al-Ain region

Spices were used as much for medical as culinary purposes: for instance, *al murr* used for stomach problems, yellow rock sulfur to cure burns, while *al anzaroot, al yaada* and *al zaater* were used to treat a variety of other complaints. Henna powder was used in both medicine, and for self-adornment.

The souqs were also the site of traditional handicrafts, including carpentry, the blacksmiths' arts and pottery.

The carpenters used a number of simple tools, including saw, chisel, adze, hammer and nails, to make household furniture, as well as larger products such as boats and dhows.

Blacksmiths typically produced agricultural tools, including *al das,* a type of agricultural plough. *Al safarrin* would polish the finished items. Wet sand was often used to clean old and rusty implements.

Pottery was made out of the local red clay, largely in Ras al-Khaimah, but goods were also imported from Oman and Iran. The pottery was fired in *al Mahraqa,* the furnace, which was made of stone with mud-lined walls, with a hole in the top to let out smoke.

Pots of all sorts were generally reddish in colour. Different types of pottery were used for different tasks, as follows: *al khers* for storing food, *al jarrah* for carrying water from wells, *al yahlah* for keeping water cool, *al borma* for cooking, *al masaab* for holding coffee, *al razem* for carrying coffee-cups, *al haalool* for giving birds and animals water to drink and *al mabkhar* to burn incense.

The traditional Arab dress was a long loose-fitting over-garment, with a head-dress, for men; and for women, a black over-garment covering the whole body, often worn with a special mask to hide the eyes. Fabrics were often purchased from India. They were measured in *waar,* equivalent to 90 centimetres (3 feet) and bolt, equivalent to 30 waar.

Jewellery was also sold in the souqs. These were important as dowry. In the 1940s the gold souq at Bur Dubai opened, followed by another at Deira in the 1950s. Typical jewellery included the 19th-century *dellal,* necklaces made of Islamic and European coins, including the Maria Theresa Dollar, often given as a present to a bride. Other traditional necklaces included *al tablah, al murtaeshah,* and *al meryah.* Various anklets, bracelets and rings were also sold in the souqs.

A number of traditional sports were enjoyed, including falconry, camel-racing and horse-racing. The falcon hunting season was in winter and spring, during the temperate season. There are different types of falcon: *al shaheen* are fast flyers and *al hur kamal* are good hunters. The birds were covered with a mask, the *burqa,* and tethered with *al mersal,* during the periods when they were not being used for hunting.

Expatriates

Until the government awarded the franchise for local taxi drivers to UAE nationals, it was possible to spend a brief holiday in the UAE without ever seeing an indigenous Arab; indeed, virtually 75 per cent of the population is made up of expatriates from India, Pakistan, the Philippines, Europe and America.

Among the 75 per cent of the population that is expatriate, Indians form the biggest group followed by Pakistanis, other Asians and non-UAE Arabs. Europeans are a small but wealthy fraction.

The biggest population centres for expatriates are the Dubai and Sharjah conurbation, with about half the total; Abu Dhabi contains about 10 per cent of the total; while the remainder of the population is split between the other five emirates.

Although Arabic is the country's official language, English is widely spoken. A large number of other languages are also spoken by the expatriate workforce, including Urdu, Hindi, Malayalam and Tagalog, reflecting the diverse ethnic and national mix among the expatriate workforce. The ethnic mix is also stratified. Many Filipinos, and people from the Indian sub-continent including Indians, Pakistanis, Bangladeshis and Sri Lankans, work in the tourist hotels, or provide manual labour for the construction industry. South Asians, especially Indians, as well as Iranians, are active in commerce and the import-export business. Westerners tend to have jobs with the multinational corporations. Meanwhile, UAE nationals have generally worked for the government or state-owned oil companies, although increasingly they are being encouraged to develop their entrepreneurial skills in the private sector. Westerners tend to have jobs with the multinational companies.

It is possible to wander around certain parts of Dubai, Sharjah or Abu Dhabi and — apart from the obvious civic cleanliness and order — feel as if you're walking through Bombay or Karachi. The Middle East has long been a trading centre attracting visitors from all over the world but, since the oil boom, it has become something of a magnet for its poorer neighbours to earn much needed foreign currency.

The massive amount of construction work in the emirates is carried out almost exclusively by migrant workers. Working conditions are tough and recent government regulations have made it more difficult for these largely male labourers to bring their wives and families to live with them.

Thus there are large numbers of male Pakistani and Indian men who live as single men — a potentially unhealthy situation but one which as yet does not seem to have resulted in crime or violence.

The service, retail and hotel industry in the UAE is dominated largely by Indian and Filipino migrant workers. As far as the Indian community are concerned, some have been in the UAE for many years and have established successful businesses. Many of the large supermarket chains such as Choitrams and Lals are run by Indian families.

The most recent visitors to the UAE are the growing numbers of Russian tourists who come attracted by the sunshine and the opportunity to purchase cheap electrical equipment which they buy in large quantities and sell on their return.

Meanwhile, the Westerners — the British, the Americans and, to a lesser extent, Australians — are generally employed at a managerial level in the larger multinational companies. Many are employed on generous expatriate terms, their company providing accommodation and a tax-free salary which allows them to live comfortably. However the expatriate community in the UAE are not all out on the golf course by two in the afternoon and the days of easy wealth may be coming to an end.

Increasingly, there is an emphasis by the UAE government on 'localization' which is the policy of promoting locals to participate in their growing economy. Thus recruitment, training and development are focused on UAE nationals rather than expatriates where possible while at the same time the government is keen to promote the nation's culture and the heritage of the UAE.

PART TWO:
A TALE OF THREE CITIES

Left: Graceful fountain near Mushrif Park, Dubai. Above: Spectacular aerial view of Dubai city. Previous pages: Happy children at the small fishing village of Qurayyah, Fujairah Emirate.

Charm, Commerce and Industrialization

The main cities in the UAE are the capital Abu Dhabi, the commercial hub of Dubai, and the bustling town of Sharjah. Abu Dhabi is situated a good two-hours' drive to the west of Dubai and Sharjah, and is a convenient jumping-off point for visits to the Liwa Oasis and Al Ain, as well as the desert dunes under which most of the country's oil and gas wealth is located.

Outside the capital, Dubai and Sharjah are by far the largest centres of population, and are located only 20 minutes' drive from each other. Sharjah is an ideal base from which to see the Northern Emirates of Ajman, Umm al-Quwain and Ras al-Khaimah, plus a convenient access point for the east coast. Dubai is a good base from which to visit the oasis of Hatta in the mountains, and the desert city of Al Ain.

These three main cities contain all that the visitor needs in terms of hotels, beaches and shopping facilities. They also have a growing number of Tourist sites of their own.

Each city has its own special character. Dubai is bustling and modern, with a wide variety of night-life and hotels. Abu Dhabi, though modern, is more sedate, perhaps reflecting the fact it is the centre of government and not just a commercial hub.

Sharjah has its own charm, with the feel of a busy Middle Eastern town — the shopping malls are on a less grand scale than in nearby Dubai, and the souqs more authentic. Each of the three cities is a convenient jumping-off point to visit the various sites in the emirates of the same name.

Because of their proximity, visitors will probably base a decision of whether to stay in Dubai or Sharjah on the type of holiday experience they are after, rather than just on the criteria of where they can travel to conveniently from the two cities.

The main advantage of Dubai is that it is

Above: Arab woman snaps her children in front of the waterfall monument, Abu Dhabi Corniche.
Right: Glass-clad skyscraper in Abu Dhabi mirrors one of the city's other high-rise attractions.

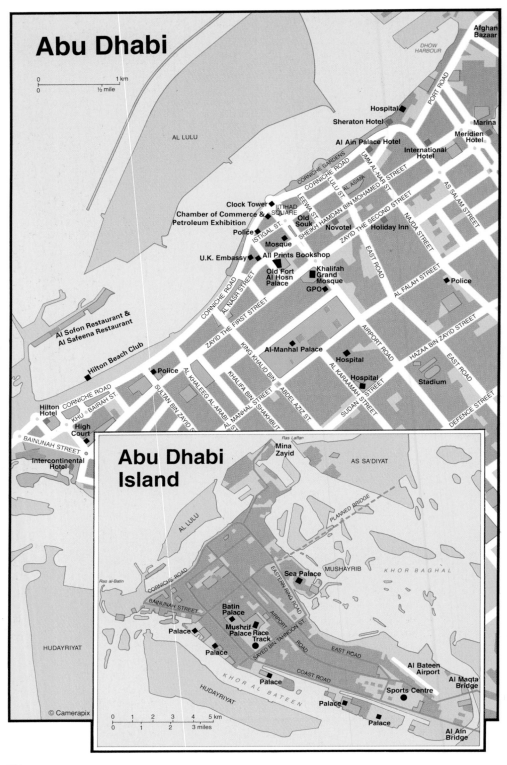

Abu Dhabi

0   1 km
0   ½ mile

AL LULU

DHOW HARBOUR

Afghan Bazaar

Hospital
Sheraton Hotel
Al Ain Palace Hotel
International Hotel
Marina
Meridien Hotel

CORNICHE GARDENS
CORNICHE ROAD
LEEWA ST.
LULU ST.
AL ASIMA
UMM AL NAR STREET
AS SALAM STREET
PORT ROAD

Clock Tower
ITTIHAD SQUARE
Chamber of Commerce &
Petroleum Exhibition
Police
Old Souk
ISTIGLAL ST.
SHEIKH HAMDAN BIN MOHAMED ST
Novotel
Holiday Inn
ZAYID THE SECOND STREET
NAJDA STREET

Mosque
U.K. Embassy
All Prints Bookshop
Old Fort
Al Hosn Palace
Khalifah Grand Mosque
GPO
Police

EAST ROAD
AL FALAH STREET

Al Sofon Restaurant &
Al Safeena Restaurant

CORNICHE ROAD
AL NASR STREET
ZAYID THE FIRST STREET

Al-Manhal Palace

AIRPORT ROAD

Hospital
Hospital
HAZAA BIN ZAYID STREET
EAST ROAD

Hilton Beach Club
Police

KING KHALID BIN
KHALIFA BIN STREET
ABDEL AZIZ ST.
AL KARAAMAH STREET
SUDAN STREET

Stadium

DEFENCE STREET

Hilton Hotel
CORNICHE ROAD
KHU... BAIRAH ST.
SULTAN BIN ZAYID S...
AL KHALEEG AL-ARABI
AL MANHAL ST.
SHAKHBUT

BAINUNAH STREET
High Court

Intercontinental Hotel

Abu Dhabi Island

Ras Laffan
Mina Zayid
AS SA'DIYAT

AL LULU

PLANNED BRIDGE

Ras al-Batin

CORNICHE ROAD
BAINUNAH STREET

MUSHAYRIB

KHOR BAGHAL

Sea Palace
EASTERN RING ROAD
AIRPORT ROAD

Batin Palace
Mushrif Palace
Race Track
SAYED BIN TAHNOON ST.
SAYED BIN TAHNOON ROAD

Palace
EAST ROAD

Palace

HUDAYRIYAT

Palace
COAST ROAD

Al Bateen Airport
Al Maqta Bridge

KHOR AL BATEEN
HUDAYRIYAT

Palace
Sports Centre

Palace

Palace

Al Ain Bridge

0 1 2 3 4 5 km
0 1 2 3 miles

© Camerapix

104

Above: Space, quality and a sense of tradition are captured in the reception area of the Meridien Hotel, Abu Dhabi

very well geared to Tourists, with luxury shopping malls, excellent hotel facilities, buzzing night-life and a relaxed attitude which allows the consumption of alcohol in main hotels. Sharjah is more traditional and the hotels are 'dry', but for many visitors the numerous old-style souqs and antique shops, and the more authentically Middle Eastern ambience, as well as more moderately priced hotel accommodation, will outweigh such considerations.

All three cities have good hotel and leisure facilities, and many visitors may prefer to put up at the main cities and simply make day trips out to the more remote and off-road tourist sites.

In the other main centres — Al Ain, Umm al-Quwain, Ajman, Ras al-Khaimah and Fujairah — the relatively slow pace means that they will appeal to most visitors more for stopovers or weekend breaks than as the main base. All are in easy reach of the three main cities with good hotels and restaurant facilities.

Abu Dhabi: Capital and Industrial Centre

Abu Dhabi is the capital of the UAE, the centre of government and of the country's oil and gas industry operations.

Getting there

Abu Dhabi can be reached by air from most major international destinations. The airport is modern and has good facilities. The duty-free shop offers a wide range of reasonably priced goods. The city centre is about 30 kilometres (20 miles) from the airport, and costs about AED 40 by taxi.

The roads are excellent and wide and, as you drive from the airport, are fringed with trees and bushes so you do not initially feel that you are in a country that is largely desert.

From the main towns of other emirates, Abu Dhabi is a two-hour drive from Dubai,

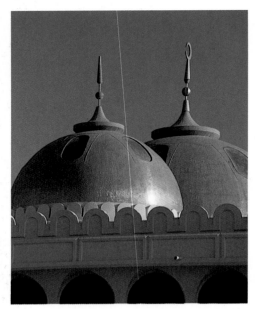

Above: Sheikh Khalifa Mosque. Right: Khalifa Gardens, Abu Dhabi.

strictly observed. As such it is best to visit outside the month. National Day on 2 December is probably the best time for those interested in the UAE culture — Abu Dhabi's ruler Sheikh Zayed has taken a leading role in promoting interest in the UAE heritage, and a number of interesting events are organized to coincide with National Day.

Where to stay
Abu Dhabi has a range of good hotels, mostly in the upper-price bracket. The best place to stay, for those who can afford a luxury hotel, is in one of the five-star hotels along the Corniche, a lovely seafront drive typical of many Gulf countries. The Hilton, particularly well situated, also has a Beach Club just a few hundred yards from the main hotel. The hotel is located in Al Khubeirah district with fine views over the clear blue waters of the lagoon. The Intercontinental is nearby, and there are also some good but cheaper hotels nearer the city centre.

Sightseeing
In Abu Dhabi, the **Corniche** runs several kilometres in a **north-easterly** direction all along the seafront — from the **Hilton Hotel** to the **Sheraton Hotel.**

The offices of **Abu Dhabi National Oil Co** (ADNOC) are located next to the Hilton Hotel, away from the town centre. Walking along the Corniche leads one past the offices of several of the major players in the UAE oil and gas industry, including **Abu Dhabi Co for Onshore Operations** (ADCO) and **Abu Dhabi Gas Liquefaction Co** (ADGAS).

A short distance from the Hilton lie two restaurants overlooking the bay opposite **Al Lulu Island**: the **As Safeena** and **As Sofon** restaurants. These are a short drive or a 20-minute walk from the Hilton Hotel, along the Corniche breakwater which stretches out like a crooked arm from the Corniche. From the shore, an old rounded

two-and-a-half hours from Sharjah, about three hours from Ras al-Khaimah, and about three hours from Fujairah. It is a one-and-a-half hours' drive from Al Ain.

The city centre may be reached by crossing one of two bridges: the Al Maqta Bridge and the Al Ain Bridge. The former runs past the Umm al-Nar oil refinery, the latter past the Sheikh Zayed Sports Centre with a good view over the Khor al-Maqta, a creek dividing Abu Dhabi island from the mainland. It is not possible to stop on the bridge.

When to go
Abu Dhabi is pleasant to visit in almost any season, with year-round sunshine. However, many nationals leave the city for cooler climes in July and August and, to make the most of a visit, spring or autumn are recommended, as for other emirates.

Abu Dhabi is a very conservative Islamic society and the holy month of Ramadan is

Following pages — three views of Abu Dhabi: Immaculate gardens at Qasr al Hosn; Dhow Harbour provides a tangible link with the past; Sentinel-like lighting structures along the Corniche are silhouetted in the soft evening light.

watchtower is visible. The restaurants have a distinctively Arabic feel — one is a wood-built floating restaurant and the other has typical Barasti-style trimmings.

The **beaches** to the **left** of the breakwater are an easy walk from the **western end** of the Corniche, sheltered from the wind and with beautiful sand, although lacking in facilities. Further along the coast to the **west,** by car, a number of **beaches** are more secluded for those who enjoy privacy.

The **Corniche Road** stretches about five kilometres (three miles) along the wide bay facing Al Lulu Island. It is pleasant both as a **walk** and a **drive.** The first two kilometres (one mile) are largely past office buildings to the right, while the seafront and beaches to the left are lined with palm trees. Further along the Corniche from the Hilton hotel towards the city centre, about a five-minute drive in the car and perhaps a 30-minute walk, the **Clock Tower** is a modern landmark at the entrance to the city's **business district,** which lies to the **south-east** of the Clock Tower. This is a good point from which to visit the city's main sights.

Ittihad Square lies just off the **Clock Tower roundabout** extending as far as the junction of **Al Nasr Street** and **Sheikh Hamdan bin Mohammad Street.** In 1996 it was redecorated, with a number of huge statues, a cannon and traditional Arab motifs.

The main **business area** lies to the **south** of the Clock Tower in the districts of **Al Hosn, Al Markaziyah** and **Madeenat Zayed;** most of the key banks and oil companies are sited in this area along **Sheikh Khalifa bin Zayed Street** and **Sheikh Hamdan bin Mohammad Street,** to the **east** of Al Ittihad Square.

Istighlal Street and **Al Nasr Street** to the west of Ittihad Square contain a number of good shops.

Nearby are the **British Embassy,** and between Al Nasr Street and the Corniche, an **exhibition** about the UAE **petroleum industry,** the **Abu Dhabi Chamber of Commerce and Industry** and the **Abu Dhabi Travel Bureau.**

Nearby is the excellent *All Prints* bookshop. Unfortunately, most bookshops in Abu Dhabi are small affairs with a handful of English titles. *All Prints* is the exception, with a **well-stocked selection** of local interest and regional historical tomes, along with standard tourist guides.

Sandwiched between Istighlal Street and Al Nasr Street, the **Khalifah Grand Mosque** is well worth a visit. It lies adjacent to the **vegetable souq.** Parallel with that, and on the other side of Ittihad Square, Abu Dhabi's **old souq** is a vivid anachronism among the sky-rise buildings on Skeikh Khalifa bin Zayed Street. To the **south** of Al Nasr street, lie the **Old Fort, Al Hosn Palace** and the **Cultural Foundation.**

The Abu Dhabi Cultural Foundation planned in 1996 to open parts of the **Qasr al-Hosn** (Al Hosn Palace) to the public as a museum. The Qasr al-Hosn was built in 1793 and is one of the oldest buildings in the UAE. It formerly served as the ruler's residence and the seat of government.

It houses the **Centre for Documentation and Research,** set up in 1968, which holds a wide-ranging collection of documents on the UAE's heritage and history, as well as that of the Gulf region.

Three sections of the **Old Fort** and its tower will be opened to the public, displaying documents, pictures and material illustrating the history and modern development of the UAE.

These will include a **natural history museum** with animal life from the desert, a **historical section** covering the setting up of the UAE and the history of Abu Dhabi emirate, as well as old pottery and other remnants of past life in the UAE.

The third section will contain an **exhibition of Abu Dhabi** as it was before the discovery of oil, as well as the founding of the UAE and its modern development. The tower will contain a **display of weapons** used through Abu Dhabi's history.

Left upper: Abu Dhabi's waterside Al Sofon Restaurant on the Corniche breakwater.
Below: Revolving restaurant at the Forte Grand Hotel.

Left: Glittering spectacle of Abu Dhabi's Zakhir Shopping Centre. Above: The prestigious Abu Dhabi Yacht Club nestles conveniently alongside the 5-star Meridien Hotel.

A second large mosque, **Sheikh Zayed the Second Mosque,** lies to the **east** of the Old Fort, directly **south** of **Zayed the First Street.** Further to the east along Sheikh Khalifah bin Zayed Street, the **Al Asima Public Garden** provides a restful haven from the busy city streets. It has a **lake** in the middle, and a small **mosque** in its **northern** corner.

To the east of the Clock Tower runs the **Corniche Gardens,** in the centre of which is a picturesque **waterfall monument.** The gardens extend as far as the Sheraton Hotel, which lies shortly before the port area. Continuing **north,** the **Port Road** leads directly to **Mina Zayed,** the site of the **Iranian souq,** formerly a bustling centre but now in decline. The **Afghan bazaar** on the **right** of the road contains a number of stalls selling Qur'ânic texts and books, and in the main section, a variety of cheap furnishings, including cushion covers and carpets from other Middle Eastern countries.

To the **west** of the Afghan bazaar, the **Dhow Harbour** is where ocean-going dhows from Iran and the Indian subcontinent dock. The area contains a number of makeshift stalls selling cheap pottery, carpets, and plants. This is a picturesque part of town to wander around. The nearby

vegetable and fruit souq is also worth visiting, with crates of fruit being unloaded from the dhows, which then refill with produce from the UAE.

Backtracking along Port Road, turn **left** in a **south-easterly** direction along the **Eastern Ring Road.** The road runs past a group of islands called **Jazirat Bu Ash Shu'um** and then past the **Qasr al-Bahr** or Sea Palace. It is a pleasant journey, with lovely views over the sea. A bridge is planned to link the island of Abu Dhabi with **Jazirat as-Sa'diyat,** about five kilometres (three miles) to the **north-east.**

From the Eastern Ring Road, one follows the road round to the **right** on **Saeed bin Tahnoon Street,** taking a **right** at **Al Karamah Street.** This leads shortly to the **Mushrif Khalifah Gardens** and **Mushrif Palace.** Nearby is the **Bateen Palace** and the **Abu Dhabi Race Track.** Directly to the **west,** along the **Khor al-Bateen,** are a number of **palaces** owned by the royal family which are not open to the public.

Head **north** again on **Sultan bin Zayed Street,** then take the **left fork** along **Bainunah Street** which takes you through the main **embassy and ministries district,** past the **Intercontinental Hotel,** and back to the main roundabout near the Hilton Hotel.

117

Dubai: Commercial, Cosmopolitan and Accommodating

Dubai is the UAE's commercial hub, with a cosmopolitan, liberal atmosphere and some excellent hotels. It is the perfect place to base yourself for a holiday, with good road links to all the other emirates. Originally a fishing village, Dubai was settled around 1830 by a branch of the Bani Yas tribe from the Liwa Oasis, led by the Al-Maktoum family who still rule the emirate.

Dubai has been a centre for entrepôt trade since the late 1800s, largely because of the liberal attitudes of the rulers which encouraged traders from Persia and India to settle. Trade remains its *raison d'être*, while traditional activities such as herding, fishing, pearl-diving and date cultivation have largely disappeared.

The discovery of oil in 1966 was a turning point in the fortunes of the emirate.

Above: Bagpipe player in the army band entertains in Dubai.

The late ruler, Sheikh Rashid bin Said al-Maktoum, carefully invested the oil revenues, building Dubai up from a backwater into the modern city it is today.

Dubai now has all modern conveniences, and the wide range of luxury hotels makes it a good base for a winter break in the sun. Also popular are two-centre holiday packages, with flights on to neighbouring Arab countries such as Oman, or to the Indian Ocean islands such as the Seychelles, Maldives or Comoros, or to Eastern and Southern Africa. What Dubai lacks is the charm that goes with discomfort and authenticity; although glimpses of old Dubai can be found in the Bastakia quarter and in the souqs.

Getting there

Dubai's International Airport, which has a good and reasonably priced duty-free shop, is the nation's busiest and has air-links with most Asian, Middle Eastern and European destinations. The taxi journey from the main international airport to the city centre costs about AED 30. Sixty-five airlines operate scheduled services through Dubai International Airport, flying to more than 100 destinations. By car, Dubai is a two-hour journey from Abu Dhabi and one-and-a-half hours from Al Ain. The city can be reached easily from Sharjah across the Garhood or Maktoum bridges in about 20 minutes.

When to go

Dubai is good all year round, although too hot for comfort in July and August when temperatures soar to 45-50°C (113-122°F). Dubai is particularly good for a Christmas or New Year break because its liberal attitudes make it one of the better places to party in the Middle East and the awareness of its possibilities as a tourist destination means that a wide variety of tours are available, even during a short break.

Where to stay

Dubai's choice of hotels is unrivalled in the Middle East. Accommodation, both in the hotels and short-term service apartments, is excellent. Most international hotels are represented. Visitors can choose according

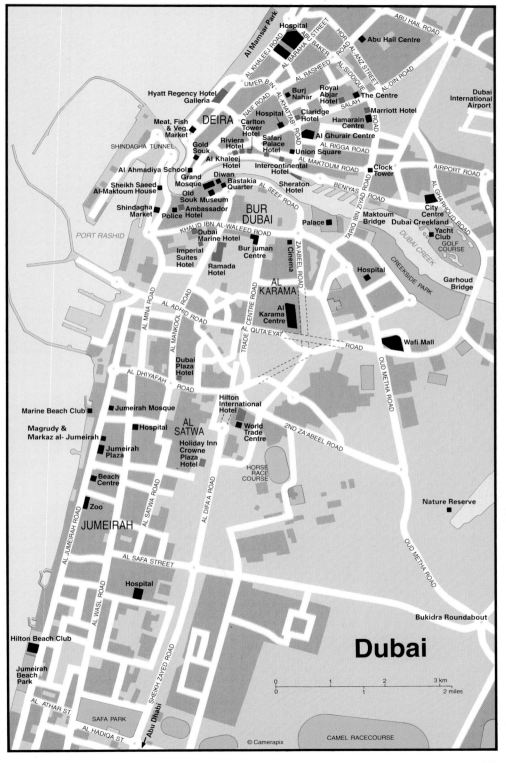

Dubai

Left: Wind tower reaches skywards in Dubai's old town.   Above: The Bastakia Quarter is well worth a closer look by visitors in search of traditional Arab culture.

to their budget, and also on their interests in Dubai.

Most historical sites are located along both sides of the creek in Deira and Bur Dubai, as are the old bazaars and the key souqs. Budget hotels abound around Beniyas Square and there are excellent luxury hotels along the creek.

For those who want a relaxed beach holiday, however, with occasional trips into the city, Jumeirah is the best bet; it is still only a 20-minute taxi drive into the city centre. Bur Dubai offers a good half-way house, lying on the west side of the creek before one reaches Port Rashid.

Sightseeing
Dubai is divided by a creek that runs through the heart of the city, and around which many of the big hotels are situated. To the east of the creek lies Deira, the commercial hub. Here there is the gold souq, old and new, and the spice souq. To the west, Bur Dubai contains the old souq,

some of the main shopping centres and the Dubai museum. Further to the west and on the sea-front, Jumeirah is a popular place for tourists, with some good beaches and beach clubs, the Dubai Zoo and some parks.

These three key areas are several kilometres apart and, as a result, getting around is easiest by taxi or by hire-car, particularly in the hot season. For those rash enough to go on foot, a steady stream of taxis will pass you, honking their horns loudly to offer a lift.

Deira
A good place to get one's bearings in Deira is at the Clock Tower, a roundabout situated just after Al-Maktoum Bridge. The clock tower is a traditional feature in the centre of many towns in the UAE and almost everyone will be able to guide you there if you get lost. From the clock tower, one walks along Al-Maktoum Road or the parallel Beniyas Road in the direction of

121

Union Square. This area contains some of Dubai's finest modern architecture: particularly striking are **Dubai Chamber of Commerce Building,** a blue tower block with a wedge-shaped top, and the **Etisalat Building,** on top of which is a concrete brown globe. A short distance from these lies **Beniyas Square,** the commercial hub, just a stone's throw from the **old souqs.**

Walking along the creek on Beniyas Road, you pass the **Intercontinental Hotel** and the **Carlton Tower** before arriving at the **Murshid Bazaar,** a collection of Indian-run shops.

The **old souq** is a few hundred metres down the same road. Off to the **right,** lie the **gold souq** and the **covered souk,** a warren of little shops selling anything from electrical equipment to Indiansilks. The Deira **meat, fish and vegetable market** is off a roundabout to the **west** of the gold souq.

Also worth a visit, in the **Ahmadiya district** of Deira, is the **school** built in the early 1900s by Ahmed bin Delmuk, a wealthy pearl trader of the day, whose house survives nearby. The school was built around a central courtyard, with arched cloisters on the ground floor and wide verandas on the upper floor. The school rooms gave off the central square. There, a mixture of Arabic, mathematics and Islamic studies was taught. The school was closed in the 1930s when the pearl trade collapsed but reopened a few years later and survived until the mid-1960s, when it was again closed.

The **Burj Nahar** in Deira is an example of a traditional round watchtower.

The souq area is the heart of Deira. Around it lie most of the good hotels and a selection of modern shopping malls including the **Al Ghurair Centre, Al Mulla Plaza,** the **Abu Hail Shopping Centre, The Galleria,** the **Al Manal Centre,** the **Hamarain Centre** and a shopping centre which calls itself simply **The Centre.**

Heading **east** from Deira along Beniyas Road past the Maktoum Bridge takes you to the **Dubai Creek Golf Club and Yacht Club** and the **Aviation Club.** The main building of the former is designed using the motif of a dhow's sail.

On the other side of the water is the lovely and extensive **Creekside Park.** The park offers beautiful views over the creek, and *abras* are available for hire, at least at some times of the year. There are a number of **gardens,** and fun **facilities** for children. **Wonderland** in Dubai was still under contstruction in 1996, but looked set to offer a number of rollercoaster and water-slide rides for children. It is located off the road leading past Creekside Park towards the Wafi Centre.

Shortly before the Golf Club lies the **City Centre shopping complex.** This huge mall was completed in 1995 and contains a French-style hypermarket, **Continent,** as well as a good range of clothes, jewellery and other shops.

Continuing east along Al-Garhoud Road, instead of going over the Al-Garhoud Bridge, leads to an area where it is possible to **hire jet skis** every afternoon for about AED 100 per half hour.

Deira also has several parks in which the footsore can relax. A short taxi journey from the souq area or the Hyatt Hotel, **Al-Mamsar park** lies beyond Hamriyyah port and, in the cool season, is a pleasant place in which to while away an afternoon. It has an **open-air theatre** for the children, several good beaches, a swimming pool and a traditional barasti-style coffee house with its own wind-tower.

Where to stay

Deira's top-end hotels include the **Intercontinental,** the **Carlton Tower,** the **Riviera** and, a bit further **south,** the **Sheraton,** all overlooking the creek. The **Al Khaleej Hotel** and the **St George's Hotel** are also on the creek, but slightly nearer the main souks. The **Hyatt Regency** is off **Al Khaleej Road,** overlooking the Gulf. Several good hotels are scattered around the area of the **Fish roundabout,** including the **Marriott,** the **Royal Abjar,** the **Four Points Sheraton, Novotel** and the **Claridge Hotel.** There are many cheaper hotels in the maze of small streets off Beniyas Square.

Dubai offers hotels for all tastes and pockets. The striking Hyatt Regency (top) is typical of those catering superbly for the top end of the market whilst excellent mid-range hotels such as the Ambassador in Bur Dubai (lower picture) provide good value.

Bur Dubai

Opposite the souq area, and just across the Dubai Creek, lies the **Dubai Old Souq** and the **Bastakia Quarter**. To get there, visitors either cross the **Maktoum Bridge** and take the road along the creek past the embassy district, or go through the **Shindagha Tunnel** and turn **left** along the water-front. A third way to get there is to cross the creek in an *abra*, a small wooden motor-launch.

The Bastakia quarter was one of the first areas to be settled in Dubai, back in the mid 1800s. Although much of it has either fallen into ruin or been destroyed, a number of old houses with traditional wind-towers are still visible.

Just opposite the Al-Faheidi roundabout at the end of Al-Musalla road, the **Majlis Art Gallery** is located in one of the few old merchant houses still in use in the Bastakia quarter. Built around a central courtyard, it contains a collection of **contemporary local art,** a selection of **handicrafts** from the Middle East, as well as **paintings** and **photographs** of local subjects. Nearby, the **Ramesh Art Gallery** offers a similar variety of *objets d'art.*

When facing the Al-Faheidi roundabout from the Al-Majlis Gallery, the road to the right leads to the Old Souq. This is the area that also contains the spectacular **Grand Mosque,** and the **Dubai Museum,** well worth an hour's visit.

Before visiting the museum and souq, however, a brief detour along the creekside is recommended. The creek is visible if you turn left from the gallery, or go straight ahead over Al Faheidi roundabout when coming from the direction of Al Musalla Road. Turning right along the dual-carriageway that runs by the creek, the **Al Boom (Dhow) restaurant** is moored a few hundred yards down Al Seef Road, opposite the Intercontinental hotel on the other side of the Creek. Al Boom offers traditional Lebanese food in an authentic renovated old dhow, and is particularly pleasant to visit for dinner. The **British Embassy** is in the same area, on the right hand side of Al Seef Road.

Return to the Al Faheidi roundabout, take a right turn at the roundabout, and after a few hundred yards, you arrive at the Dubai Museum, clearly identifiable by the stone towers and the large wooden dhow to the left of the museum entrance.

Dubai Museum is located in **Al Fahidi Fort.** The fort has a number of cannons outside. In the open courtyard inside, a variety of different **wooden boats** and other paraphernalia of Arab life are kept, as well as a typical **Arab rush house** with its windtower made of palm fronds. In adjacent rooms there are separate exhibitions covering aspects of Arab life and a good collection of **old weapons** and **musical instruments.** The museum also houses an extensive **reconstruction of a souq** in the Dubai of the 1950s, using sophisticated audio-visual techniques to recreate the atmosphere.

Al Fahidi Fort was originally built in 1800, made out of sea rocks and gypsum, and was the residence of the ruler of Dubai. In its first phase it was little more than a sur, a sort of round watchtower, but it was gradually expanded by the addition of defensive walls and additional towers.

At the start of the 20th century there were about a hundred armed men in Dubai. The fort, 41 metres by 33 metres (135 x 108 feet), comprises three towers, of which two are round and one square. The oldest is 12.5 metres (40 feet) high. The front door is made of teak, with large iron nails and brass plates that bear the name of Saeed Maktoum (1912-1958) and the Arabic phrase, *Ya Allah Muhammed.*

The fort was converted into a museum in 1971. It was fully restored in 1994, with a wide range of new exhibitions.

Right **next to the museum,** the large white modern building with traditional wind-tower motifs is the new ruler's **Diwan.** The buildings are not open to the

---

Right: Scene from Dubai Zoo. Previous pages: Dubai's huge dry-dock facilities house large tankers; Following pages: Well-appointed Dubai Yacht Club is popular with sailing enthusiasts; Fireworks burst in the night sky over Dubai, a freewheeling and cosmopolitan city.

public, although one can wander round outside with permission from the guards at the entrance to the Diwan.

Emerging from the Ruler's Diwan, the road to the right behind the museum and parallel with the creek leads past the Grand Mosque and the Old Souq area. Non-Muslims are generally not allowed to enter mosques in the UAE, but the Grand Mosque is worth visiting at Friday midday prayers, when it is visited by hundreds of devout Muslims. The **Old Souq** area lies further along from the mosque; it is a pleasant place to shop, but depite its name, has little of the atmosphere of an authentic "Oriental" bazaar.

Sheikh Saeed Al-Maktoum House, nearby on the edge of **the creek,** was the home of the former ruler from 1912 to 1958. It is located between the Falcon roundabout and Shindagha Tunnel. The house was originally built by Sheikh Maktoum, the father of Saeed, near the end of the last century. Since then it has gradually been extended as the needs of the family grew. The house was rebuilt in the 1980s after being abandoned when Sheikh Saeed died, winning the Arab City Organisation's 1988 annual architectural award. In 1996 there were plans to open it to the public.

Built on traditional Gulf Arab designs, the house has a large courtyard at the centre, around which verandas give shade to the living quarters that open onto the courtyard. Two wind-towers of the original four remain, catching the breezes from the creek and funnelling them down into the rooms below.

The lower floor contains few windows, affording the maximum privacy. Upstairs, decorated above with arched bays elaborately carved in palm-like motifs, the windows open onto the creek. The lower part of the windows stretch from the floor to a height of about 2.5 metres (eight feet), with bars to keep out burglars, and wooden shutters to keep out the sun. The house also contains a couple of large *majlis* rooms, in which the ruler attended to the needs of his citizens.

Directly **south** of Sheikh Saeed house is the **Shindagha market.** The Shindagha area also contains a splendid **square watch-**

Left: Dubai's thriving commercial centre, Deira side. Ball-topped building is Etisalat Tower.
Above: Any exertions are thirsty work!

tower, unusual in the UAE where most old watchtowers are rounded. A number of **hotels** nearby offer refreshment for the footsore and weary.

Where to stay

In Bur Dubai most of the hotels are in the vicinity of **Khaled ibn al-Waleed Road.** They include the **Ambassador,** the **Astoria,** the **Dubai Marine Hotel,** the **Imperial Suites** and the **Ramada.** Bur Dubai also contains a number of modern shopping centres including the **Bur Juman** and the **Holiday Centre,** near the World Trade Centre.

Karama

The **Al Karama** district lies in a rectangle bounded by the **Trade Centre** and **Zaabeel Roads** to the **west** and **east,** and the **Al Adhid** and **Khalid ibn al-Waleed** roads to the **north** and **south.** This area contains a **fish** and **vegetable market,** as well as a proliferation of **shops** and **restaurants** that offer a wide and interesting diet to both shopper and diner.

Above: Colourful tiles decorate this Shiite mosque. Right: Night time view of the spectacular Trade Centre Building.

Round the back of Karama, the **main Post office** on Zaabeel Road has a **Philatelic Bureau** where used and mint stamps of the UAE can be purchased. Opposite the post office, the **Lebanese Bakery** has a selection of delicious sweet and savoury pastries and baked goods, as well as snacks such as pitta bread with melted cheese, herbs or meat which cost just a few dirhams each.

From Karama, a short drive along the **Trade Centre Road** takes the visitor to the **Dubai World Trade Centre,** directly opposite which is the **Hilton Hotel** and service apartments. The World Trade Centre, one of the tallest buildings in Dubai, is mainly used as offices and a conference centre. Down the road from the Trade Centre, the **Holiday Inn-Crown Plaza** and the **Metropolitan Hotel** are recommended.

There are a number of good restaurants on the Trade Centre Road, between the Burjuman Centre and the traffic lights that mark the main turnoff into Karama. These

include the **Kamat Indian vegetarian restaurant** and the excellent **Thai Terrace**.

South of Karama, along **Al Qutaeyat Road,** on the way to the **Garhoud Bridge,** lies the **Wafi Shopping Centre.**

Al Satwa

Al Satwa lies on the way to Jumeirah, just off and around **Al Diyafah Road.** As well as **hotels** and the many tiny **restaurants,** some offering authentic **Lebanese food,** there are hundreds of **small shops** with a comprehensive range of goods. Satwa has a crowded, bustling atmosphere, and it is often difficult to park along the narrow streets.

The **Dubai Plaza Hotel,** on the main **Satwa roundabout,** contains a number of **good bars** and **restaurants** serving Mexican and Tex-Mex food. The **Al Dhiyafah Centre** is a large modern shopping mall.

Along the main road from Satwa towards Jumeirah, before a large roundabout, are a number of good resturants, in-

134

Seafaring traditions live on with the fishing dhow (left) whilst a fisherman mends his nets (above).

cluding fast food restaurants and a range of international cuisines. These include the **Istanbouli**, which serves Lebanese-style food, and which has a small grotto waterfall typical of Lebanese restaurants. A relative newcomer is the **Internet Cafe**, where you can have a snack and coffee while browsing the pages of the World Wide Web on one of the restaurant's several computers that are all hooked up to the Internet.

Following along the road towards Jumeirah, a left turn leads into Al-Wasl road, the site of the **Iranian hospital** and **mosque**. These are beautifully decorated with blue-tile mosaics. Further down Al-Wasl Road leads past **Saffa Park** on the left, popular with ornithologists because of its wealth of **bird-life**.

Jumeirah

Jumeirah offers the visitor beaches galore, and also contains one of the best mosques in the whole UAE. The **Jumeirah Mosque**, located at the end of **Beach Road** nearest to the **main port**, is built in the style of a medieval Fatimid mosque.

It comprises two graceful minarets and a large central dome surrounded by four minor domes, each with the traditional moon symbol at the top. The mosque is built of stone that gives it an almost golden glow, especially when the sun is sinking in the evening. A number of good **shopping malls** are located along Beach Road near the mosque. These include the **Markaz al-Jumeirah, Jumeirah Plaza, Magrudy's** and the **Beach Centre**. The **Dubai Marine Beach Club,** part of the Dubai Marine Hotel in Bur Dubai, has some good **restaurants,** including Lebanese. The **Profile Gallery** in Markaz al-Jumeirah contains a wide range of **antiques.**

This area of the coast is flushed by the warm clean waters of the Gulf. The **beach facilities** range from five-star at the Hilton Beach Club to dirt-tracks leading to secluded white sandy beaches.

There is a range of good hotels, most with a wide variety of **sports** and **leisure facilities.** A good choice for a visitor is the **Jumeirah Beach Club,** open to the public, although with ladies-only visiting days.

The beach club offers food and refreshments, with playgrounds for children.

Further down the coast road, hidden behind the villas on the **right-hand** side of the road, and next to the **Dubai sailing club,** a typical **fishing village** is an unexpected find after modern Dubai. The village consists of a few corrugated iron shacks, often furnished with the most basic iron-sprung beds, and is surrounded by fishing nets, other equipment and boats.

Where to stay

Jumeirah's hotels lie along the seafront. They include the **Forte Grand Jumeirah Beach,** the **Chicago Beach Hotel,** and the **Hilton Beach Club.** The latter may be used by guests of the Hilton Hotel, located at the end of the **Trade Centre Road.** The luxury **Jebel Ali Hotel** is located further out, near the **Jebel Ali Free Trade Zone.** It offers a superb beach club and beautiful grounds. Several new hotels were under construction in 1996.

Outside Dubai

A number of places worth visiting lie outside the busy centre of Dubai. These can be reached by heading along the main Dubai-Abu Dhabi road and taking the turn-off at Interchange 1 towards Nadd al-Shiba, and further off, the towns of Al-Ain and Hatta.

These include the **Nadd al-Shiba camel racetrack,** located on the road to Hatta and Al-Ain, opposite the **Dubai Golf and Racing Club,** off the Bu Kidra roundabout in the direction of the Dubai country club. **The Dubai wildlife and waterbird sanctuary,** where flamingoes can be seen during the winter, is located on the Dubai creek, off the Oud Mehta road which is reached by turning left at Bu Kidra roundabout when coming from the direction of Jumeirah.

Above: Modern architecture at Jumeirah.
Right: Jumeirah mosque.

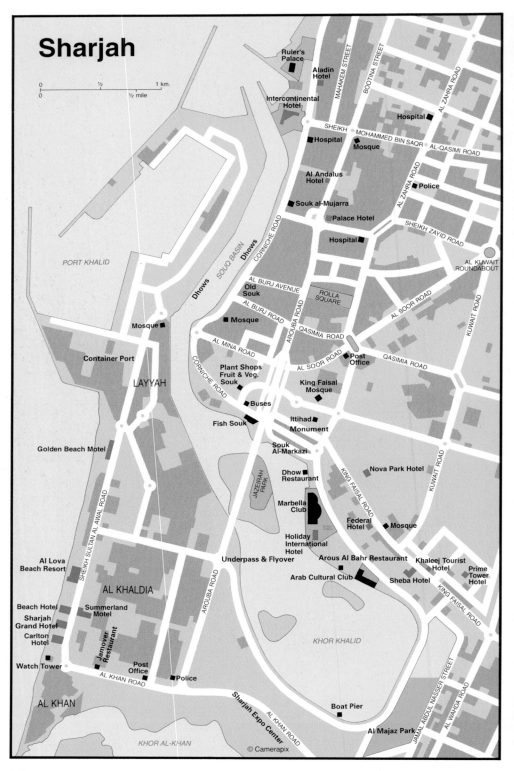

Sharjah

0   ½   1 km.
0   ½ mile

Ruler's Palace
Aladin Hotel
Intercontinental Hotel
SHEIKH MOHAMMED BIN SAQR
Hospital
Mosque
Hospital
Al Andalus Hotel
Souk al-Mujarra
Palace Hotel
Hospital
Hospital
MAHAKEM STREET
BOOTINA STREET
AL ZAHRA ROAD
AL-QASIMI ROAD
AL ZAHRA ROAD
Police
SHEIKH ZAYID ROAD
AL KUWAIT ROUNDABOUT
PORT KHALID
SOUIQ BASIN
Dhows
Dhows
Dhows
CORNICHE ROAD
AL BURJ AVENUE
Old Souk
ROLLA SQUARE
AROUBA ROAD
AL SOOR ROAD
KUWAIT ROAD
Mosque
AL BURJ ROAD
QASIMIA ROAD
AL MINA ROAD
Post Office
Container Port
CORNICHE ROAD
AL SOOR ROAD
QASIMIA ROAD
LAYYAH
Plant Shops Fruit & Veg. Souk
King Faisal Mosque
Buses
Fish Souk
Ittihad Monument
Golden Beach Motel
Souk Al-Markazi
JAZEIRAH PARK
Nova Park Hotel
KUWAIT ROAD
Dhow Restaurant
Marbella Club
KING FAISAL ROAD
Federal Hotel
Mosque
Holiday International Hotel
Al Lova Beach Resort
SHEIKH SULTAN AL AWAL ROAD
Underpass & Flyover
Arous Al Bahr Restaurant
Khaleej Tourist Hotel
Prime Tower Hotel
Arab Cultural Club
Sheba Hotel
Beach Hotel
Sharjah Grand Hotel
Carlton Hotel
Summerland Motel
AL KHALDIA
Jamover Restaurant
AROUBA ROAD
KHOR KHALID
KING FAISAL ROAD
Watch Tower
Post Office
Police
AL KHAN ROAD
AL KHAN
Sharjah Expo Center
AL KHAN ROAD
Boat Pier
Al Majaz Park
JAMAL ABDUL NASSER STREET
AL WAHDA ROAD
KHOR AL-KHAN
© Camerapix

140

Above: The luxury Sharjah Continental Hotel features a water garden and coffee shop in the foyer.

Sharjah: Tradition, Trade and Tourism

It was only in the 1950s that the emirate built its first airport and modern school, and it was not until 1967 that the first asphalt road linking Sharjah and Dubai was completed. Twenty years ago there were only two hotels — the Carlton and the Sheba. Even a decade ago, what is now the new souq was only the site of a maze of clumsy stalls and mud-brick shops.

All has changed. The city has good roads, modern hotels and other tourist facilities, and a thriving industrial area outside the main city. Despite that, Sharjah retains something of its old world charm.

Getting there

Sharjah, the capital of Sharjah emirate, lies about nine kilometres (just over five miles) north-east of Dubai, from which it is only a 20 to 30 minute drive. The road to and from Sharjah gets very busy at peak periods (from 0800-1000 in the morning and 1800-2000 in the evening), and it is best to avoid these times if possible. The Sharjah International Airport, located about 20 minutes outside the city centre, is a popular thoroughfare for visitors from Russia and Eastern Europe, largely because the airlines of the former Eastern Bloc have all chosen Sharjah as their Gulf destination.

When to go

Autumn and spring are the best times to visit Sharjah, one of whose key attractions is its proximity to the Northern Emirates.

Where to stay

There are many reasonably good, reasonably priced hotels in Sharjah and some of the best are located outside the main tourist areas. This is all very well if you want

Above: This traditional fishing craft is one of hundreds of Arab and Persian dhows which line the seafront at Sharjah. Right: Unusual monument at Kitab Corner, Sharjah, features a huge replica of the Qur'ân.

peace and quiet, but the Coral Beach Hotel or Ajman Beach Hotel in Ajman emirate probably serves the same need rather cheaper if that is all you want.

The Intercontinental at the end of the Corniche is a good halfway house, and within a couple of kilometres (a mile or so) of the tourist sites. Reasonably priced hotels such as Khaleej Tourist, the Sheba Palace and the more centrally located Palace and Nova Park hotels offer fairly basic accommodation and facilities, but are nearer the souqs and antique shops.

Sightseeing

Sharjah is as much a mix of the old and new as anywhere else in the UAE. But it is the old that penetrates most strongly there and, although there are the gleaming tower blocks and wide-open avenues that you see in Dubai and Abu Dhabi, somehow that

does not seem the key ingredient. Sharjah is one of the oldest towns in the UAE and its long tradition of seafaring and maritime-trading remains alive along the **Buheira Corniche** and in **Port Khalid.**

Sharjah's road system may be somewhat confusing. The **blue route indicators** orient the visitor to the 50 or so separate **districts** into which the city is divided, **green signs** point you in the direction of the other **emirates** and their main cities, while **brown signs** point to local **tourist sites.** The system is used in all the emirates. Unfortunately, in Sharjah the number of brown and green signs is small compared with the blue signs, which are only useful if you know the city well.

The best way to see the city is in a **clockwise loop.** Forking off to the right of the main Dubai Road, just before the second flyover, you reach a roundabout at

Following pages: Striking golden dome above Al Majaar Souq; The illuminated Dhow restaurant is a popular waterfront feature at Sharjah.

Above: The Faisal Mosque and (right) Al-Arsah souq, Sharjah.

King Faisal Square, labelled on some maps Mothercat Roundabout. Take the third exit at the roundabout, leading left into King Faisal Road, past the **Sheba Hotel** on the left, and the **Khaleej Tourist Hotel** and then **Choitrams** supermarket on the right. A couple of kilometers (a mile or so) from the roundabout, you reach a flyover shortly after the **Nova Park Hotel**, visible off to the right, and the intersection with Al-Zahra Road.

The palatial building visible to the left after the flyover is the **Souq al-Markazi**. To reach it, you need to turn 180 degrees round the huge roundabout just after the flyover. Then turn anti-clockwise under the flyover leading into the city centre, continue with the gardens whose flowers spell out the sign "Smile You Are In Sharjah" to your right, past the signs off to the wharves to your right, then back under the same road into the city centre.

The Souq al-Markazi, a gleaming blue-and-white building that looks like a palace, but in fact is a market selling anything from crude Omani pottery to vegetables.

Built in the late 1970s, the design of the souq was influenced by Islamic architecture. The souq is divided into two rows containing **eight separate halls,** each with about **100 shops,** which are connected by a covered passageway running above the dual carriageway that divides the two halves. The road is lined with old-fashioned English-style lamp posts.

The building itself is impressive, with a number of blue domes, the walls green, blue and beige, and covered with ivy and clover motifs. The wind-towers at the top of the building give an Oriental feel. The upper floor of the souq contains shops selling a variety of **Indian, Arabian** and **Persian furnishings** and **craft items,** including old carpets and antiques.

Just opposite the souq is the largest mosque in the emirate, the **King Faisal Mosque.** The tall pillar topped with gold that stands next to it is the **Ittihad,** or Unity Monument.

After the souq, turn due **south** off the main roundabout to the southern extension of the Corniche Road, right at the start of

Souqs provide a variety of offerings from caged birds (top) to hubble bubble pipes (above).

what is the **Dhow Restaurant,** moored in the **Khalid Creek** (Khor Khalid) opposite **Jazeirah Park.**

The Dhow, called *Al Boom* in Arabic, is a traditional vessel that has been rebuilt and refurbished to form a two-storey restaurant. The gangway is a springy little bridge from the shore.

The uppermost section of the restaurant offers the opportunity to lunch or dine in the open air, with a beautiful view over the bay. The decor is simple, with old wooden trestle tables covered with apricot and pink tablecloths, and paraffin lamps hanging from the ceiling. Alternatively, you can eat in the hold of the ship, on the same level as the gangway, and next to the buffet. The kitchens are at the back of the vessel, where the crew's accommodation would have been.

The restaurants serve a **buffet** on Fridays comprising no less than 30 varieties of **mezze,** freshly grilled fish including the local Gulf specialities of hammour, Sultan Abu Hamid and Sultan Ibrahim, pomfrets, and half-a-dozen varieties of dessert.

From the Dhow Restaurant, a **right** turn, takes you past the **Marbella Club** and the **Hotel Holiday International** (right). Near here, after the **Arab Cultural Club** and **Arous al-Bahr** Restaurant on the right, there is a **coffee-house,** a low thatched building, with an open-air terrace at the rear overlooking Khor Khalid and a small, uninhabited island just opposite.

The coffee-shop does not look much from the outside, and the staff do not speak English, but it is a pleasant place for a helping of **Turkish coffee** after lunch. It also contains a couple of traditional rooms, without chairs but scattered with rugs, for lunch or dinner outings.

From the coffee-shop, the road winds along the creek into **Sheikh Khalifah Road** where there is a **mooring point** for tiny boats, similar to *abras,* but with a cushioned bench at the back, in which you can take a **tour** around the creek.

Al-Majaz Park is on the left of this section of road – which incidentally has some of the biggest speed bumps you are ever likely to encounter!

This is also a favourite **spot for picnickers** especially on **Fridays** when dozens of Arab families pitch out on the grass along the creek for family barbecues. At the centre of the lagoon a fountain shoots water to a height of 100 metres (330 feet).

The **Al Khaldia, Layya** and **Al Khan** areas lie to the west of the junction that leads back to the bridge recrossing the creek from **west to east.** Go under the underpass and Layya and Khaldia are signposted.

There are a number of luxury hotels in this area, including the **Beach Hotel, Sharjah Grand Hotel** and **Sharjah Carlton Hotel,** with clean **white-sand beaches** overlooking the waters of the Gulf. The fishing village of **Al Khan** is a little-developed area, comprising mainly one-storey houses and old watchtowers. These are built of corals and sandstone.

The Khor al-Khan offers **pleasant walks** in a less-intensively urban area to the main city. Old dhows and fishing boats lie around in picturesque disarray. To the **north** of this area, **Port Khalid** is a modern **deepwater port** with 12 cargo berths, offering **container** and **ro-ro facilities.**

Crossing the Khor Khalid on the **Arouba Road** leads past the **Jazeerah Park,** the same park that is visible from the Dhow Restaurant. Jazeerah Park houses a miniature **Disneyland.** There is a fun-fair with a Big Wheel and a number of other rides. From there, heading east you are back on the mainland at the large roundabout to the **north** of the Souq al-Markaz. A **left turn** brings you to the **fruit and vegetable souq,** and **fish souq,** with the fish souq on your left. These are pleasant enough for those who like markets. Head between these, along the **northward** extension of the Corniche Road and you pass a row of **plant shops,** also selling old pottery.

At the first roundabout, the Buheira Corniche leads for about two kilometres (a mile or so) past the **souq** to the **Sharjah Continental Hotel.**

The **Old Souq** area is a must; it lies on the third road after the **blue-domed mosque** on the **right** after the roundabout. The **Al-Arsah souq** area has been resurrected after it closed down in the 1960s, and houses the **Sharjah Heritage Museum,**

Above: Roadside vegetable seller enjoys a coffee break. Right: The twin minarets of a mosque in Sharjah combine beauty with centuries-old function, calling the faithful to prayer.

along with a number of shops that sell traditional items such as **pearls, perfumes** and even **dates.** The white-washed walls and wood-beamed roofs preserve the atmosphere of a traditional souq, sparsely decorated from the outside. The **Al Arsah coffee-house** is a typical Arab coffee-shop from the old days, but with clean tables and floors.

The **Heritage Museum** at Al-Arsah Souq provides an insight into life in Sharjah in the early years of the 20th century. It is just opposite the entrance to Al-Arsah Souq. The museum is the site of the **original house** of a long-established Sharjah family, and preserves the rooms in which several generations of the family lived, ate and slept. Much of the furniture is from India, including the beautiful wooden four-poster beds, elaborately carved and raised above the floor to prevent insects from becoming unwelcome bed-partners.

Just behind the souq, off Al Burj Avenue lies the **main commercial area**. Most of the main **banks** are represented, and there are a great variety of **small shops,** as well as a

few tower blocks for offices. Sharjah is building its own **Etisalat Tower** which is expected to be ready in late 1997. It will have a spiral design, intended to fit in with the city's many minarets.

Just to the **right** of this area there are several old **merchants' houses,** topped by wind-towers. Most of these are in ruins, and less than well-preserved.

Opposite Burj Avenue, between Arouba Road and Al Zahra, **Rolla Square** is the heart of Sharjah city and, particularly on **National Day,** it becomes the site of **outdoor festivals** and entertainments. Displays of **local folk-dancing** are occasionally arranged during the **cool season** on **Fridays.** The square has a small **clocktower** and old **cannons**.

Continue along the Corniche, a spectacular brown-pink stone building laced with blue-grey decoration runs about 200 metres (650 feet) along the seafront, just before a mosque. This is the **Souq al-Mujjarah,** a relatively new building completed in 1987 which contains a variety of **luxury shops.** The modern inside of the

Above: The waterfront at Sharjah.

building contrasts with the mass of small dhows, launches, and wooden boats moored all along the sea-front. Further to the **east,** along the Corniche, one passes the **Ruler's Palace.** There is no entry to the public but it is probably worth seeing to get a sense of how the place is run.

After the palace, take a **right turn** along **Sheikh Sultan bin Saqr al-Qassimi Road** and drive straight along over six roundabouts. There, in **Al Falaj** district, a group of buildings dotted around the roundabout includes the **Sharjah Archaeological Museum** (a brown building) and the green-painted **Sharjah Cultural Centre.** Both are worth a visit.

The Archeological Museum contains finds from a number of digs in the emirate of Sharjah, dating back to the Stone and Iron Ages. The **Science Museum** is just a few hundred metres from the roundabout. It was opened in 1996, and has state-of-the-art displays from plasma balls to a wall that absorbs the shadow of anyone standing against it. There is also a **planetarium**. If your children are getting bored of cam-

els, dhows, and souqs, this is the place to head for.

From the Cultural Centre roundabout, the **Al Wahda Road** leads all the way back to the Mothercat roundabout. There is nothing special to see along the way, although there are some attractive **mosques,** and dozens of **small shops.**

This is a good place to get a feel for modern-day **Sharjah.** Most of the buildings are two- or three-storeys high, with the ground floor occupied by a shop, and the upper floors acting as accommodation, usually with laundry hanging out to dry.

Right: Fountain in Al Ittihad square, Sharjah.

PART THREE:
PLACES AND TRAVEL

Left: Not for the faint-hearted! Four-wheel-drive vehicle negotiates the top of the waterfall at Hatta Pool. Above: Life is unbelievably harsh in the Empty Quarter, as described by explorer and writer, Wilfred Thesiger after his travels there in the 1930s.

Oases, Islands and the Empty Quarter

The areas outside the main cities of the UAE are a challenge but one well worth meeting. Off-road getaways abound, while for those driving by taxi or hire-car, a varied diet from desert ice-rinks to old forts and lush oases is available.

To the west of Abu Dhabi city, a string of islands off the coast are largely under-developed and unexplored. In the south of the emirate, the Liwa Oasis offers a chance to experience an oasis at the gateway to the forbidding Empty Quarter. East of Abu Dhabi, the town of Al Ain and the nearby Jebel Hafiz Mountain have become popular weekend getaways. To the north of Sharjah, Ras al-khaimah emirate has some beautiful scenery and many archaeological sites, features shared by the eastern emirate of Fujairah — while the tiny emirates of Umm al-Quwain and Ajman offer bite-sized opportunities for a taste of life as it was lived before the coming of oil.

In 1996, with tourism still in its relative infancy in the UAE, many of the sights were often poorly documented, and not well signposted, although this situation was rapidly improving. The geography of the individual emirates, which have small enclaves outside the main body of their territory, means it is not always possible to explore the country on an emirate-by-emirate basis.

Although this is no problem while travelling, as there are no border posts between the individual emirates, it does mean that you cannot methodically *do* each emirate one at a time.

Hatta: Mountains and Off-road Adventures

Cosmopolitan Dubai is best known for its spectacular modern architecture and the fast buzz of city life. But unexpectedly, around the town itself and in its eastern enclave at Hatta, you can sample a much slower pace of life and absorb something of the traditional lifestyle.

Hatta is an easy drive from Dubai along a good road, lined by sand-dunes and camels, and is a good place to get an initial taste of the UAE countryside.

Getting there
The drive to Hatta is best made from Dubai. It takes about one-and-a-half hours through some beautiful desert dunes, and an enclave of Omani territory that stretches about 30 kilometres (18 miles). There are no border posts however, for this stretch.

When to go
Hatta is best visited in spring and autumn, though in the summer when the coastal towns are still hot, the higher altitude is a little cooler than in the sultry heat of the main cities. The Hatta Fort Hotel offers cut-price weekend breaks in the summer months.

Where to stay
The Hatta Fort Hotel is among the most pleasant getaways in the whole UAE. The entrance hall includes a traditional Bedouin *majlis,* with rugs and brass coffee-pots, and floor cushions. The swimming-pool is overlooked by a bar and open-air restaurant, open to visitors. The pool is free for hotel guests while visitors must pay a AED 40 entrance fee.

Visitors can also dine in the Jeema restaurant, or relax over a drink in the elegant Roumoul cocktail bar. The hotel includes a small par-three golf course, with a total length of 976 metres (3,200 feet). Clubs can be hired from the hotel, and golf lessons can be arranged for the uninitiated.

Right: Solitary watchtower on a rocky vantage point overlooking Hatta Heritage Village.

Above: At a time when many traditional aspects of Arab life are disappearing, Hatta Heritage Village in Dubai Emirate, an hour from Dubai city, aims to provide a valuable link with the past.

Olympic target and field archery, clay-pigeon shooting and a floodlit tennis court are also available to hotel guests.

The grounds of the hotel are superbly green and lush. The rooms comprise 54 air-conditioned doubles with satellite TV and in-house movies, as well as the usual luxuries of a good hotel. There is also a conference room which can accommodate 200 delegates, and a number of smaller rooms for meetings.

Sightseeing

Hatta, an ancient **fortress village**, nestles in the foothills of the **Hajar Mountains.** For centuries the locals have used it as a summer retreat away from the oppressive heat on the coast, and the tradition has been kept going in modern times by tourists and locals alike who now, however, tend to

stay at the Hatta Fort Hotel rather than in Hatta village itself.

The village offers a number of sites, including old **watchtowers** which at one time marked the **border** with **Oman.** A **heritage village** was still being developed in 1996, comprising about a dozen brick buildings. Nearby, a well-watered garden contains palm trees and others bearing a variety of citrus fruits including oranges.

A typical **falaj irrigation channel** is located in the grounds of the heritage village, just to the left of the main sandstone building as you enter the village. Here is a shady grove surrounded by date-palms, which can be eaten fresh from the tree by the visitor. The water irrigating the palms bubbles up fresh and cool from an underground spring into a small pond, which is a beautifully cool spot to rest your feet, es-

Following pages: The Hatta Road, heading south-east from Dubai towards the mountainous border with Oman; Ornately-dressed camel waits with its handler; The Hatta Fort Hotel pool offers a welcome relief to visitors after a hot and dusty drive.

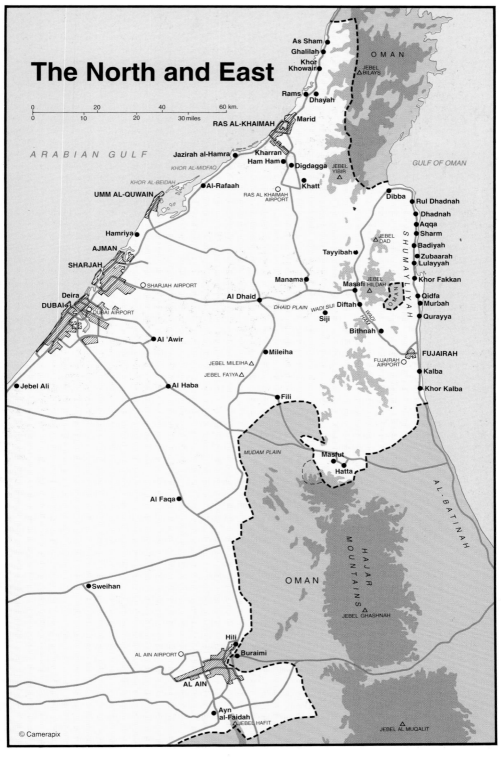

The North and East

As Sham
Ghalilah
Khor
Khowair
OMAN
JEBEL
BILAYS
Rams
Dhayah

Marid
RAS AL-KHAIMAH

ARABIAN GULF

KHOR AL-MIDFAQ

Jazirah al-Hamra
Kharran
Ham Ham
Digdagga
JEBEL
YIBIR

KHOR AL-BEIDAH

Al-Rafaah
Khatt
UMM AL-QUWAIN
RAS AL KHAIMAH
AIRPORT

GULF OF OMAN

Dibba
Rul Dhadnah
Dhadnah
Aqqa
Sharm
Badiyah
Zubaarah
Lulayyah
Khor Fakkan

Hamriya
JEBEL
DAD
Tayyibah

AJMAN
SHARJAH
Manama
Masafi
JEBEL
HILDAH
Qidfa
Murbah
Qurayya

SHUMAYLIYAH

Deira
SHARJAH AIRPORT
Al Dhaid
DHAID PLAIN
WADI SIJI
Diftah
WADI HAM
DUBAI
DUBAI AIRPORT
Siji
Bithnah

Al 'Awir
Mileiha
JEBEL MILEIHA
FUJAIRAH
AIRPORT
FUJAIRAH
Kalba

Jebel Ali
Al Haba
JEBEL FA'IYA
Fili
Khor Kalba

MUDAM PLAIN
Masful
Hatta

AL-BATINAH

Al Faqa

Sweihan

OMAN

HAJAR
MOUNTAINS

JEBEL GHASHNAH

Hili
Buraimi

AL AIN AIRPORT

AL AIN

Ayn
al-Faidah
JEBEL HAFIT
JEBEL AL MUQALIT

© Camerapix

161

pecially in the hot season when even the water in swimming pools is too warm to be really refreshing.

The Hatta Fort Hotel can also arrange 4WD safaris in the **dunes, wadis, rock pools** and **mountains** that surround Hatta for around AED 450 — well worth it if you can get a group together for the experience, but pricey if you go on your own. The hotel uses a Toyota Land Cruiser. Those who have access to a 4WD of their own may, of course, go it alone but getting lost in the dunes is a risky business. If you do decide to use your own wheels, the general advice on 4W-driving in Part Four should be observed, no matter how intrepid the driver.

The driver also needs to be aware of border issues — Oman lies immediately east and south of Hatta and, although some of the area is designated as no-man's land, going into Omani territory without a visa could cause problems.

Several routes are available. The **Hatta Fort** provides four options, lasting anywhere from three-and-a-half to six-and-a-half hours, offering a variety of terrain from towering **sand-dunes** to **scrub** and **gravel plains**, from low sunken **wadis** filled with rock pools to craggy **mountains**.

The **Hatta pools**, south of the village, are full all year round and swimming is allowed. The route to the pools is designed to avoid the concrete falaj, damaged in the past by 4WD vehicles. Visitors can get to within a short distance of the pools in a car, but have to walk the rest of the way.

North of Hatta, the mountains contain a variety of **birdlife** and attractive wadis at **Huwaylat** and **Al-Qawr**.

To the **north-west** of Hatta, on the gravel plains to the west of the mountains, the village of **Fili** includes a number of old **watchtowers**. The Hatta Fort hotel recommends that you do not enter, however, because of snakes and scorpions that sometimes lurk in the shade inside. Further on in the same direction, **Wadi Faiyah Rasta**

Opposite: The rocky terrain off-road provides a challenge to the adventure-seeking traveller.

offers a way to **high sand-dunes.** You should only drive in these when accompanied by another 4WD vehicle.

Sharjah: Road to Dhaid and Beyond

The emirate of Sharjah, outside the city of the same name, has spectacular desert scenery and is a good place to explore to get a sense of what life in the UAE was like before the discovery of oil. As you drive from Sharjah city towards the Dhaid Oasis, the desert becomes progressively redder and more sandy, giving way to large sand-dunes that are sculpted in even curves by the wind. There are many camels along the way.

From Dhaid, you can either proceed on to the east coast via Masafi, or head north towards Ras al-Khaimah after the turnoff to Manama.

Getting there
The easiest route to Dhaid is to take the road out to Sharjah International Airport, either by going right at the turnoff for Ras al-Khaimah and Fujairah on the road from Dubai to Sharjah city, or by going through Sharjah city and following signs for the airport. The journey from Sharjah to Dhaid takes between 45 minutes and one hour.

From the east coast, follow signs for Masafi; Dhaid is signposted from then on. This route takes about an hour.

When to go
The journey to Dhaid is good at any time, but as you will probably pass the town en route to other places, the time you visit will depend on your final destination. There is not much to see or do in Dhaid but it is a pleasant place to pass through on the road to Fujairah.

Where to stay
There is nowhere particularly good to stay in Dhaid, but the hotels of the east coast are only another hour's drive away. See listings for Hotels.

Above: The former beast of burden, now bred for its racing ability.

Sightseeing

From the turnoff marked towards **Fujairah** and **Ras al-Khaimah** on the main road from **Dubai** to **Sharjah,** head towards **Sharjah International Airport** and turn **right** onto the main road in that direction. At **junction four** a large **park** and **nature reserve** is located just off the main track.

At **junction eight** on the **Sharjah to Hatta road,** the **Sharjah Natural History Museum** is one of the best museums in the UAE. Run by Marika Jongbloed, the museum is divided into several exhibitions: A Journey Through Sharjah Emirate; Man and the Environment; A Journey Through Time; The Living Desert; and The Living Seas.

The museum provides a detailed introduction to the desert culture, as well as extensive information about the UAE's flora, fauna and prehistory.

Outside the museum are eight, paired **plots of land** with different soils, suitable for the types of plants being grown in them. Jongbloed intends to change the watering patterns to see if they survive better with less water. A **desert park** has also been established on the other side of the dual carriageway.

The **Dhaid Oasis** is located about 50 kilometres (30 miles) **east** of Sharjah on the same road. From the road, it is an inviting patch of green palm trees amidst the red sand-dunes through which you travel. Although it is reputed to be a holiday getaway for the wealthy, there is almost nothing to see in Dhaid. However, it is worth a brief stopover on a journey to other spots in the UAE.

From Dhaid, you may continue **east** towards **Fujairah** and the mountains, or take the road **south** through the **Dhaid Plain** through **Mleiha** to the main **Dubai-Hatta Road.**

This journey is one of the most beautiful in the UAE, particularly at sunset when the bulk of the mountains, **Jebel Mleiha** and **Jebel Fai'ya,** loom on the horizon to the right beyond the plains.

Off-road trips to these mountains can be made through the sands. The mountains are a favourite haunt of fossil-hunters and also a good place to camp.

Above: The bountiful harvest of a date palm. The dates, sometimes with 1,000 berries in a bunch, ripen in the heat of summer during July and August.

The area **south** of Dhaid has emerged as a region of considerable **archaeological interest.** In particular, archaeologists have demonstrated that the **Mudam Plain** was settled by an agricultural community, which may also have mined copper ore from the mountains to the east. The area is still relatively fertile. Scientists believe that in the past, however, rainfall levels were heavier than now, and large supplies of underground water may have been present in the shallow aquifers that run off the Hajar Mountains, allowing a heavier settlement pattern than is now supported.

Also important, **Al-Mileiha,** about 25 kilometres (15 miles) **south** of Dhaid, contains **sites** dating back to the beginning of the Christian era. The **archaeological site** is off in the sands before the main town of Mleiha, before the mountain of the same name. An experienced guide – or a great deal of patience – is needed to find them.

An ancient fort uncovered in the Mleiha area contained a **coin mould,** proving that the community minted its own bronze and silver coinage, probably the first ever minted in the emirates. At another nearby site, a **graveyard for animals** reckoned to be the oldest in the Arabian peninsula, dating back to the last couple of centuries BC, was discovered in the 1990s. Among the animal remains discovered are several two-humped camels that appear to have been ceremonially killed, perhaps as sacrifices associated with local burial customs.

A little further **south,** at **Jebel Emalah,** a group of **tombs** was found dating back 4,500 years. An **Iron Age village** dating back to 1000-500 BC was found at **Al-Thuqibah.** The village walls stand two metres (two yards) high, but are virtually covered by drifting sand.

Further down the road, just past the **Jebel Fai'ya** on the right, a left turn leads off to the town of **Fili** and its associated **archaeological site.** The site can only be reached by 4WD or on foot and is a few kilometres (a couple of miles) outside the town of Fili to the **north.**

Backtrack onto the main road, and a further 16-19 kilometres (10-12 miles) journey **south** brings you to the intersection with

Above: The impressively floodlit Ajman fort.

the **Dhaid-Hatta** road, just before the Mudam Plain. From there it is an easy journey back to **Dubai,** especially beautiful at sunset when, on the **left,** as you head **west,** the gas flare of the **Margham gas field** burns like a tall torch in the desert sands. This is the same stretch of the road described in itinerary one, before the border with Oman; but this time you will be travelling **east to west.** The road to Dubai passes the **Al Awir oases.** Al Awir can be reached by taking the right hand fork at the roundabout that leads back to Dubai and Abu Dhabi/Jebel Ali. Although there is nothing much to do in the town, the hundreds of metres of **date-palms** that line the road are worth the brief detour. The town also houses the palace of the ruler of Dubai, set in extensive gardens, but these are not open to the public.

The Northern Emirates

Getting there

The northern emirates of Ajman, Umm al-Quwain and Ras al-Khaimah are reached from Sharjah along a good asphalt dual carriageway that runs up the Gulf coast. On the left are creeks, islands, flats and sand-dunes of the Gulf; while on the right, the hills gradually give way to rocky mountains beyond Ras al-Khaimah city.

An alternative route from Fujairah emirate runs as a right fork on the road from Masafi to Dhaid, taking in views of the mountains and sands, as well as hot springs at Khatt and camel tracks at Digdaga, before reaching the main town of Ras al-Khaimah. Ras al-Khaimah emirate has its own international airport.

Where to stay

Ajman has two hotels, the Ajman Beach Hotel which has a good pool and is popular with tour groups, particularly from Eastern Europe, and the hotel Al Waha which is a small Arabic hotel in the Karama District. The beaches around here are pleasant and a good spot if you want a few days sunbathing.

Umm al-Quwain has the Umm al-Quwain Beach Hotel, the Palma Beach Hotel and the Pearl Hotel, sleepy getaways, but the beaches are not as well served.

The main deluxe hotels in the town of Ras al-Khaimah are the Al Nakheel, part of the Swiss Hotel group, and the Ras al-Khaimah Hotel, which has a wide range of sports and leisure facilities, as well as a business centre. An Intercontinental was also under construction in 1996. The Bin Majid Beach Hotel is pleasant and reasonably priced.

For visitors who want culture, shopping and scenery, Ras al-Khaimah is probably the best place to spend the night; Ajman and Umm al-Quwain might appeal most to those determinedly intent on catching rays for they offer little more than pleasant beaches.

When to Go
The Northern Emirates are good for a visit any time of the year, but bear in mind the seasonal weather patterns throughout the UAE. The area can be extremely green in the winter, although the Gulf waters become rather chilly in this season. Spring and autumn are probably the ideal times.

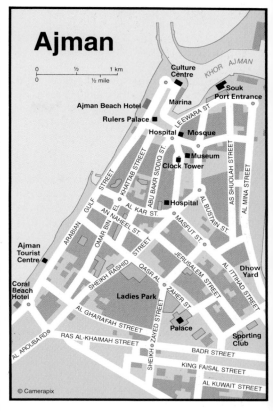

Ajman

Getting there
Ajman, the smallest of the seven emirates, comprises a stretch of coast north-east of Sharjah and south-west of Umm al-Quwain, and a couple of inland enclaves at Masfut and Manama. Driving from Sharjah on the main road to Ras al-Khaimah it is easy to travel through Ajman without even noticing it. Only the addresses on the shopfronts change.

From Sharjah Corniche, head north, with the sparkling waters of the Gulf on your left, and the road is lined with small parks, villas and occasional beachside cafes

and small restaurants on the right. After a few kilometres (a couple of miles), the **Coral Beach Hotel** is a block-like building with green and yellow awnings above the door.

Sightseeing
Beyond the hotel, after the **turnoff** to **Al Gharafa Street** and a **small mosque,** lies the Ajman Tourist Centre, a circular building with a brick-red roof. The centre contains a number of **restaurants,** including **Venice** at **Ajman Beach,** and overlooks one of the nicest beaches in the UAE, a beautiful sandy strip with beach umbrellas to keep off the intense sun. Just after the tourist centre, in the middle of the dual carriageway along the seafront, is an imposing square **watchtower.**

Further along, on the **right,** an onion-domed building with four brick watchtowers is the **Ruler's Palace.** The palace has a number of small **cannons** outside

173

and is guarded by sentries who question you if you dawdle. Do not take photographs. The palace lies just before the **Ajman Beach Hotel,** on the **left** of the road by the sea.

Bear to the **right,** past an **industrial site** on your left and the ruler's palace on the right, and the road leads past the **Ajman Culture Centre** on the left to **Ajman's Marina,** which overlooks the town's main creek.

The marina is on the **left** of the road, opposite wasteland with a small **cafeteria** in its middle. The creek is charming but not beautiful, with a **sand football pitch** on the right as you look from the marina. It is well-populated with dhows and small wooden fishing vessels, and fishing nets are strewn everywhere in colourful disarray.

Turning **right**, away from the creek and you reach a roundabout beside which is an attractive **white mosque** with blue decorative ribbing. The **third turnoff** leads to **Sheikh Humeid bin Abdul Aziz Street.** Following along this road leads to Ajman's town centre which is spread around the **central square,** which includes a **clock-tower** and, nearby, the **Ajman Museum.**

The museum is sited in a late **18th-century fort** that served originally as the ruler's palace, and then as the town's police station. The fort, with two wind-towers and two watchtowers, is fronted by a large gate and cannons. Inside, the museum's displays include old **manuscripts, weapons, archaeological finds** and reconstructions of **traditional rooms** in Arabic houses.

The museum has a reconstructed *barasti* house with a wind-tower in its forecourt, a long palm-frond house, as well as the museum shop and the Ajman Museum Cafeteria.

Al Medina and **Al Nasser souqs** lie to the **right** of the museum. These modern buildings offer nothing special to the tourist.

The area **opposite the museum** has a tangle of **small streets,** quaint but not picturesque, and crammed with small shops, restaurants, tailors, carpenters, workshops loosely dubbed **Art Shops,** an occasional **cheap hotel** and a mosque. The restau-rants offer mainly Indian and Pakistani food but do not look appetizing enough to even venture a soft drink. The whole area is dusty and rather ramshackle.

Further down **Sheikh Rashed Street** lie the more **modern areas** of the town. The road is lined with banks, modern shops and supermarkets. Turning left at the Giant **supermarket** on Sheikh Rashed Street, the road leads past a pinkish brown fort-like building towards a roundabout, off which is the **Ladies park,** used by local women and their children. The entrance to the park is on the left, after taking the right turn at the roundabout. Near here on Qasr al-Zaher Street is a palace, but this is not open to the public.

Heading back along Sheikh Rashid Street, a right hand fork in the road leads towards the sea past the **Ajman post office** and various municipal offices, behind the museum, onto **Al Mina Street,** also called **Leewara Street.** The area has a number of old fishing boats, and fruit and vegetable **markets,** as well as fish and meat markets.

The fish market should be visited early, when the catch has been freshly hauled in from the sea. Another large market sells mainly plastic household items.

Turn **right** along **Al Mina Street** and follow the road past the industrial area along the creek on the **left** out of the main town. This is the route to the **dhow-building yard;** the **black-on-white signs** for **Al Boom Marine** should be followed. Make a **U-turn** on the main road, turn **right,** follow the road until the next major road, make a **U-turn** to turn **left,** and the dhow-building yard is on the **left** past what appears to be a disused large blue **floating hotel,** beyond a **small mosque** on the right.

The dhow-building areas are actually a series of small yards, located along **Tareq bin Zayed Street,** and completely unselfconscious as tourist sites.

About 20-30 boats are built at any one time, many of them of fibreglass rather than wood. The hulls are laid on wooden frames, supported by oil drums; around the vessel sticks are propped up against each other, rather like the frame of a tepee, to hold the cross beams, and the boats are covered in blue netting to preserve the varnish.

Above: This cannon is one of several to be seen at Umm-al-Quwain Fort.

The dhows are typically about 18 metres (60 feet) long. The yards are strewn with wooden tree trunks, the wood for the hull and mast, and any amount of rubbish lies strewn around.

Back onto **Al Mina Street,** the road leads out of the emirate of **Ajman** which has a couple of **enclaves** in other parts of the UAE. These include the oasis town of **Manama,** at the **junction** of the main road from **Ras al-Khaimah,** and the road linking **Dubai** and **Sharjah** with the **east coast.**

Umm al-Quwain

Umm al-Quwain lies on a narrow finger of sand off the main road from Sharjah to Ras al-Khaimah. If Ajman is a sleepy little emirate, Umm al-Quwain positively snores; it has a small ruined fort, a few watchtowers, and a wind-tower. The tourist club offers various water sports, as do the two main hotels.

Apart from that, there is very little to see or do. Unless you are determined to soak up the relaxed atmosphere there is no reason to stay more than an hour or two. Ironically, one development that looks set to shake off Umm al-Quwain's rather sleepy image is **Dreamland**, an aqua-park that was being built in 1996 north of Umm al-Quwain on the road to Ras al-Khaimah. This promises to be the largest such theme-park in the Middle East, and among the largest aqua-parks in the world.

Getting there
Umm al-Quwain is easily reached from Ajman, simply by heading north along Al Mina Road, which meets up with a feeder road for the dual carriageway. Coming from this direction, the road actually leads back into Sharjah so you need to double back on yourself when you reach the large roundabout near the EPPCO station. If you pass Ajman Souq on your right, you have gone too far.

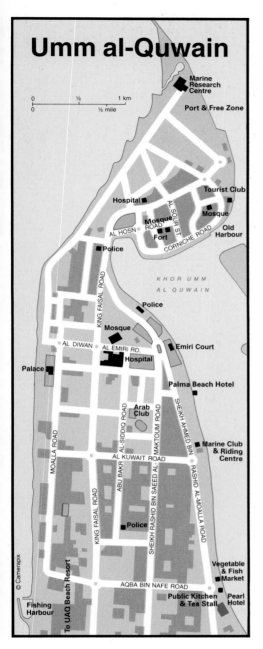

Umm al-Quwain

Marine Research Centre

Port & Free Zone

Tourist Club

Hospital

Mosque

Mosque

AL HOSN

AL SOUR ST.

Fort

Old Harbour

CORNICHE ROAD

ROAD

Police

KHOR UMM AL QUWAIN

KING FAISAL ROAD

Police

Mosque

AL DIWAN

AL EMIRI RD.

Emiri Court

Hospital

Palace

Palma Beach Hotel

Arab Club

SHEIKH AHMED BIN

MAKTOUM ROAD

AL-SIDDIQ ROAD

Marine Club & Riding Centre

AL KUWAIT ROAD

MOALLA ROAD

ABU BAKR

SHEIKH RASHID BIN SAEED AL-

RASHID AL-MOALLA ROAD

Police

KING FAISAL ROAD

AQBA BIN NAFE ROAD

Vegetable & Fish Market

Public Kitchen & Tea Stall

Pearl Hotel

To UAQ Beach Resort

Fishing Harbour

© Camerapix

The road leads past salt flats on the left and right and a Lego-like new town on the right; bulk storage tanks are visible in the distance. After 12 kilometres (8 miles), a large roundabout leads, on the left, to Umm al-Quwain and, on the right, to Falaj al-Moalla. On a small hill on the road to Falaj al-Moalla, about 160 metres (175 yards) from the roundabout, is a small archaeological dig.

From the main road to Ras al-Khaimah, a left turn at the roundabout, looping back on the dual carriageway heading back towards Sharjah, and immediately taking a right turn, leads into Umm al-Quwain. It is very clearly marked. The city centre is about 13 kilometres (eight miles) from the roundabout.

The road leading into Umm al-Quwain, King Faisal Road, crosses several small roundabouts, but there is not much to see, automobile showrooms and garages giving way gradually to small shops as the town of Umm al-Quwain gets nearer. The emir's *diwan* lies to the right of the main road, and soon after that the port area becomes visible on the right.

Sightseeing

Just before the **Emirates filling station,** to the **left,** three old **watchtowers** guard access to the town. Turn **right** along **Al Hosn Road** which leads to the **fort** and the **mosque** area. The fort is fronted by palm trees and a row of **cannons,** and has two **rounded towers,** and behind it a higher wall, now largely in ruins.

The fort is splashed with whitewash and in a sorry state of disrepair, as are the **merchants' houses** which lie behind the fort, and to your left when you look at the fort. The merchants' houses are inhabited now only by a few goats, but give authentic glimpses of the older style architecture. The houses have no windows at all on the ground floor and the arched row of windows above are made of wood and iron, with recesses for shutters.

In the one behind the fort, you can see the remains of an old wind-tower; wooden pipes jut out from the mud-brick which were used to drain away rainwater in the cool season.

Opposite: Fishing nets and traps hanging out to dry in Umm al-Quwain.

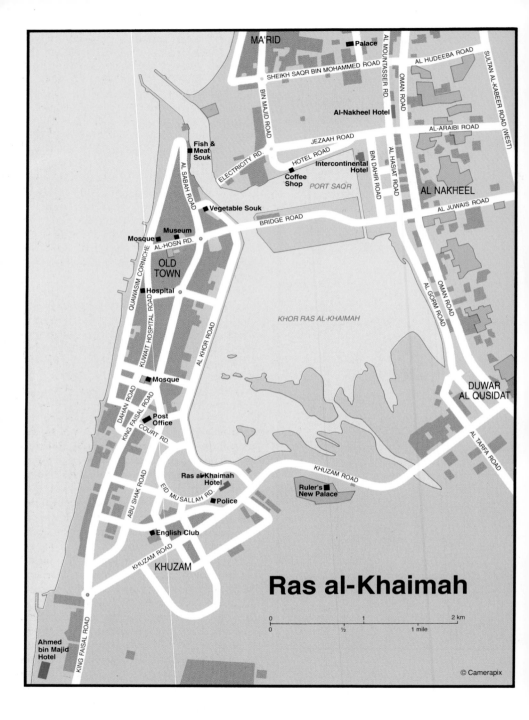

Above right: Men bathe in the Khatt hot springs. Mixed bathing is not practised in the UAE except on tourist beaches or in international hotels. Following pages: Palm plantation at Ras al-Khaimah. The area is noted for its agriculture, being blessed with good winter rainfall.

If you turn **right** from the fort you will come to the **harbour**. In 1996, a large **red cargo vessel** seemed to be permanently docked at the wharf. Further along the coast, heading **north,** a row of **derelict buildings** with decorative motifs lies on the **left.** To the **right,** the **fishing village** comprises a few dhows and onshore *barasti* huts draped with brightly coloured plastic waterproof clothing, and fishing nets, of both the metal-domed variety and cord nets for trawling behind the vessel.

A few metres further down is **Umm al-Quwain Tourist Centre,** a quiet resort with sailing dinghies and motor boats. The resort is surrounded by a palm-frond fence; beyond it a large **cruise ship** offers **tours** of the Gulf waters.

Beyond the tourist centre, heading due **north** past a couple of roundabouts, **the Umm al-Quwain Marine Research Centre** lies at the very top of the Umm al-Quwain peninsula, opposite the **Ahmed bin Rashid Port and Free Zone.** Neither the Marine Research Centre nor the Free Zone are open to the general public.

The seafront road runs about three kilometres (two miles) along the seaside, start-ing at the marine centre; a number of **watchtowers** are visible along this coast. A **left turn** as you come back down the peninsula heading south leads back to the main **King Faisal Road.** A brief detour up this road heading **north,** then bearing to the **right at the fork** in the road, leads to an old wind-tower.

The area has a few **restaurants** serving Indian and Pakistani food but they do not look anything special from the outside.

Heading out of Umm al-Quwain, the **east** coast of the peninsula may be reached by taking the left turn after the two Emirates filling stations on your right. The road is named **Sheikh Ahmed bin Rashid al-Moalla Road.** It leads past the **Emiri Court,** on the **left** at the the first large roundabout, then out past a **Marine Club** and **Riding Centre,** past a vegetable and fish **market** and the **Pearl Hotel.** After the hotel, a left turn leads to the Emir's palace; turn right and you link up with the main King Faisal Road. The **Umm al-Quwain Beach** resort lies on the sea-front to the left of the main road back into Umm al-Quwain, or to the right if you are leaving the Emirate on the same road. The resort comes to life on Fri-

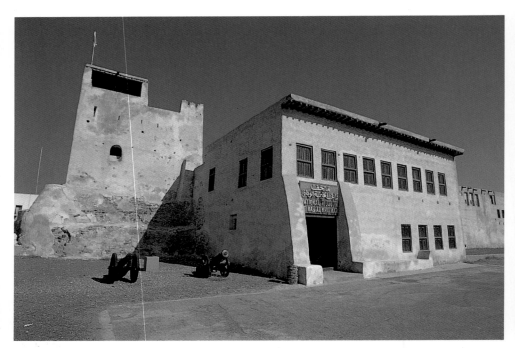

Ras al-Khaimah museum (top), housed in an 18th century fort, has rooms covering archaeology, the history of the emirate, arab jewellery and seashells, and the ruling Al Qasimi family. Exhibits include an ancient leather water bag (above).

day's when it hosts an all-you-can-consume lunch with Arabic food and dancing, for AED 150. This is well-attended by locals. The resort also has a bar and slot-machines."

While there is not much to see in Umm al-Quwain itself, **archaeological excavations** over the last few years have revealed a major site at **Al Door** on the coast. This lies to the **right** of the main **Ras al-Khaimah road,** about 10 kilometres (six miles) **north** of the **Umm al-Quwain Falaj al-Moalla** roundabout. The excavations have shown that around 2,000 years ago, Al Door was a major trading settlement in which trade flourished with countries as far afield as India to the east and the eastern Mediterranean to the west. The township was probably once known as **Omana,** a trading centre in the southern Gulf that features prominently in maps and reports by ancient geographers.

Ras al-Khaimah

Ras al-Khaimah is the northernmost emirate, and a popular getaway with people from Dubai. The emirate has been inhabited since the third millennium BC and historical texts reveal that the main town, Julfar, existed for hundreds of years just to the north of the modern city of Ras al-Khaimah.

It is the spectacular scenery, however, that will probably attract the visitor most. The narrow coastal plain rapidly gives way to steep mountains and the run-off water from these means that the emirate is among the most fertile in the UAE.

Sightseeing
The road from **Sharjah** runs first past the **ruins** at **Al Door,** opposite the thousands of tiny islands and lagoons of the **Khor al-Beidah,** facing the **Umm al-Quwain peninsula** over the water. This is a popular place with locals who like to meet on the sands, hold impromptu barbecues and nature-watch. The area is rich in **birdlife.**

About 10 kilometres (six miles) further on, you reach the village of **Al Refaah.** A

few **wind-towers** can be seen on the **eastern** side of the road. About 14 kilometres ($8^1/_2$ miles) from the turnoff to Umm al-Quwain is a **bench** with a canopy above on the **left** of the main road. Further on you pass **Khor al-Midfaq,** while on the **right,** mountains begin to loom on the horizon.

The deserted village of **Jazirat al-Hamrah** is located about 37 kilometres (23 miles) from the turnoff to Umm al-Quwain just after a **watchtower** standing on the high escarpment to the **right** of the main road. The village lies to the **left** of the road, a thin band of low houses lying on the sand flats, stippled by minarets and now and then a watchtower. The town is clearly marked. You need to do a **U-turn** on the main road and then turn immediately right. From there, the road leads past a miniature 'Eiffel Tower' on the **left,** past the **Jazirat al-Hamrah Cultural and Sporting Centre,** and you will come to a **school,** decorated outside with brightly coloured flags.

Jazirat al-Hamra is an odd place. Although of considerable archaeological and historical interest, there is nothing to explain to visitors either why the town has been deserted, or to point to the many sites of interest. Instead, you simply wander around, coming on the **ruins** of a **fort** with high **watchtowers** here, old **wind-towers** there.

In a way, it typifies the experience of many small towns in the UAE, which are remarkably self-effacing when it comes to tourists. Life tends to go on behind closed doors and, although you might see goats or other livestock and plenty of small children playing in the streets, there is little to cater for the tourist.

The odd thing about Jazirat al-Hamra is that the houses themselves are deserted. You can wander about the buildings, which are gradually falling into disrepair and ruin, examine the coral blocks that have made them and are simply falling into the roadways, and never see a living being.

The **beach** at Jazirat al-Hamra has also seen better days. Although it has good flat sands, most of it is covered with litter and detritus from the many picnic and camping expeditions that visitors have made over the years. Locals love the place for driving their 4WD vehicles and dune-buggies, but this also contributes to its less than pristine condition.

Back on the main road, heading **north,** there is little to stop for until you reach **Ras al-Khaimah city,** about 50 kilometres (30 miles) from the turnoff to Umm al-Quwain. The town now consists of two sections: the modern **Al-Nakheel area** and **the Old Town,** which are divided by **Mina Saqr,** the town's main harbour. Coming from Sharjah, you pass — on your **left** — a long line of **sand-dunes,** beyond which are good **beaches** such as that found at the **Ahmed bin Majid Hotel,** which lies to the **left** off the large roundabout a few kilometres outside the Old Town, just after the castle-like **ADNOC FOD** station whose decorative **bridge** spans the road.

The sand-dunes contain the ruins of a Persian military camp called **Khashm Nadir,** built in the 18th century, but these are not evident to a casual visitor.

Ras al-Khaimah is entered via a roundabout, above which the clock tower is in the shape of a white tent; the right turn leads to the airport, while going straight ahead takes you to the Old Town.

Heading straight on at the roundabout, you pass a mosque with a gold dome on your left; a few kilometres further on along the main King Faisal Road is a roundabout with a model of a dhow, reflecting the maritime heritage of the town. The Old Town lies a little further on, on a **small hill** with coral-built buildings. There are some small **restaurants,** including the **Omar Khayyam,** as well as a number of small coffee-shops and eateries.

The **Ras al-Khaimah Museum** is located in this area in the **old fort** on **Al-Hosn Road** – on the road directly to the **west** of the main **bridge** linking the Old Town to Al-Nakheel. A **red sign** about 160 metres (175 yards) before the roundabout opposite the bridge indicates the museum is nearby, but not very clearly. You need to take the

third exit at the roundabout, next to the **Banque du Caire** building, and drive on for about 85 metres (90 yards). The fort and museum are on your **right.**

The fort, above whose wooden door is the sign, National Museum of Ras al-Khaimah, is a distinctive white building with a garden courtyard outside. Opening hours seem to be somewhat erratic and do not always follow those specified on the sign outside the museum.

The fort was originally built in the mid-18th century, probably by Persians from the northern Gulf. It was destroyed by the British in 1819 as punishment for naval raids by the seafaring population. Originally the fort was the home of the ruling family before being converted into a prison and then restored as a museum in the 1980s.

It offers displays on the **archaeology** and **history** of the emirate, as well as interesting collections of **Arab jewellery** and **sea-shells,** and a room devoted to the ruling family, the **Al Qasimi.**

A **small garden** lies to the **left opposite,** but it is not always open to the public. The Old Town, behind the fort, offers a glimpse of the past — but only a glimpse. The main **souq** lie to the **west** of the fort, between the museum and the sea. One long street, dubbed **Kuwait Hospital Road** on a Geoprojects map, dominates this area.

The shops include a few beauty salons at which traditional henna hand-painting is practised, but apart from that there is not much to see. Mornings and late afternoons are the best time to visit the souq area.

At the **northern tip** of Kuwait Hospital Road, a small **mosque** lies at the start of the seafront road, **Qawasim Corniche.** The Corniche has a rather lost look about it, but is a peaceful place to wander about, with a few fishing nets the only sign of activity.

Walking **north** along the **Corniche road** for about a kilometre, the road then doubles back on itself heading **south** towards **Bridge Road.** Along this road lie the **fish and meat souq,** and further **south,** the veg-

---

Right: Beautiful carved door, Ras-al-Khaimah museum. Overleaf: Hilltop fort at Dhayah, near Rams, is a stark reminder of past territorial battles.

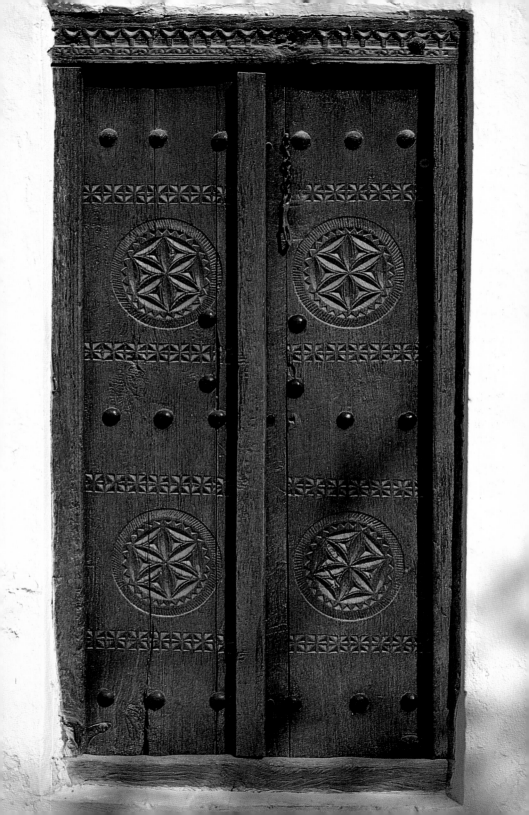

Above: No signs of the desert here! A farm at Ras al-Khaimah.   Left: Traditional Arab well.

etable souq, by the sheltered waters of the Ras al-Khaimah deep-water port.

This is the main centre of fishing activity. Behind the harbour, the steep mountains are clearly visible. Walking along the harbour of **Khor Ras al-Khaimah** is also worthwhile. There is an **old fishing port** just **north** of the bridge linking the Old Town and the modern sector of Al Nakheel, often with a number of dhows nestled together; on the other side many of the dhows have been hauled out of the water for repairs.

To enter **Al Nakheel,** you either cross **Bridge Road** or take the more scenic route all along the **creek to the south,** linking up with **Khuzam Road** at the **Ras al-Khaimah Hotel,** from which an old **watchtower** may be seen on the other side of the dual carriageway.

The road before the hotel is actually a single-lane thoroughfare, although the wide parking lot all along the creek is bordered by a hedge, giving the appearance of a dual carriageway. This can be confusing for the driver. Before the hotel, the road passes the Ras al-Khaimah **water-skiing club** on the **left,** before feeding into the dual carriageway past the hotel. This actually heads out of the city, so a **U-turn** is needed to face back in the right direction; once this has been made, the road passes the **ruler's palace** and then the Ras al-Khaimah **shooting club** on the right before reaching the **Duwar al-Qusidat district.**

About one kilometre further on, a roundabout is marked to **Digdaga** to the **right,** and **Al Nakheel** to the **left.** Al Nakheel is reached via the **Oman Road.** The Al Nakheel area is the **modern section** of Ras al-Khaimah, with fairly good shopping facilities and a few more traditional touches.

The city was building its own **Etisalat Tower** in 1996. The Ras al-Khaimah Etisalat building has been designed with windows built at an angle to the vertical to resemble the prow of a ship, emphasizing the emirate's maritime links.

Above: Prime cattle at Digdaga Dairy, Ras al-Khamaih.

Heading down the **Oman Road,** past the Al Nakeel Hotel on the **left,** the main shopping area has **banks, a currency exchange centre** and a number of larger **shops and restaurants.** A **left turn** after these shops leads to **Saqr bin Mohammed Road** in the direction of the port. Head down and at the second roundabout take a **left turn,** to a traditional **coffee-shop.**

If you continue **north** after the roundabout along the **coast road** you come to the **Maarid** area, traditionally associated with dhow-making. Before the road turns right, the **Ahmed bin Majed Arabian Navigator Museum** is on the **left;** shortly after that, **bearing right,** the road leads past a traditional **wind-tower** on the **right** and, on the **left** an **amusement park** with dodgems and other rides called **Sindbad City.**

Further on is the **Amateur Marine Fishing Association,** an out-of-the-way spot with fishing boats in the bay of Ras al-Khaimah. The nearby area of **Julan** is reputedly the site of a tiny **blacksmith's shop** which makes the traditional small axes used by the Shihuh tribes of the Musandam Peninsula.

North from Ras al-Khaimah, the Oman Road winds all the way up to the **Musandam Peninsula,** part of Omani territory. A number of **small towns** and **villages** are passed on this route and, although of little evident interest, a number of these have historical or archaeological significance. There is not much to do but the scenery is spectacular, with the sheer mountains dropping almost directly into the sea in the northern sections of the route.

The town of **Julfar** on this road was an important **port city** as early as the seventh century. Archaeological finds indicate that it traded as far afield as China and India.

Ras al-Khaimah was occupied in the 16th century by the Portuguese who were driven out by the British and Dutch navies in 1633. The town of Julfar was abandoned in ruins and most of the population migrated Ras al-Khaimah in the same year.

Nowadays, Julfar is a district like any other in the UAE, lined with residences, coffee-shops and the odd petrol station. Recent archaeological work has been done on the remains of an **old fortress** in Julfar and on the town's **old walls.**

Ras al-Khaimah emirate has a rich archaeological heritage, and almost all the sites are open to the public. Among the oldest is the village of **Shimal,** a few kilo-

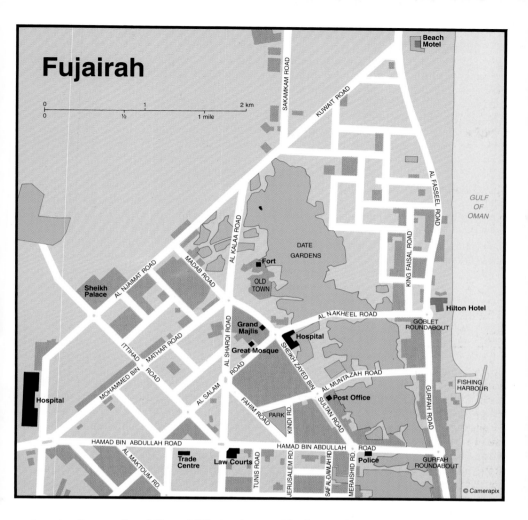

Fujairah

metres to the **north** of Ras al-Khaimah. Outside the village lies the **Qasr al-Zubba,** a set of ruined buildings so named because at one time they were thought to be the Queen of Sheba's palace.

Modern investigations suggest that the Queen of Sheba actually came from the Yemen, and that this building is unlikely to have had anything to do with the legendary queen.

However, the ruins offer evidence of a substantial military power in the Northern Emirates at least as far back as the early Islamic era; some researchers believe that the buildings could even have been used by the fourth-century AD Queen Zenobia. Further research is being conducted to date the site more accurately.

Traditional architecture is also well represented in Ras al-Khaimah. A typical **old fort** is found in the village of **Dhayah,** on top of a hill behind the modern village, and there are more ruined **fortifications** to the **south** of the hill. **Watchtowers** can be seen at the nearby town of **Rams,** the site where the British landed in 1819 during their invasion of the Arabian Gulf area. Rams is a traditional **fishing village,** with a pleasant coastline and some good beaches.

Further along the road to the Musandam Peninsula in Oman, **Mina Saqr** is a growing port and the industrial area of **Khor Khwair** nearby consists of quarries and marble-crushing plants. Mina Saqr is the avenue through which most of the emirate's growing rock and marble exports are channelled.

A large number of sites of ancient funerary architecture have been found in Ras al-Khaimah since initial investigations began in 1971. **Shimal** is one of the key centres for the **single-chambered tombs,** while ancient **two-chambered burial cairns** may be seen at **Ghalilah** beyond Khor Khwair on the road to Oman.

Various other types of tombs, including **multi-chambered tombs** of the like found at Umm al-Nar, have also been found in Ras al-Khaimah. The earliest date back to the third millenium BC; those at Ghalilah and Shimal date back to the middle of the first millenium BC.

Finally, shortly before the **Oman border,** you enter the town of **Ash Sham,** dwarfed by the mountains behind. Halfway up the mountain a number of buildings look as though they have been carved out of the rock.

From Ras al-Khaimah city, a number of spots to the **south** are also worth visiting. Within easy reach by car or service taxi, these are ideal for day-trips and visits are arranged by a number of the local hotels.

Just **south** of the city, on the road towards **Manama,** part of the emirate of **Ajman,** lies the **traditional village** of **Kharran** although its charms are at times dwarfed by the heavy traffic to the airport.

The landscape there is often extremely green in winter with the **mountains** rising on the **left** and camel-grazing grounds to the **right.** The **Saqr public park** on the **left** of this route contains good rides, including a gigantic slide. The agricultural wealth of this region is reflected in the **Ras al-Khaimah Poultry Feeding Co** and **Digdaga Dairy Farm,** which you pass en route to the airport. All around are **fields** and **greenhouses.**

Ras al-Khaimah International Airport is a modest affair, mainly serving the Eastern Bloc tourist trade and local Gulf Airlines. Just outside that lies the village of **Ham Ham** and the town of **Digdaga.**

The town of **Digdaga** is host to **camel-racing** which takes place most **Fridays** in the cool season at a track located about 10 kilometres (six miles) from the town itself. The camel races are laid on primarily for locals, as the hours suggest: the races usually begin early in the morning, starting at **0600** and ending at about **0900,** and the schedules are erratic. So it is best to check with a hotel or tour operator as to when to visit. Digdaga's camel-racing track is unusual in the UAE because it is straight, rather than round like a horse-racing track.

Khatt hot springs are located about eight kilometres (five miles) from the Ras al-Khaimah city centre, and open from dawn until well past dusk. The **bathing facilities** comprise separate hot water pools for men and women, and the water is a comfortable **36-38°C.**

The bathing pools have rocky bottoms of smoothed rocks, and the water is deep enough to swim in, or just to relax in at the side. Unfortunately, the facilities are now not in the open air but it is still a welcome change from the swimming pools in hotels.

From Digdaga, the village of **Manama** is another 40 kilometres (25 miles) drive; this is near the **turnoff** to **Dhaid,** about 53 kilometres (33 miles) from the town of Ras al-Khaimah.

There is not much to see in Manama, although the town has plentiful date-palm groves. The road soon links up with the main Dhaid to **Masafi** road. Dhaid lies 15 kilometres (9 miles) to the **west,** on the **right-hand fork,** while Masafi lies 17 kilometres (10 miles) to the **east** on the **left-hand** direction. The road to Masafi leads on to **Fujairah,** while that to Dhaid leads back to **Sharjah** or **Dubai.**

Fujairah and the East Coast

Fujairah stands alone among the seven emirates in that it does not have a shore on the Arabian Gulf. The east coast on the

Right: Cultivated palms growing in a wadi alongside the Masafi road. Following pages: Irrigated cultivation at Al Dhaid on the Sharjah-Masafi road is a desert oasis noted for its agriculture.

Top: Dibba clock tower stands amidst colourful gardens near the Fujairah/Oman border.
Above: Friday visit to the mosque at Dibba. Previous pages: Khor Fakkan port, Fujairah.

Gulf of Oman is lapped by the waves of the Indian Ocean, however, and it is there that some of the best snorkelling or scuba-diving in the UAE can be enjoyed.

The town of Fujairah is well worth a visit, with its well-stocked museum, a good fort and old town. The areas outside also have a number of sites of historical and archaeological interest, and the occasional hot spring is in the process of being developed.

However, tourist development is recent. The good asphalt road from the west coast was built only in 1976 and the rulers of Fujairah, the Sharqiyyin tribal group, have always been an independent bunch. Industrial development has so far been limited, although Fujairah has become a major bunkering centre, and both the port and airport are getting busier.

A small oil refinery is operated by Metro Oil but oil and gas exploration has proved disappointing so far, despite surveys in 1989.

It is the fresher, more spontaneous atmosphere that is the emirate's biggest attraction. Many locals regard it as the hidden jewel of travel in the UAE. Fujairah contains some of the UAE's best agricultural land and has become active in poultry and cattle-breeding. The beaches and mountains offer spectacular scenery and interesting possibilities for off-road adventures.

Getting there

The modern road that runs from Sharjah through the oasis town of Dhaid and Masafi is one of the most beautiful in the emirates. Although rather expensive by taxi (around AED 200) the journey can be made in about one-and-a-half hours, and the beautiful seaside towns of Khor Fakkan and Dibba are only a short distance away. Fujairah International Airport has become increasingly busy, both for cargo-handling and as a passenger terminal.

Where to stay

Fujairah and Khor Fakkan both have luxury hotels overlooking the seafront. The Fujairah Hilton, next to the Goblet roundabout, has excellent sports facilities. The Oceanic in Khor Fakkan is a favourite with scuba-divers and the hotel offers a variety of courses from beginners to advanced.

Alcohol is not served, as Khor Fakkan is part of the emirate of Sharjah. Further down the coast, towards Dibba, the Sandy Beach Motel has lovely beach chalets and hotel-style rooms overlooking the sea, a good but basic food menu, and serves beer and wine. A new addition is the Holiday Beach Motel which offers chalet-style accommodation near Dibba.

When to go

Fujairah is best visited in the autumn or spring when the weather is still hot and before the winter rains, which flood the Hajar Mountains. Ramadan should be avoided, but some of the hotels continue to serve food and drink discreetly during the Muslim holy month.

Sightseeing

The road from **Dhaid** leads past farms and agricultural land, including **date plantations** and a **strawberry farm** about seven kilometres (four miles) from the oasis which is open to the public.

A small road to the **right** of the main road takes the visitor to **Wadi Siji,** on the western rim of the mountains, popular for **camping** and a **historical site.** Back on the main road, nearing the **turnoff** to **Manama** on the **left,** a number of **stalls** by the roadside sell carpets, fruit and ceramic items.

The **Siji Greenhouse Company** lies on the **right-hand** side. The small town of **Masafi** at the end of the road from Dhaid is the site of a natural **mineral spring** whose waters are bottled to make Masafi spring water.

From Masafi, the road forks at a large roundabout and you can travel either **north** towards **Dibba** or **south** towards the city of **Fujairah.** Billboards on the roundabout advertise the main hotels and some of the tour sites.

Turning **right** to **Fujairah,** you pass the small town of **Diftah** at the foot of the **Jebel al-Hilqah** before entering the wide corridor of the **Wadi Ham.** The small town of **Bithna** lies about 10 kilometres (six miles) from Diftah, and 12 kilometres ($7^1/_2$

Above: Mosque at Badiyah, near Khor Fakkan, is the oldest in the UAE, dating back many centuries.

miles) before Fujairah, a few hundred metres to the **left** of the main road. It has **date plantations** and a small ruined **mud-brick fort** is visible from the road, although it is not easy to find your way down to the fort without a 4WD vehicle.

Bithna was the site of an important archaeological discovery. A **long-chambered tomb** found there dates back to the first millenium BC, and is thought to have been the site of a communal burial ground. The site was excavated in 1988.

Shortly after Bithna, a **tarmac road** leads towards the **Wadi Hail**. However, the asphalt quickly peters out and becomes loose gravel and rock suitable only for **4WD** vehicles. The Wadi is the site of a **fort** and **old palace** that used to be used by the ruling family of Fujairah. The area is a popular **camp-site.**

Heading for Fujairah, the valley becomes **coastal plain.** The exit for the **international airport** is clearly marked at a roundabout on the outskirts of the city. Before you reach the main city, the **Ain al-Madhab health re-**sort offers rest, relaxation and comfortable rooms at reasonable prices.

The **park** is open to children for AED 1, while adults pay AED 2. Rooms are available at AED 100-200, while villas can be rented for AED 300. The resort is the site of a natural **hot spring** with warm, sulphur-rich mineral water. Unfortunately, it often seems to be closed - so check in advance before visiting.

Fujairah interesting sites are in easy reach of each other, with the **fort** and **Old Town** in a small area opposite the **museum,** just behind a group of **date gardens.** At the main roundabout as you enter the town from Sharjah, the **right fork** onto **Hamad bin Abdullah Road** leads past the **Trade Centre** to a roundabout opposite the **Law Courts;** a **left turn** leads onto **Sharqi Road,** out past the **Great Mosque** and the **Grand Majlis** to the Old Town and fort.

Fujairah Museum, opened in 1991, has a well-stocked archaeological section, from excavations at the nearby villages of

Above: Giant coffee pot and cups catch the eye at a Fujairah roundabout

---

Badiyah, Qidfah and Bithna. There is a good exhibition on the **long-chambered tomb** found at Bithna, and a visit before going to the site itself is recommended.

There is also a selection of exhibits from the early days of the UAE, including **old photographs** and **household items.** Opening hours are from 0700 until 1800.

A new Etisalat Tower, construction of which was planned to begin in 1996, has a bold glass and granite design with the motif of an eight-sided Islamic star.

The Fujairah **Old Town** comprises a **300-year old fort** and the **ruins** of the buildings that used to form the town, which is now largely deserted. The fort lies on a rocky plain above the main city, with a plantation of palms at its foot. It has a large round tower, a square tower, and several other ruined towers.

From the old town and the museum, visitors should retrace their path to the **Law Courts,** then turn **left** along Hamad bin Abdullah Road in the direction of the sea. Several **government buildings** lie to the **right,** while a small **park** is on the **left** of the road.

Follow the road for just over a kilometre to the Ghurfah roundabout which offers a handsome **view** over the Indian Ocean. Turning **left** at the roundabout, you head due **north** along the **Ghurfah** and **Al Faseel Road,** the location of the two main hotels, the **Hilton** and the **Fujairah Beach Hotel.** Opposite, and down from the Hilton, are a number of pleasant restaurants: the **Diner's Inn,** the **Arous al-Bahr,** the **National,** the **New Damascus,** and the **Hafiz Irani.** Before the Hilton, you pass a **picturesque fishing harbour.**

A number of towns and villages lie around Fujairah, some on the coast and some in the mountains that form the backbone of this part of the UAE. Many have great archaeological interest, and archaeological work is ongoing in several.

To the **south** of Fujairah town, on the road towards Oman, lie the villages of **Kalba** and **Khor Kalba,** actually part of Sharjah emirate. A British team has been engaged in archeological excavations of a major **Bronze Age site** at Kalba, which was first identified when a date garden was cleared.

The town of **Kalba** lies about 12 kilometres (7 miles) **south** of Fujairah town, and has good **beaches** and one of the most bizarre hotels in the UAE.

The **Marine Hotel,** is a psychedelic version of the Bates Motel in the classic film thriller, *Psycho*. Opposite it is a small pizzeria, **Pizza at the Sea,** and the whole resort is overshadowed by an enormous radio pylon in red and white.

The decor of the small courtyard is elaborately decorated with a bright blue fountain, inexplicably bright red and yellow archways covered in fairy lights, and an even more perplexing grey concrete heart-shaped fountain with a stone dhow in the middle. Completing the effect of pleasant lunacy, a brick wishing-well stands at the entrance to the complex.

About $1^1/_2$ kilometres (one mile) further along the road, **Khor Kalba** has interesting examples of **mangrove** trees and a wealth of **birdlife.** This is a beautiful spot indeed; the mangroves lie half in and half out of the water and a small **bridge** leads into the sand-dunes along the coast. The water there is shallow, ideal for children, and beyond the bridge is a basic **playground** with children's swings.

Further **south,** narrow tracks lead out to the border with **Oman;** these are negotiable only by 4WD vehicle. A number of small villages lie in the area and there is a **hot spring** at **Ain al-Ghammour.**

To the **north** of Fujairah, a good **tarmac road** runs along the **Shumayliyah coast** with views of the narrow coastal plain and, in the background, the craggy mountains of the Hajar Range.

First of all you pass the main **port** of Fujairah, a busy industrial centre, with a small **oil refinery** and **tank farm** on the right. It is not a good idea to photograph this area too conspicuously. After this the road winds along the coast through a string of small fishing villages, including **Qurayyah, Murba** and **Qidfa.**

These are not particularly interesting in themselves but good for a brief stroll. Their boats and fishing nets line the road or the beaches. Qurayyah experienced severe floods late in 1995 when the UAE had one of its rainiest winters in decades. Another site of emerging interest is the coastal village of Qidfa, where two **Bronze Age tombs** dating back to around 1,500 BC have been discovered.

The road is interrupted by the port of **Khor Fakkan,** an important industrial and shipping area, which is part of Sharjah. The town itself is a sleepy **seaside resort.** A row of **shops** and **restaurants** is topped by wind-tower-style motifs and is followed by an open seafront lined with restaurants, **amusement parks** and lush greenery along the roadside where locals picnic and have barbecues on Fridays.

There is nothing particular to see or do there, but the restaurants, including the **Lebanon Restaurant,** offer good value food, the beach is sandy and unspoilt, and a number of places offer diving instruction.

Khor Fakkan offers one spectacular sight, but it is not a natural one: offshore, dozens of huge **oil tankers** line the horizon, lying like great grey fish in the sea. These huge tankers — Very Large Crude Carriers and Ultra Large Crude Carriers, or VLCCs and ULCCs for short — can be up to 350 metres in length.

The area off the town is a huge transhipment centre for the oil industry, and you can get a sense of the size of the UAE's oil wealth simply by looking out at the bay. Any day of the year dozens of supertankers are anchored, and at night they form a glitter of lights all along the horizon.

One kilometre further on, the **Oceanic Hotel** is a good but 'dry' stopover. The hotel has diving facilities for learners and experienced scuba-divers.

The **Wadi Wurayyah,** after the villages of **Lulayyah** and **Zubarah**, is the site of the Wurayyah **waterfall,** but it is only accessible by **4WD** vehicles. A small **dirt track** runs to the left of the main road at Zubarah into the mountains.

Back on the main road, the small town of **Badiyah** is located a few kilometres (a couple of miles) after the **turnoff** to the Wadi Wurayyah, with a few **market stalls** selling a variety of locally produced fruit and vegetables. The town has been inhabited since the third millennium BC.

It is also the site of the **oldest mosque** in the UAE, a small white-washed building with a curvy look to it that reminds you of the Spanish architect, Gaudi. The mosque is often called the Ottoman mosque, after its reputed founder Othham. On the hillside above the mosque, with a commanding view of the countryside around, a couple of ruined **watchtowers** are easily reachable after a stiff climb.

Further on along the coast, a number of small villages, including **Sharm, Aqqa, Dhadnah** and **Rul Dhadnah,** each back onto good **clean beaches.** The **scenery** is picturesque as the road winds up the rocky clefts of the mountains. It is on this stretch, before the small town of Dibba, that you stumble on the **Sandy Beach Motel.**

The Sandy Beach has a number of double and family **chalets,** all comfortably furnished, and with a tiny living room outside the main bedroom. The chalets are located close to the hotel's **restaurant,** but you can also treat yourself to an open-air barbecue, or simply drift off to the beach just yards away to sip wine after supper under the

Right: Hili Fun City at Al Ain.

Excavations have unearthed an ancient settlement (top) and a great tomb (above) at Hili, Al Ain. Some of the excavated ruins date from the third milennium BC.

Top and lower: Jahili Fort at Al Ain.

stars. The hotel has opened a second block of chalets to the north of the main hotel.

Opposite the main beach, and a short snorkel away, is **Snoopy Island,** a small cone-like peak that juts out of the water just like a shark's fin. This has a shallow reef on the shore side but on the ocean side, the corals drop away steeply into the deep blue of the Indian Ocean.

Scuba equipment can be hired from the hotel and courses in **scuba-diving** can be arranged at reasonable prices for the uninitiated. The hotel beach is a good venue for **shell-collecting** as on a low neap tide you can walk all the way to the island itself. However, the **reef** is covered in barnacles and it is wise to wear trainers if you decide to explore the island itself.

Further on down the coast, the lovely town of **Dibba** lies right on the **border** with Oman.

There is not that much to see in Dibba, but its sleepy, relaxed atmosphere and beautiful **gardens,** and the picturesque **port,** make it an ideal weekend stopover. From the port, the distant mountains of the Musandam Peninsula in Oman are higher and paler than those of the closer Hajar Range.

People compare the atmosphere to that of a Mediterranean coastal village. Historically, it was the site of the battle of Ridda in AD 633, which marked the end of the Muslim conquest of Arabia. Outside the town, a gravel plain is covered with hundreds of gravestones that mark the resting places of the fallen.

Dibba is also a site of emerging archaeological interest, with Australian teams at work in 1996-7. Sites discovered around Dibba date from the late Islamic period to as far back as the third millennium BC. Before the coming of Islam, Dibba was the capital of the whole area which now constitutes Oman and the UAE. Historical records suggest that the port town was trading as far afield as China 2,000 years ago.

From Dibba, the road is signposted back to **Dubai.** A small **circular road** takes in panoramic views of the mountains before turning **south** towards **Masafi.** The road runs through spectacular scenery of jagged mountains and wide plains and the jour-ney is particularly beautiful at sunset, as the plains stretch out to the west. Not one of the most beautiful features is the **cement plant,** a huge grey steel structure on the **right** of the main road.

A number of off-road journeys can be made in 4WD vehicles to the 1,115-metre-high (3,658-feet) **Jebel Dad,** or the innumerable small wadis that slice between the mountains. **Wadi Fay, Wadi Dhannah, Wadi Tayyibah** and **Wadi Saddar** are among these. The wadis and mountains are not well explored, if still inhabited; **small terraces, stone buildings** and some evidence of **tombs** have been found.

Al Ain Area: Abu Dhabi

Al Ain in Abu Dhabi emirate is the ancestral home of the current UAE ruler, Sheikh Zayed, and although a city of some 200,000 people, the atmosphere is more relaxed, and the traffic less frenzied, than in the main cities of Abu Dhabi, Dubai and Sharjah.

Even a couple of decades ago Al Ain was a loose-knit community of some half-dozen villages, but the villages have become a garden city, with wide tree-lined boulevards and a multitude of small parks. Around Al Ain, the Jebel Hafiz is an imposing mountain, one of the highest points in the UAE; a variety of diversions, from amusement parks to archaeological digs are also available.

Getting there
Al Ain is located about 160 kilometres (100 miles) east of Abu Dhabi, and about the same distance south-east of Dubai. It is about one-and-a-half hour's drive from either Abu Dhabi or Dubai. Both routes are well signposted, and the road is wide and perfect.

If coming from the east coast you can return to Dhaid from Masafi and take the left fork towards Mileiha and the Mudam Plain (see Sharjah Road to Dhaid and Beyond); this road eventually links up with the main road from Dubai to Al Ain. For those travelling by air, domestic and inter

national flights can be arranged to Al Ain International Airport.

When to go
Al Ain is best avoided during the summer, when the weather is simply too hot to allow extensive travel on foot at the archaeological sites and in the Jebel Hafiz. Winter is the ideal time to visit, particularly if you want to try out the hot springs, whose heat is all the more warmly appreciated during the cool season; autumn and spring are also good seasons to visit.

Where to stay
The Al Ain Hilton and Intercontinental are both extremely pleasant. The Ayn al-Faydha Hotel at the resort of the same name is the most relaxing place, and nearer the spectacular Jebel Hafiz mountain.

Sightseeing
Al Ain city is a city of parks. These are scattered all over Al Ain, which has become a popular tourist town. The **Hili Gardens** are situated outside the Al Ain city centre, on the right of the road from Dubai on the outskirts of the city, to the **right** of **Al Ain Dairy Farm.** For the children, **Hili Fun City** is the largest amusement park in Abu Dhabi Emirate. It contains the largest **ice-rink** in the UAE. There is also a good range of rides and a big wheel.

Not far from the gardens, **Hili ruins** are the scene of an ancient archaeological site which you can explore for the price of a dirham. The ruins are situated about 10 kilometres (six miles) **west** of Al Ain city and contain both **settlements** and **burial tombs.** Excavations in and around Hili have revealed settlements dating back to the third millennium BC, in the Bronze Age, as well as a number of sites from the first millennium BC (Iron Age). The ruins were originally investigated in the 1960s by a Danish team and the excavations revealed a **circular tower** made of mud bricks with a surrounding **wall** and **moat.**

The building, which contained traces of ovens and fire-places as well as ancient pottery sherds, was identified at the time as a watchtower, of the sort built in the Nizwa area of Oman.

Subsequent investigations by UAE and, later on, French archaeologists revealed several similar buildings, often with a water-well in the centre, as well as a horde of pottery fragments which suggest that the area had been populated continuously from the third millennium BC.

A number of houses in a different style were discovered in later digs, dating back to the first millennium BC, and the finds include apparently public buildings that may have been used to house travellers overnight.

Nearby **sites** at **Rumeilah Qatarrah** and at **Qarn bint Saud** revealed several **artefacts,** including arrowheads, a variety of bowls and seals, and animal figures, thought to date back to the first millennium BC. Qatarrah is the site of an existing **oasis,** with abundant **date palms** and **fruit gardens,** a stark contrast to the desert surrounding them. Ancient gold jewellery found at Qatarrah can be seen in the **Al Ain museum.**

The Al-Ain Museum is located in the compound of the **Al-Jahilia Fort,** the birthplace and former home of members of the Abu Dhabi aristocracy. The fort lies just west of the crossing of Al-Falahi Street and the road leading from the Hilton Hotel and the Al-Ain Bridge. The fort, dating back to the 18th century, has four round turrets and is fronted by cannons.

The museum is an important repository of archaeological finds in the emirates, with stone instruments dating back to 500 BC, and remains from the Umm al-Nar excavations near Abu Dhabi city, as well as the local sites at Hili and Jebel Hafiz, dating back to 2,500-3,000 BC. Early Stone Age remains from the islands off Abu Dhabi are also exhibited. The museum also has an ethnological section with life-size models of various aspects of the lives of the Bedouin in the desert. The exhibits are generally well documented, with explanatory texts in both English and Arabic.

From Hili, the road leads in through a series of roundabouts to the **Al Jimi** area, the centre of the city named after the Wadi al-Jimi. Just **south** of the wadi, between the **Al Jauw** and **Al Jimi bridges,** and past the **Al Selmi Gardens, Sheikh**

Above: Colourful Al Fayahah gardens, Al Ain.

Zayed bin Khalifa the First Street stretches all the way to the Buraimi **roundabout,** a **left turn** at which leads to the **Buraimi Oasis** in Oman. Heading straight on after the roundabout, then taking a **right turn** at the **Al Mashatel roundabout,** over the **Al Istraha** roundabout and then left at **Al Khatem** roundabout, leads to the **Al Ain Intercontinental Hotel, north** of **Wadi el-Shiq.** For the **Hilton,** simply take a **right** at the **Al Khatem roundabout.**

The **Oasis Gallery** in Al Ain is located on the ground floor of the **Al Ain Trading Centre** on the **Hilton Road** near the **Coffee-Pot roundabout.** It contains a selection of **antiques** of the Gulf area, including chests, khanjar daggers, old brass and copperware, historic maps, as well as a variety of more modern art-work.

Al Ain night-life is timid compared with that of Dubai, but it does exist at the Hilton and Inter-Continental hotels. The Hilton offers a Mexican cantina, **Pacos,** while the Inter-Continental has a couple

of music venues, **Samantha's** and **La Bamba.** The **Buraimi Hotel** near the Hilton also offers occasional entertainment. The **Hash House Harriers** also organize a number of evening events in the desert.

The **zoo** and **aquarium** are also worth a visit. These are located in the **south** of the city in the **Al Maslakh area,** just south of the **Zoo roundabout.** The zoo houses the Middle East's largest and most varied collection of wildlife, with a large collection of **indigenous species** as well as **exotic animals** from other countries. Different types of gazelle can be seen, including the world's largest herd of Arabian gazelles. The zoo also houses the **Arabian oryx,** an endangered species, as well as a variety of other rare mammals.

Around Al Ain
Jebel Hafiz is a rocky outcrop at the foot of the **Hajar Mountains,** the range that divides the UAE from the Arabian heartland. Jebel Hafiz is one of the highest

points in the country. There are two ways to see it: either you travel by car along the **tarmac road,** which winds up the sides of the mountain, with spectacular views over the **Empty Quarter,** or you can take the **right-hand fork** off the main road and drive into the rocky outcrop itself.

This route harbours the **hot springs** area. Hot springs are often associated by tourists with Japan or Germany.

In the UAE, they come as something of a surprise. The water gushes out at temperatures of about **45°C** and winds down a narrow concrete channel, into a wide public bath, before trickling off into the rocks and sand.

Visiting the springs at night is a wonderful experience; the stars out in the desert are crystal clear, and lying in the pool with the chilly breeze in winter is magical. The water is strongly ferrous, said to be good for all sorts of physical and mental ailments, and it is incredibly relaxing. There is a separate enclosed bathing area for women.

The mountain is a traditional hunting region and the habitat of the rare **Arabian tahr,** one of the few in which the animal still exists. Desert flowers, lizards and other wildlife can be found in the rocky clefts that stud the mountain.

A new hotel is planned for the top of the mountain, which promises to offer a wonderfully peaceful break from the main cities, as well as easy access to some of the area's top archaeological sites.

Near Jebel Hafiz is the **Ain al-Fayda Guest House,** operated by Abu Dhabi National Hotels Company, and part of a **resort town** comprising the main hotel and a group of chalets, set in beautiful **gardens** that include a large **boating lake.**

The resort has a range of facilities ranging from a **coffee-shop,** where you can drink traditional Arabic coffee and smoke a hubble-bubble pipe, to a **pizzeria** and fast food **take-away.**

There is also a **recreation centre** with modern video games and **pool,** and a **10-pin bowling alley.** The rest house is located over the hot springs and there are plans to develop these to allow guests to enjoy the hot mineral water which is reputed to have medicinal properties.

Buraimi Oasis lies inside the **border** with **Oman** but before the main customs point, so it is still possible to visit it, even without an Omani visa. Travellers should beware, however, as UAE driving insurance will not cover you in the eight or so kilometres (five miles) that you are in Oman, before the border post.

Buraimi has a good **vegetable market,** with a wide range of fruit from the Lebanon or as far afield as Europe, as well as offering the tourist such items as Omani chests and daggers.

The **Al Buraimi Hotel** includes the **Club Tropicana Restaurant** which serves a variety of international cuisine including Italian, Indian, Asian and American dishes.

Abu Dhabi and Beyond

Getting there
The road network to the west of Abu Dhabi is limited to the main coast road that runs all the way to Qatar, and the road down to Liwa through the oil and gas fields of the central desert. Both these roads are in reasonable condition.

However, for those who want to go off-road in a 4WD, the harsh desert sands can be a difficult and, at times, dangerous challenge. Be aware that travelling off-road without company, and without notifying friends, can be very hazardous.

When to go
For the islands, you can only visit when you get permission: the islands are protected and not readily accessible to the public.

For the coast and the Empty Quarter, avoid the summer at all costs; the coast is hot and the Empty Quarter unbearably hot.

Abu Dhabi is also much more austerely Muslim than some other emirates and, as such, the usual cautions about Ramadan apply doublefold in these areas.

Where to Stay

Choice is limited in this bleak expanse of desert. Camping is an option and there is a good hotel at Ruwais, before the turnoff to Liwa.

Sightseeing

The Liwa group of oases is situated about six hours' drive from Abu Dhabi, and the drive to it takes you through some of the most prolific oil and gas producing areas in the UAE.

There is not much to see on the way, except the **beaches** along the coast, and inland the extensive desert sands.

To get to Liwa, drive west from Abu Dhabi along the main road to Ruwais and Qatar.

For those coming from Dubai, a pleasant pit-stop about half-way to Abu Dhabi is the **Jazeerah Resort**, a beach-side hotel with swimming pool and good restaurants. The resort is signposted at the turnoff to Ghantoot. Further north along the coast from the hotel is a complex of beach chalets, each topped with a traditional wind-tower motif. Both the hotel and chalets are popular with UAE nationals during the summer.

About half way to Ruwais, after about 120 kilometres (75 miles), and past the turnoff for the coastal village of **Tarif,** the road forks to the **left** towards Liwa. First, go through the town of **Habshan,** then take the **left fork** towards **Madinat Zayed.** The road continues as far as the town of **Meziyrah,** where it forks **right** to the western villages of Liwa and **left** to the eastern towns.

The Liwa oases lie at the gateway to the forbidding **Empty Quarter,** known in Arabic as the Rub al-Khali. The crescent of oases is the home of the Bani Yas group of tribes from which the Abu Dhabi ruling family descended about 250 years ago. The main town is **Madina Liwa.** Around this, the villages are the centre of a greening project aimed at pushing back the desert. The new town of **Bida Zayed** is linked to Madina Liwa by road.

Although the traditional Bedouin lifestyle has largely died out with the coming of oil, it is still possible to see **tented en-**campments in the desert, with herdsmen and camels.

The islands off Abu Dhabi have become of major archaeological and ecological importance in recent years. As well as containing **rare species of birds and fish**, some of the earliest **archaeological discoveries** have been made there, testifying to a maritime civilization in the area that dates back as far as 7,000 BC. The Abu Dhabi Islands Archaeological Survey was established in 1992 to explore the islands and the coast for antique remains, and then to excavate them.

Recent finds have included the remains of a **Christian Church** on **Sir Bani Yas Island** dating back more than 1,400 years to the beginning of the Islamic era.

Around the church, a number of **houses** with finely plastered walls can be seen, in which pottery and glass from the **Ummayad period** were found. The site marks the furthest expansion of Christianity in the Gulf area.

Another site from the late Islamic period has been found on the island of **Balghelam,** north-east of Abu Dhabi. Digs focus on the southern coast of the island which harbours a number of sites that reveal evidence of pearling and fishing. The finds include the remains of a **fishing village** and **mosque,** a small **graveyard** and a **well.** The island appears to have been inhabited just before and after the coming of Islam.

Late **Stone Age sites** dating back around 7,000 years have been found on the islands of **Ghaghah, Al F'zaiyyah** and **Merawah,** and evidence has been found of **settlement** from as far back as 2,000 years ago on a number of other islands. The neighbouring coastline also contains a number of important archaeological finds.

PART FOUR: SPECIAL FEATURES

Above: The area around the fort at Wadi Hail, Fujairah is a popular place for camping.
Left: Practice swing at the Emirates Golf Club, Dubai.

The Rulers

The rulers of the UAE are the focal points through which the individual families, extended family groups and the citizens can shape policy. Each holds a regular *majlis* where, in theory, anyone may go and air their thoughts, complaints and plans for the future. This is viewed as a beneficial two-way process — not only does it allow citizens to feel involved in government, but it also allows the rulers to maintain a close link with their effective constituents.

Since the coming of oil, Abu Dhabi has been pre-eminent among the seven emirates, and its ruler Sheikh Zayed is a prominent symbol of national unity. But the UAE rulers govern by consensus, and hereditary right is only part of their power base. As much as anything, the ability to shrewdly manage differences and astutely develop aspirations are important qualifications.

Rule in the Emirates

Before the UAE federation, the Trucial States were ruled independently by their ruling families. The individual rulers were known as emir, equivalent to the English 'prince', hence the use of the word emirate. Other Gulf countries, such as Bahrain and Qatar, which originally might have been part of the federation, are to this day headed by their individual emirs.

Since the UAE federation was founded in 1971, the individual emirates of Abu Dhabi, Dubai, Sharjah, Ajman, Umm al-Quwain, Ras al-Khaimah and Fujairah have vested some areas of their authority in the federal government, which is bound by the UAE constitution. The ruler of each individual emirate is represented on the Supreme Council of Rulers, the UAE's top policy-making body.

The main executive body of government is the Council of Ministers, the country's *de facto* cabinet, while the country's parliament, the Federal National Council, is made up of 40 members drawn from each of the seven emirates. The make-up of the Federal National Council is determined by fixed ratios of representatives from the various emirates, based on their population: the 40-member council currently has eight members each from Abu Dhabi and Dubai, six each from Sharjah and Ras al-Khaimah, and four each from Fujairah, Umm al-Quwain and Ajman.

The cabinet includes the usual ministerial portfolios and is headed by the prime minister who is chosen by the president and the other members of the Supreme Council. The ministers may be drawn from any of the emirates although in practice, representation in the cabinet broadly reflects the demographic position in the UAE as a whole.

Abu Dhabi

The ruler of Abu Dhabi is HH Sheikh Zayed bin Sultan al-Nahyan, who is also the UAE head of state and president of the federation. Sheikh Zayed was born in about 1915 at Al Ain's Jahili fortress. From 1946-66 he was governor of Abu Dhabi's eastern province. Sheikh Zayed replaced his brother Sheikh Shakhbut (1928-1966) as ruler in 1966. Sheikh Zayed was the inspiration and founding father of the UAE federation of which he became president in 1971. Zayed was re-elected as president in 1981, 1986 and finally for a fourth consecutive five-year term in late 1991 by the Supreme Council of Rulers, which groups representatives from all seven emirates.

Sheikh's Zayed's usual residence is the Al Bahar (Sea Palace) in Abu Dhabi, but he also spends time at the Al Mushref Palace and the Al Batin Palace, also in the capital city. Zayed is closely associated with the desert city of Al Ain, where he lives at his Al Ain Palace, Al Maqam Palace, and Al Hili Palace. The presidential court is at Al Khazna. Other palaces include the Zakher Palace.

Zayed's leisure interests include falconry and hunting. His wife, Sheikhah Fatima bint Mubarak, is chairwoman of the

Above: Current issue stamps depicting the seven Emirates rulers.

Abu Dhabi Women's Society, founded in 1975.

The Crown Prince of Abu Dhabi is HH Sheikh Khalifa bin Zayed al-Nahyan, who also acts as Deputy Supreme Commander of the UAE Armed Forces. Sheikh Khalifa has also served as Abu Dhabi prime minister, minister of defence and minister of finance. He also acts as chairman of the Abu Dhabi executive council. The court of the Crown Prince has become increasingly involved in charting the development of the UAE. Sheikh Khalifa usually lives at the New Al Batin Palace in Abu Dhabi.

The Al Nahyan family are descended from the Bani Yas, a federation of more than a dozen tribes, which dominated the coastal town of Abu Dhabi, founded in

1762, the desert town of Al Ain, as well as large areas of the Liwa Oasis. The Bani Yas comprised a number of important tribes, including the Al Bu Falah who traditionally provided the rulers of Abu Dhabi. Today, the descendants of the Al Bu Falah, or the Al Nahyan as the ruling family is known, are at the helm of government in Abu Dhabi.

The Bani Yas emerged as the single most important tribal group during the 18th and 19th centuries, gradually coming to dominate the Al Ain area, and also fighting off incursions from Saudi Arabia's hard-line Muslim Wahhabist movement in the early 1800s. The rule of the Bani Yas was further consolidated during the period of rule of Sheikh Zayed bin Khalifah Al Bu Falah, who reigned between 1855 and 1909.

The historical ties between the Al Bu Falah and the areas of Al Ain and Liwa remain a factor in Abu Dhabi's planning up to this day. Sheikh Zayed has poured huge amounts of energy and money into developing these areas, which had been largely neglected during the days before the discovery of oil.

Dubai

The ruler of Dubai is HH Sheikh Maktoum bin Rashid al-Maktoum, who is also the Vice-President and Prime Minister of the UAE. Sheikh Maktoum was appointed to the chairmanship of the Dubai Lands Department in 1960, and succeeded his father, Sheikh Rashid bin Saeed al Maktoum, on his death in 1990. His father had succeeded his own father, Saeed bin Maktoum, in 1958. Sheikh Maktoum has palaces at Nad al Shiba, Al Aweer, Abu Dhabi and Al Ain.

Sheikh Maktoum is the eldest of his father's four sons, with whom he rules Dubai in a 'collegiate' system. Sheikh Rashid's second son, Sheikh Hamdan, is UAE Minister of Finance and Industry; Sheikh Mohammed is the UAE Defence Minister and Crown Prince; Sheikh Ahmed is Commander of the Central Military Region.

The ruling family of the emirate of Dubai was also descended from a branch of the Bani Yas, but from the Al Bu Falasah section of the larger tribal grouping. The Al Bu Falasah settled in Dubai in 1833. The town had been described as a prosperous trading centre as far back as 1580. The group settled at Bur Dubai under Maktoum bin Butti. The town became independent, and eight years later, in 1841, the group extended their domains to Deira, just over the creek, later also moving to Shindagha.

The Al Maktoum family has been associated for over a century with a uniquely liberal and far-sighted trading philosophy that has been largely responsible for the commercial success of Dubai emirate.

In the late 19th century, Sheikh Maktoum bin Hasher al-Maktoum instituted a number of important tax exemptions for traders who channelled commerce through the creek. By the early 20th century, business was already bustling in Deira and Bur Dubai.

After the collapse of the pearling industry, the ruling family initiated further free-trade policies that focused regional gold trade with India in Dubai emirate. The dredging of the creek in the 1950s was another astute decision by the ruling family. At a time when the creeks in other emirates were silting up, the dredging of the Dubai creek allowed the dhow trade to flourish.

The current ruler has followed the family tradition of encouraging free trade, while also developing an awareness of the emirate's traditional heritage. The establishment of the Jebel Ali Free Zone in 1985 is among the successes initiated by the ruling family.

Sharjah

The ruler of Sharjah and its dependencies is HH Sheikh Dr Sultan bin Mohammed Al Qassimi who was born in 1942 and has been ruler since the death of his brother, Sheikh Khaled, in 1972. Sheikh Sultan studied agriculture for five years at Cairo University and received his PhD from Exeter University. He served as UAE Minister of Education in 1971-72. The deputy ruler of

Above: The main tower of the ruined fort at Umm al-Quwain.

Sharjah is HH Sheikh Ahmed bin Sultan al-Qassimi.

Sheikh Sultan administers an emirate that includes the important transhipment centre of Khor Fakkan on the east coast, at which the ruler has a second palace, in addition to the one he maintains in the city of Sharjah.

Sharjah's Al Qassimi ruling family is descended from the Al Qassimi tribes, or the Qawasim, who claim descent from the prophet Mohammed, and which also provided the rulers of Ras al-Khaimah. The Qawasim emerged as a powerful force in the 18th century as a clan of the Huwalah tribe.

The current separation of Sharjah and Ras al-Khaimah, both of whose current rulers bear the name Al Qassimi, resulted from a split in the tribal grouping in 1910. The former ruler of Sharjah, Sheikh Saqr bin Mohammed al-Qassimi, was the grandson of the first ruler, Salim bin Sultan. There remain close ties between Sharjah and Ras al-Khaimah. In hotels in both emirates, the portraits of the rulers of each hang side by side, a sign of the affection between the two families.

The Northern Emirates

The Northern Emirates comprise the emirates of Ras al-Khaimah, Ajman and its dependencies, and Umm al-Quwain and its dependencies. Each of these three emirates has its own ruling family.

Ras al-Khaimah is ruled by HH Sheikh Saqr bin Mohammed al-Qassimi who took over as ruler when his uncle, Sheikh Sultan, was deposed in 1948. Sheikh Saqr, who is married to a member of the Al Ghurair merchant family in Dubai, was born in 1920. Sheikh Saqr has palaces at Ma'amourah, Khozam, and Kharran, and residences at Dubai and Huwaylat.

HH Sheikh Khalid bin Saqr al-Qassimi is Crown Prince and Deputy Ruler of Ras al-Khaimah, and HH Sheikh Sultan bin Saqr al-Qassimi also serves as Deputy Ruler.

The ruling family of Ras al-Khaimah is descended from the Qawasim tribal group, to which the ruling family of Sharjah also traces its origin. The Qawasim in the 18th and 19th centuries formed an empire based at Ras al-Khaimah, but extending over parts of modern-day Sharjah. The Qawasim's power was derived largely from its prowess at sea, and the maritime traditions of the ruling family of the emirate are still celebrated.

Ajman and its dependencies are ruled by HH Sheikh Humaid bin Rashid al-Nuaimi, whose main palace is in the town of Ajman, but who also maintains the Masfoot Farm, as well as residences at Manama and Al Zaher Palace. Sheikh Humaid was born in 1930 and served as crown prince before becoming ruler when his father Sheikh Rashid bin Humaid al-Nuaimi died in 1981. The current crown prince is HH Sheikh Ammar bin Humaid bin Rashid al-Nuaimi.

The ruling family of Ajman traces its origins to the Al Naim tribe, which originated in the Buraimi area.

Umm al-Quwain and its dependencies are ruled by HH Sheikh Rashid bin Ahmed al-Moalla. Sheikh Rashid lives in the Umm al-Quwain Palace but also has residences at Falaj al-Moalla Palace and in Dubai. Sheikh Rashid was born around 1930 and became ruler on the death of his father, Sheikh Ahmad bin Rashid al-Moalla, in 1981. HH Sheikh Saoud bin Rashid al-Moalla is the Crown Prince and Deputy Ruler of Umm al-Quwain.

The current day rulers of Umm al-Quwain are descended from the Al Ali tribe, who lived in the Ras al-Khaimah area as far back as the 17th century. The Al Ali have ruled Umm al-Quwain since 1775. Some authors trace the origin of the Al Ali to the Omani tribe of the same name.

Fujairah

The ruler of Fujairah is HH Sheikh Hamad bin Mohammed al-Sharqi, the youngest of the UAE's rulers. He was born in 1948 and became ruler in 1974 on the death of his father, Sheikh Mohammed bin Hamad al-Sharqi. He served as UAE Minister of Fisheries and Agriculture in 1970-74. In the late 1960s he studied in England and, in 1970, went to the Mons Military Academy.

Sheikh Hamad, who lives in the New Palace in Fujairah, has distinguished himself by the openness and frequency of his *majlis*, which he holds weekly on Fridays, and which is attended by people from all over the emirate. The deputy ruler of Fujairah is HH Sheikh Hamad bin Saif al-Sharqi.

The ruling family of Fujairah is descended from the powerful Sharqiyyin tribal group, which was populous across much of the area that is now Fujairah and also inhabited large tracts of the Musandam Peninsula south of the areas now held by Oman. The Sharqiyyin have a reputation of independence, reflecting their isolation from the main Gulf coast. The tribe is named after the Arabic word for east, *al sharq.*

Right: Sheikh Saeed Al-Maktoum House.

Wildlife: Amazing Adaptation

The UAE has an unexpected wealth of wildlife for a country that is more than 60 per cent desert. Many species of mammal and reptile have adapted to the harsh climate on land. Plant life is also diversified, only partly reflecting conscious attempts by the government to irrigate and 'green' the desert. The waters of the Gulf on the west coast, and on the east coast of the Indian Ocean, are a fertile breeding ground for fish both large and small, as well as a number of rare species of turtle and the sea-cow or dugong.

Many of the species are rare and endangered, however, and are unlikely to be seen by the casual visitor.

Mammals

Despite its rather harsh environment, the UAE is home to around 35 different species of mammals, some of which originate in Iran or Africa and others which are indigenous to the UAE, or at least to the Arabian Peninsula. Perhaps one of the most interesting features of the wildlife in the UAE is their ability to adapt and to survive in desert conditions.

Many of the mammals have common features which allow them to live with scarce or non-existent water and in extremely high temperatures. These creatures have adapted their behaviour in a number of ways: they tend to hunt at dusk and dawn and to seek respite in the shade during the heat of the day.

Some creatures even 'hibernate' during the summer months — though this form of behaviour in the desert is known as aestivation and, instead of sleeping through the winter, the desert mammals spend the hot season in their burrows and come out only when it becomes cooler.

In addition to behavioural adaptation, the mammals of the desert have evolved physiologically and have developed characteristics which enable them to minimize water loss and to maintain a reasonable body temperature when the sun is as its harshest. They have a wide blood temperature range, long legs, thin coats and bodies, large ears, long eye lashes, pale (or sandy) colouring as well as hairs on the soles of their feet.

Of all the desert mammals, none has adapted better to the harsh conditions of the desert than the camel which stores food in its hump in the form of fat. Though the camel is native to the region, it has become domesticated and can no longer be classified as a wild animal. Other mammals which have adapted to life in the desert include the hare, the red fox and a range of wild cats, including the Gordon's wild cat.

Sadly, many Arabian mammals have survived the desert but have not survived man's need to hunt them; consequently many are close to extinction.

The Arabian leopard (*Panthera pardus nimr*) is found only in the Arabian Peninsula and there are, according to official estimates, only 100 in existence. Whether these creatures can still be found in the wild in the UAE is not known for certain.

It seems that there are still some Arabian leopards living in the Musandam area of Oman and sightings have been reported in the Hajar Mountains. There have been sporadic kills of these creatures which would indicate that they are still around in the wild.

The animal is at home in quite inhospitable environments and its native territory is on the mountain ranges of northern Arabia from the Negev Desert to the Asir Mountains, Yemen, southern Oman and the Musandam Peninsula.

The Arabian leopard is an opportunistic feeder — meaning it will eat whatever is available, rodents, birds, goats and wild ungulates (such as ibex). In appearance it resembles an African leopard although it is slightly smaller and lighter in colour.

Though dangerous to man, its shy and secretive nature means that it is no real

Right: old and new forms of transport co-exist at the camel market, Al Ain.

Above: The beautiful Arabian oryx can be seen at Sir Bani Yas.

threat because it will disappear at the first indication that human beings are in the offing. In the past, the people of the UAE would hunt their native gazelles, oryx and birds but modern UAE takes an active role in promoting the conservation of its wildlife.

In particular, a local group called the Arabian Leopard Trust has been very active in campaigning to save the Arabian leopard as well as other rare creatures. The group has additionally been responsible for the setting up of a breeding programme for these creatures.

In 1995, the Arabian Leopard Trust rescued a young male leopard from captivity in the souk in Yemen and also was loaned a caracal lynx from Saudi Arabia's National Commission for Wildlife Conservation and Development (NCWCD).

The intention is to breed these and other animals and eventually to release them back into the wild.

The Arabian Leopard Trust also conducts research on the Arabian leopard as well as the caracal lynx and the Gordon's wild cat. During its 1995 survey, the group concluded that there could be a maximum of 20 adult leopards surviving in the Hajar mountains.

An equally rare creature, found only in the UAE and Oman, is the Arabian tahr (Hemitragus jayakari) — part of the ungulate species. This goat-like animal is found high up in the mountains — keeping itself to itself, usually at an altitude of about 600 metres (2,000 feet). The animal was thought to be extinct until a female tahr and her kid were spotted during a wildlife survey undertaken by the Arabian Leopard Trust in 1995. It is extremely vulnerable to local hunters as it needs to visit water holes every day and it also has to compete for increasingly scarce grazing territory with feral goats and donkeys.

Another wild ungulate native to the UAE is the Arabian gazelle (Gazella arabica). Some evidence of its existence in the form of distinctive dung middens was discovered during the research conducted in 1995

Above: A herd of eland at Sir Bani Yas island.

which indicates that it is present in very small numbers in the mountains of the region.

This creature and its relatives, the sand gazelle, Thomson's gazelle, the Arabian oryx, the scimitar-horned oryx, the belsa oryx and the jemsbok are all to be found in the protected environment of the Sir Bani Yas Nature Reserve.

This island, off the coast of Abu Dhabi, is the private nature reserve of President Sheikh Zayed bin Sultan al-Nahyan. Unfortunately, though these creatures were once native to the UAE, few if any survive in the wild today.

The name Abu Dhabi actually means 'father of the gazelle' and the town was apparently named when a group of gazelle hunters gathered in pursuit of the animal. Sadly over the years they accomplished their mission all too successfully.

One carnivorous animal which does appear to have survived successfully in the wild in the UAE is the lynx caracal *(Felis caracal schmitzi)* which is a reddish-brown,

medium-sized, nocturnal cat found in Africa, the Arabian Peninsula and the Middle East as far as Pakistan. It tends to avoid the heat of the day so hunts at night and is a very good jumper — able to catch birds leaping at them.

It feeds on smaller mammals and birds as well as rodents and guinea fowl. Evidence of its existence was found during the 1995 research survey referred to earlier and it has a fairly wide distribution.

Other relatively large carnivorous mammals which are known to have occurred in the UAE, but are found rarely if at all in the wild today, are the desert wolf *(Canis lupus Arabis)*, the Gordon's wildcat *(Felis silvestris gordoni)* and the striped hyena *(Hyaena hyaena)*.

Perhaps the most common carnivorous mammal in the UAE is the red fox *(Vulpes vulpes)*. It is most often found in the foothill areas of the mountains close to rural settlements although it also lives in the higher mountain areas near the larger wadis.

The Blanford's fox (*Vulpes cana*) has also been found in the UAE although this is not its native territory. Ruppell's sand fox (*Vulpes ruppelli*) is a smaller version of the red fox with large ears. This animal is a desert creature and is able to survive in extreme conditions. The Ruppell's sand fox and the fennec fox (*Vulpes zerda*) are not commonly spotted.

The Arabian desert is also home to several mammals that are members of the order insectivora, such as hedgehogs, moles and shrews which feed on insects. The Ethiopian hedgehog and the Brandt's hedgehog (*Paraechinus hypomelas*) are both found in the UAE. The former creature is more common than the latter but both mammals are ideally suited to desert conditions. They are virtually water-independent and have quite sophisticated cooling mechanisms — long legs and large ears.

There are also quite a number of bat species in the emirates including the leaf-nosed bat, the vespertilionid bat, the horseshoe, mouse-tailed and sheath-tailed bat as well as the relatively rare long-eared bat (*Otonycteris hemprichi*).

The most common of the bat species are the Egyptian fruit bats (*Rousettus aegyptiacus*), which live mainly in the fruit trees of Ras al-Khaimah, and the mouse-tailed bats (*Rhinopoma muscatellum*) which often live in caves, and finally the trident leaf-nosed bats (*Asellia tridens*) which live in underground tunnels, often near or in the *falaj* irrigation tunnels.

The UAE is also home to several varieties of shrew including the Indian house shrew — which tends to feed in inhabited areas off rubbish — as well as to the spiny mouse (*Acomys dimidiatus*), gerbils such as the baluchistan gerbil (*Gerbillus nanus*) and Wagner's gerbil (*Gerbillus dasyurus*), hares such as the cape hare (*Lepus capensis*) and jerboas.

The latter, known as the desert jerboa (*Jaculus jaculus*) is worth mentioning for its excellent ability to adapt to desert conditions. It is a member of the order rodentia and is found in north Africa, Arabia and central Asia where its natural habitat is desert and steppe.

It is a solitary, nocturnal creature which only starts to move about after sundown when it looks for food — seeds, roots and insects — from which it extracts the water it needs for survival.

Reptiles

Reptiles need sun and heat in order to survive as, unlike mammals, they do not derive all their energy from food but warm up by sun-bathing and cool down by retreating to the shade. They also can go for long periods of time without food.

They are ideally suited to the desert and therefore to the environment within the emirates. More than 50 varieties of reptile have been recorded and most are seen fairly frequently — the most common are lizards and geckos, snakes and skinks as well as marine turtles.

Snakes in general tend to be found less frequently than the other reptiles — just as well because most are venomous species of the viper. Three of these have been recorded in the UAE: the sand viper (*Cerastes cerastes*), the saw-scaled viper (*Echis carinatus*) and the Burton's carpet viper (*Echis coloratus*).

The sand viper, not surprisingly, is found in sand-dunes where it lurks amongst the vegetation looking for prey, lizards and rodents.

It sometimes buries itself in sand up to its eyes and nostrils — so look out for the telltale diagonal lines which it leaves behind or you might step on one by accident. Actually it is likely that the snake would move off at the approach of human beings.

The saw-scaled viper is more likely to be found near the sea on flat alluvial plains while the carpet viper is usually found in and around wadis or irrigated farm-land.

Other common desert snakes which are not dangerous are the desert boa (*Eryx jayakari*) which kills its prey by squeezing it, the Arabian rearfang (*Malpolon moilensis*) and the sand snake (*Psammophis schokari*). Sea snakes are also common in the UAE.

Lizards are seen frequently. They tend to live in all the various habitats: desert, mountains, gardens and parks and even houses.

The largest is the desert monitor (*Varanus griseus*) which is about one metre long and feeds on smaller lizards, birds and rodents. The more common variety of lizard is the *dhabb* or spiny-tailed lizard of which several varieties are found. They have the ability to change colour: either in response to alarm or as they warm up during the course of a day. Other varieties of lizard to be found are the spiney-tailed agamid (*Uremastryx microlepis*), the Arabian toad-head and the branded toad-head, as well as the lacertids which live in sandy areas: the spiny-foot lacertid and the desert lacertid.

The skinks which are in the desert, such as the Arabian sand skink, the ocellated skink and the mabuya skink, are interesting in terms of their high adaptability to desert conditions including the special webbed toes they have which prevent them from sinking into the sand when they run over it.

Birdlife

As the UAE develops, so does its potential for birdlife. This may seem something of an anomaly where urban, human development usually leads to reductions of the wildlife population. In the emirates, however, the considerable growth of parkland and gardens and, with it, trees and water has attracted more birds, whereas desert conditions do not suit many varieties of birds.

The fact that the UAE is on one of the main migratory routes, with as many as 300 species of birds stopping off en route to or from Asia, Europe or Africa, makes it a fascinating place for birdlife.

The best seasons for bird-watching are during the autumn (September to November) and the spring (February to May). The Natural History Group in Dubai and the Emirates Natural History Group in Abu Dhabi have done a great deal in terms of spotting and recording the various of birds.

They have spotted 360 species, made up of resident breeding birds, migratory passage-birds, birds from Europe wintering in the warmth of the UAE, as well as summer-breeding visitors.

The UAE is therefore home to exotic birds from Asia and Africa as well as common European birds such as robins, song thrushes and starlings.

Some of the best bird-watching places exist in the parks around Dubai and Abu Dhabi.

Saffa Park which is only 12 kilometres ($7^1/_2$ miles) from Dubai City centre is one of the best places in the emirates. There alone, more than 230 species have been recorded, including the common mynah, the ring-necked parakeet, the red-vented bulbul and purple sunbird. In April there are also large numbers of hoopoes, great grey shrikes as well as European bee-eaters. Birds are attracted by the park's trees and its lake which is particularly attractive to the park's wide variety of warblers, amongst which are the graceful warbler, the great reed and the clamorous reed warbler.

The lake is home to the black-necked grebe and the coot, as well as the teal, the pintail pochard and sometimes the pintail duck.

The Dubai Creek is ideal for certain varieties of waders and migrants who are drawn by the excellent feeding conditions of the shallow water and mudflats in the area.

Of particular interest is the Khor Dubai area of the creek which is a shallow lagoon about five kilometres (three miles) inland from the Dubai city centre. There you may see flocks of greater flamingo which come from their breeding sites in Russia, Iran, Afghanistan, Pakistan and Turkey; many of which are over-wintering but some of whom remain throughout the year. Common varieties seen along these shallow-watered sand banks are the dunlin, the lesser golden plover, the grey plover, the curlew sandpiper, the greenshank, the godwit and the redshank.

A recent survey by Durham University on behalf of the Dubai government discov-

Overleaf: A flock of flamingoes flies languidly above the sea.

discovered that the Dubai Creek is home to 4,000 of the world's estimated 30,000 broadbilled sandpipers.

Other good areas for ornithology around Dubai are the Emirates Golf Club, the Jumeirah Beach Park, the Mushrif National Park, the Zabeel water treatment plant, the old sewage treatment plant and the grounds of the Jebel Ali Hotel.

The great stretch of UAE coastline is attractive to birds who live on the beaches, the outlying islands, the mangroves, the rocky cliffs and the harbours of the territory.

Kalba, on the east coast, about 10 kilometres (six miles) south of Fujairah facing the Gulf of Oman, is an interesting area for bird-watching — mainly as a result of its extensive mangrove. There can be seen the relatively rare white-collared kingfisher, as well as the European kingfisher and the little green kingfisher.

Other birds in the coastal areas are: the little green heron, the booted warbler and the clamorous reed warbler, as well as wintering species such as the Indian pond heron, the little egret, the great white egret, the greater sand plover, the whimbrel and the terek sandpiper, as well as sooty, black-headed and slender-billed gulls and, very occasionally, the white pelican.

An area south of Ras al-Khaimah, near the deserted village of Jazeerah al-Hamra, known as Al Jazeerah Khor, is attractive to several varieties of plover, heron and flamingo — another area popular with birds for its mudflats and shallow waters.

In Abu Dhabi, some parts of the eastern lagoon area has been designated a bird reserve by Sheikh Zayed as a result of the survey conducted by the Emirates Natural History Group.

The area is also surrounded by mangroves which are inhabited by herons, gulls, marsh harriers, tern, plovers and egrets.

The Bateen Wood is another popular bird-watching area, home to breeding visitors such as the olivaceous and the graceful warbler, the red-vented bulbul, the palm dove as well as migrants including various warblers, the sparrow-hawk, the golden oriole and the common and bank mynah.

The garden city of Al Ain attracts the Egyptian vulture which comes to the local zoo to feed off the raw meat fed to the big cats. A visit to the top of Jebel Hafiz, the highest mountain in the UAE will reveal these and other rarer birds of prey such as the griffon vulture, the bonelli eagle, the long-legged buzzard and the lappet-faced vulture, swooping impressively around the mountain top. They float on the thermals that rise from the desert plains and nest in the mountain tops.

Fish and Sea-Life

The underwater world of the UAE is rich in variety and full of the exotic, the colourful and the rare. Not only is the marine life abundant but the UAE is also a good and relatively inexpensive place in which to learn scuba-diving. A good selection of diving schools has been established in the last 20 years.

The UAE is bordered on the west coast by the Gulf and on the east coast by the Indian Ocean. The Gulf waters are enclosed on all sides by land and have only a narrow entrance where the Gulf meets the Indian Ocean on the Strait of Hormuz, on Oman's Musandam peninsula.

As a result, the waters of the Gulf have a lower level of water exchange than other bodies of water and are also quite high in salinity, as well as subject to quite a wide temperature range (sea temperatures at the surface can drop from 35°C (95°F) in the summer to 10°C (50°F) in the winter months). Thus the number of species to be found there is restricted and some are found only in the Gulf.

Though coral reefs sometimes do not survive such cold temperatures there are nonetheless some 50 species in the Gulf of which the most common are: the *Leptoria* (a smooth, rounded coral), the *Porities* (which is a large rock like coral) and the *Acropora humilis*.

Among these corals live small creatures such as sea anemones, molluscs, crustaceans, crabs and sea urchins. There are also numerous varieties of fish to be found around the rocks and reefs and these include: catfish, batfish, hotfish, black spotted rubbertip, surgeon fish, parrot fish, angel fish, starfish and various species of grouper.

There are a number of underwater wrecks in the west coast waters of the Gulf near Abu Dhabi and Jebel Ali, some of which have been purposely sunk in order to encourage the growth of marine life.

The coral reefs and islands on this side of the emirates tend to be quite inaccessible in terms of their distance from the shore. The waters of the Indian Ocean are less saline and marine life more abundant. Thus diving sites off the coast of Fujairah, Dibba and Khorfakkan tend to offer more promise to the underwater explorer (see Sports and Leisure section). Fish to be found in the corals of these waters include dozens of colourful tropical varieties of box fish, angel fish, surgeon fish and butterfly fish. These can be easily seen by snorkellers within metres of the beach. More rarely, eels, including the moray eel, sea snakes, cuttle-fish and octopus are sighted. Filefish and pipe-fish, which have long thin bodies about 0.5 metre (one to two feet long) are also a common sight.

Among the rocks you might find a variety of molluscs including the potentially lethal cone shells (Conus striatus) and cowries and also such worms as the fire worm, the scale worm and the numertean worm.

Perhaps one of the more interesting features of the waters off the UAE is that recent research has shown they may be home to over one-third of the world's approximately 80 species of dolphins and whales. Dhow trips to watch dolphins are becoming increasingly popular among tourists but there are no whale-watching cruises from the UAE.

Some of the whales are thought to be sub-species new to marine scientists and unique to the region. Research sponsored by the Union National Bank in 1995 set out to establish baseline data regarding the status and distribution of cetaceans. The team conducting the research (in co-ordination with the Centre for Dolphin Studies in South Africa) were also looking at the effects of pollution on dolphins.

It is not always easy to document the variety of whale and dolphin species present in the Gulf but identification is done through both live spottings and also by examination of the skeletons of these marine mammals.

Evidence of the following whale species was found during the research off the UAE: the fin whale (Balaenoptera physalus), minke whale (Balaenoptera acutorostrata), blue whale (Balaenoptera musculus), sei whale (Balaenoptera borealis), Bryde's whale (Balaenoptera edeni), humpback whale (Megaptera novaeangliae) and the false killer whale (Pseudorca crassidens).

The presence of large baleen whales in the waters of the Gulf has caused marine biologists a great deal of curiosity as to their origins. With the exception of the Bryde's whale, whose natural habitat is known to be in warm waters all over the world, the other species are thought not to originate in the Gulf.

The usual pattern for baleen whales all over the world is to migrate large distances from feeding locations in polar waters to breeding locations in warmer climes. The interesting point about their appearance in the waters of the Gulf is that these whales would have had to migrate over a huge distance from the polar oceans of Antarctica across the Equator — a feat unrecorded amongst the baleen whale population.

Alternatively, if the baleen whales live year round in the Gulf, they would be unique amongst their species for doing so and thus genetically isolated — a fact which could be the crucial key to their survival.

Dolphins are frequently seen in UAE waters, the most commonly occurring species being the bottlenose (Tursiops truncatus) and the Indo-Pacific humpback (Sousa chinensis). Little is known about the Indo-Pacific humpback species although it is thought to be under threat because of its preferred habitat which is in the shallow, coastal waters.

The Dolphin Research Project found groups of around 30 Indo-Pacific humpbacks which are usually known to travel in smaller groups of between six to ten.

Other rare varieties of marine mammal spotted include the spinner dolphin *(Stenella longirostris)*, spotted dolphin *(Stenella attenuata)* and the finless porpoise *(Neophocoena phocoenoides)*. The latter is rare in the Arabian Gulf and in fact very little research has been done into this creature anywhere in the world.

Meanwhile, in the waters of the Indian Ocean off the coast of Fujairah, sperm whales *(Physeter macrocephalus)* and Risso's dolphins *(Grampus griseus)* are seen quite frequently.

The dugong *(Dugong dugon)* or sea cow, a marine mammal increasingly under threat of extinction, is being actively protected in the Gulf region which is home to the world's second largest population of the creature.

They are mainly to be found off the coast of Abu Dhabi and around the island of Merawah, although there is no estimate of exactly how many dugongs exist.

Unfortunately the dugong has been greatly affected by human encroachment on its environment — underwater explosions, oil spills, fishing nets and the dredging of sea-grass beds have all taken their toll. Until recently, dugong meat was a delicacy. The creature has now been targeted for further research and conservation.

As far as reptiles are concerned, the waters of the UAE are home to nine different species of sea snake, the most common varieties of which are: the blue-banded snake *(Hydrophis cyanocinctus)*, yellow bellied *(Pelamis platurus)*, reef sea-snake *(Hydrophis ornatus)* and yellow sea-snake *(Hydrophis spiralis)*.

It is worth noting that these sea creatures can be encountered on the surface of the water, where they lie to sun themselves and breathe. However, they are also able to remain underwater for as long as two hours during which time they breathe from air they store in their right lung.

Reptiles of a larger and more friendly nature include the green turtle *(Chelonia mydas)*, the hawksbill turtle *(Eretmochelys imbricata)*, the leather back turtle *(Dermochelys coriacea)* and the loggerhead turtle *(Caretta caretta)* as well as possibly the olive ridley turtle *(Lepidochelys olivacea)*.

The latter is known to exist in Oman and Pakistan and is therefore very likely to be present in the UAE although it has never been seen. Again, these species are all endangered. The hawksbill and the green turtles both nest on the beaches of the UAE and, like the dugong, feed off the seagrass beds and shallow coral reefs off the west coast of Abu Dhabi; the leatherback is known to feed on jellyfish which abound in the Gulf, particularly during the spring.

Like the dugong, the turtles are victims of fishermen and of the disappearance of the sea grasses they feed on. Conservationists recognize the need to preserve their grazing areas and thus to protect both the turtles and the dugong.

Flora: Indigenous and Exotic

The UAE's plant life is unexpectedly rich and diversified for a country that is more than two-thirds desert. The traditional image of deserts, inhabited only by cactuses and camels, is a long way from the reality of the UAE. More than 400 species of plant have been found throughout eastern Arabia, and most are represented in the UAE.

The UAE forms part of the Sudan vegetation zone, and the varieties of plant-life are such as are found throughout the arid north-east African countries, including Sudan, Somalia and Ethiopia. But the plants also share characteristics with plant-life in Iran, Afghanistan and Pakistan.

The plants of course have adapted to the harsh climate for, just as for the people of the UAE, availability of water is the key to their survival. The local flora have proved remarkably adaptable in their

Right: Palm trees and *falaj* irrigation at Hatta.

Above: Colourful Rumex vesicarius plant, growing at Fujairah.

ability to squeeze the water needed for life out of the harsh desert. The propagation of plants is partly mediated by the many beautiful butterflies of the Arabian peninsula, which act as pollinators.

The Arabs broadly divide plants into two categories, which they call *'ushb,* — various grasses and tender annual flowers — and *shajar,* — hardier perennials that include anything from shrublets to bushes and trees.

Trees

The trees of the UAE have many features in common with the smaller plants. The leaves of the date-palm and coconut-palm provide good examples. They are thick and leathery, preventing water-loss, while the roots stretch out horizontally, absorbing any water in a wide area around the individual tree.

Some shrubs are spiny in order to deter local animals such as sheep and goats from grazing on them. Flowering is usually an annual event when conditions are suitable.

Some shrubs are spiny in order to deter local animals such as sheep and goats from grazing on them. Flowering is usually an annual event.

The wood of the higher trees, typically ranging between three and eight metres (10-26 feet) high, has often been used to make charcoal, while the leaves have been used for a number of household purposes. Trees of this height found in the UAE include: *al ghaf; al samr; al ashkar; al artta; al ather.*

Not all the trees found in the UAE are indigenous but are hardy strains of tropical or sub-tropical species, planted in the UAE to promote the greening of the country, a vision so treasured by Sheikh Zayed. In 1994 it was estimated that about 18,000 hectares were covered in trees.

Tree Week on 15 April has been celebrated since 1981. The country has an active seed distribution programme led by Abu Dhabi, which annually sends tens of thousands of seeds to the other emirates for subsequent planting by municipalities and individuals.

Among trees commonly found in the parks and leafy urban areas, the *gulmohar* tree *(Delonix regia),* which sports beautiful red and orange blossoms each year, is a native of the island of Madagascar. This tree, more commonly called *fleur de paradis,* has a broad canopy of fronded leaves in which the flowers look like splashes of oil paint from the palette of a Fauvist painter. The tree is of the sub-species *caesalpinodeae* and family Leguminosae.

Another commonly found tree in the UAE is the umbrella tree, *Thespesia populnea,* also called the portia tree. It is of the family Malvaceae. This evergreen tree has medium-sized leaves and small yellow flowers with red bases, and fruits a small green apple.

The wood and bark may be used to make a red dye, while yellow dyes are made from the flowers and fruit. The umbrella tree is so-called because its leaves spread in a wide arch, providing cooling shade to passers-by.

The frywood tree, *Albizzia lebbek,* is also called woman's tongue because of the way the papery yellow pods clack together in the wind after it sheds its leaves during the hot season. The tree, of the sub-family Mimosoideae and family Leguminosae, has spreading leaves and tufty green and white inflorescences, each of which contains a number of tiny flowers.

The bark is used for medical purposes. The pods, hanging vertically down and about 30 centimetres (1 foot) in length, are distinctive

The babul tree, *Acacia arabica,* related to the frywood tree, is smaller in height. The tree's foliage comprises leaves made up of two rows of small petals on either side of the central stem, dotted with white circular yellow inflorescences whose stamens project a good 2.5 centimetres (1 inch) from the ball of nascent flowers. The tree has long, leathery seed-pods that are used in cattle-fodder, while its bark has been used in dyeing.

The bottle-brush tree, *Callisteman,* of the family Myrataceae, is related to the guava, clove and eucalyptus. The tree has red inflorescences and leathery leaves with oil glands that have aromatic properties.

The margosa or neem tree, *Azadirachta indica,* of the family Meliaceae, is a medium-sized tree with scythe-like leaves with serrated edges. It grows hundreds of tiny yellowish flowers during the summer. This tree is widely used for its medicinal properties, including its leaves, roots and bark. Margosa oil is obtained from the flowers.

Plants

Typically, the small plants of the UAE are characterized by small leaves, that minimize water evaporation, and shallow trailing roots that stretch for metres in a bid to absorb every available droplet out of the shallow soils. The small leaves are often more like those of a succulent, rounded and filled with sap, and with a waxy appearance. They are particularly common along the beaches.

Grasses are found all over the UAE. Among the common varieties are *al ramth,* which grows to half-a-metre (one-and-a-half feet) high, and *al russam,* which spreads lower and is often used as fodder for camels. Other grasses are found in the UAE.

which has medicinal properties is used to reduce fever. *Al shenan,* is powdered and used for soap.

In sandy areas species of plant that are typical are 'duun al faar' *(Rhynchosia minima);* 'faqi' *(Tirmania nivea);* 'zahr' *(Tribulus omanense);* 'markh' *(Leptadenia pyrotechnica);* 'nizbah' *(Silene villosa);* 'nuzaagh' *(Crotolaria aegyptiaca);* 'uzfaj' *(Rhanterium epapposum);* 'shukaa' *(Fagonia indica);* 'alqii' *(Dypterigium glaucum);* 'funuun' *(Arnebia hispidissima);* 'aaraa' *(Aerva javarica);* 'yanm' *(Plantago afra);* 'muqabiil al-shams' *(Cleome glaucescens);* 'thumuum' *(Pennisetum drivisum)* and 'thamaam' *(Panicum turgidum).*

Plants of the gravel plains include 'shubkah' *(Cuscuta planiflora);* 'ghaljah' *(Pergularia tomentosa);* 'dafrah al-hamaar' *(Iphiona aucheri);* 'naqii' *(Blepharis ciliaris);* 'kuriish' *(Glossonema varians);* 'maknaan' *(Reichardia vingitana);* 'harmul' *(Rhazya Stricta);* 'shukaa' *(Fagonia bruguieri);* 'mahandii' *(Pulicaria glutinosa);* 'du'aa' *(Aizoon canariense);* 'humaad' *(Rumex vesicarius);* 'bayaad' *(Convolvulus virgatus);* 'nufaakh' *(Pseudogaillonia hymenstephanus);* 'khawfij' *(Phystorrrrlynchus chafers)* and 'qazdii' *(Ochradenus aucheri).*

The wadis, dried-out river beds that contain water at least part of the year, are also a good place to find plants. The typical species of this habitat include 'zhafra' *(Tephrosia nubila);* 'maghaz ghaaz' *(Lavandula citriodora);* 'kubbaath' *(Launaea spinosa);* 'qatfah' *(Leucas inflata);* 'khushkhash' *(Papater dubium);* 'khuzaamah' *(Reseda aucheri);* 'muqabiil al-shams' *(Cleome rupicola);* 'marghaad' *(Lindenbergia arabica);* 'dhaanuun' *(Orobanche cernua);* 'lasf' *(Capparis spinosa);* 'rukiikah' *(Gypsophila bellidifolia);* 'qarnuwah' *(Erodium glacinatum);* 'haysh' *(Phragmitus australis)* and 'kaarii' *(Heliotroium digynum).*

A number of plants have also grown up around the plantation areas, usually comprising the date-palms that play such an important role in the life-style and furnishings of the UAE. Such plants include 'umm al-kaf' *(Chloris virgata);* 'ya'diid' *(Sonchus oleraceus);* 'uliiq' *(Convolvulus arvensis);* 'musaysim' *(Misopates antirhynnum);* 'khabiizah' *(Malva aegyptiaca);* 'hind qawq' *(Melilotus indica);* 'zaghlanatah' *(Ranunculus muricatus);* 'hamiid' *(Oxalis corniculata);* 'lankh al-mawiiyah' *(Vernonia cinerea);* 'barbiir' *(Portula oleracea);* 'kharuu' *(Ricinus communis);* 'shabr al-balbuul' *(Solanum inigrum);* desert orchid *(epipactis veratrifolia);* 'sabaahah' *(Adiantum capillus-ververis)* and 'aysh al-ghazaab' *(Fungi, coprinus possibly).*

The coasts have been the sites of settlements since time immemorial, and the population of plants there is equally impressive, partly reflecting the varied terrain which ranges from saltflats to saline swamp to rocky semi-desert. Among the plants in these areas are 'tarthuuth' *(Cynomorium coccineum);* 'dhaanuun' *(Cistanchi tubulosa);* 'qatf' *(Limorium axillare);* 'larjah' *(Helianthemum lippii);* 'ramth' *(Hammada schmidtiana);* 'hanbuuk' *(Spherocoma aucheri);* 'umm adhan' *(Ononis serrata);* 'nisii' *(Stipagrostis plumosa);* 'ashraj' *(Cassia italica);* 'hurbash' *(Lotus halopilus);* 'haad' *(Cornulaca leucacantha);* 'biishah' *(Indigofera argentea);* 'ramraam' *(Heliotropium kotschkyi);* 'qurm' *(Avicenna marina)* and 'sa'daan' *(Neurada procumbens).*

The plants that inhabit the desert proper are by definition limited. Nevertheless, more than half-a-dozen species survive in the harsh sands. These include desert hyacinth *(Cistanch tubulosa);* desert squash *(Citrullus colcynth);* 'al handhal', Sodom's apple *(Calatropis procera);* 'al ashkar'; 'al zaahar' *(Tribulus terrestri);* 'al jaad' *(Teucrium stocksianium)* and firebrush *(Calligorum comosum).*

Left: Tree in the Jabal Hafeet.

Cultural Pursuits

The traditional culture of the UAE remains closely tied to the national population's desert existence before the advent of oil wealth. Hunting and fishing were important parts of life, while the date-palm supplied many of the necessities of daily life. Camels and horses were used for transportation, and falcons for hunting. Nowadays, many aspects of the old way of life have died out.

However, camel-racing is still a popular pursuit in all of the emirates except Fujairah. And falconry is something between an art and a sport, practised by the rulers and their close colleagues.

Art and crafts

Typically the art and crafts of the UAE have a practical focus. Quite simply, daily life was too hard in the past to allow frivolity. Ceramic art has flourished. Weapons were often highly decorated, and many traditional pursuits — from dhow-building to the elaborately carved wind-towers — reveal the skill and sophistication of the country's carpenters and architects.

For many centuries henna hand-painting and jewellery have been used for self-adornment, and the many uses to which palm-fronds were put, whether in making small jewellery boxes or airy *barasti*-style houses, reveal a strong local tradition.

This inherent creative spirit has led to a resurgence of interest in art in recent years, though often focused on painting and photography. Art and craft exhibitions are held regularly in the main cities and, more and more, the works of nationals are displayed, along with those of the expatriates.

Abu Dhabi has increasingly taken the lead in the field of heritage, including art, and the Heritage Village outside Al Ain, plus galleries in the city, offer numerous items. The cultural foundation in Abu Dhabi is an important source of information on the emirates' history and culture. Sharjah is also developing its facilities and there is a heritage museum at the Al Arsah souq.

Among the venues in Dubai for the visual and plastic arts, Dubai International Arts Centre in Jumeirah was formed in 1976 by a small group of mostly British expatriates, operating out of a garage as the Dubai Arts Society.

Dubai municipality donated the use of two beachside villas for its use a couple of years later. The non-profit group aims to encourage UAE artists by providing classes and exhibition space at reasonable cost. Regular courses are held in crafts, including painting, pottery, photography, interior decorating and silk-painting. The centre also does a *Survival Arabic* course.

Despite such interest, the UAE is no great place to buy indigenous handicraft items. Most antiques in the souqs of Sharjah, Dubai and Abu Dhabi are of Indian or Omani origin. Carpets come from as far afield as Iran and Central Asia.

The gold or silver jewellery items, while beautiful and of excellent value, are mainly not locally made. The many beautiful pots and incense-burners mostly come from Oman or Iran and the making of many traditional handicraft items has fallen into abeyance with the oil-boom.

The UAE is a good place to buy a wide range of Middle Eastern handicraft items, but the visitor should be aware that these are mainly not UAE in origin. Old and traditional handicrafts are better represented in the museums than in the markets.

Natural dyes

Few of the arts and crafts of the UAE are purely ornamental. Even the most intricate motifs used in architecture and dhow building had a practical aspect. It was only on special occasions that the spartan dress of the men and women was offset by any finery, and when it was, the displays were tasteful, low-key and rooted in tradition.

Henna hand-painting

Henna hand-painting is just such a skill. Associated with shampoos and conditioners in the West, red dye from the shrub *Lawsonia inermis* has been used for centuries to adorn the hands of women.

Above: Intricate hand decoration using henna dye is a tradition, especially for weddings. The dye can remain for several weeks.

The plant grows up to two metres (just over six feet) high in Egypt, India and the Middle East. The leaves are powdered to make the henna dye, which is used for tinting hair red and dyeing nails a reddish colour. Men also use henna to dye their beard and hair, as the *Hadith (Sayings of the Prophet)* specify that men should not dye grey hair with any other dye but that of henna.

In the UAE, as in much of the Gulf, hand-dyeing is done on any special occasion, but particularly at marriages. Beauty clinics, for instance in Ras al-Khaimah, still offer to do henna hand-decorations for clients. Hand-painting treatment is increasingly available and popular with tourists.

Henna is also reputed to soften the skin and cool it against harsh sunlight. As such, it is commonly used for general cosmetic purposes. The leaves are first ground into a fine powder, using the ancient tools of pestle and mortar, and the powder is then strained through a muslin cloth to ensure a smooth texture.

The powder is mixed with eucalyptus oil and lemon juice, the paste from which becomes a moist lump after being left for two or three hours.

The henna is then applied to the hands or feet, using an instrument that resembles a modern icing bag, and left on the skin for several hours; the paste is then scraped off, and after about half a day, the colour becomes a rich pigment dyed into the skin, lasting for several weeks.

A number of intricate patterns are commonly used, usually floral. Brides-to-be have their hands, feet, wrists and ankles decorated like this, several days before the wedding ceremony.

Palm leaves

The date palm, or 'bride of the desert' as it is known in Arabic, was widely used in everyday life
. The date, was important for culinary art, while the leaves were used for making anything from houses to small decorative cosmetic cases, from boats to musical instruments. Various receptacles were fash-

237

Above: A demonstration of traditional skills at a craft village in Dubai. Overleaf: Workers at Al Khattal boat builders, Dubai.

ioned out of date-palm leaves, and used to carry and serve food. These included *al makhrafah,* in which the dates were collected. *Al mezmah,* was used to carry home the dates. And *al jefeer* was used by women to carry dates to market. *Al sarood* were small circular mats used to lay food on, while the food was covered with *al makab,* a type of conical mat.

Date-palm leaves were also used in clothing. Women used *al mashab,* a kind of simple fan, and *al geffa,* a small box, to carry around personal items. A more complex sort of box called a *shebdan* was made from straw and used as a container for perfumes.

Date-palm leaves were used to build *barasti* houses, some of which still exist today as coffee-houses. Small coastal boats were also made from palm leaves. They include the *shasha,* a few of which are still seen on the east coast.

In a typical *barasti* house, the front room was the public area, while the bedroom was found at the back. The wind-tower straddled the main living room and the bedroom. There were no windows, preserving the shady atmosphere.

Inside the main living room, furnishings were sparse, perhaps just a few wooden chests, mats and baskets. A simple *manama* bed, consisting of a rush mattress above the ground with a ladder going up to it, was used for sleeping outside in the summer.

Hide
Hides were also used to make saddles for their camels, water carriers that were slung from the camel's back or used to haul water from wells and at oases.

Hides were also used in a variety of musical instruments. These included the Bedouin fiddle, known as *rababa,* a simple instrument with a slightly mournful sound, played around the camp-fire in the desert.

The fiddle consists of a wooden frame with a goat-skin stretched over it and often only a single string made of horse hair. The instrument was either plucked or played using a bow of wood strung with horse hair.

Wood
Wood was also widely used, although lack of indigenous supplies of the harder woods meant that it tended to be only the relatively wealthy who could afford it. Carpenters used a number of simple tools, including saw, chisel, adze (a type of hand-axe), hammer and nails to fashion the wood, make household furniture, and larger products such as boats and dhows.

Dhow-building
Dhow-building has been practised for centuries along the Gulf coast, but only really underwent a revival when the ruling family of Dubai decided to fund a revival of the sport of dhow-racing. Dhow-building yards still exist — in Abu Dhabi and Ajman — but the lighter fibreglass dhows are becoming increasingly popular.

The art of dhow-making is still practised without too many modern accessories.

The templates for the main ribs of the dhow are hand-sawn from single pieces of wood. Boat builders use adzes to shape the main timbers while others use small handsaws and chisels for the finer details of the design. Steel pipes are often improvised as hammers. Boat designs are carried in the head of the master craftsman.

Other traditional uses of wood were in furniture for houses, particularly the ornamental chests, whose wood was studded with brass.

A variety of vessels were also made from wood, including the *fintas*, a huge wooden tank used to store water in the villages and towns. It consists of a wooden water-tank about three by two metres (10 x 6 feet), with a funnel and lid at the top. This was too bulky to be used by Bedouin, for whom mobility was a key concern, but in settled communities it provided a reservoir, albeit small, for rainwater.

Wool
Weaving, a traditional Bedouin pastime, is usually conducted by the women. Wool was made from the small stock of animals kept by the nomads, and fashioned into tent cloth and curtains, as well as more ornamental saddle bags, cushion covers and so on. The yarn was made from raw wool using a spindle to wind the wool into an even thread. It was then dyed using natural dyes made of ground rock, for instance sulphur, shells such as the murex and a number of plants, including henna.

The Bedouin wove on simple looms, using a wood shuttle with wool spooled around it to pass the weft threads between the warp threads, which were stretched between two metal poles or wooden sticks. Sheep's wool was typically used for rugs and furnishing, while goat's wool would be used for tent cloth.

Camel bags were used to carry trade goods and personal items on caravans, often decorated with tassels and abstract designs. Small rugs were sometimes locally manufactured but larger pieces were generally imported, as the small looms used in the desert typically made pieces under a metre wide.

Qur'ânic art
Calligraphy was the Qur'ânic art *par excellence*. Islamic art is essentially decorative and non-representational, partly because depiction of the human form is disapproved of by Islam. Even camels appear in traditional decorations in highly stylized forms because of the Qur'ân's ban on depicting living creatures.

Calligraphy took many forms, adorning the mosques, decorating walls and doors, and in the pages of the Qur'an itself. Although Qur'ânic art never reached the same heights as in the Muslim centres of Baghdad and Damascus, highly decorated Qur'âns can be bought at reasonable prices.

Metals
Jewellery is another traditional form of adornment for women, and an important element of women's dowry. Jewellery is sold everywhere in the gold and silver souqs but although traditionally a sign of wealth in the UAE, most of it was actually made in the neighbouring countries.

In the 19th century, the *dellal* consisted of a necklace of Islamic and European coins, often given as a present to a bride.

Traditional necklaces included *al tablah, al murtaeshah* and *al meryah,* as well as various anklets, bracelets and rings. Weapons were as much a form of adornment, expressing status and degree, as a military tool. At the end of the 19th century, Dubai was a key manufacturing and trading centre for weapons. Typically, blacksmiths produced farm tools, including *al das,* a type of plough. *Al safarrin* would polish the finished items and also repaired and cleaned traditional items such as the *dallah* coffee pots. Wet sand was often used to clean old and rusty implements.

The Bedu (Bedouin) used swords, daggers, spears, bows and arrows, shields of both hide and chain-mail, as well as rifles, pistols and cannons. Fiercely attached to their own tribe, the Bedouin tended their weapons carefully, often giving pet names to their favourites. Among the words from this period are the *bu falaj, bu thalatha falaj, al kattara* (scimitar) and *bu thalatha fasayel.*

Daggers were another useful accoutrement: the most famous of these are the highly decorated *khanjar,* short daggers in ornate silver curved scabbards, such as are still worn on formal occasions in Oman.

But although many of the sheikhs might have carried a *khanjar,* a variety of local daggers were also used, the best handles being of horn or ivory, usually with silver or gold decoration.

Shields were often made of shark-skin, while bows and arrows had cowrie decorations on them, as did the later-introduced cross-bows. The locals wore much of the paraphernalia of war associated with medieval knights-errant: chain-mail and helmets and the typical metal helmet with visor, like knights of yore. *Zand* wristguards were also worn.

Other weapons were of more recent origin. *Al yazer* consisted of a stick with an iron axe mounted on the end. Among the rifles that became popular, *umm fatila, umm gamaa* and *samaa* are preserved in the Dubai museum. Cannons are usually from Europe.

Ceramics

Pottery was made out of the local red clay, largely in Ras al-Khaimah, but goods were also imported from Oman and Iran. The pottery was fired in *al mahraqa,* the furnace, which was made of stone with mud-lined walls, with a hole in the top to let out smoke.

Pots of all sorts were generally reddish in colour. Different types of pottery were used for different tasks: *al khers* — for storing food; *al jarrah* — for carrying water from wells; *al yahlah* — for keeping water cool; *al borma* — for cooking; *al masaab* — for holding coffee; *al razem* — for carrying coffee-cups; *al haalool* — for giving birds and animals water to drink; *al mabkhar* — to burn incense.

Rock and coral

Traditional houses were buit mainly of date-palm fronds, although wealthier citizens used stone, often located along the creeks that stud the Gulf coast. Rocks and coral were also used.

A typical stone house consisted of a central *majlis* surrounded by verandas along the square of the inner building, and with a zigzag entrance. The house would often have a wind-tower or *baadjeer,* shaped like hands welcoming the gusts of wind, with the highest of these located above the bedroom. The wind-towers might be built of stone, or made from date-palm leaves, in the traditional *barasti* buildings. Because of the strict sense of family privacy, the houses had no windows.

Dance and Song

An old Middle Eastern proverb says the sounds that an Arab loves most are the sound of a woman's voice, running water and the chink of money.

Traditional dances revolved around the themes of love, warfare and Islam. In the days when life was split between pearling and fishing on the coasts, and the harsh life of the desert interior, singing and dancing offered a break from monotony, and a way

Left: Arab woman demonstrates traditional hand spinning techniques at a cultural centre.

Above: Ornately decorated Qu'ran dates from the tenth century.

of celebrating the inner emotions and family allegiances that dominated life.

Poetry also was a natural expression of the yearnings of the spirit in what was then a poor society; the lilting metre of the lyrical *Ghazal* poetry contrasted with the urbanity of epigramatic poetry of the main towns. Simple musical instruments were fashioned from whatever materials were available, and used as an accompaniment to the poetry.

The music is rich in emotion and spiritual feeling. Islam formed the centre of social life and gave rise to its own complex systems of chanting that dominated the towns and villages.

While the old dances and songs are now reserved for special occasions, the Arab's love of music and poetry is still alive. Many hotels organize Arabic evenings that run all night — where the songs of the great Arabic singers, Feiruz, Umm Kalthum, Sami al-Wafi and others, are performed and the audience dance with hands held above the level of their shoulders.

The old musical instruments of hide and wood have been replaced by the latest in synthesizer technology; but the lyricism of

the music remains. Meanwhile, the nasal lilt of the call to prayer by the *mu'ezzin* is chanted from every mosque to this day, from dawn prayers to sunset.

Traditional Music

The old musical instruments were made of materials readily available in the desert and along the coast: animal hide, bone, various types of wood, often decorated with silver or copper. The sound is percussive rather than harmonic.

The *tambura* was a simple type of harp, made of wood and deer-skin; the circular sound-box was covered with hide, connected to the equivalent of the bow by two simple wooden spokes, with a cross bar at the top holding the strings taut.

Percussion instruments included the *jaser*, a goat-skin drum with a wooden frame, which was draped around the neck and hung at waist-level, allowing the player to sway his hips in time with the beat.

Many instruments used materials easily found along the beaches, or among the livestock tended in the desert. The *nisk*, for instance, comprises a sound-box made of coconut, decorated all over with shells and

Above: Clay pots for sale on the Hatta road copy shapes of minarets and wind towers.

beads; while the *sheklelah* was a simple kind of tambourine, made of cloth and the hooves of goats, and worn as a waist-cloth which rattled rhythmically as the wearer danced.

Various types of wind instrument were fashioned from local materials. These included a type of metal pipe with bands of copper wire around it, a bamboo pipe with holes along the pipe in double rows, and a rosewood pipe with silver thread wrapped around it.

Some instruments were more complex. The Arabs of the UAE had their own version of the bagpipes, but the body of it was made of goat-skin with a mouthpiece of bamboo, while the pipe, or *qirbah,* was fringed decoratively with tassles of goat-hair.

Among the stringed instruments, a simple wood violin was constructed from a single piece of wood, with hefty wooden pegs on the neck to tighten the strings.

Dance

The dances these simple instruments were used to accompany were also inspired by the local environment. These were sometimes martial, sometimes lyrical, but always the aim was to bind the ties of family and tribe that were the essence of the community.

A variety of dances served as a prelude to war, although the battles between the tribes and clans were often small-scale affairs, no more than a brief raid against a hostile clan in which a few goats were stolen.

Among these, *al ayaala* extolled the virtues of courage and bravery in battle, the dancers running with swords to the sound of a heavy drum-beat. Other war-dances originated among the Bedouin living in the desert interior: these included *al arzfah* and *al harbiyah.*

Not all dances were local in origin, reflecting the importance of trade in the Gulf region centuries before the formation of the modern UAE. The *lewa* dance, for instance, originated in Africa, whence it was carried by local traders who made the long journey through the Gulf of Oman, along the horn of Africa to Zanzibar, Lamu and other East African destinations in the same dhows that today ply the creeks of Dubai and

245

Sharjah. The dance has a fast tempo and uses large drums.

A number of folk dances were associated with the various special occasions that punctuated the monotony of life in the pre-industrial UAE. These might be performed at weddings, when the pearl-diving boats returned home or went to sea, and at religious festivals.

The maritime lifestyle is celebrated in the rich lyricism of *al nahma*, a sea-song, performed without any instruments. It was sung aboard the vessel to encourage pearl divers, and expressed the longing of the crew and divers for their families.

Pearl-diving, as has been remarked, was an extremely hard lifestyle, and many divers failed to make it home after the hard months aboard the vessel. As a result, those leaving on the trip must have felt a bit like soldiers heading off for war. Returning from these journeys was equally a time for celebration, and so for song and dance.

Along with the forces of nature that dominated everyday life, Islam was the binding force in the community's spiritual life, as indeed it still is. Every child would go to the mosque to pray, while the brighter and better educated would read, and then learn by rote, the words of the holy Qur'ân.

Allah's name was chanted every day from the mosques; the mellifluous tones of the call to prayer invariably reciting the words by which every Muslim professes his faith: *Ashadu an la-Illaah ila Allah was ina Muhammadan Rasuul Allah* —I bear witness that there are no gods but Allah, and that Muhammad is the Prophet of God.

A number of dances narrated key events associated with Muhammad's life. Among the most famous in the UAE is the *maalid*, a dance narrating the biography of the Prophet Muhammad, danced to a slow drum-beat. Special heritage events are now arranged for Tourists on a more regular basis than hitherto.

Arabian nights

Many of the dances are still performed for special occasions, notably on National Day — 2 December and the week after — when a series of events celebrating the heritage of the UAE are performed. Tour operators can provide information for visitors interested in these events.

Indeed, throughout the UAE song and dance are alive and well, although the musical fare is Middle Eastern rather than specifically Gulf Arab, often reflecting the famed singers of Egypt, Lebanon, Syria and Jordan.

Hotels and clubs in the UAE hold regular Arabic evenings which are extremely well attended. The locals like to eat and then let their hair down.

Arabic evenings are for night-owls, usually only fully under way well after midnight, and going on until dawn. Often there will be a belly-dance; a dance originating in Egypt, which spread through the Ottoman Empire centred on Constantinople, and is now a somewhat bizarre addition to the typically more austere night-life of the Gulf.

Among the many weekly events, Friday at the Aviation Club in Dubai is a good place to enjoy a typical Arabic night of exotic entertainment.

Right: Gulf visitor enjoys an impromptu dance with belly dancer, Dubai.

Tastes of the Emirates

The cuisine of the UAE reflects the cultural diversity of the country and the 'melting pot' it has become. The fact that the UAE has traditionally been a centre for trading has resulted in an enormous variety of tastes.

A great selection of imported, as well as local, produce makes for an excellent culinary experience. That said, although the UAE cuisine is dominated by traditional Arabic or Middle Eastern fare, the vast majority of 'local' restaurants tend to serve Lebanese food. It is quite hard, if not impossible, to find a restaurant serving an authentic United Arab Emirates meal.

The Bedouin way of eating was to gather in one tent and eat from a communal plate with the right hand. To a large extent this tradition remains. Even today, most food is shared in such a manner and most Arabs use their hands to eat with. This method of eating is tied to the teachings of the Prophet Muhammad who taught his people to wash their hands before and after meals.

In the days before the oil boom, the traditional cuisine of the UAE consisted largely of what was available locally: fish, lamb, dates and goat, accompanied by basmati rice usually originating in Pakistan, and the flat, unleavened Arabic or pitta bread, known locally as *khubz*.

The meat or fish would normally be cooked on a barbecue or grill and flavoured with such spices as cardamom, coriander and cumin as well as those entering the Gulf from the spice routes, such as cinnamon, nutmeg, ginger, chili, saffron and turmeric.

One distinctive flavour of the Gulf region's cuisine is that of the dried lime: grown in Oman or imported from south-east Asia and dried on the tree, this ingredient is common in the cooking of the region.

The diet has changed to some extent now that there is more variety and availablity of food, particularly vegetables and dairy produce. Breakfast — *fatoor* or *re u q* as it is known — normally consists of fruit juice, bread, eggs, honey and jams accompanied by tea or coffee.

Lunch — *ghu daa* — is the most important meal of the day, and will usually be chicken, fish or meat accompanied by rice as well as fresh herbs, followed by fruit and dates. Dinner – or *aa sha* – tends to be a lighter, simpler meal: bread and cheese or meat, soup or eggs with fruit and tea.

For feasts or special occasions, citizens enjoy what is called *ouzi,* or live cooking. It is so called because the meat served is very fresh — usually a baby lamb slaughtered in the morning and served for lunch — cooked whole usually by roasting on a spit or baked in the oven, placed on a sealed tray and steeped in water.

Whatever the method, the result is the same: tender meat which falls off the bone, stuffed with a combination of rice, spices, nuts and raisins. Another tradition for special meals or occasions is the *fou alla* — a tray filled with goodies, usually sweets and served after dinner with tea and coffee. Dinner is then concluded with the ritual of incense burning and the offer of perfume to all the women.

This ceremony entails the women passing a small box filled with perfume between themselves after they have sampled its wares. They will also sample the incense by wafting it around and then passing it to their neighbour. The ritual signifies the end of a meal.

No meal would be complete without the *qahwah,* or coffee, served in the traditional style coffee-pot known as *dallah*. This tradition remains and visitors to the UAE should bear in mind that to refuse a cup of coffee from a local host is considered quite rude. In fact it would be socially acceptable to share two or three small cups of coffee with the host. The local coffee is quite light and is flavoured with cardamom - making it almost sweet and very aromatic.

The traditional method of making coffee is to roast the beans in a frying pan over direct heat, then to pound them by hand with a mortar and pestle and boil them. Of course, today the beans are more often bought ready ground and roasted.

Either way, the beans are boiled with water and then poured over a mixture of saffron, cloves and cardamom and steeped — thus producing the distinctive flavour of the Gulf coffee. The local method of indicating that one has had enough coffee is to shake the cup a little from side to side. After a heavy meal, what better way of recovering than lounging around on a floor cushion, supping coffee and partaking of a communal hubble bubble pipe. It goes without saying that this activity, at least in public, is a male domain.

Though fast disappearing, there are still a few traditional coffee-shops in the UAE. Traditionally meeting places, men gathered there to drink coffee or herbal tea from small transparent cups. They would eat boiled hot *fool* or *bahilas* (chick peas) and play chess or discuss the latest fish catch or pearl dive while lounging on wooden benches or carpets on the floors with cushions or bolsters. Nowadays, business and politics are dicussed but the old world atmosphere remains.

One such coffee-shop is in the Murshid Bazaar area on the road parallel to the creek on the Deira side in Dubai; another is in the Al Arsa souq in Sharjah. In Ras al-Khaimah there is a coffee-shop by the harbour side.

Many have now been replaced by Western style coffee-shops which are located in the modern, air-conditioned shopping malls of Dubai, Sharjah and Abu Dhabi. These attract a more international crowd, and even local women meet friends or rest there after shopping.

Arabic cuisine

The traditional method of eating in the Middle East is in evidence in the UAE, where most large hotels and some smaller restaurants provide an evening or a lunchtime buffet. Typically, this consists of several tables heaped with all manner of delicious items, always with a number of Middle Eastern specials. Some hotels have restaurants largely devoted to Egyptian, Lebanese and Iranian cuisine.

Outside the hotels, many citizens favour the authentic Middle East restaurants that serve dishes from the Lebanon. Until the Civil War in 1967, the Lebanon was the Arab culinary capital and the thousands of people who fled the country during the troubles have continued that tradition where they subsequently settled. In the UAE Lebanese restaurants often have a grotto in the back with running water and greenery.

Lebanese food is based on a selection of *mezze*, small dishes and dips — up to 25-30 available in a buffet-style restaurant, and usually five to six as the hors-d'œuvre at a sit-down meal — normally followed by a main course and dessert. In practice, you would need an enormous appetite and it is perfectly acceptable to just order *mezze*.

The dhow restaurants in Abu Dhabi, Dubai and Sharjah offer good sit-down meals during the weekend, and extremely well-furnished buffets on Fridays. These restaurants are named *al boom*, after the Arabic word for dhow.

Probably the most popular *mezze* dish is *houmos*, a paste made of finely mashed chick-peas combined with *tahini*, olive oil and lemon juice, on the top of which a few drops of olive oil is added. *Houmos* is sometimes served with minced lamb on top of the chick-pea paste.

Another popular *mezze* dish is *tabbouleh*, a herb salad made from bulgar wheat, or *burghul*, mixed with chopped onions, parsley, mint and tomato. *Fatoush* is a salad made with vegetables including fresh tomatoes, cucumber and lettuce. The distinctive feature is the pieces of toasted pitta bread mixed in the salad.

Moutabel, similar to *houmos*, is served cold on a shallow dish, but is made from egg-plant. Specially for garlic lovers, *tahini* is made from sesame, mixed with garlic and lemon and blended to form a smooth white paste. *Muhamara* is a piquant red paste topped with pine nuts.

Top right: Dates for sale in Souq al-Arsah, Sharjah. Bottom right: Sumptuous hotel buffet.

Top: There is a wide variety of fresh fruit and vegetables available in the souqs.
Above: A typical meal served in the emirates.

All these dishes are eaten with *khubz*, the flat Arabic bread — served either cold or warm — which accompanies every meal. A variant is *mafroodah*, a whiter bread without a pocket. The bread is held with the right hand and used as a scoop for the *mezze*. Almost always, a large basket of fresh vegetables such as carrot, spring onion, celery and lettuce will be served before the *mezze*, and you can use the various vegetables as scoops for the various sauces and dips, just like when eating crudités in the West.

The main courses often consist of a variety of different sorts of kebabs, typically made from lamb or chicken. In the UAE fish dishes are popular: locally caught fish include hammour, a variety of grouper, Sultan Ibrahim and safi.

Delicious prawns and other sea-food are also available. These are always freshly grilled, and many of the buffet-style Lebanese restaurants barbecue them to taste.

International

In Dubai and Abu Dhabi the proliferation of international hotels provides a complete spectrum of international cuisines. It is perfectly possible to have an aperitif in a French restaurant, a main course in a German beer *keller* and a dessert in an Italian *trattoria* — without even having to move out of the air-conditioned luxury hotel where all the restaurants are located.

European or North American tourists can travel to the UAE without risk of becoming homesick for their own food. There is also a wide variety of Western fast foods available — hamburgers, pizzas, fish and chips are in plentiful supply from all the fast food chains which will be all too familiar to the Western traveller. However, this tends not to be the case in the smaller emirates such as Ras al-Khaimah, Fujairah, Ajman and Umm al-Quwain.

The UAE is also a good place to sample authentic Indian, Pakistani, Thai and Filipino cuisine — not surprising given the make-up of the population. The visitor will find that cheap and delicious cuisine from the Indian subcontinent, and to a lesser extent southeast Asia, is widely available and many restaurants will deliver food at home at no extra charge. Equally, the small Arabic restaurants specialising in *shwarma* (chicken kebab) or *falafal* (chick-pea patties served with pitta bread) provide a tasty cheap meal.

For those who wish to visit the local markets, they will find an abundance of excellent fresh fish from the waters of the Gulf: giant prawns, barracuda, king fish and the local hammour to name but a few. In addition, excellent fruit and vegetables can be bought much cheaper and fresher there than in the modern supermarkets. The latter are well-stocked with items which would satisfy any palate and, once again, the visitor need not worry about missing food from their homeland.

Standards of hygiene are high and even the smallest restaurants are clean and well-organized. It is still possible, however, to get stomach problems which often hit travellers just through consumption of 'foreign' bacteria and microbes.

In order to avoid these kinds of problems it is best to avoid salads and uncooked vegetables and any food which has been sitting around for a while, especially meat. Also, use bottled water though many citizens drink tap water without ill effects.

Ramadan

Food is very much bound up with religion and during the holy month of Ramadan visitors should bear in mind that this is when Muslims fast from sunrise to sunset. Ramadan falls in the ninth month of the Islamic calendar — currently around January or February but the time is dependent on the moon.

During Ramadan the fast or *al summ* means that Muslims must abstain from eating, drinking, smoking and from marital relations during daylight hours. While it is of course still possible for non-Muslims to take food during this period, the visitor should bear in mind that it is a criminal offence to do so publicly.

The fact that the UAE is a Muslim country means that pork and, of course, alcohol will not be served in local restaurants. In the big hotels, however, there is no problem obtaining either item. Equally, in most large supermarkets there is a special section for pork and pork products.

Sports and Leisure

Whatever your sporting preference, you will probably find that the UAE is well equipped to cater for it particularly the larger centres of Dubai, Abu Dhabi and Sharjah. The smaller emirates tend to have fewer sophisticated sporting facilities.

Not only is there a wide variety of sport available to the Tourist in Dubai, but also the climate is ideal for most outdoor activities. Although of course in the heat of the summer it will probably be too hot to do much requiring physical exertion, even after the sun has gone down.

Water sports
The warm waters of the Gulf provide an ideal environment for a variety of water sports: sailing, windsurfing and surfing. There are a variety of marinas and sailing clubs as well as the hotels where boats and boards can be hired.

The minimal tides and currents of the Gulf make it ideal for sailing and windsurfing and visitors can hire fixed keel, dinghy or board sailing boats.

For those who prefer a faster pace, there are jet skis and water-skis available for hire through most of the larger hotels and through specialised clubs.

Marine life is rich in the Gulf and in the Indian Ocean on the east coast of the UAE at Fujairah, thus both diving and fishing are fruitful activities. Keen fishermen can hire fully equipped boats deep-sea fishing. Even fishing off the shore can bring in reasonable-sized fish.

Scuba-diving
Scuba-diving courses are run in many centres and diving equipment can be hired for those who are PADI qualified. There are numerous diving schools, with two or three located on the east coast of Fujairah, and several in Dubai, Abu Dhabi and Sharjah (see Listings).

These centres have Professional Association of Diving (PADI) or BSAC (British Sub Aqua Club) approved instructors offering the full range of PADI courses from the basic to the advanced open water course and also speciality courses.

Equipment hire is also available for those who are already PADI qualified: tanks, wetsuits and regulators as well as dive packages including boat hire. It is even possible to charter a traditional dhow for a day trips.

A proper dive course is essential because scuba-diving can be dangerous if you do not know what you are doing. The instructor will explain the various techniques by which a diver can communicate with his fellow-divers underwater, through a simple system of hand signals. These can be used to warn co-divers of unexpected danger.

The average depth for diving is 6-25 metres (20-80 feet) and the visibility ranges between 5-20 metres (16-65 feet). The water temperature varies from around 18°C (64°F) in the winter months to around 32°C (90°F) in the summer so wetsuits are really only necessary during the September to May period.

Dive sites off the east coast tend to be close to the shore. They include Marine Rock, a small underwater mountain surrounded by shoaling fish including tuna, sergeant major, moray eels, black lion fish, cuttlefish, scorpion fish and catfish. Shark Island is a popular dive site; this rock provides a sheltered site 15 metres (50 feet) down — home to lobsters and batfish amongst others.

Soft corals can be found at sites known as coral gardens and anemone gardens. They are slightly deeper at 25 metres (80 feet) for the former and 16-18 metres (50-60 feet) for the latter where there are slipper lobsters, rays, barracuda, kingfish and tuna,

Left: Marine magic of coral gardens and colourful fish. Overleaf: Scuba-divers set off for some underwater exploration with Snoopy Island, Fujairah, in the background.

as well as octopus, cuttlefish and shoaling fusiliers, rays and jacks.

There is also an underwater cave, known as the 'hole in the wall', which has a resident turtle and, north of Khorfakkan, there is a site made up of a number of cars which sank in 1985. Hard corals can be found at a site known as 'the three rocks' while Dibba Rock offers coral of both the hard and soft variety.

Golfing

The golf courses of the Middle East are usually of sand and the golfer carries a piece of artificial grass mat which is placed under the ball when he is 'on' the fairway, but not when he is 'off' the fairway. Fairway and rough look pretty much the same, and markers designate whether you are on or off the fairway.

The 'green' comprises a raised soft-sand platform along which the golfer drags a track with a heavy iron roller, then takes out an internal cup in the hole to empty out the sand before putting.

The exception to this rule is the UAE, which has beautifully green courses watered the year round by desalinated water, and underpinned by a huge net-like structure that supports the contours of the courses. The standard meets the needs even of professional golfers: it is said the best facilities for golf between Singapore and Egypt exist in the UAE. This is quite an achievement given the desert conditions.

The Emirates Golf Club, on the outskirts of Dubai, opened in 1988, has an 18-hole golf course planned by an American course designer. It is quite remarkable for the lush colour of its lawns and is said to be both challenging for the professional as well as playable by the amateur.

The Dubai Creek and Yacht Club as well as the Country Club and the Dubai Golf and Racing Club, all located in Dubai, provide good facilities for golf. There is also a nine-hole golf course at the Hatta Fort Hotel in the mountains of the Dubai Emirate.

Elsewhere, there is the Sharjah Wanderers Golf Club, the Hilton in Al Ain has a nine-hole golf course, as does the Dhafra Beach Hotel at Ruwais as well as the Abu Dhabi Golf Club. Most clubs have provisions for non-members to use their facilities, albeit sometimes during non-peak times.

Riding

Horse riding is available throughout the UAE at the Dubai Equestrian Centre, the Jebel Ali Equestrian Club, the Sharjah Equestrian Centre, the Abu Dhabi Equestrian Club and the Umm al-Quwain Marine Club and Riding Centre. These organizations offer both riding lessons as well as horse riding. Camel rides are available through tour operators who organize desert safaris which often encompass a taste of Arabia on camel-back.

Racquet sports

Tennis is very popular, and many of the main hotels in Abu Dhabi, Dubai and Sharjah have tennis courts available free to hotel guests. These can often also be used by outside visitors on payment of a fee. Squash and badminton facilities are less common, although a number of venues are available for these sports in Dubai (see Listings).

Skating and sand-skiing

Despite the desert conditions it is possible to go ice-skating in Dubai at Al Nasr Leisureland and at the Hyatt Regency Galleria. There is also a rink in Al Ain as well as Abu Dhabi. The latter, located off the Airport Road near the Zayed Sports City, is an Olympic size rink and offers ice-skating lessons as well as skate hire.

Strange as it might seem, ice-hockey is becoming increasingly popular with games taking place on Sunday evenings at Al Nasr Leisureland.

As one might expect, the mountains are not cold enough to generate snow for skiing purposes. You can, however, go sand-

Right: Top-class tennis facilities at the Hyatt Regency Hotel, Dubai.
Following pages: The Emirates Golf Club attracts overseas competitors for the Desert Classic.

skiing and in fact tour operators organize this.

Go-karting

The UAE has the Middle East's first fully equipped indoor go-kart facility which is designed for Formula One kart racing and is located on the Sheikh Zayed Road in the emirate of Dubai. The facility also has an outdoor track. Again, it is not necessary to be a member in order to spectate at the track and visitors wishing to try their hand at go-karting can do so, on race days when the club rents out one or two of its own karts. The Dubai Kart Club at Jebel Ali, founded 20 years ago, has race days on alternate Fridays from April to September.

Shooting and archery

Shooting and archery are both sports which are well catered for at the Jebel Ali Shooting Club, about 35 minutes' drive from Dubai City Centre, the Hatta Fort Hotel and Ras al-Khaimah.

Spectator sports

The UAE is quite well served for spectator sports and in fact some tour operators can arrange tours around the various events which go on regularly throughout the year. Dubai is host to several sports tournaments which attract big players, the most famous of these being the Dubai Desert Classic Golf Tournament, held at the Emirates Golf Club, the Dubai Tennis Open and the Dubai World Cup, held at Nadd al-Sheba.

It also hosts numerous smaller events and tournaments, car-racing and rallying, bowling championships, football and rugby matches (in particular the rugby sevens held in November).

The UAE is particularly well-known for its equestrian events and the Dubai World Cup, held usually in March, is a major event in the racing calendar.

The Emirates Equestrian Federation was set up in 1993 and has actively promoted horse-racing. There are race tracks in Dubai, in Abu Dhabi, in Jebel Ali and in Sharjah, as well as Sweihan, and the UAE is also very involved in horse-breeding. The UAE is also host to several watersport championships, including power-boat racing, water-skiing and sailing.

Sharjah is host to international cricket tournaments, the biggest of which is the World Masters Cricket Club.

There is a UAE football team, which qualified for the 1990 World Cup finals, and the country hosted the Gulf Cup Football Tournament in 1994 at the Zayed Sports City in Abu Dhabi. This stadium is the largest in the Arab world.

Camel-racing is a sport which is, of course, particular to the area and all the emirates have their own track. Regular race meetings are held on Thursday evenings and Fridays through the winter months, as well as special events on public holidays — National Day and Eid.

Leisure activities

The UAE is a great place for leisure activities: all the emirates have a coastline and it is certainly a place where beach activities abound. There are hotels with beach fronts, beach parks and simply beaches, depending on your preference and your budget.

The hotels which have beach locations tend to charge non-guests a fee to use their facilities. The amount varies, and tends to increase on Fridays, but is anywhere between AED 25-75. It usually entitles the guest to use of the hotel swimming pool, the hire of a towel and changing facilities and, where there is one, the use of the hotel beach-front restaurant.

It is always worth asking to see the facilities before agreeing to pay the fee as some hotels offer a better deal than others. The beach parks also charge a fee but are less expensive than the hotels — usually under AED 5.

Jumeirah Beach Park in Dubai is open on Saturdays to women and children only. Abu Dhabi has a beach park located a few minutes' drive out of the city which is called the Umm al-Nar Beach Park. It also

Left: Aerial view of Emirates Golf Course, both challenging for the professional and playable by the amateur.

Above: Presentation to a winning owner. Horse racing is highly popular in the emirates.

has its own women's beach. The latter is located near to the Presidential Palace and ensures absolute privacy by means of a high wall. Otherwise, the beach is accessible almost anywhere in the UAE at no cost.

In some areas, for example at the north end of Sharjah, in Ajman and in Fujairah, particularly around Khor Fakkan, the public beaches have been equipped with palm trees and sometimes umbrellas. Some form of shade is essential given the strength of the sun in this region.

It is worth noting that sensitivity to local customs should be observed while at the public beaches or parks and therefore women should not dress provocatively in scanty clothing.

Though swimming costumes for Western women are acceptable, topless bathing certainly is not and if you really do not want to offend, then the less revealed the better. Once inside the confines of an international hotel, however, more or less anything goes in terms of swimsuit design although, even there, topless sunbathing is not acceptable.

For those who prefer to swim in a

pool rather than in the sea, the UAE is extremely well equipped with swimming pools. Again, they are available in the larger hotels as well as in specialist clubs.

Most facilities are open to non-members for a small fee. The larger hotels also tend to be equipped with gyms, with saunas and jacuzzis, most of which can be used by non-residents on a daily basis.

The UAE also has a number of excellent parks which are usually very well kept and green, with gardens and trees being maintained even in the peak of the summer months. The parks are good places for families as many have children's play areas, barbecue pits and sports facilities including swimming pools and, if located on beaches, sheltered swimming areas patrolled by lifeguards.

Some parks charge a small amount as an entrance fee and most are open between 0800 and 2200 daily with very often one day a week reserved for women and children only.

In Dubai the Creekside Park is located between the Al Maktoum and the Al

Above: The clear, blue, warm waters of the Gulf are ideal for water-skiing.

Garhould bridges and has facilities for barbecues and an amphitheatre for live music which takes place usually on Friday evenings. It also has a variety of children's play areas and botanical gardens as well as a desert garden complete with its own *falaj* or traditional irrigation system.

Other parks in Dubai include Safa Park, which is located between the second interchange on Sheikh Zayed Road and Al Wasl Road, and is one of the oldest parks in the UAE which has children's play areas, rides such as a Ferris wheel, bumper cars as well as barbecue and sports facilities. Safa Park is also known as a good place for bird-watching.

Dubai also has a number of other parks: Al Khazzan Park, Al Hamriya Park, Al Mamzar Park, Al Wasl Park, the Jumeirah Beach Park, Mushrif Park and Rashidya Park.

All the emirates have at least one park but the most famous are the Al Jazira Fun Park at Sharjah, which has a Ferris wheel and other rides, the Hili Fun City at Al Ain, which has a good selection of rides, some quite scary, while at Abu Dhabi there is the Khalidia Park, which was the first to open in the emirates, and the Mushref Park. Both the latter have children's play areas.

Due to open towards the end of 1996, Dreamland Water Park, in the emirate of Umm al-Quwain, is said to be the biggest water park in the world. The park will have over 20 water slides, a 70 metre pool, children's pools as well as restaurants and accommodation.

The Wonderland Amusement Park, another recent addition in the emirate of Dubai, located near to the Al Garhoud Road, will have a variety of attractions including water rides, a roller coaster and a 'water cinema'.

Traditional Sports

Falconry

Falconry was known as the sport of kings in the West. In the UAE, and indeed across the Arabian Gulf, it is the sport of princes. Falcons and other raptors have been used for centuries to hunt doves, sandgrouse and the favourite prey, the houbara bustard. Among the favourite birds of prey were the peregrine falcon and the saqer falcon.

Traditional equipment for falconry included the leather glove used for carrying the falcon, known as a *mangalah*. This was worn by the falconer to protect his arms from the sharp talons of the bird.

Attached to the falcon's leg was a *subuq*, a tether made usually of leather, which in turn was connected by the leash or *mursil* to a *midwar*, or swivel.

When resting, the falcon would perch on a *wakir*, an often highly ornate wooden pole, with a metal spike at the bottom that was used to fix the perch in the sand. The falcon's head, when it is not actually hunting, is covered with a leather hood called the *burqa*.

The rulers and their retinue would normally hunt in the desert, and indeed still do, although the journey is usually made now in 4WD vehicles rather than on camel-back.

Hunting expeditions into the desert are elaborate affairs, often involving scores of people. Once there, the tracks of the prey must first be identified, and then a campsite chosen from which the hunt may be conducted.

Camel-racing

Camel-racing is another traditional pursuit, although in Fujairah, where camels are less common, the favoured sport is bull-fighting. All the other emirates have their own camel-racing tracks, some circular, while the one at Digdaga is a 1.5 kilometre (one mile) straight.

Rather like the horse in Europe, in the Arabian Peninsula the camel is bred for its racing ability. To find a good racing camel is as important as its training for the race, which is accompanied by 4WD vehicles

rushing along beside the beasts to encourage them to victory.

The camels are often jockeyed by children, because of their lighter weight.

Dhow-racing

Dhow-racing is another traditional sport which has recently undergone a revival, notably in Dubai and Abu Dhabi. Huge cash prizes are on offer in this sport, which takes a similar form to yacht-racing in the West.

Above: Falconer's paraphernalia on display at Al Ain Museum.

Right: Falconry has long been a favourite pastime of the more affluent Arabs.

Shopping

The UAE, in particular Dubai, prides itself on its shopping possibilities and in fact hosted a Shopping Festival in 1996 to celebrate its reputation as the shopping centre of the Middle East.

This was extremely successful and looks set to become an annual event.

While it is certainly true that it is possible to buy almost anything in the emirates, it is also worth bearing in mind that it is not really a place for local handicrafts as most craft items sold in the UAE are imported rather than produced locally.

What Dubai and the other main cities of the UAE do offer is reasonably priced ethnic goods from nearby Middle Eastern and South Asian countries, along with tremendous variety of modern articles, from the latest in designer clothing to top of the range high-tech items. Dubai, Sharjah and Abu Dhabi are also good places to buy Oriental rugs, a subject covered in more detail later in this chapter.

Dubai is without doubt the best place to concentrate on if you are interested in shopping for imported goods while Sharjah can offer some interesting possibilities and tends to be somewhat less expensive than Dubai or Abu Dhabi.

The smaller emirates such as Ras al-Khaimah, Fujairah, Umm al-Quwain and Ajman have a much more limited selection of items than the larger centres of Dubai, Abu Dhabi and Sharjah.

There are some general rules of thumb which apply to all visitors to the UAE who are interested in shopping in the region. This is an area where bargaining or haggling is the normal way of doing business. That means, unless you are in one of the larger European chain stores, it always pays to try and reduce the price of the item you are buying.

This is particularly the case if you are shopping in the smaller shops or souqs.

Always ask if the price is the 'best price'. If you are buying several items at the same time, always ask for a 'bulk discount'. Many local shopkeepers are receptive to this manner of shopping, so do not be embarrassed to try.

It is worth noting that many of the shops and malls in the UAE are open from 0800 to 1300 and then from 1600 to 2000, so shopping in the afternoon can sometimes be a problem. This is due to the climatic conditions. The City Centre and the Wafi shopping mall in Dubai are both open all day from 1000 to 2200 and in the afternoons on Fridays, which is the Muslim equivalent of the Sabbath and therefore a day when many shops close.

Dubai and Abu Dhabi have been very active in marketing their respective duty-free shops and, indeed, have been successful in building their reputation worldwide.

It is possible to buy electrical goods and gold at a slightly cheaper rate in the duty-free shops than in the souqs and malls of the UAE.

However, the range of goods available is quite limited and really it is hard to see why these duty-free shops are any more impressive than other such large outlets throughout the world.

Dubai

There are vast numbers of glitzy, modern shopping centres in Dubai where it is possible to find the larger European chains, department stores, designer fashion houses, electrical goods, as well as smaller gift shops, music shops, book shops and the like.

The first shopping centre to be built in Dubai was the Al Ghurair Centre, just off the Al Rigga Road in Deira, and the most recent addition to the ranks is the City Centre, also on Deira side between the Al Maktoum and the Al Garhoud bridges.

Opposite: The colourful Burjuman shopping mall, Dubai.

Above and following pages: Attractive displays in Wafi shopping mall, Dubai.

There are numerous other centres, the larger and more well equipped of these being the Bur Jurman Centre at Bur Dubai on the intersection of the Trade Centre Road and Khalid bin al-Waleed Road and the Wafi Shopping Mall on the Dubai side of the Al Garhoud Bridge. All the shopping malls have cafes or restaurants where one can stop for a break during a spot of heavy shopping.

Karama and Satwa are both areas with a concentration of Indian stores: Karama has its own market area where fish, meat, fruit and vegetables can be bought. It also has many small shops selling household items, including larger items such as furniture and smaller items such as electrical goods.

This is a place where residents can purchase 'designer' furniture: this means the local Indian and Pakistani carpenters will create copies of Habitat items at a fraction of the price. The quality may not be paramount but the price is always competitive.

The boutiques of Karama used to be renowned for copy Rolexes, copy Chanel T-shirts, and other clothes which are im-

ported from the Indian sub-continent. The copies can still be found, but are now sold under the counter because the government has clamped down on black market trade. The Karama area sprawls across a couple of kilometres (more than a mile) to the west of the Trade Centre Road on the Dubai side.

Karama has a few tailors' shops, but the main concentration is in Satwa and in Cosmos Lane in Bur Dubai. Satwa has a main street known as Al Diyafa Street, which is full of fast food outlets, small restaurants and cafes, video shops, as well as a couple of shops selling 'local' items, souvenirs of the region: coffee-pots, carpets and other 'antiques'.

Satwa and Bur Dubai are an excellent place to have clothes made up: almost anything can be copied and there are many materials available: silks, cotton, linen and synthetic fibres. Once again, the quality of the finished items is not always to be relied upon though many of the tailors do produce excellent work very quickly and can manufacture anything from ball gowns to baby clothes at a fraction of the price one would pay in a designer clothes store.

Finally, the traditional markets or souqs of Dubai still exist though they are fast disappearing. Perhaps the more interesting of these is the old spice souq on the Deira side of the creek as well as the famous gold souq - both old and new.

The former is probably the nearest you'll get in Dubai to a stepping-back into the history of the place. The small alleys which are full of merchants selling anything from cloves to saffron, to cinnamon are not too far removed from what one sees in the Dubai museum where there is a replica of the old souq. Meanwhile, the gold souq, for which Dubai is renowned, covers quite a large area of the Deira shopping region.

You can wander endlessly through rows of shops all selling seemingly the same glittering items. Much of the jewellery on offer is for the Indian market for the bridal wardrobe and is therefore very ornate and is also sold mostly in the 18, 21 and 22 carat varieties.

Prices are said to be competitive and good value and the merchandise of reliable quality. The old spice souq is located on the Deira side of the creek parallel to Al Ras Street and both the new and old gold souqs are located in the same area on either side of Sikkat al-Khail Street.

Electronic equipment and electrical items in Dubai, and in the UAE generally, are billed as being competitively priced on an international level. The UAE claims to have bargains on offer because of the fact that it has an open port with consequently low import duties.

While this may be true, the advice to any tourist planning a shopping spree in Dubai for electronic items is to first of all check the prices in your own locality and to do some thorough research on what kind of item you are looking for.

Make sure that the item you buy is adaptable to the electrical voltage where you live and also look for an international guarantee. Electrical items are available in all the shopping malls as well as in the electrical souq which is located on the Dubai and the Deira side of the creek.

Antique items are available in Dubai on a fairly limited basis: the Profile Gallery in the Markaz Al-Jumeirah shopping malls sells quality restored Arabic antique items such as local coffee-pots, Omani chests and also wooden items from India. They are cleaned up here but more expensive than those which can be bought in Sharjah in a more original state.

Having said that, many of the 'antiques' in the Sharjah souq are in fact replicas made in India. It should be noted that the most common wooden furniture item in the Gulf in the pre-oil period was the chest. Therefore most other items one sees such as tables, chairs and cupboards do not originate in this region. They may still be appealing in their own right, as many of these items are unique in design and would add an unusual touch to the home, but they are not likely to be antiques from the UAE or even the Gulf region. The Majlis Gallery in the Bastakia area in Dubai, housed in an old merchant dwelling, sells contemporary local art and other local handicrafts.

The UAE is not a good place to buy books and though most Dubai shopping malls have book shops these tend to have quite a limited range of material; very often a shop calling itself a 'book shop' is in fact a stationery shop. That said, one can usually find a good selection of books on the local region in most of the book shops in Dubai, and even Spinneys Supermarket has a book section containing a comprehensive range of books written about the UAE or indeed the Gulf region. The best selection of books can be found at Magrudy book shop in the Magrudy shopping mall on Beach Road. (See listings).

The main supermarkets in Dubai are Choitrams, Spinneys and Lals but there are numerous other well-stocked stores selling food, including the giant French hypermarket in the City Centre where shopping assistants use roller skates to cover the vast distances between aisles! Supermarkets are located in many of the shopping malls as well as near to the main residential areas: Jumeirah, Bur Dubai and Deira.

Abu Dhabi

Like Dubai, Abu Dhabi has numerous state-of-the-art shopping facilities. Its most recent shopping mall is the Central Souq, located on East Road near the Central Post Office which houses about 400 shops, a post office and a bank. The other larger malls include the Zakher Shopping Centre on Baniyas Street near to the Zakher Hotel, and the Rotana Mall on Khalidia Street near to the Prisunic Shopping Mall.

Abu Dhabi also has its share of tailors' shops where items can be repaired or copied and these can be found on Khalidia Street, Electra Road, Al Nasr Street, Salem Street and Hamdan Street. The latter is also an area where cheap clothes imported from the Indian subcontinent can be purchased.

The Abu Dhabi Cooperative Society has several branches in the city and is a competitively priced supermarket. Otherwise the well-known local chains such as Choitrams and Spinneys are reliable for their selection of food and household items.

Abu Dhabi also has a number of antique and carpet dealers.

Sharjah

The main souq in Sharjah, the Souq al-Markazi, is well known locally as the place to buy the most competitively priced carpets and rugs which originate in Iran, India or in Pakistan. For tips on how to buy these, see the section on carpets.

The Souq al-Markazi is something of a local landmark: an unmistakable building which looks more like a palace than a shopping centre. It is situated just after the intersection with Al Zahra Road near to the creek.

There is another large souq on the creek front called the Souq al-Mujjarah which is housed in a gleaming gold building but it sells a fairly simple range of clothes and household items. It looks promising from the outside but it seems rather less exciting once one is inside.

The old souq in Sharjah is really worth a trip both for the opportunities it offers of snapping up bargain ethnic objects from India and locally produced souvenirs as well as for its atmosphere.

The old souq has been in its current location for decades though it was closed in the 1970s and re-opened again in the 1990s. It is situated off the Sharjah Corniche near Burj Avenue, behind Bank Street. It is one place in the UAE which offers quite an authentic experience and remains pretty much as it has always been.

It houses the Sharjah Heritage Museum and is a covered market area with narrow alleyways leading to small shops containing treasure troves of everything from locally grown delicious dates to pearls, perfume and replica wooden dhows. There is also a traditional coffee-shop where one can sit and rest one's weary limbs after a bout of shopping.

Next to the old souq, on the left hand as one faces in the direction of the Intercontinental Hotel, parallel to the Corniche, is an old souq of a different variety: a street which is full on both sides of wonderful and unexpected Indian artifacts – anything from candle sticks to coffee-pots and larger items, including furniture.

Outside the main cities

Shopping outside the larger centres of Dubai, Abu Dhabi and Sharjah is not a particularly exciting experience. In the Northern Emirates and Fujairah, there are hundreds of small shops selling life's necessities but nothing that is particularly interesting or spectacular, or even any better value than in the larger emirates.

One exception to this is the Oasis Gallery in Al Ain which is a recently opened antique shop located at the Al Ain Trading Centre on the Hilton Road near the coffeepot roundabout.

Also, the open air souq, selling pots from Pakistan and plants, fruit and vegetables, is quite a good place to stop on the way to Fujairah. It is situated on the road

Left: Dancer provides entertainment in a Dubai shopping mall.
Previous pages: The gold souq, Dubai.

to Fujairah from Dhaid 36 kilometres (22 miles) from Fujairah and six kilometres (three-and-a-half miles) from Masafi in a valley with high mountains either side.

Buying Oriental carpets in the UAE

If you bring back one thing from the UAE as a souvenir, it is likely to be an Oriental carpet. These represent excellent value. The emirates' role as a trading centre means that carpets from all over the Middle East and Central Asia are available at relatively cheap prices in all the emirates.

Dubai and Sharjah offer the best choice and have a number of specialist shops for high-value items; Abu Dhabi arguably offers the best value for low-priced but well-made carpets; Fujairah has unexpected opportunites while the Northern Emirates of Ajman, Umm al-Quwain and Ras al-Khaimah have less wide-ranging but still good value items, although these are most often modern imported carpets from Pakistan.

Caveat emptor. Oriental carpets are big business and you are very unlikely to find a rare rug at a give-away price. In the UAE, the merchants trading in the rugs are most likely Indians, Pakistanis and Iranians, who know exactly what they are dealing with. They will be able to assess a fair value for most rugs, whether they are antiques, Persian or from one of the Central Asian republics, Arab, Turkish, or more modern fare from the many prime exporting countries, which include India, Iran and Pakistan.

The point about the UAE is that the government is keen to promote it as a tourist destination and rip-offs on the scale you see in Iran or Turkey are unlikely to occur, mainly because a vague sense of trading standards exists.

It's difficult to recommend anything in a field as complex and 'knotty' as that of bargaining for carpets; roughly, in the UAE, it would seem reasonable to assume a bargaining position of half whatever the quoted cost of the carpet might be, and to settle for something nearer to your position than the vendor's. But that is only a rough guide: and if buying a carpet, remember, it is very easy to lose all sense of proportion in your delight in the item on sale.

When you buy, first of all, work out your budget. Don't tell it aloud, but make sure you don't overspend by at least more than a sizeable fraction of what you have targeted. Having said that, don't feel obliged to say you're not going to spend more than X at the start; rug sellers have a great deal of patience and, if you close down the options too early, you will miss a good chance of seeing a lot of rugs that you won't see back in your home town.

Working out what makes an Oriental carpet worthwhile is a tricky business. Basically, the rarer it is, the more it will be worth; and the finer it is. Discerning both qualities is not easy and the vendors will invariably have the upper hand because they will have seen a hundred carpets for every one you have. It is also easy, in determining age and quality, and thus value, to completely lose sight of what, for most people, will be the only point of buying an Oriental rug: to find one that you like.

But a little knowledge is a dangerous thing and, in a funny way, too much talk of knotting and dyeing can sometimes raise the price, as the vendor will assume you feel you are on to a masterpiece, whereas if you started from a position of total ignorance, he might well sell you a non-antique, non-exceptional but still beautiful rug at a price that is quite in keeping with your budget.

Rug basics

A rug consists of two sets of threads crossing each other at right-angles: the warp threads, which act as a kind of frame, crossed horizontally by the weft threads, through which a series of knots may be tied to create the pile of the carpet. Depending on the tension of the knot, and the proximity of the warp threads, rugs of greater or lesser fineness are made.

The look of the rug also depends on the type of material used. Most rugs are made from cotton, silk or wool. The latter may be made from the hair of a number of different animals: camels, goats or sheep are the most commonly used.

The animal hair used will almost invariably be dyed: either synthetically or using natural dyes. Rug dealers tend to swear blind that their rugs are made from natural dyes, and to claim that these last much longer than synthetic dyes.

In practice, it is often quite difficult to tell a carpet made with a natural dye from one made with a synthetic dye. To say they look more 'natural' is tautologous, but they often lack the brilliance of synthetic dyes, and while blending harmoniously in the rug, they tend to be less uniform and to have organic shades.

Among natural dyes commonly used in making Oriental rugs, indigo is made from the indigo plant, *Indigofera tinctoria,* and makes a beautiful blue shade; madder comes from the plant *Rubia tinctorum,* and makes a strong red colour. Cochineal is derived from the plant *Dactylopius coccus* and makes a less warm red dye, and weld from the herb *Reseda luteola* makes a clear yellow dye.

A variety of other shades can be made by mixing dyes, or by adding small amounts of certain metals or metal salts, such as tin, iron salts, chrome, tannin and alum.

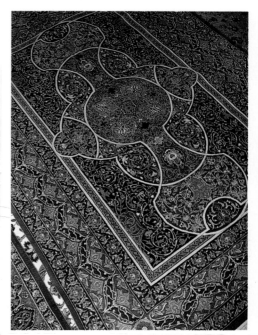

Above: Attractive carpets can be purchased, but none are actually made in the Emirates.

Rug types

The classification of the different types of rugs is complex: a variety of terms is used to define the purpose and size of the rug, the type of weave and pile, and the characteristic decoration of the rug. All these factors, as well as the age of the rug, will determine the value of the carpet.

To the lay person, the bewildering variety of the rugs available will be confusing enough: they will be presented with kilims, soumaks, prayer mats, medallion rugs; they will hear that these are Anatolian, Indian, Persian, Turkish, Baluchi, Afghani, Azeri, Kazakh, or tribal in origin; that they are silk, wool, or cotton; and be shown the clearly natural dyes and the huge amount of handiwork that has gone into the rugs.

The natural reaction is bewilderment, as the rug vendor brings out more and more fine samples from his collection. For those who get beyond this stage, making an intelligent decision from the many rugs available is not easy.

It is even harder not to make a decision given the zeal with which the vendor has

displayed his wares. Moreover, as a rule of thumb, the rug you choose will invariably be the 'jewel of the vendor's collection'. This may make you feel good, but equally is not likely to be sincere.

Brief descriptions of the terms used are given below. Reading around the subject is invaluable homework. But remember, the basic thing in assessing any rug, apart from whether you like it, is how it was made. A rug is first and foremost a manufactured item, whether it is done by hand or by machine.

Carpet shops often sell identical strips of rug that have been sown together into a larger piece, 'tribal' looking rugs made of patched together bits of dissimilar carpet, as well as smaller pieces cut down from larger items. All these will be reflected in what you see: for instance, hand-sewn joins along the weft imply the rug has been made up from smaller pieces.

The important thing is to ask the vendor about what you see, just as if it were a piece of jewellery or a coffee-pot, and to come to a decision as you would when

buying any other household item: compare prices, don't make a hasty decision; come back the next day if you're not sure.

Prayer rugs

Some rugs are defined by the purpose for which they are used. These include the well-known prayer rugs which are used by Muslims to afford them comfort when kneeling in prayer. These are often pile rugs, about 90 centimetres (three feet) by 60 centimetres (two feet) and with a square, angular or rounded arch at one end which is pointed in the direction of Mecca.

The arch represents the *mihrab*, the niche in the mosque wall that points towards the Muslim holy city. Prayer rugs are decorated with designs reflecting their purpose, including incense burners, lanterns and water jugs. The rugs are often made of wool, but fine silk rugs are also frequently found.

Bags and covers

Rugs are also used to make storage and other bags – which may be single or double pouched and often make good cushion or sofa coverings – and a variety of ornamental covers for animals, including horses and camels.

Pile carpets and flat-weave

Another way of classifying a rug is by the type of weave used. There are two basic types: pile rugs, in which knots are tied between the warp and weft threads to give the carpet a pile or depth; and flat-weave rugs, in which the warp and weft make up the carpet without knots.

Two basic types of knot are used to make a pile carpet: a symmetrical knot passing round two weft threads and then up through the middle of them; and an asymmetrical knot, wrapped around one weft thread and then looped behind the second.

The symmetrical knot is often called a Turkish or *ghiordes* knot; the asymmetrical knot is also called a Persian or *senneh* knot. These are the basic designs; regional varia-

Left: A tempting display in the carpet souq.

tions in which a single knot covers as many as four warp threads are sometimes found.

Bokharas

Pile carpets often have a central medallion, or series of medallions, either circular or polygonal, set in a rectangular border around which a larger main border is decorated with a variety of geometric or floral motifs. Bokharas are a popular type of pile carpet of Turkoman origin, usually consisting of a red background with a medallion motif that is repeated across the whole rug.

Kilims

Kilims are flat-woven rugs, that is they have no pile, and often come from Turkey, Persia or India, where they are called *dhurries*. The designs are usually fairly simple, and many are reasonably priced. Kilims can be woven in strips which are then sewn together, or made in a single piece; often the design is reversible.

Kilims use a type of weave called tapestry weave, in which the weft threads are woven in colour blocks rather than running across the whole width of the loom, with the blocks of colour totally concealing the warp threads. The 'grain' of the carpet thus goes horizontally across the warp threads but in distinct angular patches of colour. The warp threads are often undyed and you can only see them if you pull the weft threads to one side.

Soumaks

Soumaks are flat-woven rugs that use a different stitch to the kilim, and tend to have designs similar to those of some pile carpets. In a soumak, the weft is wrapped around the warp threads in loops, often taking in two parallel warp threads.

They are almost always woven in one piece and have a finer, more fiddly look to the typical kilim. Many soumaks come from the Caucasus area of Central Asia, in what used to be the Soviet Union, but they are also widely made in Iran.

Soumaks often use the technique of brocading, in which wefts or warps are added to a basic interwoven structure, and the separate threads hang off the back of the carpet, clearly visible when the rug is turned over.

Plain-weave rugs

Plain-weave rugs are produced by simply passing the weft under one warp and above the next alternately. This system creates a basic flat-weave rug of uniform thickness and design, often beautifully coloured but without great complexity. Brocade and embroidery can be used to add to the appeal of the basic plain-weave rug.

Motif

Rugs can also be designated according to the style of motif that decorates them. The range of designs is almost infinite, but certain motifs recur among rugs from different cultures and ethnic groups.

Many silk rugs from Iran and the Caucasus seen in Dubai have highly stylized bird, animal and human motifs, repeated hundreds of times across the carpet. These are usually very square-cut representations, partly because the Qur'ân proscribes showing living creatures in art.

A number of motifs recur in all types of carpet, often in many guises: for instance, the tree-of-life motif is rather like a candelabra, but can range from a simple stick-like design on tribal rugs, to highly ornate floral representations on more sophisticated rugs. *Boteh* motifs are similar to the paisley-design in neck-ties, while *herati* motifs consist of a richly four-leaf design in a diamond shape. Diamond motifs also recur in geometric patterns, as do stylized designs of amulets.

Country of origin

Finally, rugs can be classified according to their country or region of origin. The UAE has shores on both the Persian Gulf and the Indian Ocean, and the diverse ethnic mix of the expatriate population puts local dealers in contact with a huge area covering Iran, Pakistan, India, the Central Asian republics, Russia, as well as the other Gulf and Middle Eastern nations. Each country, and within that each region, has its distinctive weaving culture.

The term 'Persian carpet' usually reflects the rugs brought in by dhow from Iran, but the term masks a huge number of regional varieties, within Iran itself and also from nearby countries such as Azerbaijan. Within Iran, the ancient city of Isfahan has a strong carpet-making tradition dating back to Safavid times; Kerman, Kashan, and Tabriz have also been important centres, as has the province of Fars in the south of Iran on the Persian Gulf.

The Kurdish area of north-western Iran and north-east Iraq stretches into southern Turkey. Kurds are a separate ethnic group in these three countries, and weaving is done in the villages on simple looms.

The republics of Turkmenistan, Kazakhstan, Azerbaijan and Tajikistan, formerly part of the Soviet Union, also have their own carpet weaving traditions: Turkomen and Azeri carpets are among the most common to turn up in the souqs of Dubai and Sharjah.

Pakistan is another common source of reasonably priced carpets in the UAE: tribal rugs from the province of Baluchistan are among the most popular, but well-made modern rugs can be purchased for less than AED 100.

A number of good books are available at bookshops in the UAE giving advice on what to look for when buying an Oriental rug. The best single guide for would-be serious collectors is: *The Official Price Guide: Oriental Rugs,* by Joyce C. Ware (C) 1992, House of Collectibles, New York. There is also a wide range of larger beautifully illustrated coffee-table books.

Top: Crowds flock to the Dubai gold souq.
Above: You can buy just about anything in Dubai's Duty Free shops.

Off-Road Trips

Heading off the dual carriageways that lace the UAE opens a whole new world to the visitor: sand-dunes, wadis, pools and waterfalls; reclusive tribal villages and hidden archaeological sites.

The trouble is you need a 4-wheel-drive (4WD) to get to these off-road sites and, for the short-term visitor, hiring a 4WD, as these vehicles are called in 'expat speak' in the UAE, can be next to impossible. Although tour operators organize off-road treks, these tend to be somewhat expensive, and half of the fun, anyway, is surely to try your hand at guiding your own way through the desert sands.

The reason that few car-hire companies rent out 4WD is, quite simply, that it is not a sport for the uninitiated. Almost every instinct you have on getting into a 4WD will be wrong; from the natural urge to head off straightaway into the dunes, to the equally natural urge to brake sharply as you skim off too fast down a sand-dune. **Off-road driving is not easy; if you head off into the desert alone, it can be fatal.**

It's very easy in a country as well developed as the UAE to feel safe driving off the main road into the desert and to forget how easy it is to lose your direction, or to bog down in sand, and how rapidly the heat can affect the judgement of even the most rational individual.

Even heading for the comparatively well travelled tracks of the mountains and plains it is best to travel with others; not to do so in the desert would be sheer folly.

Picnics and barbecues

Having said that, people head off-road because it is fun, affording open-air picnics and barbecues in beautiful surroundings, as well as camping under skies that are among the clearest anywhere in the world.

The dos and don'ts in this section are not meant to daunt the reader but a bit of preparation and a little knowledge should mean that a fun trip does not turn into a nightmare. Preparing for a journey is almost as important as learning the driving

skills you will need on your trip. A plentiful supply of water is essential; in hot climates a person requires about two litres (four pints) of water a day, and this should be borne in mind when you set off.

A medical kit with cream to soothe sunburn is also a good idea. A large coolbox or two is also useful, along with containers of food. A supply of plastic bags is always useful for removing the left-over drinks cans to avoid spoiling the scenery, or for keeping sweaty clothes or wet swimming-trunks in after bathing in a wadi pool.

Remember that driving off-road is a bumpy experience; everything should be packed down as tightly as possible. For a barbecue, solid fire-lighters are useful; some of the smaller, simpler barbecues are excellent value, and pack down tightly.

Before you leave, give the car a check, particularly the oil level, but it's also worth making sure the washer bottles, brake fluid and battery levels are up to scratch. Driving accessories should include a tow-rope, a block of wood to rest the car-jack on if you get a flat tyre, a tyre-pressure gauge for when you deflate the tyres to handle desert sands, and a compressor or pump to reflate the tyres.

It is worth checking the weather forecast en route as rain can be a big problem in the desert. A shovel, planks of wood and thick rugs or rush-mats are useful to get you out if you get stuck. Finally, don't forget to check you have enough petrol.

In terms of driving skills, desert driving courses are available from the major tour groups and are a good starting point for those new to 4WD. But the first point is not to forget the normal skills of driving on any road; off-road driving is popular in the UAE, especially at the weekend, and other cars will be driving the same tracks or dunes that you are. It's all too easy to forget this when whizzing down a wadi track or up a sand-dune, but something could be coming your way. If driving in a convoy, make sure there is adequate stopping distance between yours and the car in front;

this should also avoid the risk of a shattered wind-screen from stones thrown up by the vehicle in front.

Give right of way, and don't assume the road is yours. Gears can be used for braking, just as they are in a two-wheel-drive vehicle. As with driving on main roads, caution is always the better part of valour; if the going looks like it will be rough, don't wait to find out if it is too rough; get out and check the terrain on foot, and then decide. Specific off-road driving skills are best learnt by experience, on a course, rather than by trial and error.

Instinct is often wrong: for instance, when driving through water, a natural tendency is to rush at it at full speed in the hope that momentum will carry you through. Sudden deceleration leads to an instinctive urge to take your foot off the accelerator; if you do that, water will get sucked in through the exhaust and you will stall. Instead, going in slowly, and steadily accelerating, is what you should be doing.

Similarly, if you are on soft sand, slow steady acceleration is needed, and if you brake, the vehicle will instantly bog down or, if heading down a slope, you risk toppling over. Some of the swankier UAE drivers have mastered the technique of driving on soft beaches even in a two-wheel-drive by using the same technique of slow steady acceleration. If you do need to stop on soft sand, make sure you are facing down the slope.

When you do get stuck, instinct again can make things worse rather than better. Revving the accelerator into the red does not help; it often just makes the vehicle bog down even more.

Instead, ask the passengers to get out, put the vehicle into 4WD and try to ease your way out; or if that doesn't work, rock the vehicle back and forth by alternately using the clutch and the accelerator. The bits of advice, however, should not be seen as a substitute for a proper off-road or desert-driving course. Good one- or two-day courses are available throughout the UAE from tour operators, and cost about the same as the chauffered trips available from many hotels. SNTTA Emirates Tours offer a number of courses, as well as dune and mountain safaris, and have offices in both Sharjah and the UAE.

Camping
Camping off-road is also popular in the UAE, particularly during the cooler season from November through to February. Visitors will find a number of shops in the main towns offer tents for hire, as well as foam mattresses and other accessories for more comfort.

There is little to say about camping in the UAE that makes it any different from camping anywhere else in the world.

The one crucial thing to bear in mind in the UAE is where you camp. From the 18th century onwards, explorers of the Arabian sands have cautioned against camping in or under wadis, because of the danger of flash floods. This is a danger that is unique to deserts and it is very important not to underestimate it.

Even if, when you set up camp, there is no sign of rain, do not be reassured; wadis can channel rain from miles beyond your horizon, and the speed with which rain falls really can lead to unexpected torrents of water rushing down from the mountains. Camp at the very top of wadis, or on flat land well away from the wadis.

Apart from that, hard or very soft sand can sometimes be a problem, but that would also be true in the Mediterranean in summer. Extra long tent pegs can be used in soft sand, and rocks can keep the tent strings taut if it is impossible to dig the tent pegs deep enough in rock.

Insects can also be a problem; scorpions and snakes are no myth in the desert but the usual range of medicines, such as antihistimines, and the usual precautions of zipping up the tent and taking care when rolling it up, should avoid problems.

The desert also becomes quite chilly at night, especially in higher altitudes and, while this is not a big problem in the UAE, night-time temperatures do sometimes get down to a few degrees above zero (32°F).

Overleaf: A desert safari is an experience worth sampling, but not without expert guidance.

UAE Stamps

Before the formation of the UAE in 1971, each of the then Trucial States issued its own stamps. Since federation, stamps have been issued by the central authorities.

Stamps

Dubai has the oldest post office which dates back to 1909, and was created because Dubai's and Karachi's merchant communities found it inconvenient to use the two post offices in Oman — one at Muscat, now the Omani capital, and one at Gwandar, now in southern Pakistan.

The Dubai post office was originally in the premises of the British political agent but moved to the British Bank of the Middle East in Bur Dubai in 1957. Additional post offices were set up in the early 1960s, after independence. In 1932, airmail services began using Imperial Airways planes which landed at Sharjah, because Dubai did not have its own airport.

The first stamps reflect the colonial situation: Dubai fell within the ambit of the British colonial administration in India, and stamps were denominated in Indian currency. For several months after the partition of India in 1947, stamps were over-

printed in Pakistan, because the Dubai post office remained under the control of Karachi. In 1948, the Dubai post office was transferred to the British Postal Agency, which used King George VI stamps. A special set of 11 stamps was issued by the British Postal Authority in 1961 under the name of the Trucial States.

In 1963, Dubai took control of the postal services and issued its own stamps, until 1972 when the newly created UAE federation issued their own stamps. Dubai's stamps typically carried the dhow and falcon motifs, while commemorative issues covered subjects of local interest, such as the first oil exports from Dubai in 1969, the 60th anniversary of the postal service in 1969, and the opening of the Dubai International Airport, plus broader subjects, such as education and human rights. Some issues celebrated international events, including England's 1966 victory over Germany in the World Cup.

Abu Dhabi's first post office opened in 1963, more than half a century after Dubai. Before then, the mail had largely emanated from the Abu Dhabi Petroleum Co, and was transferred to the company's Bahrain office before posting, using British stamps. The first post office was at Das Island, and shortly after its opening, Abu Dhabi issued its first set of 11 stamps, with portraits of the then Ruler Sheikh Shakbut bin Sultan al-Nahyan, his palace, plus pictures of a gazelle, an oil rig and camels. In 1967 Abu Dhabi took full control of its postal system, and a new set of stamps was issued, with the portrait of Abu Dhabi's current ruler Sheikh Zayed, as well as his palace, and the familiar antelope and falcon motifs.

Abu Dhabi's stamps tend to be more inward looking than those of Dubai — an attitude often exhibited in the emirate as a whole. Abu Dhabi's stamps carried frequently monochrome pictures of oil derricks, camels, gazelles and falcons, as well as portraits of the rulers and their palaces. Few commemorated events outside the emirate, and these tended to focus on pan-Arab themes. A notable exception was Expo 70 fair held in Japan.

The five other emirates of the UAE — Sharjah, Umm al-Quwain, Ajman, Ras al-Khaimah and Fujairah followed hard on the heels of Abu Dhabi in issuing their own stamps. By 1965, these emirates began to issue a whole range of highly elaborate pictorial stamps; many were never actually used to post letters and seem rather to commemorate the printers' talents.

Sharjah's stamps showed local scenes, including fortresses, the Dhaid oasis, the castle at Kalba and Khor Fakkan, and covered local subjects such as the scout movement. Ras al-Khaimah's stamps, and those of Ajman and Umm al-Quwain, include scenes of dhows and other marine subjects.

But the Northern Emirates and Fujairah also produced a great many apparently commemorative issues with technicolor pictures of anything from butterflies to Pekinese dogs, footballers to old master paintings, and recurrent portraits of world leaders and space travel. These are distinctively non-Arab in feel, the result probably of hiring outside contractors.

This tendency to over-issue stamps was curtailed after the formation of the UAE federation which issued its first stamps in 1973, valued between 5 fils and AED 10. The fils issue carried the UAE national flag, drawn in a sweeping circle, superimposed on a map of the Gulf and ringing the area of the seven emirates, while other denominations carried a variety of landmarks from each of the seven emirates.

Stamps issued since 1973 have carried pictures of the Jumeirah Mosque and the clock tower in Dubai, the Al Falaj Fort in Umm al-Quwain, the bay of Khor Fakkan in the enclave of Sharjah on the east coast, Abu Dhabi's Al Maqta Bridge, plus local themes such as handicrafts, traditional music, date-palms and camels. The falcon has been a recurrent symbol from the early days through to the present, reflecting the ruler's love of falconry.

Stamps issued since 1973 cover sporting events, key dates in UAE's brief history and important pan-Arab anniversaries.

Left: Examples of the colourful variety of recent issue stamps.

Dhows: Ancient Trading Craft

Dhows are seen along the sea-front in almost all the main coastal towns. These vessels have been used for thousands of years in the conduct of trade between the Gulf, South Asia and East Africa.

The Arabian Gulf and the Indian Ocean waters off Oman were an important link in the trade in spices between Europe, Persia and India, and further afield, the Far East. Their cargoes included precious stones and gold, ivory from Africa and India, and essential oils and ointments from Asia. The dhow fleets of the emirates that now form the UAE competed with dhows from Kuwait and Oman in this long-distance trade. The UAE dhow fleets, however, now carry electrical items and canned food rather than the more exotic cargoes of yesteryear.

In Dubai, dhows are still clustered all around the creek, and form a striking contrast to the ultra-modern skyscrapers behind them. Many of the dhows stopping in Dubai come from Iran and Baluchistan, now part of Pakistan. The dhow trade is also active in Sharjah; dhows here line the Buhairah Corniche, the larger ones coming from as far afield as India. But despite the concentration of the dhow trade in these commercial hubs, the vessels can be seen in every emirate: in Abu Dhabi, the dhow harbour lies off Mina Road before the entrance to the main port; in Umm al-Quwain, Ajman and Ras al-Khaimah, dhows dock in the creeks, the nucleus from which each of these towns has grown; off Fujairah Emirate, dhows are still occasionally seen plying the same waters as 350 metre-long supertankers.

Dhow-trips, including dinner cruises, can be organized through several tour operators. Full- and half-day cruises for small groups are also available from Dibba, north of Fujairah. These are not cheap, but a great way to get a whiff of the region's sea-faring past, even though the dhows are diesel- rather than wind-powered.

The waters off Dibba are rich in sea-life and the operator's promise that you will see dolphin on the trip is not idle. The cruises include breaks for snorkelling, as well as lunch and refreshments.

Dhows were traditionally made of wood and powered only by the tightly stretched lateen sail. The vessel often had a square-cut transom with a raised deck, under which lay the living quarters for the captain (al nokadah) and crew. Many dhows had a canopy over the stern as protection from the sun, and in modern dhows, this often stretches the vessel's full length.

The word dhow is not Arabic in origin. The word has been traced to the word dau in Swahili, a language widely used on the East African coast, which is a mix of Bantu and Arabic. The East African coast was, and still is, an important destination for the Gulf dhows. Different types of dhow were given their own Arabic names: al boom, al baggara, al shouee, al sambuk.

Nowadays, of course, modern technology has crept into their design: most have a diesel engine and radio as navigational aids, and racing dhows are made of light fibreglass compounds rather than wood. But the dhow heritage is being kept alive by the UAE rulers, who organize a number of dhow- and yacht-racing events. Among these, the annual President's Cup Regatta, also known as the Dubai-Muscat Sailing Race, attracts a host of traditional vessels, along with the brand-new mono-hulled and multi-hulled racing yachts.

Dhow-making is an art that many feared would be lost in the march to progress in modern UAE. But the interest in heritage dhow-making gave it a new lease of life: dhow-building yards can still be found on the Dubai creek, and outside Ajman.

Traditionally, the dhow-builder (qallaf, plural: qalaleef) built a dhow without detailed blue-prints, and using simple hand-tools such as planes, adzes and axes. First

Right: Flotilla of dhows in Dubai creek. Following pages: Silhouette against the city skyline.

Above: Craftsmen demonstrate the skilled art of dhow-making at al Khattal boat factory.

the long planks that made the hull were laid down, then the ribs and beams that formed the inside of the boat were sculpted, and the two were joined together, originally bound by rope made from coconut fibre, later by wooden dowels, and since the 20th century by iron nails. The hull of the boat was then coated with a paste know as *shahamu*, cattle-fat boiled with lime, and caulked with an oil-soaked fibre, usually cotton permeated with coconut or fish oil.

Nowadays, the dhow-builders still use traditional tools and materials, but often a dhow will be made using fibreglass, synthetic resins and modern coatings. Most of the dhows seen in the yards today are apparently types of sambuk, and many of the older varieties of dhow are now rarities.

Dhows came in a variety of different shapes and sizes. The boom was the largest type of dhow. In the past, many of them were built further up the Gulf coast in Kuwait, the busiest area for dhow-building in the 18th and 19th centuries. In the modern UAE, old dhows have been converted into floating restaurants called Al Boom in Dubai and Sharjah, and offer a pleasant outing to sample grilled fish and sea-food in traditional surroundings.

The boom dhows generally had a displacement of 150-210 tons, although the largest were about 300 tons. Typically, they would be about 30 metres (100 feet) long, six metres (20 feet) broad, and three metres (10 feet) deep. Booms were 'double-enders', that is they were narrow at the stern and at the prow.

The boom, as well as dhows such as *al baghlah* and *al bateel* were used for long-distance travel, going as far afield as India or East Africa. The sambuk were smaller but faster dhows than the boom. Typically, they would be between 75-140 tons, with a length of 24.5 metres (80 feet), beam of six metres (20 feet) and a depth of three metres (10 feet) between the gunwale and the waterline. They were often used to ferry pilgrims to Mecca. The sambuk had a roof of palm-fronds and coconut matting, which covered the cargo and living space.

The Arab navigators since the days of the 15th century Ahmed bin Majed have used the stars for navigation; indeed, the names of several of the brighter stars in the sky, even on the European star charts, have Arabic roots; for instance, the star Aldebran in the constellation Taurus. Traditionally, 48 stars were used by the Arab sailors for navigation.

Above: A traditional dhow makes an impressive display outside Dubai museum.

There were also a variety of smaller dhows, used for pearling and fishing in the waters of the Arabian Gulf or in the shallow waters near the coasts of the Indian Ocean. These smaller dhows included *al baggarah,* a smaller version of the bateel dhow, which has a painted and carved stern post. *Al shouee* and *al jalbout* were similar-sized boats. These vessels would leave for the pearl beds in the early summer, and would generally not return for three or four months. Pearling was widely practised off the Gulf until the 1930s, when the world-wide depression and the introduction of Japanese cultured pearls on the markets killed off the traditional industry. Though the waters off Bahrain were the site of the richest pearl-beds, the UAE was active in the business of pearling, with Dubai being particularly active.

Smaller vessels were also commonly used for fishing, including *houris,* which were small dug-out canoes of three to six metres (10-20 feet) long. These can still be seen, although most of them use outboard motors rather than paddles to get around. Houris and a number of other traditional fishing boats can be seen in the collection in the courtyard at Dubai Museum.

Above: Beached dhow awaiting repair.

Date-palms: Bride of the Desert

As pistachios are to Iran, and cloves are to Zanzibar, so dates are to the UAE. Of all the crops cultivated in the emirates, the date-palm is the most important. Not only did it provide a stable foodstuff in the harsh desert climate, but its trunk and leaves were widely used in making all sorts of household items, from the mats on which food was served to the boats that were used to catch the fish served up with the dates on a feast day. The date-palm, *phoenix dactilyfera,* is native to countries from North Africa to India. Its fruits are rich in sugar, and form a staple food in each of these countries. The fruits range in colour from pale yellow to a rich burnt-red colour, and during summer, they hang off the top part of the palm tree's trunk, in clusters of as many as 1,000 berries, and often a metre (three feet) in length.

Date-palms grow in all the emirates, wherever there is even a meagre supply of water to feed these hardy trees. Usually, they centred on an oasis, an area where the water table under the desert rises near enough to the surface to provide sustenance to vegetation and humans. The date-palms were watered by the ancient *falaj* irrigation channels, which channelled water from an underground spring through the groves of palm trees. These are still used, although now they are made of concrete.

Oases that support date-palm cultivation can be found in modern-day UAE at Dhaid in Sharjah, Al Awir in the emirate of Dubai, at Al Ain and Liwa in Abu Dhabi emirate, as well as in large areas of the Northern Emirates and Fujairah, particularly in the fertile emirate of Ras al-Khaimah. Extensive new plantation of dates along highway verges has been encouraged by the government.

The UAE has around 22-million date-palms, making it one of the largest date-producers in the world. There are 66 popular varieties, the best-seller being *al loulou*. Red varieties such as *al kheneizi, al khisaab,* and *al muselli* are very popular; there are also a number of yellow varieties that include *al nighal, al fardh,* and *al bagal.*

The date-palm was known as 'the bride of the desert', and was used in most aspects of daily life, to make housing, tents, agricultural implements, fishing nets and boats. Nowadays, many of these traditional items have been replaced by items made of plastic and metal; but in the emirates before the coming of oil, these modern materials were simply not available. The date-palm leaves, fronds, fibres and trunks were used for fencing, roofing, weaving, boat-building, and as a general housing material. Anything not used was burnt for firewood.

Dates were collected and carried in baskets made of the leaves of date-palms. *Al makrafah* was a container used to collect the dates in, once they had been picked from the tree, and they would be carried home in *al mezmal.* Date-palm leaves were also used to make baskets to carry the food and other items to and from the markets, as well as for the storage of personal items. The baskets used by women for carrying things to and from the markets were known as *al jefeer.* Women also used containers made of date-palm leaves for carrying their personal items, for instance, the phials of perfume, henna and kohl used for self-beautification.

As well as eating the dates, other parts of the date-palm were used in the provision, storage and serving of food. Small boats know as *shasha* were made from the leaves of the date-palm, on a skeleton of cane, and were remarkably water-tight, at least for short fishing trips in the shallow waters of the Gulf and off the coast of Fujairah. These are not much used now, but small fishing boats still use a cover of palm leaves above the vessel to keep off

Left: Date-palm with its golden yellow harvest, Abu Dhabi.

Above: Date-palm displaying unripened fruit. Right: Harvesting the now ripened crop.

the hot sun. The domed fishing-nets known as *al aliakh*, now made almost exclusively of metal, used to be made of palm leaves; palm-tree trunks were also attached to fishing nets to keep them buoyant.

Al sarood were circular mats made of date-palm leaves, on which food was served, and the individual dishes were often covered with conical covers known as *al makab*, also made of palm leaves. People would gather round the mats, squatting or lounging on their sides, depending on the formality of the occasion, and would scoop the food into their hands.

In the past, also, the date-palm leaves would be used to make the *barasti* houses that were so widely built before the coming of concrete, at a time when even houses built of mud and coral were the prerogative only of wealthy merchants. The barasti houses consisted of a wooden skeleton of supports, with the walls and room divisions made entirely of the palm leaves, which become grey-brown when they dry out. Usually, the building would

be topped by a wind-tower also made of palm leaves, open on four sides, which channelled any stirring of wind downwards into the living quarters.

Nowadays, barasti-style houses remain only in the museums: there are fine examples at Ajman, opposite the clock tower, and in the courtyard of the Dubai Museum near the Ruler's Diwan. A few coffee-shops retain the traditional barasti style, however: these can be found on the Corniche breakwater in Abu Dhabi, at Al Mamsar Park and along the creek in Sharjah, and overlooking the creek in Ras al-Khaimah.

298

A Note on the Arabic Language

The Arabic alphabet was the original inspiration for Pitman shorthand. As in Pitman shorthand, the consonants are written on the line and the vowels added by marks above and below the line. The Arabic alphabet consists of 29 letters, all of which are consonants except the letters 'a' (*alif*), 'w' (*wa*) which can be either a 'w' or 'u' sound, and 'y' (*ya*) which can be a 'y' or 'i' sound. The short vowels, 'a', 'i', 'u' are added by marks above and below the consonants.

In actual writing, for instance when you see Arabic in the newspaper, the vowels are almost always left out; it is only in important documents — among which the Muslim holy book, the Qur'ân, is far and away the most esteemed — that they are preserved. Thus when you see the word Muhammad in a newspaper, it will usually be written just with the Arabic letters m-h-m-d, and you need to know the vowels in order to divine the correct pronunciation.

Unlike European, African and some Asian languages, Arabic is written across the page from right to left.

The rules for transliterating Arabic are complex, and a number of different systems have been devised, widely different in their phonetic approach. Indeed, whole books have been written on the subject. In this guide, we have decided not to follow any single system, but simply to follow as far as possible what we saw on the street signs themselves.

Al is the Arabic word for 'the' and we have kept it in reference to local common nouns, as well as in proper nouns, such as the town Al Ain. One confusion in proper names is that the Arabic word *al* pronounced with a long 'a' rather than a short 'a' actually means 'family' rather than 'the'. Although the Arabic alphabet makes the distinction clear, it is usually lost in English transliterations: we have maintained this tradition by making no attempt to differentiate the two in our text.

Other common Arabic words that appear in names include *umm* (mother), *abu* (father), *ibn* or *bin* (son), and *abd* (servant). Thus a hypothetical name Muhammad bin Abdul Rahim might be translated as Muhammad, the Son of Abdul Rahim, and Abdul Rahim means when translated literally, Servant of the Merciful. The Merciful is one of the epithets used to describe Allah. Many common Arabic names have Islamic roots: for instance, Abdallah means literally 'Servant of God'.

Arabic words for things and people are almost always derived from a verb that has three consonants, the root verb. Each such verb can have as many as 10 different forms which give nuances of meaning to the basic three letters, by the addition of suffixes, infixes and prefixes. Each of these ten verbal forms have nouns which are derived from them.

Thus, the letters s-l-m have a root meaning 'to be safe and sound' and this gives rise to the noun *salaam*, meaning peace. When an Arab greets you with the words *As salaam aleikum* it literally means 'Peace be upon you' and when he leaves with the words *Ma'a as-salaama* it literally means, '(Go) with peace'.

The fourth form of the basic verb is *aslama*, meaning to surrender, or to become a Muslim. The word Muslim, is of course, a noun derived from this very form of the verb: a person who surrenders to God. The word Islam is similarly derived; it is the act of surrendering to God. The Biblical name Solomon is derived from the common Arabic name Suleiman, which in turn stems from the s-l-m root.

Of course, other forms of the verb have no direct religious significance, but can still be seen to derive from the basic three-consonant root verb. Thus, *istilaam* means a receipt; presumably from the fact that a receipt is issued once safe delivery of an item has been made.

Knowing the three-letter root system makes a visit to any Arab country more fun, because you can discover the culture

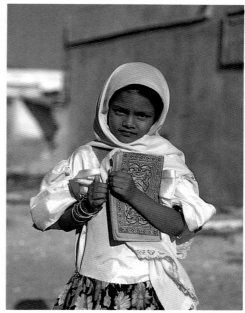

Above: Children display text books, where the Arabic script is used to teach the words of Islam.

through the words. Everyday words you will come across during your visit to the UAE suddenly become explicable.

Thus, the word souq (market) is derived from the root verb s-w-q, the second form of which means to buy or sell. In some Arab countries, although not the UAE, the word for a 'bargain purchase', *tasweeq*, comes from the same root.

The English word mosque is derived from the Arabic word *masjid*, with the same meaning, which in turn comes from the root verb s-j-d, which means 'to bow down in worship'. The initial *ma* implies it is a place where something happens: simi-lar words in Arabic are *madrasah*, a place where people study (d-r-s) and *maktab*, an office (the root here is k-t-b, which means 'to write').

Words in many different languages are derived from Arabic. The word kebab in English seems to derive from an Arabic word *kabbaab*, which in turn comes from the root k-b-b, 'to roll into a ball'. The idea seems to be that the meat was roasted in small balls on a skewer. Examples in other languages include the Swahili word for 'fish', *samaki*, which is almost identical with the Arabic word for fish, *samak*.

Following pages: Modern highway through an ancient landcape; Islam remains a dominating influence.

PART FIVE: BUSINESS UAE

The Economy

The UAE has become rich on the back of its massive oil and gas reserves, and although this remains the backbone of wealth creation in the country, its share in GDP has fallen as other industries and sectors have emerged. Most of the oil reserves are in Abu Dhabi, with enough oil there to last at least a century. In Dubai, reserves are falling, and industry estimates suggest that pumping Dubai crude will be uncommercial in about 30 years time. The UAE was a founding member of OPEC, the oil exporters' group that held the world's energy markets to ransom in 1973, and has had an OPEC production quota of more than 2-million barrels per day in recent years.

Although oil remains the backbone of the economy, the UAE has followed a process of deliberate economic diversification, and trade and the service sector in particular have become important contributors to GDP. The country's strategic location puts it in a perfect position to serve the 1.4-billion customers in emerging markets around it. Most important of these is India, but fledgling capitalism in Central Asia and rapid population growth in countries such as Pakistan, Sri Lanka and Bangladesh, also offer promise. The UAE has also played an active role in moves by the six-member Arab Gulf Cooperation Council (Bahrain, Kuwait, Oman, Qatar, Saudi Arabia and UAE) to form a GCC-wide customs union, aimed at promoting cross-border trade.

Diversification is seen as crucial to absorb the growing population. More than half UAE nationals are under 20, threatening a rise in unemployment in the coming years that can only get worse when oil revenues begin to dwindle. Perhaps partly as a result of this, but also perhaps because of a long-standing tradition of secrecy in the oil industry, the UAE divides its economic statistics into non-oil and oil data, of which little is known of the latter.

However, the exercise does give a vivid picture of just how crucial oil is to the balance of trade. The UAE's non-oil imports dwarf non-oil exports almost twenty-fold, and were more than four times as large as non-oil imports and re-exports combined, according to 1994 data.

Oil and Gas

Abu Dhabi emirate remains largely geared towards its oil industry, which dwarfs that of all the other emirates combined. Most visitors to Abu Dhabi will only see the industry in the form of the clean and efficient petrol stations: EMARAT, EPPCO and ADNOC-FOD are the three main petrol retailers. But the retail end is only the tip of the iceberg; most of the oil is exported, particularly to Japan which is Abu Dhabi's largest customer. It is from these oil exports that Abu Dhabi has earned the money to transform itself from a sleepy town with a few main roads and a population of a few thousand, into the modern commercial centre it is today.

Of total UAE oil reserves of around 98-billion barrels, Abu Dhabi holds 92-billion barrels; and its percentage share of the gas reserves is similar. About half of the hydrocarbons are onshore: easily the largest structure is the Bab field, near the coast between Abu Dhabi city and the Ruwais industrial structure, which is an important part of Murban crude, Abu Dhabi's main brand crude; but there are substantial deposits at Rumaitha and Jarn Yaphour to the north-east and at Bu Hasa to the south-west. Further inland, the fields of Sahil, Asab and Shah also contain substantial oil and gas reserves. Offshore, there are a large number of scattered smaller fields, including Zakum and Umm Shaif, which together make up the remaining half of the emirate's reserves.

The fields together yield about 1.9-million barrels per day of crude oil, but there are plans to develop the production capacity to more than 2.5-million barrels per day by the end of the century, through water- and gas-injection programmes and enhanced oil recovery techniques.

The crude oil is either exported at the Das Island loading terminal offshore or at the Jebel Dhanna terminal onshore. Crude oil that is not exported is refined at the Ruwais refinery, a 130,000 barrels per day unit, whose capacity is in the process of being doubled; or at the Umm al-Nar refinery, an 85,000 barrels per day facility just outside the capital city. Gas is sent to the liquefaction plant.

Abu Dhabi's oil industry is run by Abu Dhabi National Oil Corp (ADNOC), which together with a number of foreign companies, run the two main operating subsidiaries, ADMA-OPCO, which controls the offshore fields, and ADCO, which controls the onshore fields. The Supreme Petroleum Council, chaired by Abu Dhabi Crown Prince Khalifah bin Zayed al-Nahyan, is the top decision-making authority for oil and gas matters in the emirates.

Industry

Industry is also being developed. A number of cement factories have been built, partly to serve the needs of the local construction sector. Both light and heavy industries have found a niche: Dubai's Jebel Ali Port and Free Zone, and the large industrial estates that lie outside Sharjah, are notable in this sector.

The Jebel Ali Free Zone, lying about 50 kilometres (30 miles) from Dubai on the road to Abu Dhabi, is the non-oil industrial hub of the UAE, housing around 800 large and small companies, from more than 65 countries, largely oriented to manufacturing and industrial projects. The Jebel Ali Free Zone Authority (JAFZ), created by a Dubai government decree on 9 February 1985, is the government body charged with supervision of the zone, which now stretches over more than 100 square kilometres (38 square miles) and contains the world's largest artificial port, operated by Dubai Ports Authority. The terminal offers: 67 berths stretching along 15 kilometres (10 miles) of quays; a state-of-the-art container terminal; and vast temperature-controlled storage facilities.

Aiwa, Black and Decker, Brother, Casio, Daewoo, Goldstar, Heinz, Honda, Hyundai, Land Rover, Nokia, Reebok and Sony are among the many household names represented in JAFZ.

Jebel Ali's attractions include 100 per cent foreign ownership of a business, 100 per cent repatriation of capital and profits, and no currency restrictions. Fiscal incentives to invest in JAFZ include exemption from corporate taxes for 15 years, and, as elsewhere in the UAE, there are no income taxes. The JAFZ authority says that the tax exemption will continue even if taxes are introduced elsewhere in the UAE.

The zone's infrastructure is well developed, with modern efficient communications, ready-made factories and warehouses, and accommodation for the workforce, so the investor can simply lease these rather than build the facilities from scratch. There are no restrictions on who to employ, and the JAFZ authority will act as nominal sponsor for personnel; it also recruits staff on request.

Just outside the free zone area, Dubai Aluminium (DUBAL) operates the second-largest aluminium smelter in the Middle East, using gas from the nearby Dubai Gas (DUGAS) facilities. Dubai Cable Co (DUCAB) is also sited in the same area, and manufactures a wide range of cables using aluminium and copper as raw material.

The Northern Emirates of Sharjah, Ajman, Umm al-Quwain and Ras al-Khaimah have been slower to develop than Abu Dhabi and Dubai. Sharjah's industrial zones are an important manufacturing centre, contributing about one-third of the UAE's total manufacturing GDP; and Ras al-Khaimah's Khor Khwaiz industrial zone is gradually coming into its own.

Sharjah's industry, as has been mentioned, is already quite well developed, and a number of

large companies have preferred to base themselves in the city, where office rental is a lot cheaper than in nearby Dubai. More than 500 industries are registered in Sharjah, and annual investment in the emirate has surged to more than AED 1 billion.

Non-oil activity in Abu Dhabi has been slow to take off, and still makes up a mere one-tenth of total economic activity, and only about 15 per cent of private sector activity. An obvious derivative for the oil industry would be to set up a petrochemicals facility, and the government is in the process of choosing a partner for such a venture. Abu Dhabi is also planning to set up a number of new industrial zones; most progress has been made so far on developing the Musaffeh area outside Abu Dhabi city.

Banking

Dubai and Abu Dhabi have emerged as important regional banking centres, and their appeal has only been increased by the civic unrest suffered in Bahrain which used to be the financial hub of the entire Middle East in the early 1990s. The UAE's excellent communications, well-educated population, and the diversity of its population have contributed to this.

The banking sector has had its setbacks: the closure of the Bank of Credit and Commerce International in 1991, in which UAE nationals were major shareholders, was one of these. The Gulf crisis after Iraq invaded Kuwait in August 1990 was also a potential threat to the inflow of funds in the region.

The UAE has reacted with characteristic pragmatism. The UAE Central Bank initiated and implemented a tough new regulatory framework, setting capital adequacy ratios at even stricter levels than those initiated by the Bank of International Settlements in 1992. The banks have also been forced to develop the range of services offered to customers, because of cut-throat competition between the more than a dozen domestic banks in business. The ever-growing presence of foreign banks in the UAE looks set to hone competition further.

Trade

Re-export business has become a large money-spinner for Dubai, as it has for other Asian 'tigers' such as Hong Kong and Singapore, with which Dubai is frequently compared. The re-export business grew sharply, if erratically, in the late 1980s and early 1990s, and finally topped the AED 10-billion mark in 1993. Although annual growth is projected to slow from the 20 per cent plus rates achieved in the early 1990s, steady growth of between five to six per cent is forecast by the government for the years up to the end of this century. Dubai is the source of about 80 per cent of the UAE's total re-export business, which was valued at AED 13.2 billion in 1994. Most of the re-export business would appear to be in textiles; for instance, these made up almost a third of the UAE's re-exports to the United Kingdom in the first half of 1995. Other large categories of re-exports to the UK were machinery, including electrical equipment, and precision equipment for the medical and photographic industries.

Agriculture

Surprisingly for a country that is largely desert, agriculture has also been a minor success story, notably in the relatively fertile Northern Emirates. Subsidized supplies of seeds, equipment and fertilizers have led to a surplus in some crops, although overall the country is still far from its goal of self-sufficiency in food. The UAE has more than 22 million date trees — 15-20 per cent of all in the world — and has targeted a small range of high value-added crops, including citrus fruits, some vegetables and animal feed. The UAE is also rapidly developing its poultry and dairy farming sectors; the country has more than 50,000 head of cattle, of which about two-thirds are cows. The UAE also produces small quantities of tobacco and wheat. Fisheries remain a potential growth sector.

Tourism

Development of the service sector has become so important as part of the drive to diversify away from oil. Tourism is thriving on the back of business; about 80 per cent of all tourist arrivals in Dubai, for instance, are estimated to be business people, taking a brief holiday in the sun before a business trip to one of the GCC countries. New hotels go up by the day, and some of the most ambitious construction projects in the Gulf are related to the development of the UAE's tourism potential.

Investment

Foreign investment

To set up a company in the UAE, a foreign investor must take a local partner, who holds at least 51 per cent of the company's equity; the profit split can usually be negotiated, but most locals will expect the profit split to reflect the equity split. A good partner may well open up markets for a joint venture and genuinely contribute to its profitability; but many foreign companies complain that the local partner is all too often 'sleeping' — taking a cut of the pie without contributing to the hard work of making it.

Although the 51 per cent rule does not apply in the free zones, some foreign business people have voiced scepticism about the government's intentions in allowing 100 per cent ownership in these zones, noting that the government has invested heavily in their success, and is not likely to abandon majority local ownership if this potentially jeopardizes the success of the free zones.

The UAE offset programme started in 1990 and aims to contribute towards diversification through cooperation between foreign investors and local entrepreneurs. Under the offset programmes, all armed forces procurements and all purchases of more than US $10 million by the government or its affiliates, must be offset within a seven-year period by a contract or business venture worth at least 60 per cent of the value of the imports. All contractors must now submit offset proposals with their tenders for government projects, and failure to do so will in almost all circumstances disqualify the bid. The UAE Offsets Group monitors the extent of a company's offset obligation.

The UAE offset programme has been criticized by some foreign companies, who claim it forces them to invest in the UAE when they would prefer not to do so; in effect, they argue that they are being penalized for participating in projects, on which work should be awarded on purely commercial grounds. Tough competition for the mega-projects being developed, which shaves profit margins and leads to extremely tight contract schedules, are also cited. The UAE sees it differently; and although there are signs that the offset legislation may be made more flexible, to allow for instance for a cash sum to be paid into the offset fund, rather than actually going ahead with an offset project, there seems little chance that it will be cancelled altogether.

Company law

Foreign business people setting up in the UAE usually do so as a Limited Liability Company, LLC. The UAE Companies Law Number Eight was amended in 1988 by Federal Law Number 13 and its bye-laws, and is now implemented in all seven emirates of the UAE.

The law lays down that non-UAE nationals cannot be general partners in a company with unlimited liability. The law stipulates that only UAE nationals can be general partners with unlimited liability. Under this rule, a UAE sponsor is thus required to assume liabilities that might be incurred by the business; and the 51 per cent rule means that they must own a majority of the shares in the business. There are exceptions to this, for instance applying to companies made up of professionals such as lawyers and accountants.

The conduct of business

Opinions differ as to how easy it is to set up business in the UAE. The government paints a picture of entrepreneurial bliss in which applications to do business are quickly and efficiently processed; but expatriates remain sceptical, often comparing the UAE favourably to other Middle Eastern venues, while highlighting the long and often tedious registration procedures. The truth is no doubt somewhere in-between the official hype and the routine grumblings of would-be investors. Customs of doing business vary as much from emirate to emirate as do business procedures.

Bureaucracy is a problem in every one of the Middle Eastern countries, whose tradition of Byzantine and Ottoman seals and passes of approval seems to have survived centuries after the empires that created them have disappeared. At the same time, the UAE has a relatively efficient civil service; and the infrastructure to encourage investment is very much in place, with helpful chambers of commerce able to provide one-stop advice on anything from business regulations to finding a sponsor.

As much as anywhere, who you know in the UAE can be as important as what you know. Foreign business people make the point time and time again that whatever the broad trends in the individual emirates, a good local sponsor can enormously speed up the turnover time for setting up a business.

A local partner in tune with local developments is also invaluable when it comes to doing business. The UAE aims for transparency and openness in doing business, but word of mouth, which has survived for centuries as the prime method of information exchange among merchants, remains a key element of both identifying and getting business. Many remark that, by the time you read it, in the official gazettes or tender lists in the official *Emirates News* and other publications, you will have lost the business. Being on an inside track is essential, and personalities are important. However well-documented a proposal, UAE nationals prefer lively conversation, trust and a good idea when coming to business decisions; a respected and liked local partner is likely to be worth their weight in gold.

Types of Company

Seven separate categories of business organization are defined by the Company Law: General partnership company; Partnership-en-commendam; Share partnership company; Joint venture company; Public shareholding company; Private shareholding company; Limited liability company.

Partnership companies

Partnership companies, for instance the general partnership company, or partnership-en-commendam, are not currently encouraged. Partnership companies, however, are limited to UAE nationals only.

Joint ventures

Joint ventures are encouraged for companies working on specific projects: under this arrangement, a foreign company can join with a local company licensed to do business in the desired activity. The local partners assume all liability for the venture, while the foreign company deals with third parties under the name of the local partner. Local equity participation is a minimum of 51 per cent.

Shareholding companies

Companies engaged in banking, insurance or financial activities must be run as public shareholding companies, although foreign companies in these fields can open branch or representative offices. To set up a shareholding company, a minimum capital of AED 10 million (US $2.725 million) is required for a public company, or AED 2 million (US $0.545 million) for a private company. The chairman and a majority of directors must be UAE nationals. Shareholding companies are seen as a suitable vehicle for setting up large projects or operations, but because of the high capital requirement, will probably not be of interest to smaller investors.

Limited liability company

The final category of Limited Liability Company is viewed as a favoured vehicle for companies interested in a long-term presence in the UAE market. The requirements for setting up a LLC vary between emirates; typically in Dubai a minimum of AED 300,000 (US $82,000) must be subscribed, while in Abu Dhabi the figure is only AED 150,000 (US $41,000). The management of the company can be vested in either the foreign partners, the UAE partners, or a third party; ownership however must be a minimum 51 per cent by UAE nationals.

Branch or representative offices

Branch or representative offices of foreign companies can be set up in the UAE and can be 100 per cent foreign-owned, provided a local agent is appointed. The branch office or representative office is typically not allowed to engage in import business, although it can engage in re-export business, a huge market given the UAE's role in the entrepôt trade. The local agent must be 100 per cent UAE owned. The local sponsor does not get involved in the management of the company, but assists in obtaining visas and labour cards and so forth; the sponsor is paid a lump-sum or a percentage of profits or turnover.

Registration

The registration procedure in the UAE is painless in theory, although in practice there are wide differences between the emirates in the time taken to process applications, and the flexibility of the authorities concerned; bureaucracy can often turn what should be a quite smooth piece of paperwork into a veritable paper-mill.

LLC registration and business conduct is scrutinized initially by the local authority in the emirate in which the business is registered — usually the local municipality or, in the case of Dubai and Abu Dhabi, the economic department. The local authority will review the application for registration, and direct the applicant to discrepancies that might arise with UAE law.

To set up a LLC business, the economic department must first of all give approval for the name under which the applicant will conduct business, and the applicant must then execute the Memorandum of Association for forming the LLC. A number of documents will need to be submitted and, if originals are not available, notarized copies are often required. Notarization often has to be done in Arabic; translation costs are reasonable, however.

The following documents normally have to be submitted when making a registration for LLC status: the 'Application for Recording the Company in the Commercial Register' form; the notarized Memorandum of Association of the company; a certificate from the auditors certifying that they have been appointed, and that capital contributions by the directors of the company have been properly paid up; statements from the directors that shares have been fully paid up and duly allotted; a certificate from the bank confirming the amounts deposited by each partner, and giving undertakings about the disbursement of the sums deposited; an application form for a trade licence; a copy of the Tenancy Agreement in which business will be conducted; and passport details of all the directors.

These documents should normally be submitted at least in duplicate; the chamber of commerce or economic department can advise on the exact timetable and the number of copies required.

A number of other documents are required when the partner in the LLC is an appointee of a foreign company. These basically aim to verify that the director is indeed the person appointed to handle the business of the company in the UAE: a resolution of the board of directors specifying the duties of the company's representative, and giving a formal power of attorney on his behalf, is thus required. The foreign company's Memorandum of Association and Certificate of Incorporation will also be required. All of these must be legal documents and, as such, the stamp of a UAE embassy, backed up by that of the UAE foreign ministry, will be required; the Arabic translation of these documents will need to be authenticated by the Ministry of Justice.

Once the application has been submitted and approval has been given, you will still be some way from actually getting down to business; the Trade Licence is the grail that would-be investors require in order to get down to business, and it is often frustrating, once all the initial paperwork has been completed, to experience further delays at this stage. A trade licence will only be issued when details of the LLC have been published in the Companies Bulletin. In order to get that done, the Ministry of Economy and Commerce need to be involved.

The economic department needs to enter the company's details in the Commercial Register and then submit the key paperwork that has been gone through in order to allow this to go to the Ministry of Economy and Commerce. After paying the relevant fees to the ministry, the company's details will be published in the Companies Bulletin and a receipt issued; the ministry will then refer back to the economic department, authorizing them to issue the trade licence, and they will do so on presentation of the receipt from the ministry.

It may all sound a bit complicated, and that is largely because it is; people who have set up businesses in the UAE in the last couple of years say it takes anywhere between two and six months to go from the application stage through to actually getting the trade licence, no matter how streamlined the process is cracked up to be by the government. But as has been stated, a good local partner, active on the applicant's behalf, can speed up the process.

Branch or representative office

The procedures for setting up a branch or representative office are somewhat simpler than for setting up a LLC. The licence is applied for from the Ministry of Economy and Commerce, to whom the foreign entity must submit their agency agreement with the local sponsor.

The ministry will submit the application to the local economic department and the Federal Foreign Companies Committee for approval, and then issue the Ministerial licence specifying the activity to be practised by the foreign company. The branch must then be entered in the Commercial Register and the Foreign Companies Register of the Ministry of Economy and Commerce and, where applicable, registered with the local chamber of commerce.

Business Procedures

Once the trade licence has been issued, the bank can deliver the money to the company directors and business can proceed. The LLC, however, remains subject to a number of restrictions limiting its scope of business; for instance, the trade licence is only valid in the emirate that issued it and separate licences must be obtained to set up branch offices in other emirates. The licence must also be renewed annually.

Resolutions must also keep to the Company Law of the UAE. LLCs are subject to a complicated series of rules that cover the liability of the partners, profit-distribution and transfer of shares. These seem at least in part aimed at protecting the local partner in a venture; for instance, profits must be equally distributed between the partners unless specifically stated otherwise in the contract, and any resolution excluding a partner from profit or exempting them from loss is declared null and void. A sum equivalent to 10 per cent of net profits must be transferred to a legal reserve fund, until the fund is equivalent to half the company's paid-up capital.

There are a number of rules relating to the conduct of AGMs, such as the preparation of accounts and appointment of auditors, the keeping of registers of partners' interests and minutes of meetings of the directors. However, these present no special problem and are in keeping with good business practice in Europe or the US; if anything, rules in the UAE tend to be somewhat laxer than in the West, particularly in the field of disclosure.

In the past, the spirit of the laws relating to the establishment of companies in the Gulf Co-operation Council (GCC) has been widely flouted, but the UAE plans to toughen up its company laws to prevent these abuses, which are common throughout the GCC. These include such practices as the leasing of trade licences and the practice whereby locals allow their name to be used as the 51 per cent owner of a business for a fee. Under a new law, currently still in draft form but likely to become law by the end of 1996, fines of as much as AED 500,000, as well as imprisonment or deportation, will be meted out if such practices are detected. The new law, a draft of which was drawn up by the Ministry of Economy and has been submitted to the Ministry of Justice, is expected to be implemented by the licensing authorities in each emirate.

Free zone authorities
The Free Zones offer opportunities to operate in a more flexible business environment, and these have taken off in recent years, most of all because they offer 100 per cent ownership and other incentives that are not available under the Company Law. There is a theory that the free zones have been set up to test the waters for a greater degree of liberalization and deregulation in the UAE economy as a whole.

Dubai's Jebel Ali Free Zone (JAFZ) is by far the largest and most successful in the UAE, but a number of similar schemes have been set up in other emirates. The notes on application that follow cover the JAFZ but the broad outline will also apply to other free zones.

Applications to operate in the Jebel Ali Free Zone are relatively free of bureaucracy, but the system varies depending on the type of licence under which the company is applying to operate. All prospective investors must first of all submit a preliminary questionnaire. JAFZ will then provide a licence application, with an appendix listing the documents the company will have to produce once preliminary approval of the application is granted. A number of other forms including power-supply requests and covering environmental issues may also be required for completion at this stage.

Once preliminary approval is given, JAFZ provides a specimen lease agreement, copies of free zone notices, and relevant rules and agreements covering personnel and construction issues. The company's representative will then be called in for a meeting to discuss the details of the project, after which JAFZ prepares a lease profile, to be signed by the company, and gives conditional approval for the project. The final lease agreement is then drafted, along with any other paperwork, for signature, after which the agreed rent and licence fee is paid. The applicant company will also be required at this stage to pay insurance policies required in the agreements.

The exact documentation required at each stage will vary depending on the type of the licence being applied for. There are four types of licence available: a Special Licence, for companies legally established outside the UAE; a General Licence, for companies which already hold a valid licence to operate in the UAE from Dubai Economic Department; and a National Industrial Licence, for manufacturing in or outside the UAE, which must be owned by 51 per cent GCC entities. A fourth category of licence introduced by the Dubai government in 1992, allows a company to operate as a Free Zone Establishment (FZE), a single shareholder establishment set up within the JAFZ.

Imports and exports
The UAE is a signatory of the General Agreement on Tariffs and Trade, and as such is committed to the ideals of free and fair trade embodied in the GATT.

Customs duties are low in the UAE. Imports are mostly charged at a fixed rate of four per cent across the emirates. Goods produced within the Gulf Cooperation Council, grouping Bahrain, Kuwait, Oman, Qatar, Saudi Arabia and UAE, are exempt from any duty under the Unified Economic Agreement of June 1981. GCC origin is defined as at least 40 per cent local manufacture in terms of the final value of goods. Local citizens must own at least 51 per cent of the plant at which the goods are produced, unless the plant is 100 per cent GCC-owned. In order to claim

GCC exemption, each item must be accompanied by a certificate of origin authenticated by the appropriate government agency.

There are a variety of other exemptions from duty: for instance, a variety of foodstuffs, medicines, agriculture-related equipment and chemicals and construction materials. Any items imported for use in the UAE free zones are also exempt from duty.

Exchange control

As well as low and in many cases no duties, the UAE benefits from a freely convertible currency. The dirham is linked to the US dollar, mainly because that is the currency of the international oil trade; the current exchange rate of AED 3.675 to the dollar has not changed since around 1980. The dirham floats against other currencies.

Taxation

Apart from oil producing companies and foreign banks, there is no corporate tax in the UAE. There has been plenty of discussion of introducing taxes on corporate profits, but so far, this seems unlikely. The Dubai Business Handbook remarks, 'Direct taxation is against the traditions of the UAE and it is highly unlikely that it will be introduced in the near future.' Likewise, there are no personal taxes in the UAE; this means that companies often pay locally hired staff somewhat less than they would earn in the US or Europe.

PART SIX: FACTS AT YOUR FINGERTIPS

Visa and immigration requirements
The UAE federal authorities are primarily responsible for all immigration matters, and visitors are advised to consult their nearest UAE embassy or consulate if in doubt about visa requirements.

In general, all visitors — except citizens of the Gulf Co-operation Council states (Bahrain, Kuwait, Qatar, Oman and Saudi Arabia), British citizens with the right of abode in the UK, GCC residents of certain nationalities and professions, and transit passengers who do not leave the airport on arrival — must obtain visas before entering the UAE.

A local sponsor is required in order to apply for a visa, but the hotels are pleased to look after all such formalities on behalf of their guests. Whoever acts as your sponsor is responsible for you while you are in the UAE and it is incumbent upon them to ensure that you leave the country. The usual system for visas is that the hotel or sponsor arranging your visa will deposit it at the airport so it is awaiting your arrival in the country.

Entry is forbidden to travellers whose passports bear Israeli stamps.

Health requirements
No health certificates are required for entry to the UAE, but it is always wise to check before departure, as health restrictions may vary, depending upon the situation at the time.

International flights
There are several major international airports. Dubia International Airport is the busiest in the UAE and is served by around 65 airlines. There are International airports at Abu Dhabi, Sharjah, Ras al-Khaimah and Fujairah though the latter two are used infrequently by international travellers. Sharjah Airport is mostly used by the increasing number of tourists arriving from eastern Europe. The UAE's own airline is Emirates and flies to major destinations world-wide. Flights to the UAE are available from many destinations either in Europe or in Asia and many flights stop in Dubai or Abu Dhabi en route from Asia to Europe or vice versa.

Arrival by road
Overland routes are uncommon but it would be possible to go through the Omani border at Ras al-Khaimah or near Hatta, or at Buraimi if coming overland from Muscat. It is also possible to cross the border from Saudi Arabia at Gheweifat or to take a boat from Iran if a visa is possible.

Customs
Duty-free allowances: Cigarettes — 2,000; cigars — 400; tobacco — 2kg; alcohol (non muslim adults only) — 2 litres of spirits and 2 litres of wine; perfume — a reasonable amount.

No custom duty is levied on personal effects entering UAE.

Climate
The UAE boasts sunshine all the year round with infrequent and irregular rainfall which falls mainly in winter. Temperatures range from around 15-20°C (59-68°F) in December to around 40-50°C (104-122°F) in August.

The hot season lasts from June through September, with July and August the peak months in terms of humidity. In October temperatures begin to go down, as does the humidity. The weather is balmy from November through April, with occasional rain possible from December to March.

Clothing
Lightweight summer clothing is suitable for most of the year, but sweaters or jackets may be needed for the winter months, especially in the evenings.

Compared with certain parts of the Middle East, UAE has a very relaxed dress code. However, care should be taken not to give offence by wearing clothing which may be considered revealing, for example low-cut dresses, very short skirts or tight jeans.

Men should always wear a shirt or top in public. At the pool or on the beaches, trunks, swimsuits and bikinis are quite acceptable. Good quality sunglasses are advisable and photochromatic lenses for those who wear spectacles. Hats, or some protection for the head, are also advisable when in direct sunlight.

Culture
UAE's culture is firmly rooted in the Islamic traditions of Arabia. Courtesy and hospitality are among the most highly prized of virtues, and the visitor is sure to be charmed by the genuine warmth and friendliness of the people.

The UAE, in particular Dubai, is a relaxed and tolerant state, especially compared with the other Gulf sheikhdoms. Foreigners are free to practise their own religion, alcohol (except in

Sharjah and during Ramadan) is served in hotels and provided reasonable discretion is shown, the dress code is liberal. Women face no discrimination and may drive and move around unescorted.

Despite rapid economic development in recent years, UAE remains close to its heritage. Local citizens dress in the traditional *dishdasha* (robe) and *guttrah* (headdress). Women in public wear the black wraparound called *abbaya*. Arab culture and folklore find expression in poetry, dancing, songs and traditional art.

Weddings and other celebrations are colourful occasions of feasting and music. And traditional sports such as falconry, camel-racing and dhow-racing at sea continue to thrive.

Language
The official language is Arabic but English is widely spoken and understood. Both languages are commonly used in business and commerce.

Religion
Islam is the official religion of the UAE and there are a large number of mosques throughout the cities. Other religions are respected and in Dubai there are two Christian churches, St Mary's and Holy Trinity.

Ramadan
Ramadan is the holy month in which Muslims commemorate the revelation of the Holy Koran. The timing of Ramadan is not fixed in terms of the Western calendar, but occurs a few days earlier each year in accordance with the Muslim lunar calendar.

It is a month of fasting when Muslims abstain from all food, drinks and cigarettes during daylight hours. You will have no problem if you eat, drink or smoke in your own dwelling, for instance, the hotel room in which you are staying. However, as a general rule, visitors to the UAE should never eat, smoke or drink in public during the period of Ramadan between sunrise and sunset.

Photography
Normal tourist photography is acceptable but it may be considered offensive to photograph Muslim women.

It is courteous to ask permission before photographing men. In general, photographs should not be taken of government buildings, military installations or oil and other industrial areas.

Taxis
Taxis are plentiful and reasonably priced, but visitors should always agree on the price in advance of the journey. Taxis on stands outside hotels charge more than those flagged down on a road.

For short journeys the charge should be around AED 5. To cross the Dubai Creek will cost around AED 10 or slightly more. The journey to the town centre from Abu Dhabi or Dubai airport costs around AED 30-40 in specially registered airport taxis.

Most of the hotels operate their own transport for their guests. There are several radio taxi companies which have cars on call: numbers are available at hotels.

Car hire
Self drive cars are available and the rental company will arrange temporary local driving licences for visitors. Renters must produce their passport, two photographs and either a valid international or national licence from one of the following countries:

Australia, Belgium, Canada, Denmark, Finland, France, Germany, Greece, Holland, Ireland, Italy, Japan, Norway, Spain, Sweden, Switzerland, Turkey, UK and USA. Other nationalities must obtain a temporary UAE licence.

Roads and highways
The UAE has an extremely modern and efficient road system and this combined with a lack of other transport options, makes a car pretty much essential if you're going to do any travelling in the emirates. Tarmacked roads link the main cities, town and village, and a network of highways provide excellent routes to neighbouring countries.

Water taxis
An interesting way to travel between Dubai and Deira is by water taxi *(abra)* across the creek. The cost of this experience is 50 fils (half-a dirham).

Buses
Buses run between Dubai, Abu Dhabi and other key towns, if infrequently. There are also local buses within the cities which are used mainly by Indian and Pakistani migrant workers but there is no good information on where buses run to and from.

Currency
The monetary unit is the dirham (AED) which is divided into fils. The dirham is linked to the Special Drawing Right of the International Monetary Fund.

It has been held constant against the US Dollar since the end of 1980 at a mid-rate of approximately US\$ 1 = AED 3.675.

Banks
Many international banks are represented by branches in the emirates, providing usual commercial banking.

Transfers can be made without difficulty as

there is no exchange control and the dirham is freely convertible.

Bank hours are 0800 to 1300, Saturday through Thursday, although some also open from 1600 to 1730. Exchange houses are open from 0830 to 1300 and 1630 to 2030.

Credit cards
American Express, Diners Club, Visa, Master-Card etc are generally accepted in the main hotels and larger shops but some retailers offer better bargains for cash.

Tipping
Tipping practices are similar to most parts of the world. Some restaurants do include service; otherwise 10 per cent is adequate.

Weights and measures
Officially the metric system is followed, although the British and American standard weights and measures are understood by most merchants. Local weights and measures are also used occasionally, but seldom for international trade.

Bargaining
Bargaining is expected in the souq and is quite usual elsewhere. Vendors will usually drop the price — and often quite substantially, particularly for a cash sale.

Business hours
The weekend has traditionally been on Thursday afternoon and Friday, but some organizations now close on Friday and Saturday. Government offices are open from 0730 to 1300 (0730 to 1200 Thursday). Private sector office hours vary, but are generally from 0800 to 1300, reopening at either 1500 to 1600 and closing at 1800 to 1900.

Shop hours are similar, but the souq and most food shops remain open on Fridays, especially the smaller stores. Embassies and consulates are generally open from 0845 to 1230.

Newspapers
The Khaleej Times, The Gulf Today, Emirates News and *Gulf News* are daily English-language newspapers. Arabic newspapers include *Al Bayan, Al Itthad* and *Al Khaleej.*

Foreign newspapers, especially British, are readily available in hotel bookshops and supermarkets. *What's On* and *Connector* are colourful monthly magazines which cover social and cultural events within the UAE.

Television
There are three television stations providing programmes to millions of viewers. Leading hotels receive international news and entertainment broadcasts via satellite. The Hong Kong based Star TV network covers the UAE and features the BBC World Service.

Locally in Dubai, there are four channels: Dubai 2, 10 and 41 which show Arabic programmes, and Dubai 33, which broadcasts in English. Emirates Dubai Television broadcasts by satellite throughout the world in Arabic and English.

Radio
There are five locally based radio stations. The English-language service of UAE Radio Dubai broadcasts daily on 92 Mhz FM 24 hours a day, with main news bulletins at 0730, 0930, 1430 and 2030.

Postal services
The Postal services are reasonable. Mumtaz is the express mail service available for priority mail requiring quick delivery overseas. Leading international courier companies also operate in the UAE.

Electricity
The electricity supply in is 220/240 volts at 50 cycles. US made appliances will need a transformer.

Water
Tap water is quite safe to drink but visitors usually prefer locally bottled mineral water and this is generally served in hotels and restaurants.

Medical care
The Government-funded health system offers free medical treatment to all UAE nationals and a heavily subsidized service to expatriates. There are 35 government owned hospitals and 98 medical centres in the UAE. The UAE has some of the best medical centres in the Middle East, with specialized clinics, maternity and gynaecology hospitals.

Telephones
Telecommunications are excellent, both within the UAE and with the outside world. Telephone calls within the UAE are free except from public phone booths. Direct dialling is available to most of the countries. Internet and teleconferencing facilities are in place offering the most up-to-date communications to individuals and companies in the Middle East.

Sports clubs
The UAE is well equipped for any type of sports. The larger centres of Dubai, Abu Dhabi and Sharjah have sophisticated sporting facilities.

Marine life is rich in the Gulf and in the Indian Ocean on the east coast of the UAE at Fujairah, thus both diving and fishing are fruitful activities. There are numerous diving schools here and in Dubai, Abu Dhabi and Sharjah.

Golf courses include the Emirates Golf Club located on the outskirts of Dubai, the Dubai

Creek and Yacht Club, Dubai Golf and Racing Club and there is a nine hole golf course in Hatta at the Hatta Fort Hotel. There is also the Sharjah Wanderers Golf Club, the nine hole golf club at the Hilton in Al Ain, the Dhafra Beach Hotel at Ruwais and the Abu Dhabi Golf Club.

Riding is available throughout at the Dubai Equestrian Centre, the Jebel Ali Riding Stables, the Sharjah Equestrian Club, the Abu Dhabi Equestrian Club and the Umm al-Quwain Riding Centre.

Many of the main hotels of UAE have tennis and squash courts. Shooting and archery are both well catered for in the UAE. There is the Jebel Ali Shooting Club, the Hatta Fort Hotel and the Ras al-Khaimah Shooting Club.

Public holidays
Weekly holiday is Friday. Other fixed holidays are New Year's Day and National Day on 2 December. Moveable holidays are of Eid al-Fitr, Eid al-Adh, Hijra New Year's Day and the Prophet's Birthday.

Useful Arabic
Just a few words of Arabic will make your trip enjoyable and, at the same time, bring gleaming smiles to all Arabs with whom you speak.

Vocabulary and phrases:

Good morning	Sabah al-khayr
Good evening	Masah al-khayr
Greetings	Assalam alaykum
Hello	Marhaba
Welcome	Ahlan wasahlan
Goodbye	Massalama
Please	Min fadlak/fadlik (mas/fem)
Thank you	Shukran
How are you?	Kayf halak?
Thanks be to God	Al hamdu lillah
God willing	Inshaalah
Yes	Naam
I don't speak Arabic	Ana la atakallum al-Arabiah
My name is . . .	Esmi . . .

Taxi directions in Arabic:

Straight on	Seedha
Right/Left	Yameen/Yassar
Look	Shuf
Slowly	Shway, shway
Let's go	Yallah
Wait a moment	Stannah shwaya
Here/There	Hona/Honak

In Brief

Archaeological and Ancient Sites

Abu Dhabi
The islands of Abu Dhabi are of major archaeological and ecological importance as well as containing rare species of birds and fish. These sites are on the island of Balghelam north-east of Abu Dhabi, on the islands of Ghaghah, Al F'zaiyyah and Merawah and evidence has been found of ancient settlements.

Ajman Museum
The museum is sited in a late 18th-century fort near Sheikh Humeid bin Abdul Aziz Street in Ajman. Inside the museum's displays today include old manuscripts, weapons, archaeological finds and re-constructions of traditional rooms in Arabic houses.

Al Ain
Places of interest are the Hili Gardens just outside the Al Ain city. Hili ruins are the site of an ancient archaeological site and contain both settlement and burial tombs. Nearby sites are Rumeilah-Qatrah and Qarn bin Saud with artefacts, including arrowheads, a variety of bowls

and seals and animal figures. The zoo and aquarium in the south of the city in the Al Maslakh area are worth a visit.

Al Mileiha
South of Dhaid contains sites dating back to the beginning of the Christian era. The archaeological site is off in the sands before the main town of Mileiha, before the mountains of the same name. A fort found here contained a coin mould, proving that the community minted its own bronze and silver coinage. A group of tombs found dating back 4,500 years are found a little further south, at Jebel Emalah.

Fujairah
The old town's main sites are in easy reach of each other. There is the Fujairah Museum, Fujairah Old Town which comprises a 300-year old fort and the ruins of the buildings that formed the town, and to the south of the town lie the village of Kalba and Khor Kalba where a British team are engaged in archaeological excavations of a major Bronze Age site. The oldest mosque in the UAE is located in the small town of Badiyah. Dibba is also a site of emerging archaeological interest.

Hatta

Hatta is an ancient fortress village nestled in the folds of the Hajar Mountains, about one-and-a-half hours' drive from Dubai City. The locals have used it for centuries as a retreat from the oppressive heat of summer on the coast. It offers old watchtowers, and the Hatta Fort Hotel can arrange safaris in the dunes, wadis, rock pools and mountains that surround Hatta.

Jazirat al-Hamra

Located about 37 kilometres from Umm al-Quwain, it is of considerable archaeological and historical interest. There are remains of a fort with high watchtowers and old wind-towers.

Julfar

Julfar, situated on Oman Road was an important port city built in the seventh century. Archaeological finds indicate that it traded as far as China and India.

Mudam Plain

Area south of Dhaid has emerged as an area of considerable archaeological interest. Scientists have demonstrated that these plains were settled by an agricultural society, which may also have mined copper ore from the mountains to the east.

Persian military camp

Called Khashm Nadir, built in the 18th century, it is located on the left off the roundabout a few kilometres outside the Old Town buried amongst the sand dunes. Also around this area is the Ras al-Khaimah Museum in the old fort on Al Hasn road.

Sharjah Natural History Museum

One of the best museums in the UAE run by Jongbloed, the museum is divided into the following exhibitions: a journey through Sharjah emirate; Man and the environment; a journey through time; the living desert; and the living seas. Besides providing detailed introduction to the desert culture, it also provides extensive information about UAE's flora, fauna and prehistory.

Umm al-Quwain

Archaeological excavations have revealed a major site at Al Door on the coast at the right of the main Ras al-Khaimah road, about 10 kilometres north of the Umm al-Quwain-Falaj/al-Moalla roundabout. Excavations show that Al Door was a major trading settlement.

Wildlife Checklist

Mammals

INSECTIVORES
(Insectivora)
Brandt's Hedgehog
Ethiopian Hedgehog
Indian House Shrew

BATS
(Chiroptera)
Egyptian Fruit Bat
Horse-shoe Bat
Indent Leaf-nosed Bat
Long-eared Bat
Mouse-tailed Bat
Sheath-tailed Bat
Vespertilionid Bat

CARNIVORES
(Carnivora)
Arabian Leopard
Blanford's Fox
Fennec Fox
Red Fox
Ruppell's Sand Fox
Caracal Lynx
Desert Wolf
Gordon's Wildcat
Striped Hyena

EVEN-TOED UNGULATES
(Artiodactyla)
Arabian Gazelle
Sand Gazelle
Thomson's Gazelle
Arabian Tahr
Belsa Oryx
Scimitar-horned Oryx
Jemsbok

HARES AND RABBITS
(Lagomorpha)
Cape Hare

RODENTS
(Rodentia)
Baluchistan Gerbil
Wagner's Gerbil
Desert Jerboa
Spiny Mouse

SEA COW
(Sirenia)
Dugong

WHALES AND DOLPHINS
(Cetacea)
Bottle Nose Dolphin
Common Dolphin
Indo Pacific
  Humpback Dolphin
Risso's Dolphin
Spotted Dolphin
Spinner Dolphin
Striped Dolphin
Finless Porpoise
Bryde's Whale
False Killer Whale
Fin Whale
Humpback Whale
Killer Whale
Pygmy Killer Whale
Sperm Whale

Birds

GREBES
(Podicipidae)
Black-necked Grebe
Little Grebe

CORMORANTS
(Phalacrocoracidae)
Great Cormorant
Socotra Cormorant

HERONS, EGRETS AND BITTERNS
(Ardeidae)
Bittern
Cattle Egret
Great White Egret
Little Egret
Little Bittern
Grey Heron
Indian Pond Heron
Little Green Heron
Night Heron
Purple Heron
Reef Heron
Squacco Heron
Western Reef Heron

STORKS
(Ciconiidae)
White Stork

IBISES AND SPOONBILLS
(Threskiornithidae)
Glossy Ibis
Spoonbill

FLAMINGOS
(Phoenicopteridae)
Greater Flamingo

DUCKS AND GEESE
(Anatidae)
Cotton Teal
Ferruginous Duck
Pintailed Duck
Shelduck
Tufted Duck
Gadwall
Garganey
Mallard
Pintail Pochard
Greylag Goose
White-fronted Goose
Wigeon

**VULTURES,
EAGLES, HAWKS
AND ALLIES**
(Accipitridae)
Black Kite
Egyptian Vulture
Griffon Vulture
Lappet-faced Vulture
Marsh Harrier
Pallid Harrier
Long-legged Buzzard
Bonelli's Eagle
Lesser Spotted Eagle
Short-toed Eagle
Spotted Eagle
Steppe Eagle
Sparrowhawk

OSPREY
(Pandionidae)
Osprey

FALCONS
(Falconidae)
Hobby
Kestrel
Lesser Kestrel
Peregrine Falcon
Sooty Falcon

GAME BIRDS
(Phasianidae)
Sand Partridge
Grey Francolin

CRANES
(Balearicidae)
Common Crane

**CRAKES, COOTS
AND MOORHENS**
(Rallidae)
Coot
Moorhen
Spotted Crake

BUSTARDS
(Otididae)
Houbara Bustard

STONE CURLEWS
(Burhinidae)
Stone Curlew

PLOVERS
(Charadriidae)
Crab Plover
Greater Sand Plover
Grey Plover
Kentish Plover
Lesser Golden Plover
Lesser Sand Plover
Little Ringed Plover
Pacific Golden Plover
Ringed Plover
Red-wattled Lapwing

STILTS
(Recurvirostridae)
Black-winged Stilt
Oystercatcher

**SNIPES AND
SANDPIPERS**
(Scolopacidae)
Sanderling
Bar-tailed Godwit
Black-tailed Godwit
Broad-billed
  Sandpiper
Common Sandpiper
Curlew Sandpiper
Green Sandpiper
Terek Sandpiper
Wood Sandpiper
Common Snipe
Dunlin
Greenshank
Redshank
Little Stint
Temminck's Stint
Ruff
Turnstone
Whimbrel

SHRIKES
(Laniidae)
Great Grey Shrike
Isabelline Shrike

**COURSERS AND
PRATINCOLES**
(Glareolidae)
Cream-coloured
  Courser
Collared Pratincole

GULLS AND TERNS
(Laridae)
Armenian Gull

Black-headed Gull
Lesser Black-headed
  Gull
Slender-billed Gull
Sooty Gull
Yellow-legged Gull
Bridled Tern
Gull-billed Tern
Lesser-crested Tern
Sandwich Tern
Saunder's Little Tern
Swift Tern
Whiskered Tern
White-cheeked Tern
White-winged Black
  Tern

SANDGROUSE
(Pteroclididae)
Chestnut-bellied
  Sandgrouse
Lichtenstein's
  Sandgrouse

**DOVES AND
PIGEONS**
(Columbidae)
Collared Dove
Namaqua Dove
Palm Dove
Rock Dove
Turtle Dove

PARROTS
(Psittacidae)
Rose-ringed Parakeet

OWLS
(Tytonidae)
Barn Owl

Strigidae
Eagle Owl
Little Owl
Scops Owl
Striated Scops Owl

SWIFTS
(Apodidae)
Common Swift
Pallid Swift

KINGFISHERS
(Alcedinidae)
European Kingfisher
Little Green Kingfisher
White-collared
  Kingfisher

BEE-EATERS
(Meropidae)
European Bee-eater
Little Green Bee-eater

ROLLERS
(Coraciidae)
Indian Roller

HOOPOES
(Upupidae)
Hoopoe

LARKS
(Alaudidae)
Black-crowned Finch
  Lark
Crested Lark
Desert Lark
Hoopoe Lark
Short-toed Lark
Sky Lark

**SHEARWATERS
AND PETRELS**
(Procellariidae)
Wedge-tailed
  Shearwater
Wilson's Storm Petrel

**SWALLOWS AND
MARTINS**
(Hirundinidae)
Swallow
Pale Crag Martin
Sand Martin

**WAGTAILS AND
PIPITS**
(Motacillidae)
Grey Wagtail
White Wagtail
Yellow Wagtail
Red-throated Pipit
Tawny Pipit
Tree Pipit

BULBULS
(Pycnonotidae)
Black-cheeked Bulbul
Red-vented Bulbul
White-cheeked Bulbul
Yellow-vented Bulbul

**THRUSHES
WHEATEARS AND
CHATS**
(Turdidae)
Rock Thrush
Song Thrush
Robin
Black Redstart
Redstart
Blackcap
Bluethroat
Common Whitethroat
Desert Lesser
  Whitethroat

Lesser Whitethroat
Desert Wheatear
Hume's Wheatear
Isabelline Wheatear
Northern Wheatear
Pied Wheatear
Red-tailed Wheatear
Nightingale
Rufous Bush Chat
Stonechat

BABBLERS
(Turdodidae)
Arabian Babbler

WARBLERS
(Sylviidae)
Booted Warbler
Clamorous Reed
  Warbler
Desert Warbler
Graceful Warbler
Marsh Warbler
Menetries' Warbler
Olivaceous Warbler
Orphean Warbler
Reed Warbler
Scrub Warbler
Sedge Warbler
Willow Warbler

SUNBIRDS
(Nectariniidae)
Purple Sunbird

BUNTINGS
(Emberizidae)
House Bunting
Ortolan Bunting

WAXBILLS
(Estrildidae)
Indian Silverbill
Trumpeter Finch

WEAVERS AND
SPARROWS
(Ploceidae)
Ruppell's Weaver
House Sparrow
Pale Rock Sparrow
Yellow-throated
  Sparrow

MYNAHS AND
STARLINGS
(Sturnidae)
Bank Mynah
Common Mynah
Starling

CROWS
(Corvidae)
Brown-necked Raven
Indian House Crow

SKUAS
(Stercorariidae)
Pomarine Skua

TROPICBIRDS
(Phaethontidae)
Red-billed Tropicbird

Reptiles and Amphibians

LIZARDS
(Sauria)
Arabian Sand Skink
Mabuya Skink
Ocellated Skink
Arabian Toad-head
Branded Toad-head
Blue-headed Agama
Toad-headed Agama
Desert Lacertid
Spiny-foot Lacertid
Desert Monitor
Dhabb
Sand Fish
Spiny-tailed Agamid

SNAKES
(Serpentes)
Arabian Rearfang
Burton's Carpet Viper
Sand Viper
Saw-scaled/Carpet
  Viper
Desert Boa
Sand Snake
Sandracer

TESTUDINES
(Turtles)
Green Turtle
Hawksbill Turtle
Leatherback Turtle
Loggerhead Turtle
Olive Ridley Turtle

AMPHIBIANS
(Amphibia)
Golden-eyed Toad

Fishes

(Osteichthyes)
Emperor Angelfish
Yellow-bar Angelfish
Barracuda
Batfish
Bonito
Blue-tail Boxfish
Double-bar Bream
One-spot Bream
Sea Bream
Black Fin Butterfly
  Fish
Five-line Cardinalfish
Gold-striped
  Cardinalfish
Cobia
Cow Rays
Domino Damselfish
Humpback Damselfish
Sergeant-major
  Damselfish
Doredo
Spotted Eagle Ray
Blue-scaled Emperor
Long-faced Emperor
Red-spot Emperor
Spangled Emperor
Aerolated Grouper
Blue-spotted Grouper
Brown-spotted
  Grouper
White-blotched
  Grouper
Black-spotted Grunt
Spotted Grunt
Guitar Fish
Silver-barred

Halfbeaks
Oriental Halibut
Wolf Herring
Orange-spotted Jack
Kingfish
Frigate Mackerel
Horse Mackerel
Indian Mackerel
Spanish Mackerel
Mojarra
Mono Diamondfish
Mottled Moray Eel
Mullet
Needlefish
Parrotfish
Pennantfish
African Pomano
Black-spotted Puffer
Queenfish
Brown-spotted
  Rabbitfish
Remora
Black-spotted
  Rubbertip
Sailfish
Sardine
Big-eyed Scad
Black-tip Shark
Hammerhead Shark
Reef Shark
White Shark
Black-spot Snapper
Blue-stripe Snapper
Red Snapper
Dotted Spinecheek
Blue-spotted Stingray
Honeycomb Stingray
Sunfish
Sohal Surgeon-fish
Yellow-tail
  Surgeon-fish
Bream Threadfin
Thumbprint
Golden Trevally
Blue-throat Triggerfish
Picasso Triggerfish
Thornback Trunkfish
Mackerel Tuna
Turkeyfish
Broom-tail Wrasse
Cleaner Wrasse
Moon Wrasse

Wildlife Profile

Mammals

Brandt's hedgehog, *Paraechinus hypomelas:* Not as common as the Ethiopian hedgehog. Both species are nocturnal and ideally adapted to desert conditions, being virtually water independent and with long legs. Brandt's also has large ears. It feeds on insects and small reptiles.

Ethiopian hedgehog, *Paraechinus aethiopicus:* Found more commonly in the emirates than Brandt's. Identifiable by its dark snout and white band on forehead.

Indian mouse shrew: Largely nocturnal, living in burrows in any habitat. Also eats small animals such as worms and snails, and domestic rubbish. Originally came by sea from India; most prolific near ports.

Egyptian fruit bat, *Rousettus aegyptiacus:* Commonly found in fruit trees around Ras al-Khaimah and considered a pest. The largest species in the emirates.

Mouse-tailed bat, *Rhinopoma muscatellum:* commonly found in caves, near Ras al-Khaimah and Buraimi, identifiable by its bird-like flight.

Indent leaf-nosed bat: lives in underground tunnels especially near the *falag*. Most widespread species. Has long ears and nose flap over muzzle. Recognizable by buttterfly-like flight.

Arabian leopard, *Panthera pardus numr:* Extremely rare, possibly surviving in the Hajar Mountains, feeding on any available animals. May stray over Ras al-Khaimah/Musandam border from Oman where they are protected.

Blanford's fox, *Vulpes cana:* Not native but occasionally spotted in the emirates.

Fennec fox, *Fennecus zerda:* Very rare. Smallest of desert foxes. Fur is pale, ears large and bushy tail black tipped.

Red fox, *Vulpes vulpes:* Most common carnivore. Found in the foothills of mountain ranges, near high mountain *wadis* and rural settlements. Nocturnal, it leaves its burrows to feed on small animals, fruit and insects. Black markings on ear tips.

Ruppell's sand fox, *Vulpes ruppelli:* Rare. Smaller than the red fox, with large ears; it survives in desert conditions; shy of human habitation.

Caracal lynx, *Felis caracal schmitzi:* Rare but widely distributed. Nocturnal, feeding on birds and smaller mammals. Able to catch birds in flight. Medium-sized with sandy-red coat.

Desert wolf, *Canis lupus arabis:* Rare in the wild but apparently interbreeding with local dogs.

Wild cats: *Felis sylvesris* and subspecies *Felis sylvestris tristrami,* **Gordon's wild cat,** *Felis sylvestris gordoni,* and **Sand cat,** *Felis margarita harrisoni,* are all threatened with extinction through hunting. Feed at night on small birds and animals.

Striped hyena, *Hyaena hyaena:* Rare in the wild. Dog-like build with striped coat; lives underground during day. Very shy.

Arabian gazelle, *Gazella gazella arabica:* Extremely rare. Native of the Arabian desert where they once formed huge herds. Their sand-coloured coats act as camouflage. Now protected on Al Siniyah island off Umm al-Quwain. Found at altitudes of 600 metres. They can attain speeds of 65 kilometres an hour.

Arabian tahr, *Hemitragus jayakari:* Very rare. A species of beardless wild goat with dark, shaggy coat and short horns.

Beisa oryx, *Oryx gazella beisa:* Native to mountainous regions. Found only in Sir Bani Yas Nature Reserve.

Jemsbok, *Oryx gazella:* Native to mountainous regions. Now found only in Sir Bani Yas Nature Reserve Island.

Sand gazelle: Native to mountainous regions. Now found only in Sir Bani Yas Nature Reserve.

Scimitar-horned oryx, *Oryx dammah:* Native to mountainous regions. Now found only in Sir Bani Yas Nature Reserve Island.

Thomson's gazelle, *Gazella thomsoni:* Native to mountainous regions. Now found only in Sir Bani Yas Nature Reserve.

Cape hare, *Lepus capensis:* A large species, which survives in most conditions. Feeds on grass and low plants. Hides in shallow hollows scooped out on the sides of sand hills.

Desert jerboa, *Jaculus jaculus:* Found in desert and steppe conditions. Small mammal with black and white tipped tail. Hibernates in hottest season in burrows. Survives on stored food.

Birds

Grebes: At least four species are found in the emirates which include the **Black-necked grebe,** *Podiceps nigricollis;* often spotted in Saffa Park, Dubai.

Cormorants: The **Socotra cormorant,** *Phalacrocorax nigrogularis,* is a resident of the Gulf Islands on the west coast. Its breeding season is October to March.

Herons and egrets: These are common migrants along the coastline of UAE. Kalba is ideal for spotting the **Indian pond heron,** *Ardeloa grayii,* the **Little egret,** *Egretta garzetta,* **Great white egret,** *Egretta alba,* and the resident **Little green heron,** *Butorides striatus.* Also spotted in the shallow waters and mudflats of Al Jazeerah Khor, and Abu Dhabi Bird Reserve. **Reef herons** also reside in the mangroves of Dubai Creek.

Flamingos: Flocks of **Greater flamingo,** *Phoenicopterus ruber,* migrate to the shallow waters and mudflats of Dubai Greek as well as coastal Al Jazeerah Khor. They have benefited greatly from conservation efforts including an artificial breeding island.

Ducks and geese: Migratory visitors to the lakes of the urban parks around October. Common visitors include **Cotton teal,** *Nettapus coromandelianus,* **Pintail pochard,** *Aythya ferina,* and **Pintailed duck,** *Anas acuta.* **Garganey, Widgeon** and **Mallard** can be spotted along the inner reaches of Dubai Creek.

Vultures: The rare **Lappet-faced vulture,** *Torgos tracheliotus,* can be found on the cretaceous shales of the gravel plains near Jebel Mafit and other mountains. The common **Egyptian vulture,** *Neophron pernopterus,* is also found near Al Ain zoo and Mafit.

Ospreys: Annual visitors that feed on fish along Dubai Creek but return to their nesting grounds on uninhabited Gulf Islands.

Eagles: Bonelli's eagle may be spotted soaring on the thermals along the mountain ridge bordering Oman.

Kestrels: Previously kestrels visited the emirates on their migration further north; recently they have remained in the gardens and parks of UAE.

Kites and buzzards: The rare **Long-legged buzzard,** *Buteo rufinus,* and other birds of prey are found on Jebel Mafit as well as the high mountain bordering Oman.

Coots: These are common on the urban lake of Soffa Park. A passing migrant or winter visitor from October to May.

Lapwings and plovers: The **Lesser sand plover,** *Charadrius mongolus,* **Kentish plover,** *Charadrius alexandrinus,* and **Grey plover,** *Pluvialis squatarola,* are commonly spotted along the shallow-watered sand banks of Dubai Creek. The **Greater sand plover** is also found near coastal Kalba. Several species of plover can be spotted in the coast reserve at Abu Dhabi. **Lesser golden plovers** and grey plovers arrive along Dubai Creek in July and leave in April.

Sandpipers, godwits, curlews and **greenshanks:** The most common **Broad-billed sandpiper** has made Dubai Creek its favourite haunt. Other varieties found there include the **Curlew sandpiper,** *Calidris ferrugine,* **Black-tailed Goodwit,** *Limosa limosa,* **Greenshank,** *Tringa nebularia,* and **Redshank,** *Tringa totanus.* The **Terek sandpiper,** *Tringa cinereus,* can be spotted near Kalba.

Gulls and terns: Several species of gulls make their home along the rocky coastal cliffs and outlying islands. These include **Black-headed gull,** *Larus ridibundus,* and **Slender-billed gull,** *Larus genei.* The bird reserve in Abu Dhabi is a good place to spot these and other species as are the lagoons of Umm al-Quwain.

Doves: The **Rock dove** lives on the desert plains while the **Palm dove** prefers the bush vegetation and abundant water of villages along the wadis.

Owls: Two species may occasionally be sighted on the desert plains, namely the **Little owl** and the **Eagle owl.**

Kingfishers: The rare **White-collared kingfisher,** the **Little green kingfisher** and common **European kingfisher** can be spotted amongst the mangroves, Kalba on the east coast.

Bee-eaters: The migratory **Bee-eater,** *Merops apiaster,* found in Saffa Park, 12 kilometres from Dubai city. They are attracted by swarming bees, their staple diet. Common March to May and August to November. The **Little green bee-eater,** *Merops orientalis,* is a resident breeder not found west of Dubai.

Hoopoes: *Upupa epops,* a common visitor in April, best seen in Saffa Park, Dubai, near the lake.

Skylarks: One of the many variety of birds which inhabit the local parks and gardens. **Black-crowned finch lark, Hoopoe lark** and **Desert larks** inhabit the scrub and rocks of the desert plains.

Martins: The **Pale crag martin** previously inhabited only the steep-sided wadis and mountain sides; now they visit such gardens as Hatta Fort Hotel.

Bulbuls: These resident breeders are most commonly found in the urban parks, gardens and plantations of the emirates. The **Red-vented bulbul,** *Pycnonotus cafer,* an escaped exotic, is often seen in Saffa Park, Dubai, and Bateen Wood, Abu Dhabi. The **Black-capped bulbul,** *Pycnotus xanthopygos,* is sighted in the mountain regions and westward towards Abu Dhabi.

Shrikes: Such as the **Great grey shrike** are commonly spotted near the lake at Saffa Park, Dubai.

Thrushes: Spend the European winter in the gardens and parks of the emirates.

Robins: Spend the European winter in the gardens and parks of the emirates.

Babblers: The **Arabian babbler,** *Turtoides squamiceps* resides and breeds throughout the emirates.

Warblers: There are a wide variety of warblers in the urban parks and gardens. Amongst the most common of Saffa Park are the **Graceful warbler,** *Prinia gracilis,* the **Great reed warbler,** and the resident **Clamorous reed warbler,** *Acrocephalus stentoreus.* The **Booted warbler,** *Hippolais caligata,* and Clamorous reed warbler are also spotted along the east coast near Kalba. Warblers also visit the Bateen Wood area of Abu Dhabi, including the **Olivaceous warbler,** *Hippolais pallida.* **Scrub warbler** live among the scrub and rocks of the plains.

Sunbirds: The **Purple sunbird** is often spotted in Saffa Park, Dubai and Hatta Fort Hotel gardens.

Sparrows: The common **House sparrow** has proliferated throughout the emirates due largely to the greening of the country. The **Yellow-throated sparrow** arrives in March and spends the season along the coast.

Mynahs: The **Common mynah,** *Acridotheres tristis,* is one of many species to be seen in Saffa Park and Bateen Wood. The **Bank mynah** also visits Bateen Wood, Abu Dhabi. This aggressive bird was originally an escaped exotic.

Starlings: Spend the European winter in the gardens and parks of the emirates.

Ravens: The **Brown-necked raven** visits the local gardens and parks.

Tropicbirds: The resident **Red-billed tropicbird,** *Phaethon aethereus,* inhabits the west-coast islands and breeds between December and June.

Sealife

Crabs: Ghost crabs, *Ocypode saratan,* burrow into the sands just above tide level. Most active at night, they feed on anything including other crabs and turtle hatchlings. **Mole crabs** burrow in shove sand. Occasionally prey to Ghost crabs. **Mud crabs** burrow in coastal sands. Occasionally prey to Ghost crabs.

Dolphins and whales: The most common species in the Arabian Gulf include the **Bottlenose dolphin,** *Tursiops truncatus,* and the **Indo-pacific hump-back,** *Sousa chinensis.* The latter prefers shallow, coastal water. Rare varieties include **Spinner dolphin,** *Stenella longirostris,* **Spotted dolphin,** *Chlorostigma.* The rarest is the **Finless porpoise,** *Neophocoena phocoenoides.* The Indian Ocean is frequented by the **Sperm whale,** *Physeter macrocephalus,* and **Risso's dolphin,** *Grampus riseus.* Other whales identified in the Gulf include: **Fin whale,** *Balaenoptera physalus,* **Minke,** *Balaenoptera acutorostrata,* **Blue sei,** *Balaenoptera borealis,* **Bryde's,** *Balaenoptera edeni,* **Humpback,** *Megaptera novaeangliae,* and the **False killer whale,** *Pseudorca crassidens.*

Sea cow, *Dugong dugon,* is a protected sea mammal often found off the coast of Abu Dhabi and the island of Merawah. It feeds on seagrass found in shallow water.

Sea snakes: Several varieties including the **Blue-banded,** *Hydrophis cyanocinctus,* **Yellow bellied,** *Pelamis platurus,* **Reef sea snake,** *Hydrophis ornatus,* **Arabian Gulf sea snake,** *Hydrophis lapemoides,* and **Yellow sea snake,** *Hydrophis spiralis,* can be spotted on the surface of the Gulf waters.

Turtles: There are several species of endangered turtles, including the **Green turtle,** *Chelonia mydas,* the smaller **Hawksbill,** *Eretmochelys imbricuta,* the **Leatherback,** *Dermochelys coriacea,* the **Loggerhead,** *Caretta caretta,* and possibly **Olive ridley turtle,** *Lepidochelys olivacea.* The first two nest on the beaches of the emirates and feed on sea grasses. The Leatherback's diet also includes jellyfish, while the adult Hawksbill feeds on sponges, molluscs and other invertebrates. Green turtles have been spotted at Khor Kalba, Jazirat Badiyah and Das Island; Loggerhead at Da'biyah.

Fishes: Varieties of fishes inhabit the coral reefs and rocks of the Arabian gulf. These include **Catfish, Batfish, Black spotted rubbertip, Surgeon, Parrot fish, Angel fish, Blue spotted grouper.** The Indian Ocean is home to such species as **Leopard flounder, Spotted sole** and **Yellow-finned snake eel.**

Plant Profile

ADIANTACEAE
This family includes *Adiantum capillusveneris* (maidenhair fern), which prefers wet soil.

AIZOACEAE
The best-known member of this family is *Aizoon canariense* ('du'aa'), which prefers salty and sandy conditions.

AMARANTHACEAE
It includes *Aerva javanica* ('al-Ra'), which prefers sandy soil.

ANACARDIACEAE
The most common species is *Mangifera indica* (mango), found in plantations and wadis.

APOCYNACEAE
Members of this family occur widely in diverse habitats: it includes *Nerium mascatense* (native oleander), *Nerium oleander* (Mediterranean oleander), and *Plumeria alba* (frangipani), found in plantations and wadis; *Rhazya stricta* (harmul) is found in gravel plains and is poisonous to herbivores.

ASCLEPIADACEAE
This family includes *Calotropis procera* (Sodom apple). It prefers sandy soil and deters grazers with its poisonous sap but provides nectar for bees and wasps. *Leptadenia pyrotechnica* (broombush) is encouraged on sand dunes to stabilize them. It produces masses of small yellow flowers in March. *Periploca apylla* grows in mountain wadis.

BORAGINACEAE
There are at least four species: *Cordia sebestena* (scarlet cordia) which grows in plantations; *Moltkiopsis ciliata* and *Arnebia hispidissima* (Arabian primrose), which prefer sandy soil; and *Heliotropium kotschyi* ('ramraam'), which grows in salty soil.

CACTACEAE
The best-known member of this family is *Opuntia engelmannii* (prickly pear), which prefers sandy soil.

CAPPARIDACEAE
There are several species: *Capparis cartilaginea* (caper), found on mountains; *Capparis spinosa* ('lasf') which grows in plantations; and *Dipterygium glaucum* (sedge), which prefers sandy soil.

CARYOPHYLLACEAE
There are several species including *Cometes surattensis*, found on rocky hills and plains, *Polycarpaea spicata* and *Saponaria barbata*, which prefer sandy soil, *Sclerocephalus arabicus*, found in sandy or rocky conditions, and *Silene villosa* ('nizbah'), which grows on sand dunes.

CASUARINACEAE
The most common family member is the *Casuarina equisetifolia* (whispering pine), which grows in plantations and the shelter belt.

CHENOPODIACEAE
Several species of this family include *Arthrocnemum macrostachyum* and *A glaucum*, found in marsh or salty conditions; *Cornulaca monocantha*, which prefers sandy soil; *Cornulaca leucacantha* ('haad'); *Halopeplis perfoliata*, a succulent with red and orange fleshy leaves which grows in salty or sandy soil and is relatively common on the coast; *Hammada elegans* and *Salsola schweinfurthii*, which grow in sandy soil; *Hammada schmidtiana* ('ramth'); *Salsola baryosma*, which prefers salty soil.

COMBRETACEAE
This family includes *Terminalia catappa* (Indian almond), which is found in plantations.

COMPOSITAE
Members include *Launea capitata*, which prefers sandy soil; *Launea espinosa* ('kubbaath'); *Reichardia tingitana* ('maknaan') which grows in sand or gravel; and *C arvensis* ('luliiq').

CONVOLVULACEAE
The family includes *Convolvulus prostratus*, which is found in rocky areas; *C virgatus* ('bayaad'); *Ipomea biloba* (goat's foot), which grows in sandy soil.

CRUCIFERAE
The drought-resistant *Anastatica hierochuntica* (little rose of Jericho) grows on gravel plains and hills. It survives the harsh arid conditions through its unique ability to roll into a tight ball until the rains. *Diplotaxis harra* is found in rocky plains. *Eremobium aegyptiacum* and *Erucaria hispanica* prefer sandy soil. *Physorrhyncus chaemarapistum* grows on rocky plains. *Savignya parviflora* prefers sandy soil. *Zilla spinosa* is found in sandy or rocky areas.

CYPERACEAE
The species *Cyperus conglomeratus* (sedge) grows in sandy soil.

EUPHORBIACEAE
The *Euphorbia* comprise 1600 species. Representatives in UAE are *Euphorbia arabica*, *Euphorbia hirta* and the small-leafed *Euphorbia larica* ('isbaq') found on rocky hills; *Ricinus communis* grows in plantations.

GENTIANACEAE
The family includes *Centaurium pulchellum*, which prefers wet wadis, and *Erodium glacinatum* ('qarnuwah').

GERANIACEAE
The family includes *Erodium malacoides* and *Erodium neuradifolium*, both of which prefer sandy soil. *Geranium mascatense* grows in wadis.

GRAMINAE
Several species such as *Cenchrus ciliaris*, *Halopyrum mucronatum* (beach grass), and *Sporobolos spicatus* prefer sandy soil and are found in coastal areas.

HYDROCHARITACEAE AND CYMODOCEACEAE
Include sea grasses such as *Halodule uninervis*, *Halophila ovalis* and *Halophila stipulacea*, which grow in sedimentary shallows of the Arabian Gulf and provide essential feeding grounds for the endangered sea cow and green turtle.

LEGUMINOSAE
There are many species in the emirates: the *Acacia arabica* (Arabic gum tree) grows in plantations and sandy soil; *A auriliculiformis* prefers rocky or sandy conditions; *A decurrens* (green wattle) is found in plantations; *A ehrenoergiana* prefers sandy soil; *A tortilis* (acacia tree) with its long tap roots grows in gravel or plantations and flowers in June and July; *Albizzia lebbeck* (fry wood tree) is found in plantations; *Argyrolohium roseum* prefers gravel plains; *Astragalus fasciculifolius* grows on mountains; *Cassia italica* ('senna') prefers sandy soil or wadis and discourages grazing by camels as it causes diarrhoea; *Indigofera arabica* is found in rocky plains and wadis; *Indigofera intricata* (indigo plant); *Caesalpinea bonduc* (Indian nut) grows in plantations; *Melilotus indica* ('hind qawq') is found in sandy areas or plantations; *Lotus halophilus* ('hurbash') prefers salty soil; *Parkinsonia aculeata* (Jerusalem thorn), *Peltophorum inerme* (rusty shieldbearer), *Pongamia glabra* (pongam) and *Prosopis juliflora* (mesquite) grow in plantations; *P spicigera* (ghaf tree) is found on sand dunes where its long tap roots and ability to absorb water through its leaves keep it alive for up to five years without rainfall. It produces yellow catkin-like flowers March to April.

LILIACEAE
This family contains *Aloe vera* (aloe), which grows in plantations, and *Asphodelus fistulosus* (lily), which prefers sand or gravel.

LYTHRACEAE
Lawsonia inermis (henna) is found in plantations and similar situations.

MALVACEAE
The best-known member of this family is the *Hibiscus rosa sinensis* (Chinese shoe flower) which grows in plantations. *Malva aegyptiaca* ('khabiizah') prefers sandy soil while *Malvaviscus arboreus* (Turk's hat hibiscus) and *Thespesia populaea* (Aden apple) are found in plantations, gardens and parks.

MORACEAE
This family includes *Ficus benghalensis* (banyan), which is found in plantations; *F carica* (common fig); *F nitida* (laurel fig), which prefers wadis and mountains; *Morus nigra* (mulberry), which grows in mountains or plantations.

MORINGACEAE
Moringa oleifera (drumstick tree) grows in plantations.

MYRTACEAE
The best-known member of this family is the *Callestemon speciosus* (Australian bottle brush), found in plantations, parks and gardens. Others are *Eucalyptus camaldulensis* (red gum), found in the shelter belt, and *Melaleuca leucadendron*, which grows in plantations.

NYCTAGINACEAE
This family includes *Boerhaavia elegans* ('hadimdam'), which prefers rocky areas; *Bougainvillea glabra* and *B spectabilis*, which grow in plantations, urban parks and gardens.

OLEACEAE
The species of the Oleaceae family found in the emirates are *Jasminum sambac* (Arabian jasmine), growing in plantations, and *Olea europaea* (olive tree), which prefers sandy soil.

ORCHIDACEAE
Epipactis veratrifolia (orchid) grows in plantations, city gardens and parks.

OROBANCHACEAE
Includes the parasitic *Cistanche tubulosa* (desert hyacinth), which prefers sandy or salty soil.

PALMACEAE
Cocos nucifera (coconut palm), *Phoenix dactylifera* (date palm) and *Washingtonia robusta* (Californian fan palm) are found in plantations and similar conditions.

PLANTAGINACEAE
Plantago afra ('yanm') and *P ovata* grow in sandy conditions.

PLUMBAGINACEAE
Dyerophytum indicum, is found in wadis; purple-flowering *Limonium axillare* (sea lavender) and *Plumbago capensis* (leadwort) prefer the sandy, elevated soils between Abu Dhabi and Dubai.

POLYGONACEAE
Much valued by the Bedu, *Calligonum comosum* (firebush) grows in sandy conditions. It retains water in its fleshy roots and remains dormant during droughts. It bears small white fruits in February to March. *Antigonon leptopus* (coral vine) grows in sandy conditions while *Rumex vesicarius* ('humaad') prefers rocky plains.

PORTULACACEAE
Two members of this family are *Portulaca grandiflora* and *P olereaca* ('barbiir'), which grow in sandy soil.

PRIMULACEAE
This family includes the species *Anagallis arvensis* (blue pimpernel), found in plantations, city gardens and parks.

RHAMNACEAE
Common members of this family are *Ziziphus jujuba* (Chinese date) and *Z spina-christi* (crown of thorns), which grow in plantations.

RHIZOPHORACEAE
Avicennia marina (grey mangrove) grows in marsh and coastal areas and is subject to several replanting programmes. Common in Ras al-Khaimah and Khor Kalba.

SALVADORACEAE
One member of this family is *Salvadora persica* (rak bush), found on low mountains.

SAPINDACEAE
Dodoea viscosa grows in plantations.

SCROPHULARIACEAE
This family includes *Schweinfurthia papillionacea*, found in wadis and coastal areas, and *Scrophularia deserti*, which grows on rocky plains.

SOLANACEAE
Two members of this family are *Lycium shawii* (desert thorn), found in low mountains, and *Solanum nigrum* ('shabr al-balbuul'), which grows on plantations.

TAMARICACEAE
This family includes *Tamarix aphylla*, *T articulata* and *T passerinoides*, which prefer salty soil.

VERBENACEAE
This family includes the species *Clerodendron inerme* (wild jasmine), *Lantana camara* (common lantana) and *Lippia nodiflora*, usually found in plantations, while common lantana also grows in mountainous areas.

VITACEAE
The species *Vitis vinifera* (grape vine) grows on plantations.

ZYGOPHYLLACEAE
Fagonia indica ('shukaa') is found on rocky plains while *Tribulus omanense* ('zahr'), *Tribulus terrestris* (tribulus) and *Zygophyllum simplex* prefer sandy conditions. *Zygophyllum hamiense* grows in salty soil and contains a herbivore deterrent which causes diarrhoea.

Demographic Profile

Location
A federation of seven emirates formerly known as the Trucial States, the UAE is situated on the east coast of the Arabian Peninsula, sharing a border with the neighbouring Sultanate of Oman.

About 65 per cent of the UAE is desert, extending from the western-most tip of Abu Dhabi, where it borders Saudi Arabia, eastwards to the land border with Oman and the Indian Ocean; in the north, the coast runs along the Persian Gulf as far as Oman, which is at the tip of the peninsula opposite the Strait of Hormuz. The coasts of the UAE are separated by the Musandam Peninsula.

Area
The emirates have a territory of about 85,000 sq km (32,818 sq mls). Abu Dhabi is the largest, covering an area of approximately 65,000 sq km (25,096 sq mls). Abu Dhabi covers almost all the western and central areas of the UAE.

Dubai is the second largest, covering an area of 3,900 sq km (1,505 sq mls). It extends from the industrial zone of Jebel Ali in the west to the neighbouring emirate of Sharjah to the northeast. On the east, the enclave of Hatta lying on the border with Oman is part of Dubai territory.

The emirates of Ajman, the UAE's smallest emirate is a tiny enclave of 260 sq km (100 sq mls), Umm al-Quwain consisting of a narrow lagoon with an area of 780 sq km (301 sq mls) in the north is Ras al-Khaimah which covers 1,690 sq km (652 sq mls).

To the east of the other Northern Emirates, Fujairah covers an area of 1,170 sq km (451 sq mls).

Topography
The topography is varied: a line of low mountains stretches all along the eastern coast of the UAE, and gives way to the sandy coastline of Fujairah; in the west and north, the desert changes from sandy, with spectacular, reddish or pink-coloured sand-dunes, to arid scrubby sand or gravelly rock. Sandy beaches and salt flats stretch all along the Gulf coast.

More than two-thirds of the UAE's total area is covered by sandy desert, studded by the occasional oasis. The mountains are dominated by the Hajar (rock) Range in the east which divide the

Gulf coastline from the deeper waters of the Indian Ocean. The mountains are rugged with some of the cliff facing almost vertical.

The coast is bordered with reefs, shoals, lagoons and low-lying islands. There are more than 200 islands.

Population
The UAE has a population of almost 2.377 million per the 1995 census. Males outnumber females by a wide margin, making up 66 per cent of the total population, largely as a result of the large numbers of immigrants.

Abu Dhabi is the most populous, with a total population of more than 900,000 or 39 per cent of the total; Dubai has 675,000 people, or about 28 per cent of the population; followed by Sharjah with little over 400,000 people, representing 17 per cent of the population. The rest of the emirates are scantily populated. Ajman's population is 120,000, Ras al-Khaimah has a population of 144,000 people; Fujairah has about 75,000 people; Umm al-Quwain a tiny 35,000 people.

The above figures include foreigners living in the UAE. The local Arabs make up about a quarter of the total population.

Language
The oficial language is Arabic but English is widely spoken and understood. Both languages are commonly used in business and commerce.

Religion
Islam is the official religion of the UAE and there are a large number of mosques throughout the city. Other religions are respected and Dubai has two Christian churches, St Mary's (Roman Catholic) and Holy Trinity (inter-denominational).

Literacy
There are well over 290,000 children at government schools throughout the country. Each small desert or mountain village has its school for younger children, while secondary schools with boarding facilities are in larger towns.

Outside the government sector, there is a wide range of 300 private schools, attended by over 150,000 students. Further education is also available for citizens through a number of technical colleges, like the Dubai Aviation College, linked to Dubai's Department of Civil Aviation, the Emirates Banking Training Institute, or the Career Development Centre of the Abu Dhabi National Oil Company.

Health service
There has been heavy investment in health care for the past couple of decades, both in preventive medicine, and an extensive health education programme. There is a smaller but thriving private health care industry with 9 hospitals, 44 multipurpose poly-clinics, and nearly 1,300 doctors in private practice. There are 35 hospitals and 98 medical centres in the Government sector.

Considerable attention has also been paid to preventive medicine. Over 95 percent of new-born children are now vaccinated against tuberculosis, and 85 per cent against diphtheria, whooping cough, tetanus and polio. Malaria has been virtually eliminated, while immunisation against diseases like measles and German measles has helped to reduce infant mortality rates to 11.8 per 100,000 of the population, comparable to developed nations. Life expectancy has risen to 73.5 for women and 71 for men.

Gazetteer

(Distances between Emirates in kilometres)

Abu Dhabi
Ajman 185, Dubai 165, Fujairah 200, Ras al-Khaimah 252, Sharjah 181, Umm al-Quwain 203

Ajman
Dubai 20, Fujairah 110, Ras al-Khaimah 67, Sharjah 5, Umm al-Quwain 17, Abu Dhabi 185

Dubai
Fujairah 120, Ras al-Khaimah 87, Sharjah 16, Umm al-Quwain 38, Abu Dhabi 165, Ajman 20

Fujairah
Ras al-Khaimah 120, Sharjah 115, Umm al-Quwain 110, Abu Dhabi 200, Ajman 110, Dubai 120

Ras al-Khaimah
Sharjah 71, Umm al-Quwain 49, Abu Dhabi 252, Ajman 67, Dubai 87, Fujairah 120

Sharjah
Umm al-Quwain 22, Abu Dhabi 181, Ajman 5, Dubai 16, Fujairah 115, Ras al-Khaimah 71

Umm al-Quwain
Abu Dhabi 203, Ajman 17, Dubai 38, Fujairah 110, Ras al-Khaimah 49, Sharjah 22

Listings

Dialling Codes

Abu Dhabi	02
Ajman	06
Al Ain	03
Dubai	04
Fujairah	09
Ras al-Khaimah	07
Sharjah	06
Umm al-Quwain	06

Air Charter Companies

Abu Dhabi
Abu Dhabi Aviation
PO Box 2723
Tel: 449100
Fax: 449081

Aero Gulf
PO Box 10566
Tel: 823157
Fax: 823028

Dubai
Emitex Aviation Services (Citylink seaplane)
PO Box 8619
Tel: 820101
Fax: 820100

Airlines

Abu Dhabi
Aeroflot Russian International Airlines
PO Box 25111
Tel: 315016
Fax: 316247

Air France
PO Box 806
Tel: 215815
Fax: 343002

Air India
PO Box 46889
Tel: 322300
Fax: 327376

Airlanka Limited
PO Box 2086
Tel: 212057
Fax: 340391

Air Malta
PO Box 2911
Tel: 331511
Fax: 324312

Al Yemda (Air Yemen)
PO Box 346
Tel: 335028
Fax: 392142

Balkan Bulgarian Airlines
PO Box 1200
Dubai
Tel: 778877
Fax: 788887

Biman (Bangladesh Airlines)
PO Box 4356
Tel: 342597
Fax: 344664

British Airways
PO Box 267
Tel: 341328
Fax: 349205

Cathay Pacific Airways Limited
PO Box 279
Tel: 323586
Fax: 216855

Cyprus Airways
PO Box 346
Tel: 342300
Fax: 317012

Czechoslovak Airlines
PO Box 2838
Tel: 784455
Fax: 793378

Egypt Air
PO Box 45222
Tel: 212100
Fax: 347775

Emirates Airlines Bin Harmal Travel and Tourism
PO Box 47470
Tel: 315777/888

Ethiopian Airlines
PO Box 346
Tel: 333153
Fax: 317012

Garuda Indonesia
PO Box 278
Tel: 328124
Fax: 392425

Gulf Air
PO Box 573
Tel: 331700
Fax: 321410

Iran Air
PO Box 278
Tel: 324266
Fax: 311546

KLM Royal Dutch Airlines
PO Box 3264
Tel: 323280
Fax: 341365

Kuwait Airways
PO Box 46147
Tel: 770555
Fax: 725157

Lufthansa German Airlines
PO Box 26382
Tel: 213200
Fax: 213566

Malev (Hungarian Airlines)
PO Box 7364
Tel: 339861
Fax: 316101

Pakistan Int Airlines Corp
PO Box 698
Tel: 320638
Fax: 314662

Philippine Airlines
PO Box 2086
Tel: 351700
Fax: 331313

Royal Air Maroc
PO Box 3644
Tel: 774950
Fax: 782479

Singapore Airlines
PO Box 267
Tel: 221110
Fax: 311353

Sudan Airways
PO Box 698
Tel: 335867
Fax: 342531

Swissair
PO Box 47077
Tel: 343430
Fax: 335812

Syrian Arab Airlines
PO Box 346
Tel: 335821
Fax: 317012

United Airlines
PO Box 267
Tel: 339841
Fax: 315654

Yemen Airways
PO Box 5027
Tel: 338700
Fax: 392790

Zas Airline of Egypt
PO Box 698
Tel: 331511
Fax: 324312

Ajman
Emirates Airline
PO Box 1446
Tel: 641111
Fax: 660004

Gulf Air
PO Box 1757
Tel: 654882
Fax: 658789

Al Ain
Emirates Airlines Bin Harmal Travel and Tourism
PO Box 1446
Tel: 641111

Dubai
Aer Lingus
PO Box 1515
Tel: 228151
Fax: 225973

Aeroflot Russian International Airlines
PO Box 1020
Tel: 222245
Fax: 227771

Air Canada
Al Naboodah Travel Agencies
PO Box 1200
Tel: 270500
Fax: 279488

Air Comoros
Al Abbas Travel Agency
PO Box 327
Tel: 511171
Fax: 521200

Air Djibouti
Naseer Air Travel and Shipping Agencies
PO Box 1520
Tel: 214455
Fax: 211016

Air France
Al Naboodah Travel Agencies
PO Box 1200
Tel: 667773
Fax: 629877

Air Hong Kong Limited
PO Box 8312
Tel: 822801
Fax: 822813

Air India
PO Box 1701
Tel: 276747
Fax: 271293

Airlanka Limited
PO Box 12889
Tel: 225951
Fax: 234245

Air Malta
PO Box 12863
Tel: 319990
Fax: 214560

Air Tanzania
Al Zohra Travel
PO Box 13020
Tel: 234390
Fax: 823599

Alitalia
Naseer Air Travel and Shipping Agencies
PO Box 6594
Tel: 284656
Fax: 236148

American Airlines
PO Box 70
Tel: 518185
Fax: 359256

Azerbaijan Airlines
PO Box 13033
Tel: 263555
Fax: 262566

Astro Airline House of Travel
PO Box 1515
Tel: 281510
Fax: 224085

Austrian Airlines
Al Naboodah Travel Agencies
PO Box 1200
Tel: 224159
Fax: 279488

Balkan Bulgarian Airlines
PO Box 1200
Tel: 222156
Fax: 238033

Biman (Bangladesh Airlines)
PO Box 1515
Tel: 283767
Fax: 278451

British Airways
PO Box 1989
Tel: 314141
Fax: 310731

British Midland
PO Box 53226
Tel: 314299
Fax: 310583

Canadian Pacific
Al Rais Travel and Shipping Agencies
PO Box 24713
Tel: 519519
Fax: 520700

Cargolux Airlines International
PO Box 5977
Tel: 822071
Fax: 822442

Cathay Pacific Airways Limited
PO Box 4868
Tel: 239355
Fax: 279954

China Airlines Asian Travels
PO Box 1187
Tel: 221511
Fax: 274631

Continental Airlines
Al Rais Travel and Shipping Agencies
PO Box 24713
Tel: 520100
Fax: 520700

Cyprus Airways
Nasser Air Travel
PO Box 1520
Tel: 215325
Fax: 211016

Czechoslovakia Airlines
PO Box 1810
Tel: 212142
Fax: 233054

Daalo Airlines
PO Box 21297
Tel: 255808
Fax: 264464

Eastern Airlines
Al Rais Travel and Shipping Agencies
PO Box 24713
Tel: 520100
Fax: 520700

East West Airlines
Al Naboodah Travel Agencies
PO Box 1200
Tel: 270500
Fax: 279488

Egypt Air
PO Box 12919
Tel: 248555
Fax: 273300

Emirates Airlines Telephone Sales
Dubai Airline Centre
PO Box 686
Tel: 215544/271234

Ethiopian Airlines Asian Travels
PO Box 7140
Tel: 237963
Fax: 273306

Eva Air
PO Box 52156
Tel: 556776
Fax: 368226

Federal Express
PO Box 9239
Tel: 821066
Fax: 821703

Finnair
PO Box 576
Tel: 552121
Fax: 552377

Flying Cargo Shuttle Freight Forwarders
PO Box 12962
Tel: 529905
Fax: 521591

Garuda-Indonesian Airlines
AASA Travel and Tours
PO Box 16741
Tel: 232955
Fax: 821046

German Cargo
PO Box 5545
Tel: 822111
Fax: 822221

Gulf Air
PO Box 4410
Tel: 231700
Fax: 286665

Iran Air
PO Box 4389
Tel: 222698
Fax: 237487

Japan Airlines
Al Futtaim Travel and Cargo
PO Box 7880
Tel: 239433
Fax: 233846

Jes Air
Al Naboodah
PO Box 1200
Tel: 224159
Fax: 279488

Jet Airways Tourism and Travel
PO Box 20485
Tel: 226371
Fax: 222490

Kenya Airways
PO Box 24713
Tel: 289222
Fax: 511964

Kish Air
Al Rais Travel and Shipping
PO Box 50508
Tel: 682602
Fax: 682923

KLM Royal Dutch Airlines
PO Box 1696
Tel: 244747
Fax: 245916

Korean Airlines
Pan World Air Travel Agency
PO Box 24775
Tel: 228183
Fax: 271216

Kuwait Airways
PO Box 1984
Tel: 285896
Fax: 281807

Libyan Arab Airlines
PO Box 55870
Tel: 210400
Fax: 234970

Lot Polish Airlines
Nasser Air Travel
PO Box 1520
Tel: 284292
Fax: 211016

Lufthansa German Airlines
PO Box 5545
Tel: 221191
Fax: 221192

Malaysian Airlines
PO Box 24713
Tel: 521221
Fax: 527286

Malev (Hungarian Airlines)
PO Box 1200
Tel: 224159
Fax: 279488

Middle East Airlines
PO Box 1515
Tel: 237080
Fax: 237280

Northwest Orient United Tourist Services and Travel
PO Box 8023
Tel: 668939
Fax: 233613

Olympic Airways
Nasser Air Travel and Shipping Agencies
PO Box 3761
Tel: 228689
Fax: 222821

Oman Aviation Services Co
PO Box 24713
Tel: 518080
Fax: 520700

Pakistan Int Airlines (PIA)
PO Box 12858
Tel: 222154
Fax: 232289

Philippine Airlines
United Tourist Services and Travel
PO Box 16736
Tel: 358999
Fax: 275374

Polish Airlines
PO Box 1520
Tel: 284292
Fax: 211016

Qatar Airways
PO Box 13142
Tel: 668284
Fax: 682266

Qantas
PO Box 1515
Tel: 228151
Fax: 278857

Royal Brunei Airlines
PO Box 1515
Tel: 519331
Fax: 519334

Royal Jordanian
PO Box 4534
Tel: 232855
Fax: 236977

Royal Nepal Airlines
Elisa Travels
PO Box 13174
Tel: 287122
Fax: 284200

Sabena Belgian
World Airlines
PO Box 1515
Tel: 228151
Fax: 214560

Saudia
Al Ghaith and Al
Moosa Travels
PO Box 1770
Tel: 236455
Fax: 230730

Scandinavian
Airline System
Emirates Travel
Agency
PO Box 262
Tel: 219200
Fax: 371080

Shaheen Airlines
Al Sayegh Travels
PO Box 6055
Tel: 252020
Fax: 451818

Singapore
Airlines
PO Box 3358
Tel: 282486
Fax: 218357

S African
Airways
PO Box 21593
Tel: 517766
Fax: 526431

Somali Airlines
United Tourist
Services and
Travel
PO Box 8023
Tel: 231610
Fax: 233613

Sudan Airways
Emirates Travel
Agency
PO Box 626
Tel: 219200
Fax: 271420

Swissair
PO Box 1515
Tel: 283151
Fax: 216037

Syrian Arab
Airlines
Al Ghaith and Al
Moosa Travels
PO Box 1810
Tel: 214441
Fax: 233054

Tarom Romanian
Airlines
Al Majid Travel
Agency
PO Box 1020
Tel: 211176
Fax: 275863

Thai Airways
PO Box 13142
Tel: 681701
Fax: 681703

Trans World
Airways
Al Ghaith and Al
Moosa Travels
PO Box 1810
Tel: 211164
Fax: 233054

Tunis Air
PO Box 1020
Tel: 211176
Fax: 275863

Turkish Airlines
Al Naboodah
Travel Agencies
PO Box 1200
Tel: 237230
Fax: 279488

Uganda Airlines
Naseer Air Travel
PO Box 1520
Tel: 238052
Fax: 211016

United Airlines
PO Box 1515
Tel: 2033791
Fax: 287246

US Air
PO Box 53226
Tel: 314299
Fax: 310583

Yemen Airways
PO Box 4951
Tel: 520100
Fax: 224888

Yugoslav Airlines
Al Rais Travel
and Shipping
Agencies
PO Box 24713
Tel: 520600
Fax: 520700

ZAS Airline
of Egypt
House of Travel
PO Box 1515
Tel: 281510
Fax: 224085

Fujairah
Emirates Airline
PO Box 686
Dubai
Tel: 221543
Fax: 222986

Emirates Airlines
D N A T A
Bank Sedarat Iraq
Building
PO Box 445
Tel: 222985/1543

Gulf Air
Tel: 226979
Fax: 226809

Ras al-Khaimah
Air India
PO Box 3193
Tel: 356635
Fax: 364694

Emirates Airline
PO Box 686
Dubai
Tel: 229413
Fax: 222262

Gulf Air
Tel: 229523
Fax: 225300

Sharjah
Aeroflot Russian
Int Airlines
PO Box 22748
Tel: 526252
Fax: 525323

African Airlines
PO Box 24001
Tel: 593816
Fax: 593952

Air China
PO Box 6577
Tel: 371529
Fax: 540307

Air India
PO Box 3193
Tel: 356635
Fax: 364694

Air Malta
PO Box 17
Tel: 351411
Fax: 374968

Air Plan Int
(Zaire)
PO Box 6769
Tel: 366379
Fax: 545365

Al Ahli Travel
and Tourist
Agency
PO Box 789
Ajman
Tel: 448877
Fax: 445350

B S P Gulf Area
IATA
PO Box 22633
Tel: 351029
Fax: 364680

British Airways
PO Box 4033
Tel: 357241
Fax: 361498

Buhaira Travel
Agency
PO Box 4841
Tel: 352593
Fax: 523885

Egypt Air
PO Box 4080
Tel: 352163
Fax: 373343

Emirates Airline
PO Box 686
Dubai
Tel: 351411
Fax: 374968

Gulf Air
PO Box 5015
Tel: 371366
Fax: 354354

Indian Airlines
PO Box 1477
Tel: 548789
Fax: 372789

Iran Air
PO Box 1477
Tel: 369649
Fax: 355074

Kuwait Airways
PO Box 17
Tel: 378126
Fax: 366877

Moscow Airways
PO Box 20
Tel: 522855
Fax: 364595

Sudan Airways
PO Box 17
Tel: 378124
Fax: 374968

Trans
Mediterranean
Airways SAL
PO Box 8
Tel: 581027
Fax: 581147

Uzbekistan
Airways
PO Box 23088
Tel: 543732
Fax: 548322

Yemen Airways
PO Box 1139
Tel: 353830
Fax: 364175

Umm al-Quwain
Emirates
PO Box 686
Dubai
Tel: 656615
Fax: 655549

Airports

Abu Dhabi
Abu Dhabi Int
Airport
PO Box 20
Tel: 757500
Fax: 757285

Al Ain
Al Ain Int
Airport
PO Box 1554
Tel: 855555
Fax: 855000

Dubai
Dubai Int
Airport
PO Box 2525
Tel: 245555
Fax: 244074

Fujairah
Fujairah Int
Airport
PO Box 977
Tel: 226222
Fax: 224205

Ras al-Khaimah
Ras al-Khaimah
Int Airport
PO Box 501
Tel: 448111/
229523
Fax: 448199

Sharjah
Sharjah
International
Airport
PO Box 8
Tel: 581111
Fax: 581051

Art Galleries

Abu Dhabi
Aati Gallery
PO Box 27538
Tel: 780101
Fax: 317575

French House
Decoration
PO Box 44219
Tel: 728255

Dubai
Aati Gallery
PO Box 2623
Tel: 345145
Fax: 375888

Abrash Gallery
PO Box 14430
Tel: 317748
Fax: 317825

Al Abbar
PO Box 1626
Tel: 449207
Fax: 378607

Al Majlis Gallery
PO Box 11934
Tel: 536233
Fax: 535550

Art Shoppe
PO Box 60840
Tel: 622080
Fax: 698575

Green Art Gallery
PO Box 25711
Tel: 449888
Fax: 447449

Intra Gallery
PO Box 10672
Tel: 696963
Fax: 699596

Joumana Arts
PO Box 11970
Tel: 318914
Fax: 489843

Banks

Abu Dhabi
ABN Amro Bank
PO Box 2720
Tel: 335400
Fax: 330182

Abu Dhabi
Commercial Bank
PO Box 939
Tel: 720000
Fax: 776499

Abu Dhabi Fund
for Arab
Economic
Development
PO Box 814
Tel: 725800

Abu Dhabi
Investment
Authority
PO Box 3600
Tel: 213100

Abu Dhabi
Investment
Company
PO Box 6309
Tel: 328200

ANZ Grindlays
Bank PLC
PO Box 241
Tel: 330876
Fax: 331767

Arab African
International
Bank
PO Box 928
Tel: 323400
Fax: 216009

Arab Bank for
Investment and
Foreign Trade
PO Box 46733
Tel: 721900
Fax: 793497

Arab Bank PLC
PO Box 875
Tel: 334111
Fax: 336433

Banca
Commerciale
Italiana
PO Box 3839
Tel: 324330
Fax: 323709

Bank Melli Iran
PO Box 2656
Tel: 345802
Fax: 314992

Bank of Baroda
PO Box 2303
Tel: 330244
Fax: 335293

Bank of
Sharjah PLC
PO Box 27391
Tel: 794936
Fax: 795843

Bank of Tokyo
Limited
PO Box 2174
Tel: 339622
Fax: 331410

Bank Saderat Iran
PO Box 700
Tel: 335155
Fax: 325062

Banque du Caire
PO Box 533
Tel: 328700
Fax: 323881

Banque Indosuez
PO Box 46786
Tel: 338400
Fax: 338581

Banque Libanaise
pour le
Commerce
PO Box 3771
Tel: 320920
Fax: 213851

Banque Nationale
de Paris
PO Box 930
Tel: 332530
Fax: 320634

Banque Paribas
PO Box 2742
Tel: 335560
Fax: 215138

Barclays Bank
PLC
PO Box 2734
Tel: 335313
Fax: 345815

British Bank of
the Middle East
PO Box 242
Tel: 332200
Fax: 331564

Citibank NA
PO Box 999
Tel: 800-4000
Fax: 744742

Commercial Bank
of Dubai Limited
PO Box 2466
Tel: 345700
Fax: 334120

Credit Lyonnais
PO Box 4725
Tel: 337493
Fax: 344995

Credit Suisse
PO Box 47060
Tel: 325048
Fax: 324109

Dubai Islamic
Bank
PO Box 3863
Tel: 346600
Fax: 346643

El Nilein Bank
PO Box 46013
Tel: 729300
Fax: 762139

Emirates Indl
Bank
PO Box 2722
Tel: 339700
Fax: 326397

First Gulf Bank
PO Box 3662
Tel: 323000
Fax: 216653

Gulf International
Bank (BSC)
PO Box 27051
Tel: 318080
Fax: 311966

Habib Bank AG
Zurich
PO Box 2681
Tel: 322838
Fax: 351822

Habib Bank
Limited
PO Box 897
Tel: 330188
Fax: 333620

Investment Bank
for Trade and
Finance LLC
PO Box 2875
Tel: 794594
Fax: 795792

Janata Bank
PO Box 2630
Tel: 331400
Fax: 348749

Mashreqbank
PO Box 858
Tel: 332300
Fax: 345935

Airport Road
Branch
PO Box 2933
Tel: 335600
Fax: 212822

Al Salam
Branch
PO Box 44930
Tel: 786500
Fax: 742482

Middle East Bank
PO Box 46077
Tel: 328400
Fax: 332520

National Bank of
Abu Dhabi
PO Box 4
Tel: 335262
Fax: 336078

National Bank of
Bahrain (BSC)
PO Box 46080
Tel: 335288
Fax: 333783

National Bank of
Dubai Limited
PO Box 386
Tel: 778200
Fax: 346152

National Bank of
Fujairah
PO Box 786
Tel: 333300
Fax: 211336

National Bank of
Oman Limited
PO Box 3822
Tel: 325358
Fax: 216153

National Bank of
Ras al-Khaimah
PO Box 2289
Tel: 782227
Fax: 328732

National Bank of
Sharjah
PO Box 43153
Tel: 337255
Fax: 320828

National Bank of
Umm al-Quwain
PO Box 3915
Tel: 775100
Fax: 779644

Oman Finance
Company Ltd
PO Box 3773
Tel: 328491
Fax: 325335

Rafidain Bank
PO Box 2727
Tel: 335882
Fax: 326886

Standard
Chartered Bank
PO Box 240
Tel: 330077
Fax: 341511

Union Bank of
Switzerland
PO Box 3744
Tel: 325024
Fax: 327652

Union National
Bank
PO Box 3865
Tel: 321600
Fax: 786080

United Arab Bank
PO Box 3562
Tel: 325000
Fax: 338361

United Bank Ltd
PO Box 237
Tel: 326597
Fax: 344090

Ajman
Bank of Credit
and Commerce
Tel: 422313

Bank Saderat Iran
PO Box 16
Tel: 422232
Fax: 426190

First Gulf Bank
PO Box 414
Tel: 423450
Fax: 446503

Mashreqbank
PO Box 11
Tel: 422017
Fax: 426690

National Bank of
Abu Dhabi
Tel: 422996

Oman Finance
Company Ltd
PO Box 1494
Tel: 425252
Fax: 427233

United Arab Bank
PO Box 2700
Tel: 424335
Fax: 423727

Al Ain
ANZ Grindlays
Bank PLC
PO Box 1100
Tel: 643400
Fax: 645121

Abu Dhabi
Commercial Bank
PO Box 15180
Tel: 660000
Fax: 643105

Arab Bank for
Investment and
Foreign Trade
PO Box 16003
Tel: 655133
Fax: 655590

Bank Saderat Iran
PO Box 1140
Tel: 641556
Fax: 668875

British Bank of
the Middle East
PO Box 1147
Tel: 641812
Fax: 657094

Citibank NA
PO Box 1430
Tel: 641090
Fax: 665942

Dubai Islamic
Bank
PO Box 1232
Tel: 644111
Fax: 661897

Investment Bank
for Trade and
Finance LLC
PO Box 1933
Tel: 644446
Fax: 645335

Mashreqbank
PO Box 80800
Tel: 669968
Fax: 668895

Al Ain Branch
PO Box 1111
Tel: 667700
Fax: 645602

Middle East Bank
PO Box 15095
Tel: 642885
Fax: 644883

National Bank of
Dubai Limited
PO Box 16122
Tel: 644345
Fax: 668515

National Bank of
Umm al-Quwain
PO Box 17888
Tel: 513000
Fax: 513500

Oman Finance
Company Limited
PO Box 15244
Tel: 656495

Standard
Chartered Bank
PO Box 1240
Tel: 641253
Fax: 654824

Union National
Bank
PO Box 1812
Tel: 644551/2
Fax: 664505
Telex: 34065

Dubai
ABN Amro Bank
PO Box 2567
Tel: 512200
Fax: 511555

Abu Dhabi
Commercial Bank
PO Box 5550
Tel: 228141
Fax: 279632

Alahli Bank of
Kuwait (KSC)
PO Box 1719
Tel: 224175
Fax: 215527

American Express
Bank Limited
PO Box 3304
Tel: 223236
Fax: 213516

ANZ Grindlays
Bank PLC
PO Box 4166
Tel: 228171
Fax: 222018

Arab African
Int Bank
PO Box 1049
Tel: 223131
Fax: 222257

Arab Bank for
Investment and
Foreign Trade
PO Box 5549
Tel: 212100
Fax: 234311

Arab Bank PLC
PO Box 11364
Tel: 221905
Fax: 285974

Arab Emirates
Investment Bank
PO Box 5503
Tel: 222191
Fax: 274351

Bank Brussels
Lambert
PO Box 4296
Tel: 515600
Fax: 512795

Bank Melli Iran
PO Box 1894
Tel: 268207
Fax: 269157

Bank of Baroda
PO Box 3162
Tel: 531955
Fax: 536962

Bank Saderat Iran
PO Box 4182
Tel: 221161
Fax: 215961

Beniyas Road
Branch
PO Box 4182
Tel: 265834
Fax: 266543

Dubai Side
Branch
PO Box 4182
Tel: 511110
Fax: 529415

Banque Banorabe
PO Box 4370
Tel: 284655
Fax: 236260

Banque du Caire
PO Box 1502
Tel: 225175
Fax: 212801‏

Banque Indosuez
PO Box 9256
Tel: 314211
Fax: 313201

Banque Libanaise
pour le
Commerce
PO Box 4207
Tel: 222291
Fax: 279861

Banque Paribas
PO Box 7233
Tel: 525929
Fax: 521341

Barclays Bank
PLC
PO Box 1891
Tel: 283116
Fax: 282788

British Bank of
the Middle East
PO Box 66
Tel: 535000
Fax: 531005

Deira Branch
PO Box 66
Tel: 227161
Fax: 281714

Jebel Ali Branch
PO Box 66
Tel: 816433
Fax: 816378

Citibank NA
PO Box 749
Tel: 522100
Fax: 511302

Commercial Bank
International PLC
PO Box 4449
Tel: 275265
Fax: 279038

Commercial Bank
of Dubai Limited
PO Box 2668
Tel: 523355
Fax: 514310

Dubai Islamic
Bank
PO Box 1080
Tel: 214888
Fax: 237243

Emirates Bank
International
PO Box 2923
Tel: 256256
Fax: 268005

Al Karama
Branch
PO Box 2923
Tel: 373498
Fax: 346575

Al Maktoum
Branch
PO Box 52088
Tel: 220266
Fax: 276987

Al Qiyadah
Branch
PO Box 2923
Tel: 692330
Fax: 625742

Al Satwa
Branch
PO Box 2923
Tel: 445040
Fax: 494495

Al Shindagha
Branch
PO Box 2923
Tel: 538585
Fax: 530477

Al Souk Branch
PO Box 11954
Tel: 533545
Fax: 530630

Bander Taleb
Branch
PO Box 2923
Tel: 265013
Fax: 253263

Beniyas Square
Branch
PO Box 2923
Tel: 283101
Fax: 213489

Galleria Branch
PO Box 2923
Tel: 236109
Fax: 275430

Jebel Ali
Free Zone
PO Box 2923
Tel: 815551
Fax: 815545

Emirates
Industrial Bank
PO Box 5454
Tel: 211300
Fax: 232320

First Canadian
Capital Corp
PO Box 414
Tel: 310888
Fax: 310118

First Gulf Bank
PO Box 52053
Tel: 278627
Fax: 278636

Habib Bank AG
Zurich
PO Box 3306
Tel: 214535
Fax: 284211

Habib Bank Ltd
PO Box 888
Tel: 268423
Fax: 260198

Investment Bank
for Trade and
Finance LLC
PO Box 12955
Tel: 285551
Fax: 220818

Janata Bank
PO Box 3342
Tel: 223360

Lloyds Bank PLC
PO Box 3766
Tel: 313005
Fax: 313026

Mashreqbank
PO Box 1250
Tel: 229131
Fax: 238830

Beniyas Square
Branch
PO Box 5208
Tel: 220206
Fax: 233787

Bur Juman
Branch
PO Box 2469
Tel: 527103
Fax: 522035

Hor Al Anz
Branch
PO Box 5508
Tel: 623100
Fax: 662887

Jebel Ali Branch
PO Box 55355
Tel: 815355
Fax: 816628

Khor Dubai
Branch
PO Box 8499
Tel: 534000
Fax: 531854

Naif Road
Branch
PO Box 5507
Tel: 222195
Fax: 233786

Riqa Branch
PO Box 5511
Tel: 211120
Fax: 233785

Satwa Branch
PO Box 24993
Tel: 312645
Fax: 312713

Suk Al Kabir
PO Box 5509
Tel: 264176
Fax: 266783

Merrill Lynch
International and
Company
PO Box 3911
Tel: 311222
Fax: 318273

Middle East Bank
PO Box 5547
Tel: 256256
Fax: 255322

Al Dhyiyafa
Branch
PO Box 5547
Tel: 451149
Fax: 455739

Al Riqqa Branch
PO Box 5547
Tel: 211448
Fax: 235136

Murshid Bazaar
Branch
PO Box 5547
Tel: 256685
Fax: 256706

National Bank of
Dubai Limited
PO Box 777
Tel: 267000
Fax: 268939

National Bank
Fujairah
PO Box 2979
Tel: 511700
Fax: 526001

National Bank of
Ras al-Khaimah
(PSC)
PO Box 1531
Tel: 226291
Fax: 281312

National Bank of
Sharjah
PO Box 13006
Tel: 281456
Fax: 216453

National Bank of
Umm al-Quwain
PSC
PO Box 8898
Tel: 228000
Fax: 236112

Oman Finance
Company Limited
PO Box 14090
Tel: 288444
Fax: 228189

Royal Bank of
Canada
PO Box 3614
Tel: 225226
Fax: 215687

Standard
Chartered Bank
PO Box 999
Tel: 520455
Fax: 526679

UBS
Representative
Office Limited
PO Box 4530
Tel: 285429
Fax: 285446

United Arab Bank
PO Box 4579
Tel: 220181
Fax: 274309

United Bank Ltd
PO Box 1367
Tel: 267191
Fax: 514525

Fujairah
Bank Saderat Iran
PO Box 55
Tel: 222241
Fax: 229451

British Bank of
the Middle East
PO Box 21
Tel: 222221
Fax: 227150

Central Bank
Tel: 224040

Dubai Islamic
Bank
PO Box 1007
Tel: 221550
Fax: 229249

Mashreqbank
Dibba Branch
PO Box 11600
Tel: 444230
Fax: 443831

Fujairah Branch
PO Box 270
Tel: 222754
Fax: 226860

Kalba Branch
PO Box 11033
Tel: 777430
Fax: 778950

Khorfakkan
Branch
PO Box 10170
Tel: 385259
Fax: 387189

National Bank of
Abu Dhabi
Tel: 222633

National Bank of
Fujairah
PO Box 887
Tel: 224518
Fax: 224516

National Bank of
Ras al-Khaimah
PO Box 11171
Kalba
Tel: 778707
Fax: 778881

National Bank of
Sharjah
PO Box 10308
KFN
Tel: 385735
Fax: 387475

Dibba Branch
PO Box 12005
Tel: 444295
Fax: 443549

National Bank of
Umm al-Quwain
PO Box 1444
Tel: 232100
Fax: 232220

Oman Finance
Company Limited
PO Box 615
Tel: 222262
Fax: 227522

Ras al-Khaimah
Abu Dhabi
Commercial
Tel: 332200

Arab Bank
Tel: 228437

Banque Libanaise
pour le
Commerce
PO Box 771
Tel: 333880
Fax: 335067

British Bank of
the Middle East
PO Box 9
Tel: 333544
Fax: 330200

Commercial Bank
International
PO Box 793
Tel: 227555
Fax: 227444

Dubai Islamic
Bank
PO Box 1522
Tel: 224888
Fax: 224788

Habib Bank
Tel: 33549

Mashreqbank
Al Nakheel
Branch
PO Box 5279
Tel: 221695
Fax: 221880

Ras al-Khaimah
Branch
PO Box 700
Tel: 333644
Fax: 333620

Middle East Bank
PO Box 5198
Tel: 221366
Fax: 222467

National Bank of
Abu Dhabi
Tel: 333643

National Bank of
Ras al-Khaimah
(PSC)
PO Box 5300
Tel: 221127
Fax: 224202

Oman Finance
Company Limited
PO Box 1856
Tel: 351855
Fax: 353150

United Arab Bank
PO Box 615
Tel: 333556
Fax: 330922

Sharjah
ABN Amro Bank
PO Box 1971
Tel: 355021
Fax: 546036

Abu Dhabi
Commercial Bank
PO Box 4377
Tel: 542211
Fax: 369151

ANZ Grindlays
Bank PLC
PO Box 357
Tel: 359998
Fax: 357046

Arab Bank PLC
PO Box 130
Tel: 353994
Fax: 357182

Bank Melli Iran
PO Box 459
Tel: 522510
Fax: 350565

Bank of Baroda
PO Box 1671
Tel: 354231
Fax: 543025

Bank of Sharjah
PO Box 1394
Tel: 352111
Fax: 350323

Bank Saderat Iran
PO Box 316
Tel: 522470
Fax: 547589

Banque Banorabe
PO Box 5803
Tel: 593361
Fax: 593361

Banque du Caire
PO Box 254
Tel: 356317
Fax: 365427

Banque Libanaise
pour le
Commerce
PO Box 854
Tel: 354561
Fax: 367843

Barclays Bank
PO Box 1953
Tel: 355288
Fax: 543498

British Bank of
the Middle East
PO Box 25
Tel: 350055
Fax: 374440

Citibank NA
PO Box 346
Tel: 522533
Fax: 373378

Commercial Bank
International
PO Box 793
Tel: 227555
Fax: 379858

Dubai Islamic
Bank
PO Box 1409
Tel: 374444
Fax: 374555

Habib Bank AG
Zurich
PO Box 1166
Tel: 354468
Fax: 379958

Habib Bank Ltd
PO Box 300
Tel: 356116
Fax: 526473

Investment Bank
for Trade and
Finance LLC
PO Box 1885
Tel: 355391
Fax: 546683

Janata Bank
PO Box 5303
Tel: 357032

Mashreqbank
PO Box 2082
Tel: 351366
Fax: 372903

Dhaid Branch
PO Box 12705
Tel: 822899
Fax: 822416

Middle East Bank
PO Box 5169
Tel: 356166
Fax: 356492

National Bank of
Dubai Limited
PO Box 22
Tel: 656151
Fax: 655151

National Bank of
Sharjah
PO Box 4
Tel: 547745
Fax: 543483

National Bank
Umm al-Quwain
PSC
PO Box 800
Tel: 655225
Fax: 655440

Oman Finance
Company
PO Box 6035
Tel: 350939
Fax: 526588

Standard
Chartered Bank
PO Box 5
Tel: 357788
Fax: 546676

United Arab Bank
PO Box 881
Tel: 354111
Fax: 374965

United Bank Ltd
PO Box 669
Tel: 522666
Fax: 361245

Umm al-Quwain
Mashreqbank
PO Box 127
Tel: 666948
Fax: 664948

Middle East Bank
PO Box 315
Tel: 656670

National Bank of
Umm al-Quwain
(PSC)
PO Box 800
Tel: 655225
Fax: 655440

Business
Associations

Abu Dhabi
Abu Dhabi
Chamber of
Commerce and
Industry
PO Box 662
Tel: 214000
Fax: 215867
Telex: 22449

Federation of
UAE Chambers of
Commerce,
Industry and
Agriculture
PO Box 3014
Tel: 214144
Fax: 339210
Telex: 23883

Ajman
Ajman Chamber
of Commerce and
Industry
PO Box 662
Tel: 422177
Fax: 427591
Telex: 69523

Al Ain
Abu Dhabi
Chamber of
Commerce and
Industry
PO Box 1778
Tel: 643945
Fax: 645357

Dubai
Dubai Chamber
of Commerce and
Industry
PO Box 1457
Tel: 221181
Fax: 211646
Telex: 45997

Federation of
UAE Chambers of
Commerce,
Industry and
Agriculture
PO Box 8886
Tel: 212977
Fax: 235498
Telex: 48752

Fujairah
Fujairah
Chambers of
Commerce,
Industry and
Agriculture
PO Box 738
Tel: 222400
Fax: 221464
Telex: 89077

Sharjah
Sharjah Chamber
of Commerce and
Industry
PO Box 580
Tel: 541444
Fax: 541119
Telex: 68205

Umm al-Quwain
Umm al-Quwain
Chamber of
Commerce and
Industry
PO Box 436
Tel: 656915
Fax: 657066

Car Hire Companies

Abu Dhabi
Abu Mansoor
Rent A Car
PO Box 8095
Tel: 795577
Fax: 795588

Abu Mubarak
Cars Exhibition
PO Box 5140
Tel: 477150

Al Ahram Car
Rental Est
PO Box 3003
Tel: 770881
Fax: 779964

Al Amal Rent
A Car
PO Box 399
Tel: 329998
Fax: 770880

Al Asad Car Est
PO Box 70526
Tel: 311209

Al Barq Rent
A Car
PO Box 5495
Tel: 785079
Fax: 770684

Al Borj Rent
A Car
PO Box 43115
Tel: 770353
Fax: 316494

Al Dhafra Rent
A Car Est
PO Box 44313
Tel: 722788
Fax: 722899

Al Dhaheri Rent
A Car
PO Box 384
Tel: 452554
Fax: 454655

Al Dyar Rent
A Car
PO Box 70126
Tel: 771701
Fax: 793613

Al Fahad Rent
A Car
PO Box 866
Tel: 788454
Fax: 791683

Al Ghazal Taxi
PO Box 8200
Tel: 447787
Fax: 444719

Al Jazeera Rent
A Car
PO Box 43372
Tel: 727449

Al Kahf Rent
A Car
PO Box 5313
Tel: 450228
Fax: 456306

Al Marfa Rent
A Car
PO Box 2415
Tel: 775441
Fax: 767445

Al Mulla Rent
A Car
PO Box 521
Tel: 779277
Fax: 788227

Al Nasseri Rent
A Car
PO Box 3330
Tel: 791933
Fax: 792721

Al Otaibi Rent
A Car
PO Box 80999
Tel: 795577
Fax: 793376

Al Rahhala Car
Rental
PO Box 5778
Tel: 768800
Fax: 767769

Al Reef Rent
A Car
PO Box 7791
Tel: 786047
Fax: 721960

Al Rimal Rent
A Car
PO Box 4482
Tel: 786464
Fax: 784788

Al Ruwais Rent
A Car
PO Box 7585
Tel: 336338
Fax: 310507

Al Sahraa Cars
Exhibition
PO Box 397
Tel: 465000
Fax: 462000

Al Sholla Rent
A Car
PO Box 8182
Tel: 432222

Al Zafra Rent
A Car
PO Box 44313
Tel: 727686
Fax: 722899

Arabian National
Rent A Car
PO Box 16024
Tel: 641829

Automobile and
Touring Club
PO Box 27244
Tel: 332719
Fax: 348315

Avis Rent A Car
PO Box 3237
Tel: 323760
Fax: 330734

Bin Gharib Rent
A Car
PO Box 970
Tel: 787172
Fax: 785831

Bin Habroosh
Rent A Car
PO Box 3457
Tel: 777115
Fax: 776703

Bin Ham Rent
A Car
PO Box 46918
Tel: 795377
Fax: 446459

Bin Kardous Rent
A Car
PO Box 7765
Tel: 769595
Fax: 762840

Bin Mussalem
Rent A Car
PO Box 25628
Tel: 311997
Fax: 348879

Bin Nassra Rent
A Car Est
PO Box 70206
Tel: 788840
Fax: 787184

Bright Star Rent
A Car
PO Box 195
Tel: 331331
Fax: 322002

Budget Rent
A Car
PO Box 3292
Tel: 334200
Fax: 331498

Cars Rent A Car
PO Box 44933
Tel: 334334
Fax: 336166

City Rent A Car
PO Box 7700
Tel: 771188
Fax: 780894

Dana Gulf Rent
A Car
PO Box 80040
Tel: 645783

Dana Rent A Car
PO Box 17345
Tel: 664184

Delmon Rent
A Car
PO Box 45889
Tel: 777644
Fax: 777733

Devcon Rent
A Car
PO Box 46333
Tel: 348844
Fax: 393096

Dolphin Rent
A Car
PO Box 10809
Tel: 324325
Fax: 330468

Eagle Rent A Car
PO Box 730
Tel: 351671
Fax: 323919

Eisa Car Hire
PO Box 294
Tel: 335297
Fax: 344430

Emco Rent A Car
PO Box 46761
Tel: 338933
Fax: 316494

Euro Dollar Rent
A Car
PO Box 42228
Tel: 338899
Fax: 332933

Europcar Inter
Rent
PO Box 4399
Tel: 319922
Fax: 346565

Excellent Rent
A Car
PO Box 7378
Tel: 781735
Fax: 778093

Express Rent
A Car
PO Box 25431
Tel: 393833
Fax: 344627

Faris Rent A Car
PO Box 43135
Tel: 723288
Fax: 783518

Fas Rent A Car
PO Box 41140
Tel: 655667
Fax: 655154

Fast Rent A Car
and Gen
Transport
PO Box 3848
Tel: 786611
Fax: 786622

Freedom Rent
A Car
PO Box 26818
Tel: 432222
Fax: 455030

Hathboor Rent
A Car
PO Box 45644
Tel: 313848
Fax: 343663

Hibah Rent
A Car Est
PO Box 5207
Tel: 391642

Jarnas Rent A Car
PO Box 1845
Tel: 666515

Lotus Rent A Car
PO Box 411
Tel: 791505
Fax: 791404

Magic Carpet
Rent A Car
PO Box 46226
Tel: 780377

Mansour Rent
A Car
PO Box 15528
Tel: 662449

Moon Rent
A Car Est
PO Box 7875
Tel: 393747
Fax: 324285

Safety Car
PO Box 861
Tel: 330187
Fax: 392514

Sahari Rent A Car
PO Box 3042
Tel: 456417
Fax: 453342

Seven Stars Rent
A Car
PO Box 26883
Tel: 721816
Fax: 791914

Silver Valley Rent
A Car
PO Box 44112
Tel: 393950
Fax: 320374

Sports Rent
A Car
PO Box 2331
Tel: 723433
Fax: 788287

Star Rent A Car
PO Box 43261
Tel: 323971
Fax: 315660

Thrifty Car
Rental
PO Box 5216
Tel: 727777
Fax: 723999

Top Car Rent
A Car
PO Box 25172
Tel: 770994
Fax: 792080

Tourist Rent
A Car
PO Box 4018
Tel: 319878
Fax: 311489

334

Zamil Rent A Car
PO Box 26128
Tel: 785919
Fax: 790919

Ajman
Al Ameen Rent
A Car
PO Box 508
Tel: 455677
Fax: 455668

Al Haytham Rent
A Car
Tel: 444676

Ali Shamsi Rent
A Car
PO Box 738
Tel: 421366

Al Soud Rent
A Car
Tel: 426414

Al Ain
Al Ain Rent
A Car
PO Box 4550
Tel: 330724
Fax: 697743

Al Dana Rent
A Car
Tel: 664184

Al Ghazal Taxi
Tel: 644484

Al Hisn Rent
A Car
Tel: 650673

Al Reyami Rent
A Car
Tel: 654464

Arabian National
Rent A Car
PO Box 16024
Tel: 641829

Avis Rent A Car
Tel: 687262

Castel Rent A Car
Tel: 643478

Dana Gulf Rent
A Car
PO Box 80040
Tel: 645783

Dana Rent A Car
PO Box 17345
Tel: 664184

Jarnas Rent A Car
PO Box 1845
Tel: 666515

Mansour Rent
A Car
PO Box 15528
Tel: 662449

Dubai
Abdulla Al Harmi
Rent A Car
PO Box 2922
Tel: 510232

Abdulla Al Zabbi
Rent A Car
PO Box 4894
Tel: 289700
Fax: 235904

Abdul Zabbi Rent
A Car
PO Box 4894
Tel: 668092
Fax: 666522

Access Rent
A Car
PO Box 50378
Tel: 312913
Fax: 315139

Ahmed Rashed
Qasemi Rent
A Car
PO Box 55020
Tel: 274543
Fax: 287565

Al Ain Rent
A Car
PO Box 4550
Tel: 330724
Fax: 697743

Al Araf Rent
A Car
PO Box 10061
Tel: 621212

Al Baraha Rent
A Car
PO Box 55253
Tel: 277278
Fax: 226888

Al Doha Rent
A Car
PO Box 12111
Tel: 211234
Fax: 238305

Al Ghusais Rent
A Car
PO Box 19997
Tel: 612121
Fax: 616696

Al Marmoom
Rent A Car
PO Box 23161
Tel: 280459

Al Moalem Rent
A Car
PO Box 4817
Tel: 271210
Fax: 278356

Al Najah Rent
A Car
PO Box 570
Tel: 359909/49
Fax: 359949

Al Nashab Rent
A Car
PO Box 7538
Tel: 269787
Fax: 253866

Al Obaid Rent
A Car
PO Box 52606
Tel: 367176
Fax: 348511

Al Ramah Al
Zahabiyah Rent
A Car
PO Box 20117
Tel: 238382
Fax: 234743

Al Rehab Rent
A Car
PO Box 20093
Tel: 221162
Fax: 221185

Al Salmia Rent
A Car
PO Box 9330
Tel: 225297
Fax: 210627

Al Samsam
Transport and
Rent A Car
PO Box 11650
Tel: 223303
Fax: 240814

Al Sayara Al
Zahabia
PO Box 51836
Tel: 347677

Al Shiba Rent
A Car
PO Box 8323
Tel: 823977
Fax: 823574

Al Siri Rent A
Car Est
PO Box 4215
Tel: 344011

Al Zajel Rent
A Car
PO Box 11325
Tel: 225273
Fax: 219892

Alice Rent A Car
PO Box 16469
Tel: 277886
Fax: 275057

American Rent
A Car
PO Box 11631
Tel: 344888
Fax: 367765

Appollo Rent
A Car
PO Box 13611
Tel: 690008

Arrow Tourism
and Rent A Car
PO Box 11387
Tel: 281116
Fax: 232718

Asia Rent A Car
PO Box 4450
Tel: 237237
Fax: 226600

Autobahn Car
Rental
PO Box 15978
Tel: 695100
Fax: 626340

Auto Drive Rent
A Car
PO Box 10376
Tel: 225764
Fax: 234339

Autojet Rent
A Car
PO Box 13499
Tel: 211228
Fax: 210507

Autolease Rent
A Car
PO Box 50555
Tel: 375333
Fax: 825656

Automobile Rent
A Car
PO Box 55765
Tel: 278300
Fax: 235578

Autorent Car
Rental
PO Box 2692
Tel: 662770
Fax: 694912

Auto Speed Rent
A Car
PO Box 10376
Tel: 237171
Fax: 288838

Avis Rent A Car
PO Box 6891
Tel: 282121
Fax: 279807

Avislease
PO Box 6891
Tel: 800-5454
Fax: 279807

Awan Car
Rentals
PO Box 4816
Tel: 235588
Fax: 225123

Balmar Rent
A Car
PO Box 50916
Tel: 288633
Fax: 281717

Beniyas Rent
A Car
PO Box 2097
Tel: 212762
Fax: 274993

Barly Rent A Car
PO Box 24248
Tel: 493366
Fax: 494418

Bin Kenand Rent
A Car
PO Box 12116
Tel: 494696
Fax: 495038

Bin Saifan Tourist
Services and Rent
A Car
PO Box 7839
Tel: 521141
Fax: 275057

Borar Rent A Car
PO Box 4422
Tel: 225225
Fax: 226225

Budget Rent
A Car
PO Box 8323
Tel: 823030
Fax: 823574

Buhaira Rent
A Car
PO Box 16667
Tel: 667800
Fax: 622765

Cars Rent A Car
PO Box 5239
Tel: 692694
Fax: 623813

Concord Rent
A Car
PO Box 7974
Tel: 212164
Fax: 274260

Creek Rent A Car
PO Box 20330
Tel: 225144
Fax: 227784

Cruise Rent
A Car
PO Box 14961
Tel: 235303
Fax: 234094

Daitona Rent
A Car
PO Box 60130
Tel: 211133
Fax: 231032

Daker Rent A Car
PO Box 55130
Tel: 694669
Fax: 667487

Delta Rent A Car
PO Box 4499
Tel: 660696
Fax: 694731

Discovery Rent
A Car
PO Box 21281
Tel: 277555
Fax: 276665

Dorar Rent A Car
PO Box 4422
Tel: 221221
Fax: 226225

East Coast Rent
A Car
PO Box 24632
Tel: 377666
Fax: 375522

Emirates Rent
A Car
PO Box 5020
Tel: 281184
Fax: 666054

Eurodollar Rent
A Car
PO Box 10990
Tel: 312121
Fax: 313099

Europcar (Dubai
Rent A Car)
PO Box 2533
Tel: 520033
Fax: 527692

Express Rent
A Car
PO Box 50004
Tel: 218999
Fax: 282439

Fancy Transport/
Rent A Car
PO Box 2329
Tel: 348770
Fax: 366854

Fasten Rent
A Car
PO Box 16535
Tel: 219955
Fax: 212191

Flash Rent A Car
PO Box 50054
Tel: 365577
Fax: 365559

Formula Rent
A Car
PO Box 359
Tel: 289090
Fax: 289928

Gulf Rent A Car
PO Box 1038
Tel: 225545
Fax: 239024

Hajar Rent A Car
PO Box 14700
Tel: 222555
Fax: 219611

Hanco Emirates
Rent A Car
PO Box 21971
Tel: 699544
Fax: 699659

Hertz
PO Box 7976
Tel: 824422
Fax: 824822

Hestinic Rent
A Car
PO Box 2316
Tel: 344733

Ibis Rent A Car
PO Box 20127
Tel: 270864
Fax: 232167

Inter Emirate
Rent A Car
PO Box 7974
Tel: 621333
Fax: 621813

Jumairah Rent
A Car
PO Box 2538
Tel: 373000
Fax: 365371

Kamali Rent
A Car
PO Box 55275
Tel: 625452
Fax: 696088

Lima Rent A Car
PO Box 20117
Tel: 274567
Fax: 234743

Limousine Rent
A Car
PO Box 13182
Tel: 664040
Fax: 278509

Lisphona Rent
A Car
PO Box 373
Tel: 288699
Fax: 233211

London Rent
A Car
PO Box 1120
Tel: 228696
Fax: 226888

Makki Rent
A Car
PO Box 50669
Tel: 376433
Fax: 360377

Marblau Rent
A Car
PO Box 22328
Tel: 270727
Fax: 279386

Master Rent
A Car
PO Box 10960
Tel: 368080
Fax: 364780

Metro Rent A Car
PO Box 220
Tel: 228017
Fax: 271605

Middle East Rent
A Car
PO Box 2097
Tel: 520415
Fax: 511915

Midland Rent
A Car
PO Box 52292
Tel: 360521
Fax: 360523

Milano Rent
A Car
PO Box 21230
Tel: 274095
Fax: 289928

Murree Rent
A Car
PO Box 55682
Tel: 212628
Fax: 275768

Patriot Rent
A Car
PO Box 16457
Tel: 214440
Fax: 273386

Rahnoomah Rent
A Car
PO Box 2097
Tel: 348400
Fax: 368328

Rally Dubai Rent
A Car
PO Box 3724
Tel: 691114
Fax: 691434

Reems Rent
A Car
PO Box 4596
Tel: 211336
Fax: 234233

Regency Rent
A Car
PO Box 16535
Tel: 272333
Fax: 212191

Rennie Rent
A Car
PO Box 13850
Tel: 626263
Fax: 624437

Rent A Wreck
PO Box 1047
Tel: 623111
Fax: 692090

Road Star Rent
A Car
PO Box 5280
Tel: 270300
Fax: 277616

Rocket Rent
A Car
PO Box 55801
Tel: 696662
Fax: 683868

Royal Motor Rent
A Car
PO Box 22050
Tel: 229697
Fax: 226465

Saba Rent A Car
PO Box 21220
Tel: 222300
Fax: 232761

Safeenat Nooh
Rent A Car
PO Box 20800
Tel: 219234
Fax: 592483

Sahari Dubai
Rent A Car
PO Box 13697
Tel: 277335
Fax: 274792

Saif Bin Jarsh
Rent A Car
PO Box 11483
Tel: 226442
Fax: 223317

Sapo Car Rentals
and Leasing
PO Box 60901
Tel: 822333
Fax: 822330

Self Drive Rent
A Car
PO Box 3310
Tel: 212777
Fax: 231665

Seven Stars Rent
A Car
PO Box 26883
Abu Dhabi
Tel: 215121
Fax: 215177

Super Star Rent
A Car
PO Box 3006
Tel: 222992
Fax: 277110

Swift Rent A Car
PO Box 2872
Tel: 456060
Fax: 453816

Teepad Rent
A Car
PO Box 13708
Tel: 222247
Fax: 219794

Territory Rent
A Car
PO Box 1847
Tel: 210099
Fax: 277355

Thrifty Car
Rental
PO Box 2622
Tel: 370743
Fax: 345364

Time Rent A Car
PO Box 7595
Tel: 216194

Top Gear Rent
A Car
PO Box 3310
Tel: 217666
Fax: 217585

Turbo Rent A Car
PO Box 7877
Tel: 210333
Fax: 235290

Unicar Auto
Rental
PO Box 4791
Tel: 273455
Fax: 280167

United Car
Rentals
PO Box 8138
Tel: 666286
Fax: 692001

Victoria Rent
A Car
PO Box 5424
Tel: 218344
Fax: 210627

Waikiki Rent
A Car
PO Box 20326
Tel: 215121
Fax: 215177

Warba Rent
A Car
PO Box 14394
Tel: 227233
Fax: 231849

Fujairah
Al Asad Rent
A Car
PO Box 1064
Tel: 226298

Al Fujairah Rent
A Car
PO Box 11824
Tel: 224693

Al Nawres Rent
A Car
PO Box 10610
Tel: 385123
Fax: 387123

Al Rashdy Tours
and Travels
PO Box 824
Tel: 227107
Fax: 223152

Al Saada Rent
A Car
PO Box 224
Tel: 223994
Fax: 232176

Al Savana Rent
A Car
PO Box 773
Tel: 227994

Al Sharqi Rent
A Car
PO Box 4
Tel: 226900
Fax: 226388

Al Tawson Rent
A Car
PO Box 202
Tel: 227276

Al Zaabi Group
PO Box 11339
Tel: 778884
Fax: 776826

Al Zaabi Trading
PO Box 1108
Tel: 222064
Fax: 225052

Autobahn Car
Rental
PO Box 4259
Tel: 360600
Fax: 355911

Avis Rent A Car
Hilton Hotel
PO Box 231
Tel: 222021

City Rent A Car
PO Box 10653
KFN
Tel: 387186

Dubai Rent A Car
Tel: 221318

East Coast Rent
A Car
PO Box 956
Tel: 224456
Fax: 226161

Eurodollar Rent
A Car
PO Box 345
Tel: 224816
Fax: 223065

Inter Rent A Car
Tel: 224816

Faisal Rent A Car
PO Box 11339
Kalba
Tel: 387471
Fax: 776826

Happy Rent
A Car
PO Box 152
Tel: 227942

International Rent
A Car
PO Box 4661
Tel: 237391

Miami Rent
A Car
PO Box 195
Tel: 229829

National Rent
A Car
PO Box 11339
Kalba
Tel: 778303
Fax: 776826

Omar Traders
PO Box 479
Tel: 223318
Fax: 223317

Thrifty Car
Rental
PO Box 1291
Tel: 225582

Ras al-Khaimah
Al Arabi Rent
A Car
PO Box 1099
Tel: 333327
Fax: 333399

Al Auf Rent
A Car
PO Box 4865
Tel: 227374

Al Ikhlas Rent
A Car
PO Box 676
Tel: 330442

Al Muntaser Rent
A Car
PO Box 4616
Tel: 236245

Al Nakheel Rent
A Car
Tel: 228183

Al Oraibi Rent
A Car
Tel: 333327

Al Rasheed Rent
A Car
PO Box 5141
Tel: 223583

Al Sawaleh Rent
A Car
PO Box 1148
Tel: 331831

Al Wadi Rent
A Car
Tel: 331655

Amal Rent A Car
PO Box 5599
Tel: 222211
Fax: 224415

Beach Rent A Car
PO Box 221
Tel: 332032

Cars Rent A Car
PO Box 779
Tel: 228668
Fax: 224143

Damascus Rent
A Car
PO Box 5659
Tel: 229948

National Rent
A Car
Tel: 228657

Union Rent A Car
PO Box 5719
Tel: 226457
Fax: 222910

Youths Rent A
Car Office
PO Box 1568
Tel: 228192

Sharjah
Al Azad Rent
A Car
PO Box 2961
Tel: 356661

Al Darari Rent
A Car
PO Box 21133
Tel: 367755

Al Dhaid Rent
A Car
PO Box 12712
Dhaid
Tel: 822638
Fax: 823218

Al Dooki Rent
A Car
PO Box 472
Tel: 362810

Al Faraj Rent
A Car
PO Box 19889
Tel: 525574

Al Jamal Rent
A Car
PO Box 4564
Tel: 356282
Fax: 352883

Al Salam Rent
A Car
PO Box 6159
Tel: 597883

Al Shaab Rent
A Car
PO Box 1871
Tel: 544455
Fax: 379955

Apollo Rent
A Car
PO Box 533
Tel: 367844

Arezona Rent
A Car
PO Box 22119
Tel: 593283

Autobahn Car
Rental
PO Box 4259
Tel: 360600
Fax: 355911

Auto Fleet Rent
A Car
PO Box 20506
Tel: 525166

Autohire Rent
A Car
PO Box 20601
Tel: 549777
Fax: 541154

Autolease Rent
A Car
PO Box 616
Tel: 375333
Fax: 524095

Autorent Car
Rental
PO Box 611
Tel: 590333
Fax: 524095

Avis Rent A Car
PO Box 6318
Tel: 280437
Fax: 283193

Awacs Rent
A Car
PO Box 355
Tel: 355506
Fax: 526283

Budget Rent
A Car
PO Box 3283
Tel: 373600
Fax: 362143

Buhaira Rent
A Car
PO Box 6781
Tel: 590483

Crescent Rent
A Car
PO Box 128
Tel: 371188
Fax: 522299

Delta Rent A Car
PO Box 3952
Tel: 590222
Fax: 593446

Diana Universal
Tourist and
Cargo
PO Box 22043
Tel: 363617
Fax: 355056

Dollar Rent
A Car
PO Box 7100
Tel: 365563

Eject Rent A Car
PO Box 4959
Tel: 599566

Eurodollar Rent
A Car
PO Box 3464
Tel: 590815
Fax: 598044

Europe Car Rent
A Car and
Tourist
PO Box 5151
Tel: 546655
Fax: 522699

Everest Rent
A Car
PO Box 20918
Tel: 372118

Gulf Coast Rent
A Car
PO Box 21221
Tel: 376212
Fax: 362145

Holiday Rent
A Car
PO Box 6673
Tel: 366636
Fax: 525238

Hunter Rent
A Car
PO Box 3304
Tel: 541185

Interhome Rent
A Car
PO Box 21794
Tel: 800-6008
Fax: 544788

Isis Rent A Car
PO Box 478
Tel: 599888
Fax: 591888

Laywad Rent
A Car
PO Box 22122
Tel: 363833

Majid Rent A Car
PO Box 1991
Tel: 597744

Metro Rent A Car
PO Box 1496
Tel: 376120
Fax: 523908

Middle Gulf Rent
A Car
PO Box 5949
Tel: 590626

Milano Rent
A Car
PO Box 6177
Tel: 543171
Fax: 357997

Modex Rent
A Car
PO Box 5855
Tel: 597836
Fax: 597837

Ragait Rent A
Car
PO Box 2177
Tel: 522577
Fax: 367656

Rally Rent A Car
PO Box 21112
Tel: 544000
Fax: 547333

Riviera Rent
A Car
PO Box 1415
Tel: 358000

Ruby Rent A Car
PO Box 22525
Tel: 354772
Fax: 544257

Sano Rent A Car
PO Box 40346
Tel: 545309
Fax: 336969

Sharjah Rent
A Car
PO Box 1448
Tel: 599288
Fax: 594152

Solar Rent A Car
PO Box 20565
Tel: 367227
Fax: 367772

Speed Rent A Car
PO Box 6298
Tel: 333222
Fax: 336026

Super Rent A Car
PO Box 7268
Tel: 391711
Fax: 392722

Warda Rent
A Car
PO Box 19979
Tel: 363313
Fax: 377661

West Coast Rent
A Car
PO Box 20174
Tel: 372212
Fax: 546470

Wheelers Rent
A Car
PO Box 3604
Tel: 522145
Fax: 547971

World Wide Rent
A Car
PO Box 331
Tel: 355547

Umm al-Quwain
Al Lolouh Rent
A Car
Tel: 656131

Orient Rent
A Car
Tel: 651064

Royal Rent A Car
Tel: 656362

Cinemas

Abu Dhabi
Abu Dhabi
Cinema
PO Box 2014
Tel: 215861

Al Firdous
Cinema
Tel: 771126

Al Jazira
Tel: 431116

Eldorado
PO Box 45084
Tel: 763555

New Al Mariah
Cinema
PO Box 45084
Tel: 776020
Fax: 741197

Ajman
Royal Cinema
PO Box 1186
Tel: 422636

Al Ain
Cinema Jimi
PO Box 17287
Tel: 634666

Club Cinema
PO Box 1113
Tel: 664121

Dubai
Al Nasr Cinema
PO Box 1186
Tel: 374353

Al Massa
Tel: 443244

Deira Cinema
PO Box 403
Tel: 223551

Dubai Cinema
PO Box 2953
Tel: 660632
Fax: 273366

Galleria
Tel: 2064094

Plaza Cinema
PO Box 138
Tel: 532683
Fax: 533944

Rex Drive-In
Cinema
PO Box 10946
Tel: 886447

Strand Cinema
PO Box 574
Tel: 370304
Fax: 378404

Fujairah
Plaza Cinema
PO Box 676
Tel: 224037

National Cinema
Kalba
PO Box 123
Kalba
Tel: 777488
Fax: 549841

Ras al-Khaimah
Ras al-Khaimah
Cinema
PO Box 544
Tel: 222416

Sharjah
Al Hamra Cinema
PO Box 277
Tel: 523953

Concorde Cinema
PO Box 277
Tel: 523956

Metro Cinema
PO Box 123
Tel: 285583
Fax: 549841

Sharjah Cinema
PO Box 123
Tel: 522241
Fax: 549841

Umm al-Quwain
Umm al-Quwain
Cinema
PO Box 185
Tel: 656240

Clubs and Associations

Abu Dhabi
Abu Dhabi Chess
and Cultural Club
PO Box 7513
Tel: 725564
Fax: 782246

Abu Dhabi Club
PO Box 658
Tel: 731111
Fax: 731113

Abu Dhabi
Educational Zone
Parents' Council
PO Box 25320
Tel: 478101
Fax: 474737

Abu Dhabi
Equestrian Club
PO Box 590
Tel: 455500
Fax: 465111

Abu Dhabi
Folklore Society
PO Box 7902
Tel: 432682

Abu Dhabi
Golf Club
PO Box 4555
Tel: 463226
Fax: 461423

Abu Dhabi Int
Marine Sports
Club
PO Box 45656
Tel: 765566
Fax: 767666

Abu Dhabi
Malayalee
Samajam
PO Box 2779
Tel: 343115
Fax: 338736

Abu Dhabi
Marina Club
PO Box 4869
Tel: 721300
Fax: 723981

Abu Dhabi
Tourist Club
PO Box 28
Tel: 723400
Fax: 772516

Abu Dhabi
Women's
Association
PO Box 4088
Tel: 669982
Fax: 669909

Al Khulood Club
PO Box 3102
Tel: 329979
Fax: 320291

Al Wahda Sports
Club
PO Box 4388
Tel: 433000
Fax: 433001

Automobile and
Touring Club
PO Box 27244
Tel: 332719
Fax: 348315

Bangladesh
Association
PO Box 25273
Tel: 334536
Fax: 327086

Dhabian Woman
Society
PO Box 623
Tel: 667911

Emirates Banks
Association
PO Box 44307
Tel: 322578
Fax: 324158

Indian Islamic
Centre
PO Box 4190
Tel: 724488
Fax: 760570

Indian Social
Centre
PO Box 816
Tel: 772225
Fax: 786895

Oriental Karate
and Kobudo
Club
PO Box 70236
Tel: 778878
Fax: 771272

Pakistan Centre
PO Box 70831
Tel: 476914
Fax: 4752288

Red Crescent
Society
PO Box 3324
Tel: 434300
Fax: 450777

UAE Equestrian
and Racing
Federation
PO Box 3234
Tel: 434333
Fax: 435133

Ajman
Ajman Cultural
Sporting Club
PO Box 85
Tel: 422441
Fax: 444244

Al Ain
Al Ain Sports
Club
PO Box 1113
Tel: 635866
Fax: 320291

Pakistan Centre
PO Box 1779
Tel: 679848
Fax: 672282

Dubai
Al Ahli Sports
Club
PO Box 1551
Tel: 660628
Fax: 662885

Al Nasr
Leisureland
PO Box 2652
Tel: 371234
Fax: 374952

Al Wasl Sports
Club
PO Box 3888
Tel: 374488
Fax: 345664

Arabian Leopard
Trust
PO Box 24444
Fax: 499894

Association for
Humanistic
Studies
PO Box 11032
Tel: 277884
Fax: 690084

Aviation Club
PO Box 55400
Tel: 824122
Fax: 824751

Basket Ball
Association
PO Box 5130
Tel: 660101
Fax: 666008

Club Aqua
(Chicago Beach
Hotel)
Tel: 480000

Club Olympus
(Hyatt Regency)
PO Box 5588
Tel: 2064841
Fax: 211868

Creek Football
Club
PO Box 24665
Tel: 331291
Fax: 823010

Darjeeling Cricket
Club
PO Box 52058
Tel: 331746
Fax: 331746

Dubai Archery
Group
PO Box 9099
Tel: 442591
Fax: 442591

Dubai Bowling
Centre
PO Box 50005
Tel: 283819
Fax: 238881

Dubai Country
Club
PO Box 5103
Tel: 331155
Fax: 331409

Dubai Equestrian
Centre
PO Box 292
Tel: 361394
Fax: 363934

Dubai Exiles
Rugby Club
PO Box 4987
Tel: 331198

Dubai Flying
Association
PO Box 1897
Tel: 883326

Dubai Folklore
Society Theatre
PO Box 1848
Tel: 669922
Fax: 621906

Dubai
Racing and
Golf Club
PO Box 52872
Tel: 363666
Fax: 363717

Dubai International Art Centre
PO Box 11816
Tel: 444398
Fax: 449477

Dubai International Marine Club
PO Box 24883
Tel: 451112
Fax: 845839

Dubai International Seafarers Centre
PO Box 5811
Tel: 452951
Fax: 452969

Dubai Karate Centre
PO Box 11696
Tel: 447797
Fax: 625241

Dubai Kart Club
Tel: 06-356411

Dubai Marine Beach Club
PO Box 5182
Tel: 441221
Fax: 446526

Dubai Offshore Sailing Club
PO Box 11881
Tel: 381669
Fax: 381596

Dubai Polo and Equestrian Club
PO Box 7477
Tel: 331188
Fax: 330846

Dubai Water Sports Assoc
PO Box 13413
Tel: 342031
Fax: 341684

Emirates Golf Club
PO Box 24040
Tel: 480222
Fax: 481888

Emirates Racing Club
PO Box 1178
Tel: 313311
Fax: 313322

Griffins Health Club (J W Marriott Hotel)
PO Box 16590
Tel: 624444
Fax: 626264

Highland Lodge
PO Box 9332
Tel: 379470
Fax: 379471

Hilton Beach Club
PO Box 26878
Tel: 445333
Fax: 446222

Indian Association
PO Box 342
Tel: 511082
Fax: 511091

Indian Sports Club
PO Box 679
Tel: 371112
Fax: 378880

Jebel Ali Recreation Club
PO Box 3258
Jebel Ali
Tel: 846628
Fax: 845245

Jebel Ali Sailing Club
PO Box 11764
Tel: 846444
Fax: 845291

Jebel Ali Shooting Club
PO Box 9232
Tel: 836555
Fax: 837551

Jordan Social Club
PO Box 1910
Tel: 371065
Fax: 359349

Nasir Al Sayer Scout Camp Association
PO Box 5011
Tel: 663730
Fax: 622610

Norwegian Seamen's Centre
PO Box 2404
Tel: 370062
Fax: 368246

Petroleum Wives Club of Dubai
PO Box 11713
Tel: 442389

Sports City
PO Box 50129
Tel: 214575
Fax: 289490

UAE Athletics Association
PO Box 6756
Tel: 231838
Fax: 217850

UAE Basketball Association
PO Box 5130
Tel: 668800
Fax: 666008

UAE Chess Assoc
PO Box 11110
Tel: 665293
Fax: 665036

UAE Football Association
PO Box 5458
Tel: 823444
Fax: 823700

UAE Olympic Committee
PO Box 4350
Tel: 223242
Fax: 225576

UAE Table Tennis Association
PO Box 6224
Tel: 669362
Fax: 668142

Fujairah
Kalba Union Sports Cultural Club
PO Box 11019
Kalba
Tel: 777245
Fax: 777457

Khorfakkan Public Stage
PO Box 10002
Tel: 385002
Fax: 384730

Ras al-Khaimah
Al Nakheel Billiards Centre
PO Box 4742
Tel: 221001
Fax: 224226

Billiard Centre
PO Box 646
Tel: 352255

Emirates Sports Cultural Club
PO Box 23
Tel: 351411
Fax: 351677

Ras al-Khaimah Sports and Cultural Club
PO Box 550
Tel: 222411
Fax: 225523

Ras al-Khaimah Water Ski Club
PO Box 1881
Tel: 354444
Fax: 354545

Sharjah
Al Shaab Sports and Cultural Club
PO Box 959
Tel: 232266
Fax: 232274

Arab Cultural Club
PO Box 1913
Tel: 351555
Fax: 542996

Guides Association
PO Box 3644
Tel: 522414
Fax: 545988

Indian Association Sharjah
PO Box 2324
Tel: 358845
Fax: 356805

Sharjah Chess Club
PO Box 6277
Tel: 241819
Fax: 247152

Sharjah Equestrian Club
PO Box 1991
Tel: 581155
Fax: 581177

Sharjah Sports Club
PO Box 55
Tel: 322666
Fax: 322214

Sharjah Wanderers Sports Club
PO Box 1767
Tel: 357505
Fax: 353826

Umm al-Quwain
Umm al-Quwain Marine Club and Riding Centre
PO Box 624
Tel: 666644
Fax: 665446

Umm al-Quwain Tourist Centre
PO Box 1129
Tel: 651185
Fax: 651186

Dreamland Water Park
PO Box 23
Tel: 681888

Courier and Freight Services

Abu Dhabi
A N E Express Parcel Service
PO Box 7974
Tel: 773344
Fax: 723369

Aramex International Courier
PO Box 27449
Tel: 322888

D H L International
PO Box 47041
Tel: 432940

I M L Air Couriers
PO Box 43234
Tel: 335578

KRT — Kanoo Rapid Transit
PO Box 245
Tel: 727898
Fax: 787956

Overseas Courier Services
PO Box 316
Tel: 348358

T N T Express
Worldwide
PO Box 7860
Tel: 794448

UFF — Unique
Freight
Forwarding Co
PO Box 5631
Tel: 792200

UPS/IML Air
Couriers
PO Box 50875
Tel: 335578

Al Ain
Overseas Courier
Services
PO Box 1372
Tel: 513151

Dubai
ANE Express
Parcel Service
PO Box 7974
Tel: 663062

Aramex
International
Courier
PO Box 3841
Tel: 821578

Elite Express
Parcel
PO Box 19664
Fax: 228005

Federal Express
PO Box 9239
Tel: 821821

Flying Dolphin
PO Box 60315
Tel: 821967
Fax: 821806

General Postal
Authority
(Mumtaz Post)
PO Box 8888
Tel: 371243

IML Air Couriers
PO Box 50875
Tel: 344646

JK Express
Transportation
PO Box 14468
Tel: 289272

KRT
PO Box 290
Tel: 375175

Memo Express
PO Box 13001
Tel: 364400

Overseas Courier
Services
PO Box 1545
Tel: 625757

Sky Express
Services
PO Box 7141
Tel: 826399

Swift Freight
International
PO Box 50177
Tel: 369595
Fax: 377325

Total Freight
International
PO Box 50379
Tel: 519924
Fax: 519925

TNT Express
Worldwide
(UAE) LLC
PO Box 15321
Tel: 665050

UFF — Unique
Freight
Forwarding Co
PO Box 5631
Tel: 526000

Universal Express
PO Box 825
Tel: 368877

UPS/IML Air
Couriers
PO Box 50875
Tel: 344646

Sharjah
Azemarch Group
PO Box 40663
Tel: 539995
Fax: 539996

DHL
International
PO Box 5771
Tel: 800-4004

Ducalguild
Emirates
PO Box 2496
Tel: 376000

General Postal
Authority
(Mumtaz Post)
PO Box 8888
Tel: 541281

KRT — Kanoo
Rapid Transit
PO Box 153
Tel: 354691

Skysom Express
PO Box 6195
Tel: 544153

TNT Express
Worldwide
PO Box 3746
Tel: 373857

Credit Card Representa-tives

Abu Dhabi
American Express
International Inc
PO Box 806
Tel: 213045
Fax: 314692

MasterCard
(Abu Dhabi
Comm Bank)
PO Box 939
Tel: 725552
Fax: 783470

Dubai
American Express
International Inc
PO Box 290
Tel: 365000
Fax: 366006

MasterCard
(Abu Dhabi
Comm Bank)
PO Box 5550
Tel: 214512
Fax: 279632

Network
International
PO Box 2923
Tel: 255600
Fax: 256552

Sultan Special
System
PO Box 7982
Tel: 826682
Fax: 826788

Sharjah
MasterCard
(Abu Dhabi

Comm Bank)
PO Box 4377
Tel: 542211
Fax: 369151

Diving Courses and Equipment

Abu Dhabi
Scuba
International
PO Box 4869
Tel: 790377
Fax: 790377

Dubai
Dubai Diving and
Watersports
Centre
PO Box 9154
Tel: 441693
Fax: 492441

Inner Space
Diving Centre
PO Box 23520
Tel: 310203
Fax: 310204

Lukhma Divers
PO Box 52958
Tel: 446944
Fax: 448237

Scuba Dubai
PO Box 51753
Tel: 317433
Fax: 310680

Scuba
International
PO Box 51753
Tel: 313416
Fax: 313107

Scubatec
PO Box 11468
Tel: 348988
Fax: 366461

Fujairah
Ocean Divers
(Scuba Int)
PO Box 10444
Tel: 385031
Fax: 382971

Sandy Beach
Diving Centre
PO Box 10528
Tel: 445050
Fax: 445900

Scuba
International
PO Box 51753
Tel: 382971
Fax: 382971

Sharjah
Unique Systems
PO Box 20904
Tel: 590059
Fax: 590060

Emirates Airlines Overseas

Australia
South Pacific
Express Level 13
257 Collins Street
Melbourne
Vic 3000
Tel: 6504900

South Pacific
Express Level 17
456 Kent Street
Sydney
N S W 2000
Tel: 267355

Austria
Kustritz Touristik
Ges M B H
Gesselgasse 10
1238 Vienna
Tel: 81872222

Bahrain
Al Bader Travel
and Tourism
Al Bader House
Government Rd
PO Box 505
Manama
Tel: 244444/
224444

Bahrain Int
Travel
Chamber of
Commerce Bldg
Ground Floor
PO Box 1044
Manama
Tel: 257156

Yusuf Bin Ahmed
Kanoo W L L
26 Abu Obeida
Avenue
PO Box 45
Manama 304
Tel: 257156

Bangladesh
ABC Air Limited
58 Agrabad
Commercial Area
Chittagong
Tel: 505647

ABC Air Limited
64 Motijheel
Commercial Area
Dhaka
Tel: 243797/1760/
863493

ABC Air Limited
11 Idris Market
Zinda Bazar
Sylhet
Tel: 821-2159

Canada
Global Aviation
Limited
2800 Skymark
Ave Suite 403
Mississaugua
Ontario
Tel: (905)
6298368/(800)
567-3944

Comoros
Hahaya
International
Airport
Moroni
Tel: (269) 732814

Cyprus
Amathus
Navigation
Company Ltd
Larnaca Airport
Tel: 643070/323

66E Archbishop
Makarios III
Avenue
PO Box 1601
Nicosia
Tel: 374010/612/
302

Egypt
Baron Hotel
Heliopolis
Cairo
Tel: 2907730

Cairo Marriott
Hotel
PO Box 33
Zamalek
Cairo
Tel: 3401142/02/
087

France
Nice Aeroport
Cote d'Azur
Terminal 1
06056 Nice Cedex
Tel: 05063325/
4495944/214659

Germany
Schwindstrasse 3
60325 Frankfurt
Tel: 740621

Greece
Manos Welcome
Services Limited
6-10 Charilaou
Trikoupi Street
GR 10679 Athens
Tel: 3304023/24

Hong Kong
Suite 3707/8
37th Floor
Gloucester Tower
Landmark
Building
Central Hong
Kong
Tel: 25267171

India
Kanchenjunga
Building
18 Barakhamba
Road
New Delhi
Tel: 332-4803/
4665/9884

Mittal Chambers
Office No 3
Ground Floor
228 Nariman
Point
Bombay
Tel: 2871649/50/
1-2

Indonesia
Sahid Jaya Hotel
2nd Floor
Jalan Jend
Sudiman
Jakarta
Tel: 5742440

Iran
2nd Floor
Block No 74
Argentine Square
Tehran
Tel: 871-2700/
1257/6412

Italy
Emirates
Via Paolo Da
Cannobio 10
5th Floor
20122-Milan
Tel: 72000366/48

Via Toscana 1
00187 Rome
Tel: 42903841/3/6

Japan
Air System Inc
^{C}/o Hommachi N
S Building 7F
2-5 3 Hommachi
Chuo-ku,
Osaka 541
Tel: 06-243-2222

Air System Inc
^{C}/o Tranomon
TBL Building 7F
19-9 1 Tranomon
Minato-Ku
Tokyo 105
Tel: 03-3593-6720

Jordan
Al Sayegh
Commercial Ctr
11th Floor
Al Abdaly
PO Box 910325
Amman
Tel: 643341/7/53

Kenya
View Park Towers
20th Floor
Adjacent to A M
Bank House
Nairobi
Tel: 211900/2990/
5994

Korea
Woore Agency
Corporation
5th Floor
Soonhwa Bldg
Soonhwa-Dong
Chung-Gu Seoul
Tel: 02-319-0059

Kuala Lumpur
Maples Travel
(M) SDN BHD
2 46-2 49 2nd Flr
Wisma Stephens
88 Jalan Raja
Chulan
50200 Kuala
Lumpur
Tel: 2443288

Kuwait
Boodai Aviation
Agencies
Kuwait Finance
House Building
Al Hilali Street
13058 Safat
PO Box 5798
Al Kuwayt
Tel: 2425566/
40666

Lebanon
Gefinor Building
Ground 2
Section D
No 60-63
Al Harma Area
Beirut
Tel: 865233/4/5/
602190/270/
370790

Malaysia
Maple Travel (M)
SDN BHD
G 125 Ground
Floor Holiday
Plaza
Taman Century
80250 Johor
Bahru
Tel: 3325828/218

Maple Travel (M)
SDN BHD
Phase 2B Lot 4-32
Komtar Level 4
10000 Penang
Tel: 2631100

Maldives
Maldives Air
Services Limited
Fashana Building
Boduthakurufaan
Magu Male 20-05
Tel: 322436-8

Nepal
Universal Tours
and Travel Ltd
PO Box 939
Kathmandu
Tel: 212080/6080/
4192

Netherlands
Air Support
Kruisweg 635
2132 NB
Hoofddorp
Schiphol Airport
Amsterdam
Tel: 4466180

Pakistan
1-D Rehmat Plaza
Jinnah Avenue
Blue Area
Islamabad
Tel: 223145/
819833

265 R A Lines
Sarwar Shaheed
Rd Karachi 74200
Tel: 5684500/805/
1663

Emirates House
1717 Kutchery Rd
Multan
Tel: 513737/0747/
580727

Regent House 3
Imtiaz Plaza
85 The Mall
Lahore
Tel: 6372990-2

95-B Saddar Road
Peshawar
Tel: 273744/5912

Philippines
Country Space
Cond Building
Sen Gil Puyat
Ave Salcedo
Village Makati
Metro-Manila
Tel: 816-0744/
0809/0830/0832

Qatar
Abdulla Bin
Jassem Street
PO Box 22488
Dohar
Tel: 418877/
425577

Saudi Arabia
Al Adlia Travel
and Tours
Abu Baker Al
Saddeuq Street
Al Ayoon
Building
PO Box 2321
Medina
Tel: 8268244/
7097/8164

Al Adlia Travel
and Tours
Cercon Bldg No 4
Mousa Bin
Nousair Road

Olaya
PO Box 57475
Riyadh 11574
Tel: 465-5485/
7117/8687/464-
4207

Al Adlia Travel
and Tours
Corner King
Khaled/Dhahrain
Street
PO Box 561
Al Khobar
Tel: 832-5249

Al Adlia Travel
and Tours
City Centre
Building
Medina Road
PO Box 41142
Jeddah 21521
Tel: 665-9405

Singapore
435 Orchard Road
19-06 Wisma
Atria
Tel: 735335

South Africa
Office Tower
5th Floor
Sandton City
6 Rivonia Road
Sandton
Johannesburg
Tel: 8838420/9260

Spain
Viajes AA
International S L
Barquillo 13
28004 Madrid
Tel: 5219763

Sri Lanka
World Trade Ctr
8th Floor Echelon
Square
Colombo 1
Tel: 438878/6620/
440709

Sweden
World
Connection
Marketing
Salmaetargatan 5
113 59 Stockholm
Tel: 314220

342

Syria
Manal Tours and
Travel
29 Ayyar Street
Damascus
Tel: 422887/8032/
416303

Taiwan
Sentra Travel
Service Limited
4F 112 Sec 2
Chung Hsiao E Rd
Taipei
Tel: 2-3966891

Thailand
2nd Floor
B B Bldg
54 Asoke Road
Sukhumvit 21
Khet Prakanong
Bangkok 10110
Tel: 2607873-5/
400/-4

Turkey
Inonu Caddesi 96
Gumussuyu
Instanbul
Tel: 2935050/-2/4

United Kingdom
First Floor
Gloucester Park
95 Cromwell Rd
London SW7 4DL
Tel: 171-8080808

Suite 11
Manchester
International
Office Centre
Styal Road
Manchester M22
5TT
Tel: 161-437-9007

**United States of
America**
405 Park Avenue
Suite 1002
New York 10022
Tel: 800-777-3999
(212 758-2786)

5718 Westheimer
Road
Suite 1090
Houston
Texas 77057
Tel: (713) 2665491
(800) 7773999

Vietnam
The Landmark
5B Ton Duc Thang
District 1
Ho Chi Minh City
Tel: (848) 228000

West Australia
South Pacific
Express
Level 7 City
Arcade Office
Tower
207 Murray Street
Perth
Tel: 3210133

Foreign
Diplomatic
Missions

Abu Dhabi
Algeria
PO Box 3070
Tel: 448949
Fax: 447068
Telex: 23414

Argentina
PO Box 3325
Tel: 436838
Fax: 431392
Telex: 23998

Austria
PO Box 3095
Tel: 324103
Fax: 343133
Telex: 22675

Bahrain
PO Box 3367
Tel: 312200
Fax: 311202

Bangladesh
PO Box 2504
Tel: 668375
Fax: 667324
Telex: 22201

Belgium
PO Box 3686
Tel: 319449
Fax: 319343
Telex: 22860

Brazil
PO Box 3027
Tel: 665352
Fax: 654559
Telex: 23815

China
PO Box 2741
Tel: 434276
Fax: 463837
Telex: 23928

Croatia
PO Box 41227
Tel: 311700
Fax: 338366

Czech
PO Box 27008
Tel: 782800
Fax: 316567
Telex: 22106

Denmark
PO Box 46666
Tel: 325900
Fax: 351690
Telex: 23677

Egypt
PO Box 4026
Tel: 445566
Fax: 449878

Finland
PO Box 3634
Tel: 328927
Fax: 325063
Telex: 23161

France
PO Box 4014
Tel: 435100
Fax: 434158
Telex: 22325

Germany
PO Box 2591
Tel: 435630
Fax: 435625
Telex: 22202

Greece
PO Box 5483
Tel: 316818
Fax: 316306

Hungary
PO Box 44450
Tel: 660107
Fax: 667877

India
PO Box 4090
Tel: 664800
Fax: 651518
Telex: 22620

Indonesia
PO Box 7256
Tel: 669233
Fax: 653932
Telex: 22253

Iran
PO Box 4080
Tel: 447618
Fax: 448714

Italy
PO Box 46752
Tel: 435622
Fax: 434337
Telex: 23861

Japan
PO Box 2430
Tel: 435696
Fax: 434219
Telex: 24411

Kenya
PO Box 3854
Tel: 666300
Fax: 652827
Telex: 24244

Korea
PO Box 3270
Tel: 435337
Fax: 435348

Kuwait
PO Box 926
Tel: 446888
Fax: 444990
Telex: 22804

Lebanon
PO Box 4023
Tel: 434722
Fax: 435553
Telex: 22206

Malaysia
PO Box 3887
Tel: 656698
Fax: 341091
Telex: 22630

Mauritania
PO Box 2714
Tel: 462724
Fax: 465772
Telex: 22512

Morocco
PO Box 4066
Tel: 433973
Fax: 433917
Telex: 22549

Netherlands
PO Box 46560
Tel: 321920
Fax: 313158
Telex: 23610

Oman
PO Box 2517
Tel: 463333
Fax: 464633

Pakistan
PO Box 846
Tel: 447800
Fax: 447172

Philippines
PO Box 3215
Tel: 345664
Fax: 313559

Poland
PO Box 2334
Tel: 465200
Fax: 436171
Telex: 23283

Qatar
PO Box 3503
Tel: 435900
Fax: 434800
Telex: 22664

Romania
PO Box 70416
Tel: 666346
Fax: 651598
Telex: 23546

Russia
PO Box 8211
Tel: 721797
Fax: 788731
Telex: 24464

Saudi Arabia
PO Box 4057
Tel: 445700
Fax: 462324
Telex: 22670

Slovak
PO Box 3382
Tel: 321674
Fax: 315839

Somalia
PO Box 4155
Tel: 669700
Fax: 651580
Telex: 22624

Spain
PO Box 46474
Tel: 213544
Fax: 313944
Telex: 23340

Sri Lanka
PO Box 46534
Tel: 666688
Fax: 667921
Telex: 23333

Sudan
PO Box 4027
Tel: 666788
Fax: 654231
Telex: 22706

Sweden
PO Box 2609
Tel: 337772
Fax: 332904

Switzerland
PO Box 46116
Tel: 343636
Fax: 216127
Telex: 22824

Syria
PO Box 4011
Tel: 448768
Fax: 449387
Telex: 22729

Tunisia
PO Box 4166
Tel: 661331
Fax: 660707
Telex: 22370

Turkey
PO Box 3204
Tel: 655466
Fax: 662691
Telex: 23037

United Kingdom
PO Box 248
Tel: 326600
Fax: 318138
Telex: 22234

United States of
America
PO Box 4009
Tel: 436691
Fax: 434171

Yemen
PO Box 2095
Tel: 448457
Fax: 447978
Telex: 23600

Dubai
Australia
PO Box 9303
Tel: 313444
Fax: 314812
Telex: 49393

Bangladesh
PO Box 4336
Tel: 628966
Fax: 628965
Telex: 49484

Canada
PO Box 52472
Tel: 521717
Fax: 517722

China
PO Box 9348
Tel: 453357
Fax: 456267

Egypt
PO Box 2575
Tel: 511222
Fax: 511033
Telex: 45837

Finland
PO Box 1042
Tel: 823338
Fax: 823041
Telex: 45998

France
PO Box 3314
Tel: 232442
Fax: 270887
Telex: 49699

Germany
PO Box 2247
Tel: 523352
Fax: 528138
Telex: 47270

India
PO Box 737
Tel: 519666
Fax: 524453
Telex: 46061

Iran
PO Box 2832
Tel: 521150
Fax: 512069
Telex: 45585

Italy
PO Box 24910
Tel: 314167
Fax: 317467
Telex: 49284

Jordan
PO Box 2787
Tel: 517500
Fax: 524675

Kuwait
PO Box 806
Tel: 284111
Fax: 232024
Telex: 46335

Lebanon
PO Box 7800
Tel: 239524
Fax: 274893
Telex: 48611

Malaysia
PO Box 4598
Tel: 285695
Fax: 319994
Telex: 47000

Netherlands
PO Box 7726
Tel: 528700
Fax: 510502
Telex: 46502

Pakistan
PO Box 340
Tel: 524412
Fax: 527975
Telex: 48285

Romania
PO Box 1404
Tel: 383580
Fax: 385992
Telex: 45880

Somalia
PO Box 23900
Tel: 223030
Fax: 274570

Sweden
PO Box 2609
Tel: 457716
Fax: 332904

Switzerland
PO Box 9300
Tel: 313542
Fax: 313679

Syria
PO Box 7801
Tel: 663354
Fax: 698277
Telex: 47971

Turkey
PO Box 9221
Tel: 314788
Fax: 317317
Telex: 49444

United Kingdom
PO Box 248
Tel: 521070
Fax: 527095
Telex: 45426

United States of
America
PO Box 9343
Tel: 313115
Fax: 314043

Yemen
PO Box 1947
Tel: 520213
Fax: 522901

Hospitals

Abu Dhabi
Abu Dhabi
Central Hospital
PO Box 233
Tel: 214666
Fax: 313664

Al Jazirah
Hospital
PO Box 2427
Tel: 214800
Fax: 216007

Al Mafraq
Medical Centre
PO Box 46266
Tel: 51-23100
Fax: 315321

Al Noor Hospital
PO Box 46713
Tel: 727222
Fax: 781148

Charter Medical
(Cayman Islands)
Limited
PO Box 3984
Tel: 727912
Fax: 720120

Corniche Hospital
PO Box 3788
Tel: 724900
Fax: 720782

Dar Al Shifaa
Hospital
PO Box 2519
Tel: 435555
Fax: 434144

Delma Island
Hospital
PO Box 50561
Tel: 81888
Fax: 81885

Emirates
Polyclinic
PO Box 26285
Tel: 339888
Fax: 351227

Ghayathi Hospital
PO Box 11795
Tel: 41666
Fax: 42008

Mafraq Hospital
PO Box 2951
Tel: 5123100
Fax: 5121549

Medinat Zayed
Hospital
PO Box 50018
Tel: 088-46888
Fax: 088-47825

Ajman
Ajman Hospital
PO Box 402
Tel: 422227
Fax: 441144

Al Zahraa
Hospital
PO Box 402
Tel: 422235

Al Ain
Al Ain Hospital
(ALJIM)
PO Box 1006
Tel: 635888
Fax: 634322

Al Saad Hospital
PO Box 15220
Tel: 826893

Emirates
International
Hospital
PO Box 18088
Tel: 669888
Fax: 510888

Oasis Hospital
PO Box 1016
Tel: 641251
Fax: 666007

Swaihan Hospital
PO Box 9877
Tel: 747233

Dubai
Al Amal Hospital
PO Box 11425
Tel: 444010
Fax: 496433

Al Dowali Pte
Hospital
PO Box 914
Tel: 212484
Fax: 278894

Al Maktoum
Hospital
PO Box 1899
Tel: 284584
Fax: 277921

Al Wasl Hospital
PO Box 9115
Tel: 341100
Fax: 341515

Al Zahra Private
Medical Centre
PO Box 23614
Tel: 315000
Fax: 314369

Dubai
Gynaecology and
Fertility Centre
PO Box 8729
Tel: 344300
Fax: 346919

Kuwaiti Hospital
Tel: 691200
Fax: 690757

Rashid Hospital
PO Box 4545
Tel: 371111
Fax: 368152

Red Crescent
Society of Islamic
Republic of Iran
PO Box 2330
Tel: 440250
Fax: 440321

Fujairah
Dibba Fujairah
New Hospital
PO Box 11414
Tel: 444711
Fax: 442119

Kalba Hospital
PO Box 11195
Kalba
Tel: 777011
Fax: 772004

Khorfakkah
Hospital
PO Box 10449
Tel: 386941
Fax: 383653

New Fujairah
Hospital
PO Box 10
Tel: 224611
Fax: 229072

Ras al-Khaimah
Al Zahrawi
Hospital
PO Box 5442
Tel: 228544
Fax: 228558

Saif Bin Ghobash
Hospital
PO Box 4727
Tel: 223555
Fax: 222760

Saqr Hospital
PO Box 5450
Tel: 223666

Shaam Hospital
PO Box 67466
Tel: 666465

Sharjah
Al Zahra Private
Hospital
PO Box 3499
Tel: 375533
Fax: 377042

Dhayd Hospital
PO Box 12550
Dhaid
Tel: 822221
Fax: 826667

Falaj Al Moalla
Hospital
PO Box 11020
Tel: 824851

Kuwaiti Hospital
PO Box 5735
Tel: 242111
Fax: 242100

Sarah Hosman
Hospital
PO Box 12
Tel: 522824
Fax: 540929

Zulekha Hospital
PO Box 457
Tel: 378866
Fax: 372299

Umm al-Quwain
Umm al-Quwain
Hospital
PO Box 24
Tel: 656888
Fax: 656588

Hotels

Abu Dhabi
Abu Dhabi Gulf
Hotel
PO Box 3766
Tel: 414777
Fax: 414537

Abu Dhabi
International
PO Box 3789
Tel: 779900
Fax: 721897

Al Ain Palace
Hotel
PO Box 33
Tel: 794777
Fax: 795335

Beach Hotel
PO Box 45200
Tel: 743000
Fax: 742111

Centre Hotel
Novotel
PO Box 47136
Tel: 333555
Fax: 3436333

Corniche
Residence
PO Box 6677
Tel: 211200
Fax: 344596

Dana Hotel
PO Box 47300
Tel: 761000
Fax: 766650

Delma Centre
PO Box 46320
Tel: 332100
Fax: 329228

Dhafra Beach
Hotel
PO Box 11828
Tel: 81-71600
Fax: 81-71002

Emirates Plaza
Hotel
PO Box 5295
Tel: 722000
Fax: 723204

Federal Hotel
PO Box 43067
Tel: 789000
Fax: 794728

Habara House
PO Box 47173
Tel: 431010
Fax: 342885

Holiday Inn Abu
Dhabi
PO Box 3541
Tel: 335335
Fax: 335766

Hilton
International
Abu Dhabi
PO Box 877
Tel: 661900
Fax: 669696

Holiday Inn
Abu Dhabi
PO Box 3541
Tel: 335335
Fax: 335766

Hotel Inter-
Continental
Abu Dhabi
PO Box 4171
Tel: 666888
Fax: 669153

Jazira Resort
PO Box 26268
Tel: 5629100
Fax: 5629035

Khalidia Palace
Hotel
PO Box 4010
Tel: 662470
Fax: 660411

Le Meridien
Abu Dhabi
PO Box 46066
Tel: 776666
Fax: 727221

Mina Hotel
PO Box 44421
Tel: 781000
Fax: 791000

Oasis Residence
PO Box 46336
Tel: 351000
Fax: 313213

Park Residence
PO Box 47878
Tel: 742000
Fax: 785656

Sheraton Abu
Dhabi Resort
and Towers
PO Box 640
Tel: 773333
Fax: 725149

Zakher Hotel
PO Box 932
Tel: 327900
Fax: 326306

Ajman
Ajman Beach
Hotel
PO Box 874
Tel: 423333
Fax: 423363

Hotel Al Waha
PO Box 2869
Tel: 424333
Fax: 426272

344

Al Ain

Ain Al Fayda Hotel
PO Box 15798
Tel: 838333
Fax: 838900

Al Ain Hilton
PO Box 1333
Tel: 686666
Fax: 686888

Al Ramaha Rest House
PO Box 15798
Tel: 772400
Fax: 838900

Hotel Inter-Continental
PO Box 16031
Tel: 686686
Fax: 686766

Dubai

Airport Hotel
PO Box 13018
Tel: 823464
Fax: 823781

Al Aman Hotel
PO Box 8187
Tel: 265188
Fax: 265134

Al Ahrar Hotel
PO Box 12978
Tel: 271000
Fax: 232373

Al Buteen Plaza
PO Box 8384
Tel: 263888
Fax: 264759

Al Diwan Hotel
PO Box 55652
Tel: 287118
Fax: 213624

Al Firdous Apts
PO Box 15482
Tel: 252420
Fax: 252425

Al Hashemi Hotel
PO Box 13214
Tel: 233333
Fax: 214717

Al Hili Hotel
PO Box 5322
Tel: 288878
Fax: 289264

Al Ittihad Hotel
PO Box 1590
Tel: 238455
Fax: 255005

Al Jawhara Hotel
PO Box 7217
Tel: 223141
Fax: 232049

Al Jazeera Hotel
PO Box 8814
Tel: 262322
Fax: 251150

Al Jazira Arabia Fara Hotel
PO Box 50644
Tel: 267151
Fax: 267898

Al Julus Hotel
PO Box 537
Tel: 251252
Fax: 251533

Al Karnak Hotel
PO Box 5118
Tel: 268799

Al Kawakeb Hotel
PO Box 55543
Tel: 261202

Al Khail Hotel
PO Box 8384
Tel: 269171
Fax: 269226

Al Khaima Hotel
PO Box 12185
Tel: 255774
Fax: 256015

Al Khaleej Hotel
PO Box 10559
Tel: 211144
Fax: 237140

Al Khaleej Palace Hotel
PO Box 3720
Tel: 231000
Fax: 211293

Al Khayam Hotel
PO Box 1219
Tel: 264211
Fax: 265825

Al Madani Hotel
PO Box 55543
Tel: 283040
Fax: 275827

Al Mashariq Al Arabia Hotel
PO Box 4043
Tel: 260773

Al Muraqabat Plaza
PO Box 20127
Tel: 690550
Fax: 699779

Al Nakhuda Shelter Hotel
PO Box 53122
Tel: 277903
Fax: 277436

Al Rabat Hotel
PO Box 12845
Tel: 266694
Fax: 266444

Al Rukun Al Hadi Hotel
PO Box 5464
Tel: 258880

Al Saadah Hotel
PO Box 41121
Tel: 284440
Fax: 232569

Al Salam Hotel
PO Box 1570
Tel: 256660

Al Saqer Hotel
PO Box 12185
Tel: 252796

Al Shara Hotel
PO Box 2388
Tel: 265213
Fax: 254668

Al Tawon Hotel
PO Box 4021
Tel: 267600

Al Wasel Hotel
PO Box 1013
Tel: 210621
Fax: 289160

Al Yasat Hotel
PO Box 174
Tel: 266460
Fax: 266899

Al Zahara Hotel
PO Box 13580
Tel: 221704
Fax: 210665

Ambassador Hotel
PO Box 3226
Tel: 531000
Fax: 534751

Arabian Island Hotel
PO Box 50644
Tel: 267151
Fax: 267998

Aras Hotel
PO Box 20832
Tel: 258527

Arbella Hotel
PO Box 1590
Tel: 226688
Fax: 272645

Arvand Hotel
PO Box 12247
Tel: 258800
Fax: 261001

Astoria Hotel
PO Box 457
Tel: 534300
Fax: 535665

Atlas Hotel
PO Box 15664
Tel: 281919
Fax: 275827

Avon Hotel
PO Box 1041
Tel: 258877
Fax: 252061

Baku Hotel
PO Box 21755
Tel: 243600
Fax: 236874

Bin Sadoon Hotel
PO Box 12430
Tel: 264236
Fax: 259825

Bristol Hotel
PO Box 1471
Tel: 224171
Fax: 232765

Cape Town Hotel
PO Box 4577
Tel: 255888
Fax: 256283

Captain Hotel
PO Box 20832
Tel: 289507
Fax: 289544

Carlton Tower Hotel
PO Box 1955
Tel: 227111
Fax: 228249

Casablanca Hotel
PO Box 19218
Tel: 289111
Fax: 289123

Chicago Beach Hotel
PO Box 11416
Tel: 480000
Fax: 482273

City Gold Hotel
PO Box 4428
Tel: 263600
Fax: 264373

City Hotel
PO Box 55986
Tel: 214300
Fax: 214033

Claridge Hotel
PO Box 1833
Tel: 227141
Fax: 232072

Concord Palace Hotel
PO Box 7052
Tel: 512555
Fax: 520194

Country Hotel
PO Box 8734
Tel: 286222
Fax: 279080

Deira Hotel
PO Box 1390
Tel: 221904

Deira Park Hotel
PO Box 51110
Tel: 239922
Fax: 239893

Doha Palace Hotel
PO Box 19335
Tel: 212288
Fax: 282469

Down Town Hotel
PO Box 22324
Tel: 260777
Fax: 268655

Dreamland Hotel
PO Box 7409
Tel: 288300
Fax: 288845

Dreams Hotel
PO Box 10397
Tel: 254333
Fax: 262476

Dubai Benta Hotel
PO Box 1590
Tel: 212525
Fax: 234059

Dubai Inter-Continental Hotel
PO Box 476
Tel: 227171
Fax: 284777

Dubai Inter-diplomat Hotel
PO Box 14223
Tel: 220700
Fax: 246882

Dubai Marine Hotel
PO Box 5182
Tel: 520900
Fax: 521035

Dubai Metropolitan
PO Box 24988
Tel: 440000
Fax: 441146

Dubai Palm Hotel
PO Box 21969
Tel: 210021
Fax: 212312

Dubai Park Hotel
PO Box 22380
Tel: 487111
Fax: 487222

Dubai Plaza Hotel
PO Box 24621
Tel: 454545
Fax: 454700

Dubai Shangrila Hotel
PO Box 5800
Tel: 211334
Fax: 222916

Emirates Hotel
PO Box 3210
Tel: 220191
Fax: 222044

Forte Grand-Dubai
PO Box 10001
Tel: 824040
Fax: 825540

Forte Grand Jumeirah Beach
PO Box 24970
Tel: 845555
Fax: 846999

Glass Suites Hotel
PO Box 55808
Tel: 278800
Fax: 286655

Hatta Forte Hotel
PO Box 9277
Tel: 085-23211
Fax: 085-23561

Heathrow Hotel
PO Box 19479
Tel: 239555
Fax: 212816

Hilton International
PO Box 927
Tel: 314000
Fax: 313383

Hotel Bristol
PO Box 1471
Tel: 224171
Fax: 232765

Hotel Copper Chimney
PO Box 8144
Tel: 524005
Fax: 513181

Hotel Delhi Darbar Bombay
PO Box 6962
Tel: 267474
Fax: 266464

Hotel Diamond Rock
PO Box 16412
Tel: 277333

Hotel Dubai Orient
PO Box 1041
Tel: 261233
Fax: 252061

Hotel Heathrow Palace
PO Box 19471
Tel: 256425
Fax: 256542

Hotel La Paz
PO Box 52441
Tel: 268800
Fax: 269797

Hotel Mermaid
PO Box 14089
Tel: 288555
Fax: 280480

Houf Hotel
PO Box 8384
Tel: 268282
Fax: 263093

Hyat Palace Hotel
PO Box 12185
Tel: 252273

Hyatt Regency
PO Box 5588
Tel: 221234
Fax: 211868

Imperial Palace Hotel
PO Box 51509
Tel: 211344
Fax: 223770

Imperial Suites Hotel
PO Box 52444
Tel: 515100
Fax: 511647

Intercity Hotel
PO Box 55450
Tel: 213000
Fax: 272785

Isteqal Hotel
PO Box 10076
Tel: 265935
Fax: 251994

Jamal Palace Hotel
PO Box 9833
Tel: 278687
Fax: 220892

Jebel Ali Hotel
PO Box 9255
Tel: 836000
Fax: 835543

JW Marriott
PO Box 16590
Tel: 624444
Fax: 626264

Kams House Hotel
PO Box 12769
Tel: 519111
Fax: 254888

London Hotel
PO Box 20514
Tel: 254888
Fax: 225287

Maarab Hotel
PO Box 8384
Tel: 266050
Fax: 266603

Marakesh Hotel
PO Box 19479
Tel: 259545
Fax: 273432

Maredias Hotel
PO Box 14140
Tel: 289393
Fax: 288600

Mariana Hotel
PO Box 19335
Tel: 259333
Fax: 259186

Marina Star Hotel
PO Box 21755
Tel: 288872
Fax: 236874

Marmar Hotel
PO Box 21548
Tel: 275550
Fax: 239038

Metro Hotel
PO Box 1439
Tel: 260040
Fax: 262098

Metropolitan Beach
PO Box 24454
Tel: 845000
Fax: 846547

Middle East Hotel
PO Box 1590
Tel: 261111
Fax: 255005

Mirage Hotel
PO Box 55582
Tel: 260004
Fax: 260293

Montana Hotel
PO Box 15950
Tel: 272300
Fax: 283253

Moon Hotel
PO Box 51214
Tel: 252400
Fax: 252860

Najim Al Khaleej Hotel
PO Box 6219
Tel: 256555
Fax: 256462

Nazwa Hotel
PO Box 5464
Tel: 255300
Fax: 252314

Nia Waren Hotel
PO Box 10076
Tel: 286403
Fax: 259155

Novotel Dubai
PO Box 24990
Tel: 235000
Fax: 285000

Odeon Hotel
PO Box 7941
Tel: 233123
Fax: 270311

Oman Hotel
PO Box 1388
Tel: 222308
Fax: 217556

Omid Hotel
PO Box 3930
Tel: 251811
Fax: 265165

Onesis House
PO Box 4803
Tel: 287474
Fax: 228101

Oxeen Hotel
PO Box 20514
Tel: 288830
Fax: 225287

Palm Beach Hotel
PO Box 5822
Tel: 525550
Fax: 528320

Panorama Hotel
PO Box 14703
Tel: 518518
Fax: 518028

Penninsula Hotel
PO Box 23749
Tel: 533000
Fax: 535010

Phoenicia Hotel
PO Box 4467
Tel: 227191
Fax: 221629

President Hotel
PO Box 6715
Tel: 346565
Fax: 368915

Qaser Sherine Hotel
PO Box 12978
Tel: 255700
Fax: 255543

Qasr Al Seyaha Hotel
PO Box 21457
Tel: 255855
Fax: 255636

Ramada Hotel
PO Box 7979
Tel: 521010
Fax: 521033

Red Sea Hotel
PO Box 1613
Tel: 264281
Fax: 265249

Regent Palace
Hotel
PO Box 51712
Tel: 535555
Fax: 535111

Rex Hotel
PO Box 10482
Tel: 212834
Fax: 289232

Riga Hotel
PO Box 21125
Tel: 217555
Fax: 229299

Riviera Hotel
PO Box 1388
Tel: 222131
Fax: 211820

Royal Abjar Hotel
PO Box 8668
Tel: 625555
Fax: 697358

Royal Crystal
Hotel
PO Box 60192
Tel: 288222
Fax: 2888828

Royal Prince
Hotel
PO Box 16382
Tel: 270476
Fax: 219757

Sadhna Hotel
PO Box 2881
Tel: 216611
Fax: 210867

Saeed Hotel
PO Box 11011
Tel: 268200
Fax: 219059

Sahwa Hotel
PO Box 15933
Tel: 255201
Fax: 265249

Salalah Hotel
PO Box 1662
Tel: 252440

Sas Hotel
PO Box 5464
Tel: 258881
Fax: 252314

Sea Palace Hotel
PO Box 7217
Tel: 264964

Shams Al Sahra
Hotel
PO Box 2388
Tel: 253666
Fax: 266899

Shangrila Hotel
PO Box 5800
Tel: 211334
Fax: 285236

Shata Al Arab
Hotel
PO Box 6421
Tel: 260355

Shell Inn Hotel
PO Box 20715
Tel: 551000
Fax: 551441

Sheraton Dubai
PO Box 4250
Tel: 281111
Fax: 213468

Shiraz Hotel
PO Box 1123
Tel: 254800
Fax: 254867

Shirazi Hotel
PO Box 13163
Tel: 216464
Fax: 226142

Sina Hotel
PO Box 2413
Tel: 252323
Fax: 252606

Sira Hotel
PO Box 15806
Tel: 262111
Fax: 270865

Sochi Hotel
PO Box 21754
Tel: 242500
Fax: 236874

St George Hotel
PO Box 3944
Tel: 251122
Fax: 261661

Stars Hotel
PO Box 20117
Tel: 266000
Fax: 253739

Strand Hotel
PO Box 14188
Tel: 255990
Fax: 231908

Sulaf Hotel
PO Box 5275
Tel: 264246
Fax: 212928

Summer Land
Hotel
PO Box 14107
Tel: 219500
Fax: 277984

Sun Rock Hotel
PO Box 24607
Tel: 514222
Fax: 515755

Swiss Hotel
PO Box 50128
Tel: 212181
Fax: 538121

Taj Mahal Hotel
PO Box 852
Tel: 279000
Fax: 275638

Tara Hotel
PO Box 13253
Tel: 272424
Fax: 273755

Tehran Hotel
PO Box 3938
Tel: 282244
Fax: 222823

Time Palace Hotel
PO Box 12769
Tel: 532111
Fax: 534899

Toofan Hotel
PO Box 15304
Tel: 258511
Fax: 259751

Tourist Hotel
PO Box 23618
Tel: 229388
Fax: 271853

Tourist Palace
Hotel
PO Box 21457
Tel: 255855
Fax: 255636

Vendome Plaza
Hotel
PO Box 20331
Tel: 222333
Fax: 213222

Victoria Hotel
PO Box 4428
Tel: 269626
Fax: 269575

Vienna Hotel
PO Box 3983
Tel: 218855
Fax: 212928

Weekend Hotel
PO Box 21899
Tel: 271700
Fax: 239697

White Beach
Hotel
PO Box 73453
Tel: 263695
Fax: 264694

Yasmin Hotel
PO Box 174
Tel: 250166
Fax: 250568

Fujairah
Fujairah Beach
Motel
PO Box 283
Tel: 228051
Fax: 228111

Fujairah Plaza
PO Box 1199
Tel: 232000
Fax: 232111

Hilton
International
Fujairah
PO Box 231
Tel: 222411
Fax: 226541

Holiday Beach
Motel and Chalets
PO Box 1433
Tel: 445540
Fax: 445580

Marine Motel
Kalba
PO Box 11323
Tel: 778877
Fax: 776000

Sandy Beach
Motel
PO Box 659
Tel: 445353
Fax: 445207

Ras al-Khaimah
Al Nakheel Hotel
PO Box 5333
Tel: 222822
Fax: 222922

Bin Majed Beach
Hotel
PO Box 1946
Tel: 352233
Fax: 353225

Khat Family Rest
House
PO Box 5456
Tel: 448181
Fax: 448182

Ras al-Khaimah
Hotel
PO Box 56
Tel: 352999
Fax: 352990

Sharjah
Al Buhaira
Residence (Apts)
PO Box 22909
Tel: 391818
Fax: 592633

Al Hormoodi Pal
PO Box 20722
Tel: 378222
Fax: 529958

Beach Hotel
Sharjah
PO Box 5977
Tel: 281311
Fax: 525422

Coral Beach Hotel
PO Box 5524
Tel: 221011
Fax: 274101

Federal Hotel
PO Box 5143
Tel: 354106
Fax: 541394

Golden Beach
Motel
PO Box 1198
Tel: 281331
Fax: 284962

Holiday
International
Hotel
PO Box 5802
Tel: 357357
Fax: 372254

Khaleej Tourist
Hotel
PO Box 5504
Tel: 597888
Fax: 598999

Marbella Resort
Sharjah (Chalets)
PO Box 5017
Tel: 357123
Fax: 378050

Sharjah Airport
Hotel
PO Box 6125
Tel: 581110
Fax: 581300

Sharjah Carlton
Hotel
PO Box 1198
Tel: 283711
Fax: 284962

Sharjah
Continental Hotel
PO Box 3527
Tel: 371111
Fax: 524090

Sharjah Grand
Hotel
PO Box 6059
Tel: 285557
Fax: 282861

Sharjah Plaza
Hotel
PO Box 204
Tel: 377555
Fax: 373311

Sheba Hotel
PO Box 486
Tel: 522522
Fax: 354357

Summerland
Motel
PO Box 1083
Tel: 281321
Fax: 285422

Umm al-Quwain
Pearl Hotel
PO Box 887
Tel: 666678
Fax: 666679

Umm al-Quwain
Beach Hotel
PO Box 158
Tel: 666647
Fax: 667273

Libraries and Book Shops

Abu Dhabi
Al-Mutanabi
Bookshop
PO Box 71946
Tel: 340319
Fax: 317706

All Prints
Bookshop
PO Box 857
Tel: 338572

The Cultural
Foundation
Library
Tel: 215300

Dubai
Al Siddique Book
Centre and
Circulating
Libraries
PO Box 9261
Tel: 535583

Archies Library
PO Box 23428
Tel: 365402
Fax: 365491

British Council
Bookshop/Library
PO Box 1636
Tel: 371540

Dubai Lending
Library
Tel: 446480

Islamic Library
PO Box 3811
Tel: 221355

Shopping Mall
Magrudy's
Tel: 444192

Reading for All
Bookshop
PO Box 11032
Tel: 663901
Fax: 690084

Ras al-Khaimah
Student Library
PO Box 42
Tel: 236132

Sharjah
Al Qairwan
Library
PO Box 244
Tel: 548837

Arabian Library
PO Box 2226
Tel: 549315
Fax: 522754

Shaikh Adbulla
Ali Al Mahmood's
Library
PO Box 4211
Tel: 377822
Fax: 376666

Student Library
PO Box 2578
Tel: 582157

Media

Abu Dhabi
Agence France
Presse (AFP)
PO Box 3790
Tel: 334563
Fax: 348572

Al Fajr
Newspaper
PO Box 505
Tel: 478300
Fax: 474326

Al Khaleej
Newspaper
PO Box 7353
Tel: 771355
Fax: 727360

Emirates Printing
Publishing and
Distribution Co
Limited
PO Box 44788
Tel: 456500
Fax: 456665

Gulf News
PO Box 7441
Tel: 723100
Fax: 316018

Khaleej Times
PO Box 3082
Tel: 336000
Fax: 336424

Kuwait News
Agency
PO Box 2947
Tel: 666994
Fax: 666935

Malik News
Agency
PO Box 7580
Tel: 764676
Fax: 764636

Reuters Middle
East Limited
PO Box 7872
Tel: 328000
Fax: 333380

Dubai
Agence France
Presse (AFP)
PO Box 3790
Tel: 218111
Fax: 242949

Dublin
Commercial
Intermediary
PO Box 55777
Tel: 237373
Fax: 276668

Emirates Printing
Publishing and
Distribution Co
Limited
PO Box 60499
Tel: 623920
Fax: 663768

Gulf News
PO Box 6519
Tel: 447100
Fax: 449139

Khaleej Times
PO Box 11243
Tel: 382400
Fax: 383345

Sharjah
Dar Al Khaleej
PO Box 30
Tel: 598777
Fax: 599336

Malik News
Agency
PO Box 1588
Tel: 351872

United News
of India
PO Box 2027
Tel: 378123
Fax: 375547

Museums

Abu Dhabi
Al-Hosn Fort
PO Box 2380
Tel: 212900
Fax: 332610

Cultural
Foundation
PO Box 2380
Tel: 215300
Fax: 336059

Petroleum
Exhibition
Tel: 6065050

Ajman
Ajman National
Museum
PO Box 2829
Tel: 423824
Fax: 441202

Al Ain
Al Ain Museum
PO Box 15715
Tel: 641595
Fax: 658311

Dubai
Dubai Museum
PO Box 5818
Tel: 531862
Fax: 539445

Sheikh Saeed Al-
Maktoum House
PO Box 5818
Tel: 535928
Fax: 539269

Fujairah
Fujairah National
Museum
PO Box 1
Tel: 229085
Fax: 229539

Ras al-Khaimah
Ahmed bin Majed
Arabian Navigator
Museum
Tel: 228226

National Museum
PO Box 94
Tel: 333411
Fax: 315564

Sharjah
Sharjah Museum
PO Box 5119
Tel: 366466
Fax: 376334

Sharjah
Archaeological
Museum
PO Box 5119
Tel: 366366
Fax: 376334

Sharjah Natural
History Museum
PO Box 24444
Tel: 311411
Fax: 311000

Sharjah Science
Museum
PO Box 25700
Tel: 514777
Fax: 514733

Night Spots and Bars

Abu Dhabi
Al Finjan
Le Meridien
Tel: 776666

Al Karya
Sheraton Hotel
Tel: 7030240

Al Sahara
Nightclub
International
Hotel
Tel: 779900

Ally Pally Corner
Al Ain Palace
Hotel
Tel: 794777

Anarkali
Zakher Hotel
Tel: 329300

Asian Bar
International
Hotel
Tel: 779900

Bounty
Jazira Beach
Resort
Tel: 5629100

Bugsy's
Federal Hotel
Tel: 789000

Caza Brazil
Le Meridien
Tel: 776666

Cheers
Al Ain Palace
Hotel
Tel: 795288

Churchill's
Zakher Hotel
Tel: 329300

Club One
Zakher Hotel
Tel: 329300

Cozy Corner
Jazira Beach
Resort
Tel: 5629100

Diwan Nightclub
Emirates Plaza
Tel: 722000

El Sabre Lounge
Sheraton Hotel
Tel: 773333

Falcon
Dhafra Beach
Hotel
Tel: (081) 71600

Finnegan's
Forte Grand
Hotel
Tel: 742020

49ers
Dana Hotel
Tel: 761000

Harambee
Zakher Hotel
Tel: 329300

Harvesters
Holiday Inn
Hotel
Tel: 335335

Hemingway's
Hilton Hotel
Tel: 661900

Horse and Jockey
Inter-Continental
Hotel
Tel: 686686

Island Exchange
Forte Grand
Hotel
Tel: 742020

Jhankar
Emirates Plaza
Tel: 722000

La Bamba
Inter-Continental
Hotel
Tel: 686686

La Bodega
Zakher Hotel
Tel: 329300

Maikhana
International
Hotel
Tel: 779900

Manila Bay Disco
Emirates Plaza
Tel: 722000

Mombasa
Emirates Plaza
Tel: 722000

Mood Indigo
Novotel
Tel: 333555

Odyssey
Khalidia Palace
Hotel
Tel: 662470

Pearl Club
Zakher Hotel
Tel: 329300

Rababa Nightclub
Gulf Hotel
Tel: 414777

Rameses
Novotel
Tel: 333555

Ranch, The
Gulf Hotel
Tel: 414777

Red Lion
International
Hotel
Tel: 779900

Rhapsody Lounge
Holiday Inn
Hotel
Tel: 335335

Samantha's
Inter-Continental
Hotel
Tel: 686686

Sampaguita
Zakher Hotel
Tel: 329300

Sargum
Emirates Plaza
Tel: 722000

Scorpio
Discotheque
International
Hotel
Tel: 779900

Shahrazad
Emirates Plaza
Tel: 722000

Shamiana
Dana Hotel
Tel: 761000

Southern Comfort
International
Hotel
Tel: 779900

Taj Mahal
Zakher Hotel
Tel: 320400

Talk of the Town
Khalidia Palace
Tel: 622470

Tavern Disco
Sheraton Hotel
Tel: 773333

Tavern, The
Sheraton Hotel
Tel: 7030240

Tramp, The
Mina Hotel
Tel: 781000

Tiffany Bar
Khalidia Palace
Tel: 662470

Trap, The
Dana Hotel
Tel: 761000

Zino
Meridian
Tel: 776666

Dubai
Al-Nakheel
Carlton Tower
Tel: 227111

Al-Sayyad
Claridge Hotel
Tel: 227141

Alamo, The
Dubai Marine
Beach Club
Tel: 441221

Amy's Key Club
Airport Hotel
Tel: 823464

Anartaki
Sun Rock Hotel
Tel: 514222

Aphrodite's
Chicago Beach
Tel: 480000

Atlantic
Nihal
Tel: 278800

Bangkok Cellar
Highland Lodge
Tel: 824040

Baron's Table
Peninsula
Tel: 533000

Biggles
Airport Hotel
Tel: 823464

Billy Blues
Dubai Plaza
Hotel
Tel: 454545

Boardwalk, The
Dubai Creek and
Yacht Club
Tel: 825777

Butterfly Night
Club
Carlton Tower
Tel: 227111

California
Swiss Hotel
Tel: 212181

Carlton Pub, The
Carlton Tower
Tel: 227111

Carpenters
Hyatt Regency
Hotel
Tel: 221234

Cheers Bar
Highland Lodge
Tel: 379470

Chelsea Arms
Sheraton Hotel
Tel: 281111

Club Joumana
Jebel Ali Hotel
Tel: 835252

Colony Bar
Chicago Beach
Tel: 480000

Constellation Bar
Aviation Club
Tel: 824122

Country Bar
Claridge Hotel
Tel: 227141

Crazy Horse
Regent Palace
Tel: 535555

Der Kellar
Chicago Beach
Tel: 480000

Diwan
Sheraton Hotel
Tel: 281111

Down Under Bar
Dubai Creek and
Yacht Club
Tel: 825777

Dubliners, The
Forte Grand
Tel: 824040

English Pub, The
Inter-Continental
Tel: 222691

Equator Bar
Highland Lodge
Tel: 379470

Escobar
Al Khaleej Palace
Tel: 231000

Falcon
Hilton Hotel
Tel: 314000

Fox and Hound
Novotel
Tel: 235000

Garfield's
Swiss Plaza
Tel: 533737

George and
Dragon
Ambassador
Hotel
Tel: 531000

Harley's
Metropolitan
Hotel
Tel: 440000

Harry's Bar
Royal Abjar
Tel: 625555

Harvesters
Holiday Inn
Crowne Plaza
Tel: 311111

Hawker's
St George Hotel
Tel: 251122

Humphrey's
Hilton Hotel
Tel: 314000

Hunter's Bar
Imperial Suites
Hotel
Tel: 515100

Indian Night
Club
Phoenicia Hotel
Tel: 227191

Jules Bar
Forte Grand
Tel: 824040

Layalina
Metropolitan
Tel: 440000

Le Cave
Inter-Continental
Hotel
Tel: 227171

Le Mirage
Chicago Beach
Tel: 480000

Lodge, The
Highland Lodge
Tel: 379470

Los Angeles
Swiss Hotel
Tel: 212181

Mahal
Regent Palace
Tel: 535555

Mexican Bar
Royal Abjar
Tel: 625555

Oasis
Royal Abjar
Tel: 625555

Old Vic
Ramada Hotel
Tel: 521010

Oriental Night
Club
Phoenicia Hotel
Tel: 227191

Pancho's Villas
Astoria Hotel
Tel: 534300

Pearl Bar
Forte Grand
Tel: 824040

Philippino Night
Club
Phoenicia Hotel
Tel: 227191

Piano Bar
Holiday Inn
Crowne Plaza
Tel: 311111

Picasso's
Inter-Continental
Tel: 227171

Premiere
Hyatt Regency
Tel: 221234

Rany Mahal
Swiss Hotel
Tel: 212181

Red Lion Pub
Metropolitan
Tel: 440000

Rockefellas
Highland Lodge
Tel: 379470

Sampaguita
Claridge Hotel
Tel: 227141

Sanjam
Sun Rock Hotel
Tel: 514222

Shama
Sun Rock Hotel
Tel: 514222

Sharif
Metropolitan
Tel: 440000

Sharif Bar
Swiss Hotel
Tel: 212181

Shooting Club
Jebel Ali Hotel
Tel: 836555

Silsila
Sun Rock Hotel
Tel: 514222

Sinatra's
Al Khaleej Palace
Tel: 231000

Stanley's Bar
Peninsula
Tel: 533000

Studio 61-62
Sun Rock Hotel
Tel: 514222

Tahiti Garden
Highland Lodge
Tel: 379470

Tartan Bar
Higland Lodge
Tel: 379470

Taverna, The
Dubai Marine
Beach Club
Tel: 441221

TGIT
Astoria Hotel
Tel: 534300

Thatcher's
Dubai Marine
Tel: 520900

Tiptop Disco
St George Hotel
Tel: 251122

Tony Bar/
Grasshopper
Palm Beach Hotel
Tel: 525550

Tower Restaurant
Aviation Club
Tel: 824122

Up On The Tenth
Inter-Continental
Hotel
Tel: 221691

Valentino's
Peninsula
Tel: 533000

West Coast Bar
Jebel Ali Hotel
Tel: 835252

Fujairah
Tropicana
Fujairah Hilton
Hotel
Tel: 222411

Ras al-Khaimah
Paradise Disco
Bin Majed Beach
Hotel
Tel: 352233

Umm al-Quwain
Hot Beat Club
Pearl Hotel
Tel: 666678

Shopping Centres

Abu Dhabi
Al Ahlia Prisunic
PO Box 4033
Tel: 662800
Fax: 669593

Ayoun Al Reem
Ladies Shopping
Centre and Salon
PO Box 15155
Tel: 513334
Fax: 665144

Zakher Shopping
Centre
PO Box 932
Tel: 337427
Fax: 326306

Ajman
Ajman Souk
PO Box 2585
Tel: 444333
Fax: 444488

Dubai
Abu Hail
Shopping Centre
PO Box 5005
Tel: 669600
Fax: 695722

Al Dhiyafah
Centre
PO Box 133
Tel: 450347/
492222

Al Ghurair
Centre
PO Box 69999
Tel: 232333
Fax: 285356

Al Manal Centre
PO Box 4455
Tel: 277701
Fax: 287425

Al Mulla Plaza
PO Box 59
Tel: 665885
Fax: 625438

Beach Centre
PO Box 53500
Tel: 449045
Fax: 497737

Bur Jumain
Centre
PO Box 8022
Tel: 520222
Fax: 510824

The Centre
PO Box 1714
Tel: 693155
Fax: 692548

City Centre
PO Box 60811
Tel: 232344
Fax: 684550

Hamarain Centre
PO Box 16739
Tel: 621110
Fax: 626004

Holiday Centre
PO Box 11393
Tel: 317755
Fax: 313533

Inter-Continental
Plaza
PO Box 8811
Tel: 232279
Fax: 245777

Jumaira Plaza
PO Box 9287
Tel: 497111
Fax: 490919

Markaz Al Jumeira
PO Box 894
Tel: 443085
Fax: 449801

Magrudy's
Shopping Mall
PO Box 1155
Tel: 444192
Fax: 444954

Wafi Shopping
Mall
PO Box 721
Tel: 367125
Fax: 369075

Taxis

Abu Dhabi
Al Amal Rent
A Car
PO Box 399
Tel: 329998
Fax: 770880

Al Ghazal Taxi
PO Box 8200
Tel: 447787
Fax: 44719

Eurodollar Rent
A Car
PO Box 42228
Tel: 338899
Fax: 332933

Al Ain
Al Ghazal Taxi
Tel: 644484

Dubai
Emirates Taxi
PO Box 23661
Tel: 515515
Fax: 515551

Golden Taxi
PO Box 2622
Tel: 365444
Fax: 348529

Gulf Radio Taxis
PO Box 10779
Tel: 236666
Fax: 275418

Inter Taxi
PO Box 10990
Tel: 666333
Fax: 695525

Limousine Dubai
PO Box 1768
Tel: 627333
Fax: 697388

Sharjah
Delta Taxi
PO Box 3952
Tel: 598598
Fax: 594949

Inter Taxi
Tel: 545464

Travel and Tour Agents

Abu Dhabi
Abdul Jalil Travel
Agency
PO Box 279
Tel: 333210
Fax: 349395

Advanced Travel
and Tourism
PO Box 5561
Tel: 347900
Fax: 325334

Agab Travel and
Tourism Est
PO Box 2072
Tel: 333720
Fax: 311133

Al Aweidha
Travel Bureau
PO Box 10
Tel: 324333
Fax: 322104

Al Badie Travel
Agency
PO Box 2838
Tel: 792400
Fax: 793378

Al Bait Travel
and Tourism Est
PO Box 25454
Tel: 213944
Fax: 213588

Al Dhaheri Air
Services
PO Box 45057
Tel: 337474
Fax: 332727

Al Fandi Al
Mazroui Travel
and Tourism
PO Box 2151
Tel: 772227
Fax: 776363

Al Faraj Global
Services (Travel
Section)
PO Box 47184
Tel: 773486
Fax: 785408

Al Ghaith Travel
and Tourism
PO Box 268
Tel: 341169
Fax: 316438

Al Hadidi Travel
and Tourist
Agency
PO Box 3644
Tel: 774950
Fax: 782479

Al Harmoudi
Tourism and
Travel Est
PO Box 5502
Tel: 316533
Fax: 393680

Al Khalila Travel
and Cargo
PO Box 43185
Tel: 725576
Fax: 785809

Al Khatem
Travel Tourism
and Cargo
PO Box 27448
Tel: 347788
Fax: 342286

Al Madina Travel
Agency
PO Box 4759
Tel: 722826
Fax: 778153

Al Mansoor
Travel Agency
PO Box 4141
Tel: 326246
Fax: 316016

Al Masaood
Travel
PO Box 322
Tel: 772000
Fax: 776689

Al Masaood
Travel and
Services
PO Box 806
Tel: 212100
Fax: 325323

Al Muhairy
Travel Bureau
PO Box 3365
Tel: 327898
Fax: 329424

Al Otaiba Travel
and Tourism Est
PO Box 25139
Tel: 338718
Fax: 341164

Al Qamzan Travel
and Tourism
Agency
PO Box 363
Tel: 326131
Fax: 391595

Al Rayed Travel
and Tourism
PO Box 3277
Tel: 338897
Fax: 795170

Al Sarraj Travel
and Services
Bureau
PO Box 3655
Tel: 345251
Fax: 342128

Alwathba Travel
and Tourism
PO Box 3837
Tel: 778877
Fax: 788387

Al Yousef Travel
Agency
PO Box 3733
Tel: 339145
Fax: 316247

Al Zaabi Travels
PO Box 2053
Tel: 312424
Fax: 319979

Al Zubarea Travel
and Tourism
PO Box 275
Tel: 720096
Fax: 772755

Arabian Travel
and Shipping Est
PO Box 46067
Tel: 330626
Fax: 340212

Arabic Wings
Travel and
Tourism Est
PO Box 26367
Tel: 393444
Fax: 392112

Atiq International
Tours and Travel
PO Box 43731
Tel: 315445
Fax: 316995

Atlas Travel
Tourism and
Transport
PO Box 2086
Tel: 337272
Fax: 331313

Bin Batoota
Travels
PO Box 7223
Tel: 339865
Fax: 393720

Bin Brook Group
PO Box 879
Tel: 776686
Fax: 764663

Bin Ham Travel
and Tourism
Agency
PO Box 27242
Tel: 393366
Fax: 393663

Bin Harmal
Travel and
Tourism
PO Box 47470
Tel: 315888
Fax: 345511

Bin Sabha Travel
Agency
PO Box 26190
Tel: 393539
Fax: 322947

Delma Travel
Agency
PO Box 2760
Tel: 322928
Fax: 328454

Dhafir Travel
Services (DTS)
PO Box 6344
Tel: 786700
Fax: 776786

Eastern Travels
PO Box 472
Tel: 335928
Fax: 314837

Emirates Express
(Gulf Group)
PO Box 25298
Tel: 311322
Fax: 346262

Emirates Travel
and Tourism
PO Box 6
Tel: 212131
Fax: 391231

Falcon Tours and
Travel
PO Box 43832
Tel: 216824
Fax: 351008

Faris Travel and
Tourism
PO Box 6877
Tel: 783233
Fax: 765233

Frontier
International
Travels
PO Box 4260
Tel: 776778
Fax: 768336

Garuda Indonesia
PO Box 278
Tel: 328124
Fax: 392425

Golden Falcon
Travel and
Tourism
PO Box 508
Tel: 777033
Fax: 787831

Gulf Express
Travel
PO Box 2007
Tel: 343498
Fax: 325759

Horizon Travel
and Tours
PO Box 3154
Tel: 347464
Fax: 315214

352

Idex Travel
Agency
PO Box 47380
Tel: 444427
Fax: 444288

Image Travel and
Tourism
PO Box 4018
Tel: 311900
Fax: 333824

Inter-Continental
Travels
PO Box 4494
Tel: 777534
Fax: 741816

Jet Air Travel
and Cargo
PO Box 46434
Tel: 451526
Fax: 454451

Khoony Travel
PO Box 46235
Tel: 326520
Fax: 217033

Majid Travel
Tourism and
Cargo
PO Box 26656
Tel: 776474
Fax: 793635

Narwas Travels
PO Box 3981
Tel: 211112
Fax: 211889

Net Tours and
Tourism
PO Box 43933
Tel: 794656
Fax: 721188

Oman Travel
and Tourism
PO Box 7364
Tel: 339861
Fax: 316101

Omeir Travel
Agency
PO Box 267
Tel: 344476
Fax: 315654

Orient Tours
PO Box 4171
Tel: 657256
Fax: 657244

Salem Travel
Agency
PO Box 346
Tel: 333323
Fax: 317012

Shaheen Travel
and Tourism
PO Box 3142
Tel: 393200
Fax: 347477

Sultan Bin Yousuf
and Sons Travel
Agency
PO Box 698
Tel: 331511
Fax: 324312

Sunshine Tours
PO Box 8200
Tel: 449914
Fax: 446856

Trans Orient
Travel and
Tourism
PO Box 4870
Tel: 337865
Fax: 313167

Ulfat Travels
PO Box 7277
Tel: 331004
Fax: 319963

Zas Airline of
Egypt
PO Box 698
Tel: 331511
Fax: 324312

Ajman
Ajman National
Travel Agency
PO Box 641
Tel: 422300
Fax: 427537

Al-Ahli Travel
and Tourist
Agency
PO Box 789
Tel: 423044
Fax: 455628

Al Hadidi Travel
and Tourist
Agency
PO Box 438
Tel: 423066
Fax: 449854

Al Matrooshi
Travel Agency
PO Box 444
Tel: 425555
Fax: 429300

Al Noaimi
International
Company
PO Box 210
Tel: 421176
Fax: 422022

Al Safa Travel
PO Box 999
Tel: 421939
Fax: 427922

Al Zora Travel
and Cargo
Agency
PO Box 333
Tel: 423789
Fax: 444441

Galadari Travel
and Tours
PO Box 1087
Tel: 423057
Fax: 428752

Sahara Travel
Agency
PO Box 2765
Tel: 443956
Fax: 443924

Al Ain
Automobile and
Touring Club
PO Box 26880
Tel: 775607

Al Ain Express
Travel
PO Box 43185
Tel: 348834
Fax: 348830

Al Amaan Travel
and Tourism
PO Box 1615
Tel: 656777
Fax: 657572

Al Badeena Int
Travel and
Tourism
PO Box 15911
Tel: 644811
Fax: 668450

Al Darmaki
Travel and
Tourism
PO Box 15113
Tel: 642447
Fax: 668450

Eastern Travel
Bureau
PO Box 15035
Tel: 643044
Fax: 510035

Emirates Travel
Express
PO Box 1557
Tel: 655571
Fax: 664522

Malik Travel
Agency
PO Box 1470
Tel: 641661
Fax: 642478

Prime Travel
and Tours
PO Box 16569
Tel: 664772
Fax: 664550

Target Travels
and Tourism
PO Box 17103
Tel: 663393
Fax: 658380

Union Express
Travel and
Tourism
PO Box 15398
Tel: 641115
Fax: 645888

Dubai
Abdulla Al
Ghaith Travels
and Air Cargo
PO Box 3969
Tel: 552233
Fax: 552763

Adha Travel
PO Box 14199
Tel: 286996
Fax: 233922

Airlink
International
UAE
Tel: 821050
Fax: 821644

Ajman National
Travel Agency
PO Box 13142
Tel: 212882
Fax: 226284

Al Abbas Travels
PO Box 327
Tel: 511171
Fax: 513284

Al Arabi Travel
Agency
PO Box 24904
Tel: 455885
Fax: 451173

Al Bai Tourism
PO Box 21332
Tel: 255116
Fax: 266002

Al Barakat
National Travel
Agency
PO Box 298
Tel: 220873
Fax: 223490

Al Fajr Tourism
PO Box 1600
Tel: 286446

Al Faraena
Tourism and
Cargo
PO Box 23400
Tel: 243700
Fax: 234615

Al Fardan Travel
and Tourism
PO Box 24696
Tel: 346777
Fax: 379256

Al Futtaim Travel
PO Box 7880
Tel: 213030
Fax: 230534

Al Ghaith and Al
Moosa Travels
(ALTA) LLC
PO Box 1810
Tel: 211164
Fax: 233054

Al Kanz Tourism
and Travel
PO Box 16437
Tel: 684666
Fax: 684184

Al Khaleej Travel
PO Box 267
Tel: 539995
Fax: 536765

Al Majid Travel
Agency
PO Box 1020
Tel: 211176
Fax: 275863

Al Naboodah
Travel Agencies
PO Box 1200
Tel: 285691
Fax: 279488

Al Owais Travel
Agency
PO Box 150
Tel: 222756
Fax: 233677

Al Rais Travel
and Shipping
Agencies
PO Box 24713
Tel: 520800
Fax: 520700

Al Sayegh Travels
PO Box 6055
Tel: 213869
Fax: 217626

Al Shafar Travel
Agency
PO Box 7725
Tel: 525800
Fax: 529737

Al Shamsi Travel
Tourism and
Cargo
PO Box 1943
Tel: 212371
Fax: 233635

Al Shirawi Air
Travel and
Tourism
PO Box 6325
Tel: 821211
Fax: 821385

Al Tayer Travel
Agency
PO Box 2623
Tel: 236000
Fax: 229460

Al Yousef Travel
Agency
PO Box 21297
Tel: 255808
Fax: 264464

Al Zora Travel
and Cargo
Agency
PO Box 13028
Tel: 823990
Fax: 823988

Anta Holidays
PO Box 13142
Tel: 422300
Fax: 226284

Arabian
Adventures
PO Box 686
Tel: 317373
Fax: 314696

Arabian Incentive
Company
PO Box 772
Tel: 512111
Fax: 510699

Arabian Travel
Agency Limited
PO Box 4516
Tel: 216789
Fax: 217765

Asian Air Travel
and Tours
Agency
PO Box 1187
Tel: 221511
Fax: 274631

Bond Aviation
PO Box 55867
Tel: 221188
Fax: 228181

Breeze Travels
PO Box 13033
Tel: 263555
Fax: 262566

City Travels
PO Box 7130
Tel: 267111
Fax: 268585

Coastline Leisure
PO Box 23863
Tel: 450867
Fax: 452497

Concord Travels
and Tours
PO Box 294
Tel: 345000
Fax: 344550

Continental
Travels
PO Box 8488
Tel: 237777
Fax: 218059

Daallo Airlines
PO Box 21297
Tel: 255808
Fax: 264464

Destinations of
the World
PO Box 19950
Tel: 666369
Fax: 661986

Dial A Travel
PO Box 23377
Tel: 519999
Fax: 519888

Diners World
Travel
PO Box 1711
Tel: 237339
Fax: 239591

Discover the
World Marketing
PO Box 53226
Tel: 314285
Fax: 310583

Ditce Beach Club
PO Box 7428
Tel: 661925
Fax: 661929

DNATTA
PO Box 1515
Tel: 228151
Fax: 239817

Dubai Star
Tourism and
Cargo
PO Box 14414
Tel: 218777
Fax: 218779

Dubai Travel and
Tourist Services
PO Box 2533
Tel: 313818
Fax: 313130

Eisa Travels
PO Box 11266
Tel: 237348
Fax: 284200

Egypt Air Tours
Division
PO Box 12919
Tel: 236551
Fax: 273300

Emirates
Holidays
PO Box 686
Tel: 317373
Fax: 314696

Emirates Travel
Agency
PO Box 626
Tel: 219144
Fax: 271420

Europcar
PO Box 2533
Tel: 515153
Fax: 527692

Fly High Tourism
and Travels
PO Box 51702
Tel: 526383
Fax: 513454

Golden Tourist
PO Box 16347
Tel: 623355
Fax: 626181

Gulf Dunes
PO Box 6655
Tel: 714506
Fax: 714633

Gulf and World
Tours and Travels
PO Box 5527
Tel: 454004
Fax: 451625

Gulf Ventures
PO Box 70
Tel: 346838
Fax: 365973

Gulf Wings
Travel Agency
PO Box 1247
Tel: 664623
Fax: 660746

House of Travel
PO Box 7654
Tel: 662000
Fax: 823452

International
Travel Services
PO Box 7283
Tel: 351135
Fax: 516435

Jaber Nasser
Tourism and
Cargo Services
PO Box 3172
Tel: 536536
Fax: 538484

Kanoo Travel
PO Box 290
Tel: 521100
Fax: 524532

Kazim Travel
Agency
PO Box 705
Tel: 522171
Fax: 527126

Khalid Al Shirawi
Tourism Cargo
and Rent A Car
PO Box 5008
Tel: 274062
Fax: 216140

Larstan Tourism
and Freight Est
PO Box 16137
Tel: 266630
Fax: 254940

Leads Tourism
Services
PO Box 10281
Tel: 330995
Fax: 330997

Life Tourism
Cargo
PO Box 9170
Tel: 212134
Fax: 236611

Local Tours
PO Box 6117
Tel: 365554
Fax: 369118

Majid Obaid
Travel and Cargo
PO Box 20317
Tel: 629550
Fax: 622185

Middle East
Express
PO Box 50253
Tel: 268244

MMI Gulf
Ventures
PO Box 70
Tel: 251548
Fax: 251633

MMI Travel
Centre
PO Box 70
Tel: 346706
Fax: 345029

Mombasa
Tourism and
Cargo
PO Box 20424
Tel: 682828
Fax: 682826

Moonlight
Tourism
PO Box 6292
Tel: 271227
Fax: 233674

Mystic Tours
and Cargo
PO Box 21112
Tel: 239800
Fax: 359834

Nasser Air Travel
and Shipping
Agencies
PO Box 1520
Tel: 214455
Fax: 211016

National Travel
and Tourist
Agency
PO Box 298
Tel: 272222
Fax: 223490

Nerwin Tourism
and Cargo
PO Box 55176
Tel: 288455
Fax: 237202

Net Tours and
Travels
PO Box 50777
Tel: 668661
Fax: 668662

Nordic Middle
East
PO Box 5950
Tel: 518800
Fax: 518802

Oman Travels
PO Box 24924
Tel: 535420
Fax: 535450

Omest Travels
PO Box 4203
Tel: 222838
Fax: 226186

Orient Travel and
Touring Agency
PO Box 13808
Tel: 549333
Fax: 282946

Overseas Travels
PO Box 12579
Tel: 533338
Fax: 532229

Pan World Air
Travel Agency
PO Box 4775
Tel: 282779
Fax: 271216

Planet Travel
Tours and Cargo
PO Box 55645
Tel: 822199
Fax: 826867

Remni Tourism
and Shipping
PO Box 1750
Tel: 255946
Fax: 255896

Royal Caribbean
Cruises Limited
PO Box 53226
Tel: 314299
Fax: 310583

Safeen
PO Box 53226
Tel: 310737
Fax: 310583

Salt Lake Tourism
and Cargo
PO Box 4732
Tel: 267755
Fax: 250215

Sharaf Travel
LLC
PO Box 576
Tel: 552121
Fax: 511648

Sharjah National
Travel and
Tourist Agency
(SNTTA)
PO Box 8845
Tel: 225550
Fax: 273844

Sky Masters
PO Box 8019
Tel: 212121
Fax: 210515

Stalco Travel and
Tourism
PO Box 464
Tel: 250946
Fax: 250994

Sultan Travel and
Tourism
PO Box 16741
Tel: 232955
Fax: 239049

Tamra Travel
(WLLC)
PO Box 4861
Tel: 279988
Fax: 273281

Target Travels
and Gen Cargo
Agency
PO Box 1151
Tel: 262666
Fax: 262249

Tarik Travel
Agency
PO Box 13039
Tel: 534355
Fax: 532303

Thomas Cook Al
Rostamani LLC
PO Box 10072
Tel: 236060
Fax: 283318

Time Travel and
Cargo
PO Box 52120
Tel: 360560
Fax: 359345

Tourcare
PO Box 2565
Tel: 224883
Fax: 224001

Tourlink
PO Box 55619
Tel: 272181
Fax: 287460

Trans Orient
Travel and
Tourism Services
PO Box 10856
Tel: 233803
Fax: 217633

Transworld Air
Travels
PO Box 1859
Tel: 211853
Fax: 219078

Travelink
Tourism and
Cargo
PO Box 8666
Tel: 359696
Fax: 359393

Travel Market
PO Box 14480
Tel: 664455
Fax: 682111

Travel Way
Tourism and
Cargo
PO Box 1857
Tel: 256336
Fax: 252233

Trust Travel and
Tours
PO Box 6950
Tel: 277727
Fax: 277737

Unasco (LLC)
Union National
Air Land and Sea
Shipping Co
PO Box 8821
Tel: 538113
Fax: 539949

Unique Travel
PO Box 4744
Tel: 210444
Fax: 210001

United Tourist
Services and
Travel
PO Box 8023
Tel: 668939
Fax: 694327

Uralinteravia
PO Box 52120
Tel: 360560
Fax: 359321

Uranus Travel
and Tours (LLC)
PO Box 8611
Tel: 255444
Fax: 265222

Via Dubai
PO Box 13517
Tel: 218440
Fax: 218858

White Sands
Tours
PO Box 22072
Tel: 826800
Fax: 826500

World of Travel
PO Box 10471
Tel: 690889
Fax: 694748

World Wide
Tours
PO Box 2301
Tel: 344242
Fax: 377005

Yousco Tourism
PO Box 22254
Tel: 697746
Fax: 697743

Yousuf Habib Al
Yousuf
PO Box 25
Tel: 267092
Fax: 266660

Zabeel Travel
Agency
PO Box 7647
Tel: 534800
Fax: 534844

Fujairah
Al Awael Tours
and Travel
Agency
PO Box 1321
Tel: 226066
Fax: 229811

Al Barood Travel
Agency
PO Box 195
Tel: 232397
Fax: 232398

Al Musharif Rent
A Car and Haj
Company
PO Box 978
Tel: 446123

Al Rashdy Tours
and Travels
PO Box 824
Tel: 227107
Fax: 223152

Al Sharqi Travel
Agency
PO Box 208
Tel: 227183
Fax: 231278

Al Yamahi
Tourist Travel
Agency
PO Box 479
Tel: 223163

Al Zoaaby Tours
and Travels
PO Box 598
Tel: 231434
Fax: 231435

Arabian Air
Travel Agency
PO Box 638
Tel: 221561
Fax: 221461

Bin Majed Tours
and Travels
Agency
PO Box 92
Tel: 225522
Fax: 225858

Dicontinental
Tours and Travel
Agency
PO Box 11557
Dibba
Tel: 444841
Fax: 442474

Emirates Wings
Tours
PO Box 1158
Tel: 231661
Fax: 231660

Fujairah National
Air Travel
Agency
PO Box 96
Tel: 222316
Fax: 222555

Fujairah Tours
and Travel Centre
PO Box 989
Tel: 226969
Fax: 226949

Gulf Travel
PO Box 169
Tel: 223831
Fax: 229485

Safari Tours and
Travel
PO Box 925
Tel: 225313
Fax: 232355

Siberian World
Travel and Cargo
Agency
PO Box 77
Tel: 232700
Fax: 232288

Ras al-Khaimah
Al Ain
Automobile and
Touring Club
PO Box 4610
Tel: 229811

Emirates Travel
and Golden
Tourism
PO Box 1315
Tel: 225872
Fax: 224336

Express Tours
and Cargo
PO Box 1883
Tel: 333265
Fax: 337200

Jamal Travel and
Tourist Agency
PO Box 71
Tel: 225211
Fax: 228288

Ras al-Khaimah
Maritime and
Mercantile
International
PO Box 4888
Tel: 221427
Fax: 225313

Ras al-Khaimah
National Travel
Agency
PO Box 5214
Tel: 221536
Fax: 221255

Sharjah
Al Gazzal Tours
PO Box 4297
Tel: 526663
Fax: 352826

Al Ghaith and Al
Moosa Travels
(ALTA) LLC
PO Box 624
Tel: 221888
Fax: 231628

Al Khalidiya
Tourism
PO Box 13131
Tel: 546611
Fax: 538706

Al Mazroei
Travel and
Tourist Agency
PO Box 3835
Tel: 525969
Fax: 526999

Al Naboodah
Travel Agencies
PO Box 17
Tel: 351105
Fax: 374968

Al Wahda Air
Travel and Cargo
Agency
PO Box 6825
Tel: 330477
Fax: 337041

Arabianlink
Tours
PO Box 821
Tel: 373000
Fax: 524095

Arabian Travel
Agency Limited
PO Box 1477
Tel: 350000
Fax: 355074

Buhaira Travel
Agency
PO Box 4841
Tel: 352593
Fax: 523885

Cordial Tours
PO Box 4614
Tel: 545080
Fax: 365576

Delmon Tours
and Cargo
Agency
PO Box 20359
Tel: 363733
Fax: 522933

Diana Universal
Tourist and
Cargo
PO Box 22043
Tel: 363617
Fax: 355056

Express Tourism
Services
PO Box 3891
Tel: 369999
Fax: 369888

Gray Mackenzie
and Partners
PO Box 186
Tel: 355330
Fax: 540351

Gulf and Baltic
Travel
PO Box 4743
Tel: 238381
Fax: 592061

Hamad Al Tonaiji
Travel and
Tourist
PO Box 1766
Tel: 543743
Fax: 541140

Inter-Continental
Travel and
Tourist
PO Box 21220
Tel: 363553
Fax: 371441

Isis Tourist
PO Box 911
Tel: 526222
Fax: 365757

Kanoo Travel
PO Box 153
Tel: 356058
Fax: 364694

Marhaba Tourism
and Travels
PO Box 5394
Tel: 355320
Fax: 355300

Nata Tourist
Agency
PO Box 20757
Tel: 356444
Fax: 374000

North South
Tourism and
Cargo
PO Box 12389
Tel: 325538
Fax: 325537

Oman Travel
Agency
PO Box 15
Tel: 357929
Fax: 366369

Omest Travels
PO Box 22998
Tel: 529066
Fax: 529044

Orient Tours
PO Box 772
Tel: 668661
Fax: 525077

Sandset Tours
PO Box 9166
Tel: 547979
Fax: 549925

Sharjah National
Travel and
Tourist Agency
(SNTTA)
PO Box 17
Tel: 548296
Fax: 374968

Sky Line Travel
and Tourism
and Shipping
PO Box 40085
Tel: 355923
Fax: 367968

Sun Shine Tours
PO Box 1198
Tel: 324939
Fax: 324936

Trans
International
Travel and
Tourist Agency
PO Box 1116
Tel: 544515
Fax: 372396

Victoria Travels
PO Box 2752
Tel: 352642
Fax: 357359

Umm al-Quwain
Umm al-Quwain
National Travel
Agency
PO Box 601
Tel: 656615
Fax: 655549

United Arab Emirates Tourist Offices Abroad

France
Dubai Commerce
and Tourism
Promotion Board
15 bis Rue de
Marignan
75008 Paris
Tel: (01) 44958500
Fax: (01) 45631314

Germany
Dubai Commerce
and Tourism
Promotion Board
Neue Mainzer
Strasse 57
D-60311
Frankfurt/Main
Tel: (069) 253422
Fax: (069) 253151

Hong Kong
Dubai Commerce
and Tourism
Promotion Board
Suite 1203-4 Shui
On Centre
6-8 Harbour Road
Tel: 802-9002
Fax: 827-2511
Telex: 62390

Italy
Dubai Commerce
and Tourism
Promotion Board
Piazzetta Pattari 2
20122 Milan
Tel: (02) 7202-2466
Fax: (02) 7202-0162

Japan
Dubai Commerce
and Tourism
Promotion Board
One-Win Yoyogi
Building 4th Flr
3-35-10 Yoyogi
Shibuya-ku
Tokyo 151
Fax: (03) 3379-9313

North America
Dubai Commerce
and Tourism
Promotion Board
8 Penn Centre
Philadelphia
PA 19103
Tel: (251)751-9750
Fax: (252) 751-9551

UK and Ireland
Dubai Commerce
and Tourism
Promotion Board
34 Buckingham
Palace Road
London
SW1W ORE
Tel: (071) 828-5961
Fax: (071) 828-4891

Index

(Illustrations are indicated in bold)

358